The Write Start
with Readings
SENTENCES TO PARAGRAPHS

The Write Start with Readings

SENTENCES TO PARAGRAPHS

Lawrence Checkett

Gayle Feng-Checkett

St. Charles County Community College

Longman

New York   San Francisco   Boston
London   Toronto   Sydney   Tokyo   Singapore   Madrid
Mexico City   Munich   Paris   Cape Town   Hong Kong   Montreal

To the best teachers
we've ever had . . . our parents.

Publisher: Joe Opiela
Senior Acquisitions Editor: Steve Rigolosi
Marketing Manager: Melanie Goulet
Supplements Editor: Donna Campion
Media Supplements Editor: Nancy Garcia
Production Manager: Mark Naccarelli
Project Coordination, Text Design, and Electronic Page Makeup: Nesbitt Graphics, Inc.
Cover Designer/Manager: Wendy Ann Fredericks
Cover Photos: Plants: ©Nick Dolding/Stone; Clouds: ©PhotoDisc
Photo Researcher: Diana Gongora
Senior Manufacturing Buyer: Roy Pickering
Printer and Binder: Quebecor World-Taunton
Cover Printer: Coral Graphic Services

For permission to use copyrighted material, grateful acknowledgment is made to the copyright holders on pp. 415–417, which are hereby
made part of this copyright page.

Library of Congress Cataloging-in-Publication Data

Checkett, Lawrence.
    The write start with readings : sentences to paragraphs / by Lawrence Checkett, Gayle Feng-Checkett.
      p. cm.
    Includes index.
    ISBN 0-321-09084-5   ISBN 0-321-09085-3 (annotated instructor's edition)
      1. English language—Paragraphs. 2. English language—Sentences. 3. English
language—Rhetoric. 4. English language—Grammar. 5. Report writing. I. Feng-Checkett,
Gayle. II. Title.

PE1439 .C48 2000
808'.042–dc21   00-056734

Please visit our website at http://www.ablongman.com/checkett

ISBN 0-321-09084-5

3 4 5 6 7 8 9 10—QWT—03 02

BRIEF CONTENTS

PART 3

Writing Effective Essays   253

The Writer's Resources   275

Readings   345

DETAILED CONTENTS

PART 3

Writing Effective Essays   253

Chapter 22

The Essay   255

The Writer's Resources   275

PARTS OF SPEECH   276

Readings   345

PREFACE

TO THE INSTRUCTOR

More and more nontraditional students are enrolling in two- and four-year colleges. While adding to the rich diversity of the educational landscape, their arrival is posing challenges for faculty, particularly in the area of enhancing student-writing abilities. *The Write Start with Readings: Sentences to Paragraphs* addresses the strategies necessary for writing success in school, on the job, and in social communications. By emphasizing the basic elements of good writing, *The Write Start* helps developing writers achieve a solid foundation that will facilitate their evolution as writers as they continue through their academic and other life experiences. Throughout the text, our main goal has been simplicity and clarity. Equally important, and in keeping with the title of the text, we have stressed the importance of *writing from the start*. In other words, we believe that students learn to write by *writing*, not by completing fill-in-the-blank grammar exercises.

Overview

Unlike most texts for developing writers, *The Write Start* begins with sentence formation, moves to paragraph organization, and ends with one chapter on the full essay. While this is one suggestion for a course outline, the chapters are self-contained units allowing for flexibility of design depending on the instructor's own needs and that of the class. Within the text, references are made to other chapters and to the Writer's Resources section when appropriate.

Organization of the Text

To the Student: Chapters 1 and 2

This section introduces developing writers to the importance of writing well. It stresses the idea that writing is difficult but, like other life skills, it can be mastered with the proper attitude, information, and hard work.

Writing Effective Sentences: Chapters 3 to 12

This section helps developing writers understand the fundamentals of good sentence building and establishes the importance of sentence variety in writing. Ten different sentence types are each given their own chapter. Each chapter contains examples to illustrate instruction. Multiple practice sets allow for the transference of specific skill-building ideas into clear, concise, and complete sentences.

Writing Effective Paragraphs: Chapters 13 to 21

This section teaches developing writers how to organize and construct body paragraphs in a variety of rhetorical modes. The chapters incorporate both professional and student paragraph models, as well as technique questions that focus on the elements necessary for effective paragraphs. Specific detail and sentence variety are an integral part of each paragraph chapter.

Writing Effective Essays: Chapter 22

The final product of most writing programs—developmental programs included—is the essay. For instructors who wish to include the essay in their courses, Chapter 22 introduces developing writers to the process of constructing a clear, concise essay. Using the skills learned in preceding sections on sentence variety and paragraph development, the demands of the essay are taught: writing the introductory paragraph, organizing and developing support in the body paragraphs, and coming to a conclusion that is appropriate for the essay's approach.

The Writer's Resources

The Writer's Resources are more than a listing of tables on parts of speech. Rather, to keep the instructional chapters "clean" so that students remain focused on the specific topic under discussion, The Writer's Resources section is a veritable warehouse of information on parts of speech, usage, punctuation, mechanics, and spelling. Examples and exercises accompany the material for illustration, clarification, and additional practice. References to The Writer's Resources are made in the text chapters where appropriate. Material helpful to English as a Second Language students is included in The Writer's Resources and appears in a special section of the accompanying Instructor's Manual.

Additional Readings and Read All About It

An exciting feature of *The Write Start* is that most professional paragraph examples excerpted in the text can be found in full—with accompanying apparatus—in the Readings section. Instructors have the flexibility of showing their students the full context of specific paragraphs and how they are integrated into the whole essay. This feature is invaluable in showing student writers how developing specific subtopics works in developing the major topic. The essays were chosen to serve as models for the modes being taught in the text.

Answer Section

At the end of *The Write Start,* an answer key contains one half of the answers to the in-text Practice exercises. This approach allows for ultimate flexibility: Students can check half their answers to gauge their development, and instructors can use the remaining questions for homework or in-class work. (A complete answer key is included in the Annotated Instructor's Edition.)

Special Features of *The Write Start*

The features embedded in *The Write Start* make it an invaluable tool for both instructors and students.

▼ *Clarity and Simplicity.* Writing, mechanics, and grammar instruction are taught as quickly and simply as possible without losing core content, focusing on valuable insights and meaningful suggestions. Key terms and concepts are boldfaced and defined in each chapter as they are introduced, with ample examples for clarification. Key terms and definitions are repeated in the glossary.

▼ *Things You Need to Know.* In anticipation of instructors choosing to teach Chapters 3 to 12 in a different order than they appear in the book, prerequisites are mentioned at the beginning of certain chapters. These prerequisites, labeled "You Need to Know," direct instructors and students to specific information in preceding chapters that is necessary for a clearer understanding of the material under discussion. In other words, visiting the prerequisite material first will make the current chapter material easier to understand.

▼ *Student Writing.* *The Write Start* gives equal weight to professional and student writing. While professional writing models often are engaging and prove that good writers actually do use the techniques and processes taught in writing classes, developing writers sometimes view professional writing with suspicion. They simply don't believe that they will ever approach that level of expertise. *The Write Start* uses equal amounts of student-generated and professional writing to make an important point: that developing writers use the same rules, processes, and techniques as their professional counterparts.

▼ *End-of-Chapter Review Boxes.* The highlighted reviews help developing writers identify and remember key terms and concepts that are to be utilized in writing, revising, and editing.

▼ *English as a Second Language Instruction.* Material aimed at students for whom English is not the first language is embedded throughout the text, but it is not labeled as such. In other words, *The Write Start* uses current ESL research and pedagogy to reach all developing writers, while not singling out specific ESL "problems." In addition, the Writer's Resources includes specific lists, charts, and exercises for ESL-specific concerns, such as verb form/tense, phrasal verbs, irregular verbs, articles, and idiomatic prepositional phrases. Finally, *The Writer's Resources* section offers ESL icons to point out the basic material most needed by ESL students.

▼ *Vocabulary.* Most developmental writing textbooks have vocabulary lists following the readings. In *The Write Start,* each essay is prefaced by a list of challenging words found in the essay. Readers are asked to look up the definitions of these words prior to reading the essay so that they can focus more easily on the essay's content.

The Write Start Series

More and more two- and four-year colleges are identifying levels of developmental writing students and are instituting developmental writing course sequences. *The Write Start* is a two-book series whose aim is to answer this need. While the content of the two books is complementary for sequenced instruction, each book can be used effectively as a stand-alone text for different levels of instruction. The series is designed for students with a variety of skill levels and for students with a variety of challenges in learning Standard English. *The Write Start with Readings: Sentences to Paragraphs* focuses primarily on sentence variety and paragraph development, with essay writing as the concluding section. *The Write Start with Readings: Paragraphs to Essays* (available in 2001) begins with a review of paragraph construction in the rhetorical modes and moves to the thorough development of longer essays in the rhetorical modes, followed by a review of sentence grammar and variety. Both books share the same features, pedagogy, and easy-to-read format.

The Teaching and Learning Package

Each component of the teaching and learning package has been crafted to ensure that the course is rewarding for both instructors and students.

The **Annotated Instructor's Edition** is a replica of the student text, but includes all answers printed directly on the fill-in lines provided in the text. 0-321-06115-2

The **Instructor's Manual with Transparency Masters** provides information on the following: *Using the Text, Syllabus Preparation, Answer Keys, Student and Professional Reading Selections, Thesis Sentences, Outlining, Proofreading Checklists, Peer Editing, English as a Second Language/English as a Foreign Language (ESL/EFL), Diagnostic Pre-Test,* and *Transparency Masters.* 0-321-06116-0

The **Test Bank** provides a wealth of printed quizzes and additional practice exercises for each chapter in the text. The test bank is formatted in a way that simplifies copying and distribution. 0-321-06117-9

In addition, an **Electronic Test Bank for Writing** is also available. Available in December 2000, this electronic test bank features more than 5,000 questions in all areas of writing, from grammar to paragraphing, through essay writing, research, and documentation. With this easy-to-use CD-ROM, instructors simply choose questions from the electronic test bank, then print out the completed test for distribution. 0-321-08117-X

Each copy of *The Write Start with Readings: Sentences to Paragraphs* is packaged with a free copy of the **Writer's ToolKit Plus CD-ROM.** This CD-ROM offers a wealth of tutorial, exercise, and reference material for writers. It also includes model documents, writing prompts, and a mini-handbook. It is compatible with either a PC or Macintosh platform, and is flexible enough to be used either occasionally for practice or regularly in class lab sessions.

For additional exercises, summaries, and interactive activities, be sure to visit our **companion website at http://www.ablongman.com/checkett.** The *Write Start Online* provides a wealth of resources, including gradable quizzes, e-mail capabilities, and interactive chat. Stop by for a visit!

The Longman Developmental English Package

In addition to the book-specific supplements discussed above, a series of other skills-based supplements are available for both instructors and students. All of these supplements are available either free or at greatly reduced prices.

For Additional Reading and Reference

The Dictionary Deal. Two dictionaries can be shrinkwrapped with this text title at a nominal fee. *The New American Webster Handy College Dictionary* is a paperback reference text with more than 100,000 entries. *Merriam Webster's Collegiate Dictionary,* tenth edition is a hardback reference with a citation file of more than 14.5 million examples of English words drawn from actual use.

Penguin Quality Paperback Titles. A series of Penguin paperbacks is available at a significant discount when shrinkwrapped with any Longman Basic Skills title. Some titles available are: Toni Morrison's *Beloved,* Julia Alvarez's *How the Garcia Girls Lost Their Accents,* Mark Twain's *Huckleberry Finn, Narrative of the Life of Frederick Douglass,* Harriet Beecher Stowe's *Uncle Tom's Cabin,* Dr. Martin Luther King, Jr.'s *Why We Can't Wait,* and plays by Shakespeare, Miller, and Albee. For a complete list of titles or more information, please contact your Longman sales consultant.

***The Pocket Reader,* First Edition.** This inexpensive volume contains 80 brief readings (1-3 pages each) on a variety of themes: writers on writing, nature, women and men, customs and habits, politics, rights and obligations, and coming of age. Also included is an alternate rhetorical table of contents. 0-321-07668-0

100 Things to Write About. This 100-page book contains 100 individual assignments for writing on a variety of topics and in a wide range of formats, from expressive to analytical. Ask your Longman sales representative for a sample copy. 0-673-98239-4

Newsweek Alliance. Instructors may choose to shrinkwrap a 12-week subscription to *Newsweek* with any Longman text. The price of the subscription is 57 cents per issue (a total of $6.84 for the subscription). Available with the subscription is a free "Interactive Guide to *Newsweek*"—a workbook for students who are using the text. In addition, *Newsweek* provides a wide variety of instructor supplements free to teachers, including maps, Skills Builders, and weekly quizzes.

Electronic and Online Offerings

The Longman English Pages Website. Both students and instructors can visit our free content-rich Website for additional reading selections and writing exercises. From the Longman English pages, visitors can conduct a simulated Web search, learn how to write a resume and cover letter, or try their hand at poetry writing. Stop by and visit us at **http://www.awl.com/englishpages.**

The Longman Electronic Newsletter—Twice a month during the spring and fall, instructors who have subscribed receive a free copy of the Longman Basic Skills Newsletter in their e-mailbox. Written by experienced classroom instructors, the newsletter offers teaching tips, classroom activities, book reviews, and more. To subscribe, visit the Longman Basic Skills Website at **http://www.awl.com/basicskills,** or send an e-mail to **BasicSkills @awl.com.**

Daedalus Online. Addison Wesley Longman and The Daedalus Group are proud to offer the next generation of the award-winning Daedalus Integrated Writing Environment. Daedalus Online is an Internet-based collaborative writing environment for students. The program offers prewriting strategies and prompts, computer-mediated conferencing, peer collaboration and review, comprehensive writing support, and secure, 24-hour availability.

For educators, Daedalus Online offers a comprehensive suite of online course management tools for managing an online class, dynamically linking assignments, and facilitating a heuristic approach to writing instruction. For more information, visit **http://daedalus.pearsoned.com,** or contact your Longman sales representative.

***Teaching Online: Internet Research, Conversation, and Composition,* Third Edition.** Ideal for instructors who have never surfed the Net, this easy-to-follow guide offers basic definitions, numerous examples, and step-by-step information about finding and using Internet sources. Free to adopters. 0-321-07760-1

***Researching Online,* Fourth Edition.** A perfect companion for a new age, this indispensable new supplement helps students navigate the Internet. Adapted from *Teaching Online,* the instructor's Internet guide, *Researching Online* speaks directly to students, giving them detailed, step-by-step instructions for performing electronic searches. Available free when shrinkwrapped with any Longman text. 0-321-08408-X

For Instructors

Competency Profile Test Bank, Second Edition. This series of 60 objective tests covers ten general areas of English competency, including fragments; comma splices and run-ons; pronouns; commas; and capitalization. Each test is available in remedial, standard, and advanced versions. Available as reproducible sheets or in computerized versions. Free to instructors. Paper version: 0-321-02224-6. Computerized IBM: 0-321-02633-0. Computerized Mac: 0-321-02632-2.

Diagnostic and Editing Tests, Third Edition. This collection of diagnostic tests helps instructors assess students' competence in Standard Written English for purpose of placement or to gauge progress. Available as reproducible sheets or in computerized versions, and free to instructors. Paper: 0-321-08382-2. Computerized IBM: 0-321-08782-8. Computerized Mac: 0-321-08784-4.

ESL Worksheets, Third Edition. These reproducible worksheets provide ESL students with extra practice in areas they find the most troublesome. A diagnostic test and post-test are provided, along with answer keys and suggested topics for writing. Free to adopters. 0-321-077652-2

80 Practices. A collection of reproducible, ten-item exercises that provide additional practices for specific grammatical usage problems, such as comma splices, capitalization, and pronouns. Includes an answer key, and free to adopters. 0-673-53422-7

CLAST Test Package, Fourth Edition. These two 40-item objective tests evaluate students' readiness for the CLAST exams. Strategies for teaching CLAST preparedness are included. Free with any Longman English title. Reproducible sheets: 0-321-01950-4 Computerized IBM version: 0-321-01982-2 Computerized Mac version: 0-321-01983-0

TASP Test Package, Third Edition. These 12 practice pre-tests and post-tests assess the same reading and writing skills covered in the TASP examination. Free with any Longman English title. Reproducible sheets: 0-321-01959-8 Computerized IBM version: 0-321-01985-7 Computerized Mac version: 0-321-01984-9

Teaching Writing to the Non-Native Speaker. This booklet examines the issues that arise when non-native speakers enter the developmental classroom. Free to instructors, it includes profiles of international and permanent ESL students, factors influencing second-language acquisition, and tips on managing a multicultural classroom. 0-673-97452-9

For Students

Learning Together: An Introduction to Collaborative Theory. This brief guide to the fundamentals of collaborative learning teaches students how to work effectively in groups, how to revise with peer response, and how to co-author a paper or report. Shrinkwrapped free with any Longman Basic Skills text. 0-673-46848-8

A Guide for Peer Response, **Second Edition.** This guide offers students forms for peer critiques, including general guidelines and specific forms for different stages in the writing process. Also appropriate for freshman-level course. Free to adopters. 0-321-01948-2

Acknowledgments

We would like to thank everyone at Longman for participating in the publishing of *The Write Start*. To our Acquisitions Editor, Steven Rigolosi, whose vision, insight, advice, and timely cheerleading made this project a realization. To our Development Editor, Dave Cohen, whose contributions to style, content, and structure have given the project a voice and direction far beyond our original scope. To Jennifer Krasula, who kept the parts in good order and answered our questions and found out the answers to questions with speed and good spirits. To our students, who contributed paragraphs and essays to the text and demonstrated through their own writing that our techniques are sound while always challenging us to do it better. We also owe many thanks to the devoted English instructors who reviewed our text in all stages of its development: Linda Austin, Glendale Community College; Marianne Dzik, Illinois Valley Community College; Tim Florschuetz, Mesa Community College; Carlotta Hill, Oklahoma City Community College; Patsy Krech, University of Memphis; Irma Luna, San Antonio College; Raymond Mort, Oakland Community College; Linda Rollins, Motlow State Community College; Athene Sallee, Forsyth Technical Community College; Phil Skerry, Lakeland Community College; John Thornburg, San Jacinto College-Central; and Suzanne Weisar, San Jacinto College-South.

Lawrence Checkett
Gayle Feng-Checkett

To the Student: Getting Started

In the following chapters, you will learn why writing is important at home, school, and work. You will learn that writing, like driving a car, hitting a ball, or preparing a nutritious meal, is a learned skill. You also will learn about two common problems associated with poor writing skills: unclear meaning and the negative perception that others might have of you. As you read through these chapters, you will learn that writing is a skill that will help you throughout your life.

1

The Importance of Writing

The first question most students ask when starting to read a book on writing is "Why is writing that important?" The simple answer is that being able to write well and express yourself will help you throughout the rest of your life. Consider the three situations in which you'll find yourself most: school, work, and home.

▼ For school, you will be called on to write essays, reports, analyses, and research papers to show what you've learned.
▼ For work, you'll be asked to write memos, business letters, and reports to communicate clearly with co-workers, your boss, and even employees at other companies. Moreover, before getting that job, you'll need to write résumés and cover letters to your prospective employers.
▼ For personal business, you will need to write notes, letters, and e-mail to everyone from your children's teachers to local politicians and even your family and friends.

Whatever form your writing takes, and wherever you use it, you must learn to write well. Your writing for school, work, or personal business will have to express your ideas clearly. Organizing and developing your writing to achieve this clarity is one of the most important skills you can learn.

The key words in the previous paragraph are "learn" and "skills." No one is born with good writing skills. Just as you must learn how to keyboard, repair an engine, solve math problems, or install a plumbing fixture, you also must learn how to write well.

How do you learn to write well? You learn how to write well in the same way you develop any other skill. Consider some of your other talents:

▼ Are you a good free-throw shooter in basketball?
▼ Are you a whiz at setting up a new program on a computer?
▼ Can you make a dress from a pattern in no time?

Why are you so successful at a particular skill? Why does it seem so easy? Is the answer "a little hard work and practice?" If so, then why should learning how to write well be any different? Remember, writing is a skill just like any other skill. If you make a commitment to learn the skill of writing, you will learn how to write and do it well.

Avoiding the Two Major Problems of Poor Writing

There are two obvious problems arising from a poor piece of writing. The first problem is one of understanding. For example, what do the following sentences mean?

1. The chef, made primarily of noodles, served the fettuccine Alfredo to his customers.
2. The truck hit the wall, and it was damaged.
3. Throwing confetti, the parade floats moved slowly down the boulevard.

Can you understand these sentences? In the first sentence, the fettuccine Alfredo is made of noodles, not the chef. In the second sentence, the pronoun "it" does not refer clearly to either truck or wall, so the reader cannot know which of the two was damaged. In the third sentence, the confetti was thrown by spectators (not mentioned), not by the parade floats.

In each of these sentences, the meaning is confused and unclear because of poor writing, but the problems are not that difficult to correct. A bit of re-arranging or the addition of a key word should do the trick:

1. The chef served fettuccine Alfredo, made primarily of noodles, to his customers.
2. The truck hit the wall, and the wall was damaged.
3. The spectators threw confetti as the parade floats moved slowly down the boulevard.

The second problem arising from poor writing is one of perception. When people read writing that is difficult to understand or that contains punctuation errors, poorly constructed sentences, and misspelled words, their opinion of the writer lessens. They think that the writer is either not very intelligent or at least careless (for not proofreading the writing for errors), or possibly both. When the people making such assessments are bosses, professors, school principals, co-workers, human resource managers, and admission directors, the consequences can be devastating.

Poor writing can lead to not being admitted to college or to a failing grade on an assignment. It can mean not getting the job interview or a poor performance review. It can be the reason an issue is not taken seriously by your local city council, or why your children are not getting the help they need at school. Learning to write well can help open those same doors that now seem closed.

Writing as a Life Skill

If you don't believe that writing well is a necessary "life skill," look in the classified ad section of your local newspaper and count how many help-wanted ads have a phrase in them that states "good communication skills necessary." You might be surprised at the number of jobs that require good writing skills, including those in which you thought writing wasn't even necessary.

Talk to people who have applied for jobs or applied to a variety of colleges, and ask them if the application asked them for a writing sample. You will find that most job and college applications do, and the reason should be no surprise. Your writing demonstrates to the reader how well you think, organize information, analyze, and communicate your thoughts to others—all skills necessary for success in school, work, or your personal business.

Writing well is a learned skill. Like any other skill, it takes a certain amount of commitment, practice, and hard work. In not too many weeks, however, if you keep at it, you can learn how to raise the level of your writing substantially. For a few weeks' investment in time and energy, you can enjoy a lifetime of success in school, work, and your personal business.

Visit *The Write Start* Online!

For additional practice with the materials found in this chapter, visit our Website at:

http://www.ablongman.com/checkett

The Website also features additional readings, quizzes, writing activities, and Internet links, as well as a bulletin board and interactive chat.

For More Practice with Your Grammar and Writing Skills

For further exercises designed to improve your writing and grammar skills, use the Writer's ToolKit Plus CD-ROM included with this text. The toolkit provides a wealth of computerized tutorials and practice activities.

2 Elements of Good Writing

What does it take to write well? Like many students, you might find that writing assignments are time-consuming, difficult, and no fun at all. If so, you're not alone. Many writers, including well-known professionals, find that writing is a chore. A good number of writers, though, find writing to be a joy, and by mastering some of the basic elements of good writing, perhaps you can too.

Good Writing: Four Misconceptions

There are four basic misconceptions about good writing that can make it seem like a chore:

▼ Good writing has to be complicated.
▼ Good writing has to be long.
▼ Good writing means writing just like you talk.
▼ Good writing means good ideas—punctuation is of secondary importance.

In reality, the first two of these misconceptions are often misunderstood, while the last two are simply wrong. After all, the whole point of writing is to get information across clearly and concisely to someone else.

Good Writing Doesn't Have to Be Complicated

When people say "complicated," what they really mean is "developed." Keep your writing as simple as possible without leaving out any important information, and make certain you explain each idea fully. Concentrate on details that clearly express the main idea, not on words that the reader has to run to a dictionary to look up.

Complicated/Unclear

Televised educational programming should facilitate the pedagogical manifestations embedded in the internalized psyche of the community's concern for children's edification in discreet categories.

7

It would take 20 minutes using a dictionary and a thesaurus to figure out the meaning of this information.

> ### Developed/Clear
> Children's educational television shows, such as *Sesame Street, The Electric Company,* and *Mister Rogers,* should reflect parents' concerns in regard to math, reading, and writing. The instruction should reflect the proper age and level of childrens' development.

Notice how simple the language is, yet the content is clear.

Good Writing Doesn't Have to Be Long

Some assignments dictate length by their very nature. For example, a research paper on the causes of World War II would necessarily be long. However, in most writing cases, short and simple is better. Most people in the business world and academia do not have unlimited time to read communications coming across their desks. They want information that is clear and as short as possible without leaving out any important facts or ideas. However, you don't want your writing to be so brief that it becomes monotonous, immature, and uninformative.

> ### Too Short
> Tom is a Democrat. Yuri is a Republican. Yasheef is an Independent. Tom voted. Yuri voted. Yasheef voted. Senator Brown was reelected.

Here, the sing-song rhythm of the sentences is immature, and the information is insufficient. For example, is Senator Brown a Democrat, Republican, or an Independent?

> ### Too Long
> Tom, a Democrat, likes chocolate ice-cream and riding his bicycle in the countryside on weekends, while Yuri, a Republican, enjoys reading science articles and owns a two-story brick house. Furthermore, Yasheef, an Independent, has a red convertible and started his own business two years ago. Tom, Yuri, and Yasheef all voted in last Tuesday's election. Because it was a bright, sunny day and the forecast predicted a continuation of good weather, many other people came out to vote, as well. Most of the voters in the district—a full 62 percent—were Democrats, while 34 percent were Republican and 4 percent were Independent. Senator Brown, a Democrat, received the most votes and was reelected.

Here, the inference is clear that Senator Brown was reelected because Democrats were the majority of voters in the district and the good weather boosted the voter turnout, but the sentences are too long and meandering. Also, most of the information has nothing to do with the topic.

Clear/Concise

Tom, a Democrat representing the majority of voters in the district, voted along with Yuri, a Republican, and Yasheef, an Independent. Also, the weather boosted voter turnout. Later that evening, it was announced that the Democratic incumbent, Senator Brown, was reelected.

Here, all the necessary information is present, using clear, simplified language.

Good Writing and the Way You Speak

Writing, with the possible exception of short notes and memos to family members, friends, and co-workers, is more formal than talking. When you talk, you use slang, intonation, facial expressions, and other body language to get your point across. As a result, the exact words you use can be informal or imprecise, and your audience will still understand you. When writing, though, words are all you have to get your point across, so those words need to be more precise and more formal. Therefore, word choice, sentence structure, and paragraph organization become more important. In business and academia, do not use slang and confusing expressions that do not mean what their individual words suggest.

Slang

John F. Kennedy was a *cool* president, and he never *disrespected* his *posse*.

Appropriate Language

John F. Kennedy was *an effective* president, and he never *showed disrespect for his supporters*.

Confusing Expression

After the receiver dropped the pass, the coach *had a cow*.

Appropriate Language

After the receiver dropped the pass, the coach *became angry*.

The purpose of good writing is to get across information to someone in a clear and concise manner. Slang and confusing expressions are unacceptable in formal writing for several reasons.

Slang and confusing expressions are often used by a select group of people, usually belonging to a particular social club, profession, age group, or culture. The meaning of slang and confusing expressions is usually understood only by the select group. Also, slang and confusing expressions do not have an exact meaning, making it difficult for the reader to understand the intended meaning. You might use a word or an expression to mean one thing, while your reader might interpret it to mean something else. "That song is bad." To one group "bad" might mean "awful," while to another group, it might mean "good." A good example is the expression "The man was so angry, he had a cow." To a foreigner or to a person outside of the group familiar with its actual meaning, "having a cow" would certainly be confusing;

the reader would have no way to figure out the cause and effect relationship between a man being angry and his having a cow.

When you write, try to use exact language that is easy to understand and clarifies ideas, not confuses them. Omit slang and confusing expressions, and use precise language to get your points across.

Good Writing and Punctuation

Proper punctuation is essential to attain clear meaning. Punctuation has two prime functions: First, it divides information into smaller groups, making it easier for the reader to understand; and second, it creates rhythm so that the sentences flow easily together.

By way of comparison, think of punctuation as having a similar function in writing as traffic signals do on the road. Traffic signals keep the traffic (like words in writing) moving with a coordinated ease. The signals also divide traffic into smaller, more manageable groups to regulate flow and allow everyone to travel at a reasonable rate. For instance, you might think of a period as a red light (full stop), a semicolon as a flashing red light (a full stop but not quite as long as a nonflashing red light), and a comma as a flashing yellow light (a slowing down but not a full stop).

Without Punctuation

The secretary having finished at least for the day her stack of communications was then confronted with another set of demands without help from an assistant it would take her at least another four hours consequently she called with permission from her boss a temporary employment agency.

This sentence is difficult to follow, and finding a place to take a breath is almost impossible.

With Punctuation

The secretary, having finished at least for the day her stack of communications, was then confronted with another set of demands. Without help from an assistant, it would take her at least another four hours; consequently, she called, with permission from her boss, a temporary employment agency.

Notice how the punctuation helps to clarify the content by breaking the information into smaller units. Punctuation also helps to create rhythm in the writing by making the reader slow down and pause at certain places.

The Computer, Writing, and You

Now that you're in college, many instructors will expect you to use a computer on which to do your writing. Some courses will even require you to submit your papers and essays on a hard disk or even to send them electronically to a folder for the instructor's or your classmates' comments. But don't panic. If your instructor doesn't spend time in class teaching you how to accomplish this, your school probably has an instructional center where tutors can instruct you individually or in special classes. In a few short weeks you'll become comfortable with using the computer to help you with all your writing assignments.

Although you may have heard a few horror stories about students losing their entire paper into cyberspace or a file being destroyed by an Internet virus, millions of students just like you are discovering how computers can help them write their papers more efficiently, more accurately, and more professionally.

The computer can help you with a multitude of tasks that are necessary to complete a variety of writing assignments. You can use the computer to help you during all phases of the writing process.

Writing
▼ Brainstorming
▼ Freewriting
▼ Rough drafts (save multiple drafts for comparison)
▼ Inserting and/or deleting sentences (also helps you achieve sentence variety)
▼ Moving paragraphs (to help you organize and develop your ideas)
▼ Thesaurus (to help you find synonyms and antonyms)
▼ Spellchecker
▼ Grammarchecker
▼ Printing (italics, boldface, font size, highlighting, and many other features)

Research
▼ Use the Internet and World Wide Web to find information.
▼ Access online library catalogs.
▼ Write to others about your assignment using e-mail.
▼ Talk live in "chat" rooms.
▼ Exchange files and folders.
▼ Post assignments to class archives and forums.

Using a computer to write can offer many advantages when working on your assignments. As you gain experience, you will learn to access information more quickly, focus your research, organize your ideas and communicate a developed point of view, and produce a professional looking final draft. The new tools available to writers today can make many writing tasks and processes easier and quicker to accomplish.

CHAPTER REVIEW

▼ *Good writing doesn't need to be complicated.* Good writing must be developed, but it isn't necessarily complicated. Keep writing as simple as possible without leaving out any important information.
▼ *Good writing doesn't need to be lengthy.* While some specific assignments demand length, for most writing cases, short and simple is better. Most people don't have unlimited time to read communications coming across their desks; so, keep your writing short and to the point.
▼ *Good writing is more formal than talking.* When writing, don't use slang or confusing expressions that might get in the way of clear understanding. In writing, word choice, sentence structure, and paragraph organization become of utmost importance.

▼ *Good writing is a combination of content and proper punctuation.* Proper punctuation is essential to attain clear meaning. Punctuation divides information into smaller groups, making it easier for the reader to understand. It also creates rhythm so that the sentences flow easily together.

Hopefully, the examples you've been shown have erased some misconceptions about the writing process. Yes, writing can be difficult—but don't get discouraged—we're just getting started. The instructional chapters of this book have been designed to give you information and techniques in a clear and concise manner so that your writing experience will be as productive as possible.

You don't have to be a professional to write well. This book also shares with you the thoughts and styles of many student writers just like you. The finished student writings that you will read are the product of the instructional chapters that went into the making of this book. These students were just like you when they began, and with work and dedication, you will be writing just like them in a relatively short time. There is a voice within you that is waiting to be discovered and developed. Let's go!

Visit *The Write Start* Online!

For additional practice with the materials found in this chapter, visit our Website at:

http://www.ablongman.com/checkett

The Website also features additional readings, quizzes, writing activities, and Internet links, as well as a bulletin board and interactive chat.

For More Practice with Your Grammar and Writing Skills

For further exercises designed to improve your writing and grammar skills, use the Writer's ToolKit Plus CD-ROM included with this text. The toolkit provides a wealth of computerized tutorials and practice activities.

PART 1

Writing Effective Sentences

In the following chapters, you will learn the basic rules of grammar and the basic sentence types. You also will learn the technique known as "sentence combining" that allows writers to create a more interesting and mature style of writing. Almost every aspect of your life at home, school, and work demands longer pieces of writing (memos, letters, reports, essays, research papers) with which to communicate to family, friends, teachers, and colleagues. All of these forms of writing are created using the grammar rules that make up standard English. Without these rules, neither sentence variety nor longer pieces of writing would be possible.

3

The Simple Sentence and the Independent Clause

The sentence is the building block of all writing. Paragraphs, memos, letters, reports, and even essays and books are built out of sentences. But what are sentences built out of? A properly constructed sentence must have a **subject,** a **verb,** and sufficient meaning.

In this chapter, we will practice identifying subjects and verbs in **simple sentences.** A simple sentence has one subject and one verb. This is also called an **independent clause.** Sentences can have more than one subject and one verb; compound subjects and verbs are presented at the end of the chapter.

The Subject

The subject of a sentence is usually a noun or a pronoun.

Nouns

A **noun** names persons, places, and things. Nouns either can be *common* (not capitalized) or *proper* (always capitalized). Notice that common nouns name general persons, places, and things while proper nouns name particular persons, places, and things.

Common	Proper
(general)	(particular)
city	Los Angeles
boy	Peter
photocopier	Xerox

Examples

Proper Noun/Person: *Fred* drove to the store.

Common Noun/Person: The *manager* counted the day's receipts.

Proper Noun/Place: *New York* is a city with many tall buildings.

Common Noun/Place: The *countryside* was very open but very quiet.

Proper Noun/Thing: The *Washington Monument* was circled by tourists.

Thing: The large *table* was filled with birthday gifts.

Pronouns

Pronouns are used to take the place of nouns.

Commonly Used Pronouns

I	we	me	it
you	they	this	that
everyone	something	nobody	which

For a complete list of pronouns, see The Writer's Resources, Parts of Speech, Pronouns (page 278).

When we want to eliminate using the same noun too many times, we use a pronoun to reduce repetition.

In the following sentence, the repetition of the nouns "children," "soda," and "potato chips," makes the sentence sound awkward and almost like it was written for a very young child's reader.

The children wanted to have a party, but the children did not have enough soda and potato chips. The children ran to the store and bought more soda and potato chips.

In the next sentence, noun repetition is eliminated by substituting pronouns for nouns. The pronoun substitutions are *italicized*.

The children wanted to have a party, but *they* did not have enough soda and potato chips. *They* ran to the store and bought *them*.

Once the main nouns have been established, we can use pronouns to eliminate repetition. However, overuse of pronouns can lead to the common problem called *pronoun reference*. A pronoun reference error occurs when the pronoun that is replacing a noun does not clearly refer to that noun.

Example

The truck ran into the light pole, and *it* was damaged.

Which noun, "truck" or "light pole," does the pronoun "it" refer to? There is no way for the reader to understand which reference the writer meant. Always be sure that when you substitute a pronoun for a noun, the pronoun refers clearly to that noun.

▼
PRACTICE 1

Underline the subject in each of the following sentences.

Example: <u>Heathrow Airport</u> was crowded with vacationers returning home.

1. The airliner flew the "red eye" from London to New York.

2. A thick fog had settled over the airport.

3. The runway lights flashed blue and yellow.

4. The jet circled JFK for over an hour.

5. The air traffic controller gave the pilot landing clearance.

6. The pilot landed the aircraft successfully.

7. Passengers emptied into the large terminal.

8. Flight attendants helped children and senior citizens.

9. Signs written in many languages helped passengers find their way.

10. Luggage was picked up from the baggage carousel.

▼
PRACTICE 2

Underline the subject in each of the following sentences.

1. Frank Lloyd Wright wanted to study architecture at the University of Wisconsin.

2. It did not offer architecture courses.

3. Civil engineering became his major area of study.

4. The Adler and Sullivan Company hired him as a designer.

5. "Organic architecture" was a style he created.

6. This philosophy held that a building should develop out of its natural surroundings.

7. He created many wonderful buildings using this idea.

8. The carport was one of his inventions.

9. Air conditioning was first used in a Frank Lloyd Wright building.

10. Frank Lloyd Wright became a pioneer in modern architecture.

▼ PRACTICE 3

Underline the subject in each of the following sentences.

1. The Yukon Territory is located in northwestern Canada.

2. The vast area (186,300 sq mi) is bordered by Alaska and British Columbia.

3. Its mineral wealth and scenic vistas are two of its main attractions.

4. The name Yukon is taken from an Indian expression meaning "great river."

5. High plateaus occupy most of the south and central portions of the territory.

6. The St. Elias Mountains separate the Yukon from the Pacific Ocean.

7. Forests cover about 40 percent of the total land area.

8. White spruce is the most common species of tree.

9. A subarctic climate prevails with severe winters and hot summers.

10. The annual precipitation ranges from 9 to 13 inches.

▼ PRACTICE 4

Supply a person, place, thing, or pronoun for the subject in the following sentences.

1. _____ called to his friend Osama to see if he wanted to go for a walk.

2. The _____ sped down the road at breakneck speed.

3. _____ enjoyed going to the movies every Saturday.

4. Three _____ landed on the deck of the aircraft carrier.

5. _____ sparkled in the clear, evening sky.

6. The thick, wool _____ kept the camper warm while she slept.

7. Many _____ visit the Grand Canyon every year.

8. _____ read many books every summer.

9. _____ listened to rock, jazz, and classical music.

10. _____ is a popular Italian pasta dish.

PRACTICE 5

Write a sentence using the subject provided.

1. Tornado— _____

_____

2. Cabdriver— _____

_____

3. Actors— _____

_____

4. Apartment— _____

_____

5. Detective— _____

_____

6. Table— _____

_____

7. Grapefruit— _____

_____

8. Motorcycle— _____

_____

9. Movie— _____

_____

10. Lasagna— _____

_____

Subjects and Prepositional Phrases

There is an old saying in writing: all subjects are nouns, but not all nouns are subjects. When looking for subjects, you might be confused by the noun in a prepositional phrase.

A **prepositional phrase** is a group of words containing a preposition, such as *in, of, on,* or *to,* and a noun as its object.

Preposition	+	Object	=	Prepositional Phrase
in	+	a minute	=	in a minute
of	+	the nation	=	of the nation
on	+	the roof	=	on the roof
to	+	the moon	=	to the moon

Many sentences contain prepositional phrases at or near the beginning where the subject noun is located. It is sometimes confusing to figure out which of the two nouns is the subject. The object noun of a preposition is never the subject.

In the morning, coffee is a favorite beverage.

     ↑   ↑

   noun   noun

Two nouns side-by-side in front of the verb can be confusing. One method to identify the subject noun is to cross out the prepositional phrase (and the noun in it); the noun that remains will be the subject.

~~In the morning~~, coffee is a favorite beverage.

Once "in the morning" is crossed out, the remaining noun "coffee" is easily identified as the subject.

Learn to recognize prepositions so that you can eliminate their object nouns as possible subjects.

Here is a list of commonly used prepositions you should become familiar with:

Commonly Used Prepositions		
about	beside	off
above	between	on
across	by	over
after	during	through
against	except	to
along	for	toward
among	from	under
around	in	until
at	into	up
before	like	with
behind	of	without

For a complete list of prepositions, see The Writer's Resources, Parts of Speech, Prepositions (page 308).

▼ PRACTICE 6

In each of the following sentences, cross out the prepositional phrases. Then, underline the subjects.

Example: ~~At the zoo~~, most <u>animals</u> are still kept ~~in cages~~.

1. In the wind, kites are difficult to control.

2. The carton of oranges floated in the water.

3. Bill was safe in the space under the bridge.

4. Between the two hills, the houses are made from cedar logs.

5. The microwave on the counter in the kitchen was very clean.

6. During the week and on the weekend, homework is a constant activity.

7. Except on casual day, the workers always wore suits to the office.

8. Over the river and through the woods, the wolf raced to Grandmother's house.

9. The couple arrived at the wedding reception without a gift.

10. Three of the guitarists are alternative musicians.

▼ PRACTICE 7

In each of the following sentences, cross out the prepositional phrases. Then, underline the subjects.

1. In a presidential election, the incumbent has to choose a running mate.

2. Until the process ends, the party's campaigning cannot start.

3. At the beginning of the process, many candidates are considered.

4. Before the interviews, the candidates' party credentials are inspected.

5. After the elimination of some candidates, a short list is assembled.

6. From the short list, interviews are scheduled.

7. Without the interview process, the final choice cannot be made.

8. During the interview, the candidate must clarify specific positions.

9. By the end of the process, the incumbent can make a clear choice for the party.

10. Behind each political partnership, a lot of work has to be done.

▼ **PRACTICE 8**

In each of the following sentences, cross out the prepositional phrases. Then, underline the subjects.

1. In the plane, the tour passengers slept peacefully.

2. The rocking motion of the plane was very relaxing.

3. Most of the passengers slept with a pillow under their heads.

4. Outside the cabin, the stars shone like small fireflies in the dark.

5. There was a hushed silence inside the cabin.

6. In most cases, smaller children slept on their parent's laps.

7. The people with older children were free to roll over on their sides if they wanted to.

8. After the flight landed, the passengers walked to the baggage carousel.

9. On the waiting ramp, the passengers were required to show tickets to the skycaps.

10. During the trip to the hotel, their bags were carried on the top of the bus.

The Verb

As a developing writer, there are three types of verbs you should become familiar with: *action verbs, linking verbs,* and *helping verbs.*

Action verbs describe an activity the subject is performing:

Commonly Used Action Verbs		
arrive	soar	eat
study	run	smile
speak	construct	race
climb	called	leave

Examples

The mailman *arrives* with a package.

The dog *races* the squirrel to the tree.

The wind *climbs* high above the cliffs.

The defense lawyer *speaks* with a Southern drawl.

▼
PRACTICE 9

Underline the action verb in each of the following sentences. To help you find the action verb, circle the subject. Cross out any prepositional phrases.

Example: ~~On average~~, (Tiger Woods) hits a golf ball over 290 yards off the tee.

1. As a young child, he learned the proper mechanics of the swing.

2. His father guided his golf instruction.

3. The youngster progressed rapidly as a golfer.

4. He garnered three Junior Amateur championships in a row.

5. Without hesitation, Woods won three straight Amateur championships.

6. On the professional tour, Tiger arrived at the Masters tournament as a tour rookie.

7. He regularly launched 300 yard drives on the longer holes.

8. His length off the tee catapulted him to victory again.

9. Tiger stunned the golfing world with his outstanding and exciting play.

10. Woods earned over a million dollars his first full year on the professional tour.

PRACTICE 10

Underline the action verb in each of the following sentences. To help you find the action verb, circle the subject. Cross out any prepositional phrases.

1. A letter arrived at Marjorie's apartment.

2. She opened the letter on the kitchen table.

3. A handwritten note fell from the envelope.

4. She unfolded the piece of paper.

5. For no apparent reason, she read the message out loud.

6. Tears of happiness flowed from her eyes.

7. A major airline selected her name from a list of contest entrants.

8. After calming down, Marjorie called her mother and father on the phone.

9. She told them the happy news.

10. She won round trip tickets for four to London.

PRACTICE 11

Underline the action verb in each of the following sentences. To help you find the action verb, circle the subject. Cross out any prepositional phrases.

1. Most people participate in outdoor activities.

2. One man scuba dives in the Caribbean.

3. Another skis in the mountains of Colorado.

4. People on both Florida coasts fish for trophy marlin and swordfish.

5. A group from Vermont searches for rare birds in the deep forests.

6. "Spelunkers" crawl through narrow caves.

7. Missourians ride bikes on the scenic Katy Trail.

8. Individuals connected with ropes climb the faces of steep cliffs.

9. Others leap from bridges with bungee cords attached to their ankles.

10. Small groups in military garb play "paintball" in the woods.

▼
PRACTICE 12

Write a sentence using the action verb provided.

1. Starts— _____

_____

2. Jumps— _____

_____

3. Study— _____

_____

4. Bake— _____

_____

5. Swerves— _____

_____

6. Builds— _____

_____

7. Travels— _____

_____

8. Speaks— _____

_____

9. Looks— _____

_____

10. Crashes— _____

_____

Linking verbs indicate a condition or state of being. The linking verb connects the subject with a word or phrase identifying or describing something about the subject:

Commonly Used Linking Verbs

act	feel	look
appear	grow	seem
be (am, is, are, was, were, have been)	become	taste

Examples

Dr. Smith *is* a surgeon.

The wool sweater *feels* rough.

The desert sand *is* cool in the evening.

Aretha *appears* tired and sluggish.

PRACTICE 13

There is a linking verb in each of the following sentences. To help identify the linking verb, circle the subject, and draw a line to the word or words that describe the subject. Then, circle that word or group of words. Finally, underline the linking verb between the two circles.

Examples:

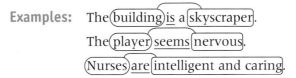

The (building) is a (skyscraper).
The (player) seems (nervous).
(Nurses) are (intelligent and caring).

1. The concert was very exciting.

2. The foyer looked buffed and polished from floor to ceiling.

3. The hall felt cold and stuffy.

4. People in the audience seemed nervous.

5. Members of the orchestra were relaxed.

6. The symphony orchestra sounded confident and well rehearsed.

7. The cookies served during intermission smelled heavenly.

8. The music remained controlled throughout the evening.

9. The conductor appeared pleased with the orchestra members' effort.

10. At the concert's end, the applause became louder with each bow.

PRACTICE 14

There is a linking verb in each of the following sentences. To help identify the linking verb, circle the subject, and draw a line to the word or words describing the subject. Then, circle that word or group of words. Finally, underline the linking verb between the two circles.

1. My life was not wonderful.

2. I appeared surly and cantankerous to my friends.

3. My family said I looked depressed.

4. My job became boring and uninteresting.

5. Even food smelled dull and tasteless.

6. I had become lazy and indifferent.

7. I felt disassociated with my true self.

8. These unproductive states of mind were not acceptable.

9. I turned to a counselor for help.

10. After many months, the therapy seems to be helping.

PRACTICE 15

Write a sentence using the linking verb provided.

1. Was— _____

_____

2. Seem— _____

_____

3. Is— _____

_____

4. Feel— _____

_____

5. Have— _____

_____

6. Am— _____

_____

7. Appear— _____

_____

8. Were— _____

_____

9. Has— _____

_____

10. Are— _____

_____

Helping verbs combine with a main verb to form a group of words called a *verb phrase*. The helping verb gives the main verb a specific time reference or meaning.

Commonly Used Helping Verbs		
can	could	may
might	must	shall
should	will	would
forms of the irregular verbs *be*, *do*, and *have*		

For a list of irregular verbs, see The Writer's Resources, Parts of Speech, Irregular Verbs (pages 287–290).

Examples
The manager *can* fire employees if they break regulations.
Keeping a diary *might* help you better understand yourself.
Studying *will* enhance your grade point average.
A positive attitude *should* make your day more enjoyable.

PRACTICE 16

There is a helping verb and a main verb in each of the following sentences. To help identify the helping verb, circle the subject. Then, cross out any prepositional phrases. Finally, underline the entire verb phrase.

Example: Studies of all ages indicate that (exercising) can help overall mental and physical health for most people.

1. People of all ages should exercise.

2. However, exercising must be done on a regular basis.

3. Working out three times a week can create a more healthy person.

4. On the other hand, exercising too much may be detrimental to your health.

5. An effective workout must include exercises for both muscles and the cardiovascular system.

6. Lifting weights should be accompanied by an aerobic exercise.

7. Some experts think walking might be as beneficial as jogging.

8. Mental health also will be stimulated by physical exercise.

9. Good mental health could facilitate success in other areas of your life.

10. Regular exercising would lower health-related costs nationally.

PRACTICE 17

There is a helping verb and a main verb in each of the following sentences. To help identify the helping verb, circle the subject. Then, cross out any prepositional phrases. Finally, underline the entire verb phrase.

1. How do you start a hobby?

2. First, you can buy a hobby magazine and learn the varieties of hobbies available.

3. Then, you should ask your friends and neighbors what hobbies they have.

4. You will need to figure out how much time and money you have to invest in the hobby.

5. Knowing this may help you narrow your choices.

6. Of course, you must ask for advice at a hobby shop near you.

7. This could put you in touch with other enthusiasts interested in the same hobby as you.

8. Joining a hobby club will be an invaluable resource for furthering your enjoyment.

9. Being a member of a club also might get you discounts on materials and publications.

10. Also, other members would assist you with difficult aspects of your hobby.

Write a sentence using the helping verb provided. You also will have to choose a main verb to combine with the helping verb as you create each sentence.

Example: Can— I <u>can</u> *ride* a unicycle for five minutes before losing my balance.
      ↑   ↑
   helping main
    verb   verb

1. Could— _____

_____

2. May— _____

_____

3. Can— _____

_____

4. Might— _____

_____

5. Must— _____

_____

Verb Tense (Time)

In writing, time is called *tense*. Because tense is shown primarily through the *verb*, time is more accurately called **verb tense.** It is important to know whether an action or linking verb is in the past, present, or future tense. After all, you would certainly react differently if something had already happened, was happening at present, or was not going to happen until later. This section deals with the simplest forms of past, present, and future verb tense in regard to the action and linking verbs we have already studied.

For additional information regarding verb tense, see The Writer's Resources, Parts of Speech, Verb Tense (page 286).

Examples of Simple Past, Present, and Future Verb Tense

Past	I talked
	I worked
	He talked
	He worked
Present	I talk
	I work
	She talks
	She works
Future	I will talk
	I will work
	They will talk
	They will work

For a complete list of tenses, see The Writer's Resources, Parts of Speech, Verb Tense (page 286).

Examples

Past Tense Linking Verb: Juan *was* a student at USC last year.

Present Tense Linking Verb: Juan *is* a student at USC this year.

Future Tense Linking Verb: Juan *will be* a student at USC next year.

Past Tense Action Verb: Amy *skated* yesterday.

Present Tense Action Verb: Amy *is skating* today.

Future Tense Action Verb: Amy *will skate* tomorrow.

▼ **PRACTICE 19**

Complete the following sentences by filling in the blank spaces with the past tense form, the present tense form, and the future tense form of the verb provided.

1. Verb: practice

Past Tense: The girls' soccer team _____ for the tournament.

Present Tense: The girls' soccer team _____ for the tournament.

Future Tense: The girls' soccer team _____ for the tournament.

2. Verb: dance

Past Tense: The ballerina ———————— *Swan Lake* for the first time.

Present Tense: The ballerina ———————— *Swan Lake* for the first time.

Future Tense: The ballerina ———————— *Swan Lake* for the first time.

3. Verb: cook

Past Tense: I ———————— seafood gumbo for my guests.

Present Tense: I ———————— seafood gumbo for my guests.

Future Tense: I ———————— seafood gumbo for my guests.

4. Verb: play

Past Tense: Jasmine ———————— the guitar for her boyfriend.

Present Tense: Jasmine ———————— the guitar for her boyfriend.

Future Tense: Jasmine ———————— the guitar for her boyfriend.

5. Verb: clean

Past Tense: Melvin ———————— his school locker.

Present Tense: Melvin ———————— his school locker.

Future Tense: Melvin ———————— his school locker.

▼ PRACTICE 20

Complete the following sentences by filling in the blank spaces with the past tense form, the present tense form, and the future tense form of the verb provided.

1. Verb: corner

Past Tense: The dog ———————— the cat in the alley.

Present Tense: The dog ———————— the cat in the alley.

Future Tense: The dog ———————— the cat in the alley.

2. Verb: assume

Past Tense: The professor ———————— the students had read the chapter.

Present Tense: The professor ———————— the students have read the chapter.

Future Tense: The professor ———————— the students will read the chapter.

3. Verb: consume

Past Tense: The crocodile _____ a large portion of meat for its daily meal.

Present Tense: The crocodile _____ a large portion of meat for its daily meal.

Future Tense: The crocodile _____ a large portion of meat for its daily meal.

4. Verb: type

Past Tense: The secretary _____ a letter for the Vice President.

Present Tense: The secretary _____ a letter for the Vice President.

Future Tense: The secretary _____ a letter for the Vice President.

5. Verb: camp

Past Tense: The scientist _____ deep in the Amazon rain forest.

Present Tense: The scientist _____ deep in the Amazon rain forest.

Future Tense: The scientist _____ deep in the Amazon rain forest.

▼ **PRACTICE 21**

Complete the following sentences by filling in the blank spaces with the past tense form, the present tense form, and the future tense form of the verb provided.

1. Verb: trust

Past Tense: The employees _____ their boss.

Present Tense: The employees _____ their boss.

Future Tense: The employees _____ their boss.

2. Verb: coordinate

Past Tense: The manager _____ all cleaning responsibilities.

Present Tense: The manager _____ all cleaning responsibilities.

Future Tense: The manager _____ all cleaning responsibilities.

3. Verb: exercise

Past Tense: Felicia _____ every morning at 4 a.m.

Present Tense: Felicia _____ every morning at 4 a.m.

Future Tense: Felicia _____ every morning at 4 a.m.

4. Verb: juggle

Past Tense: The executive _____ a long list of activities.

Present Tense: The executive _____ a long list of activities.

Future Tense: The executive _____ a long list of activities.

5. Verb: jump

Past Tense: The kangaroo _____ over the fence guarding the field.

Present Tense: The kangaroo _____ over the fence guarding the field.

Future Tense: The kangaroo _____ over the fence guarding the field.

PRACTICE 22

Supply a present, past, or future tense verb in the space provided in each of the following sentences. In the parentheses, identify the tense for the verb you wrote.

Example: The eagle <u>glides (present tense)</u> over the river searching for salmon.

1. The girls _____ (_____) on the freshly mowed lawn.

2. The space shuttle _____ (_____) into the sky over Florida.

3. The college student _____ (_____) for the History 101 final exam.

4. The cyclist _____ (_____) toward the finish line.

5. The kittens _____ (_____) together in the warmth of the sunbeam.

6. All 100 senators _____ (_____) the healthcare legislation.

7. Jennifer _____ (_____) the customer choose the correct pair of glasses.

8. The judge _____ (_____) the gavel on her desk to restore order.

9. José _____ (_____) three dozen fajitas for the party.

10. The choir _____ (_____) the gospel song with feeling and emotion.

▼ **PRACTICE 23**

Supply a present, past, or future tense verb in the space provided in each of the following sentences. In the parenthesis, identify the tense for the verb you wrote.

1. The skater _____ (_____) on the frozen pond.

2. Kitaro _____ (_____) the chemistry exam.

3. Tina _____ (_____) lifting weights during gym class.

4. The bird _____ (_____) its feathers after a dip in the bird bath.

5. The engine _____ (_____) as the dragster reached the start line.

6. The senator _____ (_____) at the fund raiser banquet.

7. Icebergs _____ (_____) as they float aimlessly in the ocean.

8. The grasshopper _____ (_____) in the field of golden corn.

9. The severe storms _____ (_____) across the Midwest.

10. Donny _____ (_____) while riding the roller coaster.

Compound Subjects

To this point, we have been using single subjects and single verbs. However, compound subjects and compound verbs also can be used in simple sentences. First, we explore compound subjects. A **compound subject** consists of two or more nouns or pronouns connected by *and, or, either/or,* or *neither/nor*. Some special relationships exist between certain compound subjects and their verb complements. For a discussion with exercises, see The Writer's Resources, Parts of Speech, Compound Subjects, and also Parts of Speech, Subject/Verb Agreement on pages 296–300.

Examples

Bill and Raul drove to the cineplex.

Either you or I will have to pick Melanie up at the train station.

Neither Venice nor Rome are ignored by tourists.

Compound subjects can be separated by other words, but they are still considered one subject as long as they are doing the same action or being the same thing.

Examples

Charles the dentist, *Clyde* the doctor, and *Phyliss* the chiropractor, met for dinner.

In this sentence, Charles, Clyde, and Phyliss are having dinner together.

Large, powerful *St. Bernards*, sleek, fast *Russian Greyhounds*, and small, aggressive *English Terriers*, are popular pets around the world.

In this sentence, the various types of dogs share a common experience.

▼ PRACTICE 24

Underline the compound subjects in the following sentences. To help you identify the subjects, cross out any prepositional phrases you find, and circle the verb.

1. The child's ears and nose looked just like its mother's.

2. Neither my golf coach nor my swimming coach were ever professionals.

3. Jupiter, Mars, and Venus are planets in our solar system.

4. After the dance, Joan and Jillian drove to a private party.

5. The antique sofa, the art deco clock, and the abstract painting were sold at auction.

6. At Chicago's Navy Pier, Fred and Dianna bought three sweaters and a necklace.

7. The slithery snake, the prickly hedgehog, and the colorful parrot are the most popular animals at the children's zoo.

8. In the middle of the room, the food, the drinks, and the cake covered the table.

9. *Hamlet* and *Macbeth* are two of Shakespeare's most famous plays.

10. Either the cat or dog knocked the lamp and vase onto the floor.

▼ **PRACTICE 25**

Underline the compound subjects in the following sentences. To help you identify the subjects, cross out any prepositional phrases you find, and circle the verb.

1. For their new business venture, Jamal and Nerita purchased two computers.

2. Brad Pitt, Harrison Ford, and Tom Cruise are popular movie stars.

3. At the auto show, neither Mick, Tina, nor Jacki bought a car.

4. The lawn mower, the edger, and the cultivator sat unused in the garage.

5. *His* and *Hers* are popular monograms on bath towels.

6. Either you or I will have to make dinner for the cub scouts.

7. Chrysler, General Motors, and Ford are known as the "Big Three" auto makers.

8. In the middle of the night, snoring, cat calls, and crying infants can reduce sleep.

9. The brightly colored yellow finch, the aptly named red-breasted grosbeak, and the red-winged blackbird are favorite subjects for bird watching clubs.

10. Nike, Adidas, and Reebok are best-selling athletic shoes.

Compound Verbs

Like subjects, verbs also can be compound. A **compound verb** consists of more than one verb. With few exceptions, compound verbs are almost always connected by the conjunction *and*.

> **Examples**
> Janet *laughed and cried* during the movie.
> The horse *ran and jumped* as part of the rodeo contest.
> Paris *dazzles and excites* visiting tourists.

In the sentences above, notice that the subject is not repeated in front of the second verb. We do not write: *Paris dazzles* and *Paris excites* visiting tourists. Writing "Paris" twice is unnecessarily repetitive, and it makes the rhythm of the sentence choppy and awkward.

Underline the compound verbs in the following sentences.

1. The horse trotted and galloped around the track.

2. The mechanic tuned the engine and lubricated the chassis of the car.

3. The audience laughed and cried at the actor's performance.

4. The broker bought and sold the investor's energy stocks.

5. The motel room was clean and smelled of lilacs and roses.

6. A fax machine can save money and hasten communications.

7. In New York City, skateboarders ride on subways and skate in parking garages.

8. Ramon caught and cleaned a bucketful of fish.

9. The legislature argued and voted on fifty-three bills this current session.

10. The police chased and arrested the bank robber.

Underline the compound verbs in the following sentences.

1. Lightning cracked and popped in the darkened sky.

2. In the auditorium, students clapped their hands and stomped their feet.

3. The two elk rivals snorted and brandished their antlers at one another.

4. The old fire engine jiggled and rattled down the cobblestone street.

5. A distant waterfall roared and thundered across the plain.

6. After the huge meal, the diners moaned and groaned.

7. The truck skidded, jackknifed, and crashed into the barrier.

8. Sea birds fly, dive, swim, and float while searching for food.

9. The bull lowered its head, scraped its hooves, and charged the matador.

10. The dancers twirled and leaped in unison with the music.

Write sentences for the following compound subjects and verbs. Provide compound subjects for the compound verbs listed and compound verbs for the compound subjects when given.

Examples: Bill/Ted—Bill and Ted <u>laughed and cried</u> during the movie.

Dribbled/Shot—<u>Jill and Teiko</u> dribbled and shot during the game.

1. Stewardess/Passenger _____

_____

2. Swam/Lifted Weights _____

_____

3. Truck/Car _____

_____

4. Shivered/Trembled _____

_____

5. Ira/Sheila _____

_____

6. Camped/Hiked _____

_____

7. Flower/Tree _____

_____

8. Ate/Drank _____

_____

9. Teacher/Student _____

_____

10. Stumbled/Fell _____

_____

Correcting Sentence Fragments

A simple sentence consists of a single **independent clause.** An independent clause is a series of words with a subject, verb, and sufficient meaning. This means that the independent clause can stand on its own as a simple sentence. When you are writing sentences, be certain that each independent clause has a subject and a verb and sufficient meaning. If the subject, verb, or sufficient meaning is missing from the independent clause, then a sentence fragment error is committed.

> **Examples of Sentence Fragments**
>
> **1.** The kicked the football. (no subject—who or what kicked the football?)
> To correct, add a subject:
> The <u>football player</u> kicked the football.
> **2.** The chef the fettuccine Alfredo. (no verb—what did the chef do in relation to the fettuccine Alfredo?)
> To correct, add a verb:
> The chef <u>prepared</u> the fettuccine Alfredo.
> **3.** The announcement of the new dress code caused all the employees. (insufficient meaning—what did the dress code cause the employees to do?)
> To correct, add additional information to create sufficient meaning:
> The announcement of the new dress code caused all the employees <u>to buy uniforms</u>.

▼ PRACTICE 29

Correct and rewrite the following sentence fragments using the three techniques listed above.

1. Marathon runners, training for the Olympics, as many as 100 miles every week.

_____

2. Build nests and lay eggs.

_____

3. It was time for the archeologists.

_____

4. Cooks in a short amount of time.

_____

5. The man wearing the red vest.

_____

6. The gigantic iceberg a hole in *Titanic's* hull.

_____

7. George a computer at a discount store to save money.

_____

8. Can earn money by investing in mutual funds.

_____

9. Broken racket strings was the reason for her.

_____

10. Spilled the platter of ravioli on her Aunt Vidalia's new dress.

_____

▼
PRACTICE 30

Correct and rewrite the following sentence fragments using the three techniques listed above.

1. Ate the delicious apple strudel for dessert.

_____

2. Ramon 14 hours a day to save enough tuition money for school.

_____

3. The rugby team rode a bus for 14 hours in order.

_____

4. A chipped tooth caused the movie star to.

_____

5. The wine steward the list of the restaurant's entire stock.

_____

6. Measured the foundation before pouring the concrete.

_____

7. The entered the dark cave looking for a place to sleep.

_____

8. The baker sifted the flour before.

_____

9. The watchman to the third floor to make certain the doors were locked.

_____

10. The cleaned all the desks, mopped the floors, and emptied the wastebaskets.

_____

CHAPTER REVIEW

▼ A simple sentence contains a subject and verb, and has sufficient meaning. This also is the definition of an independent clause.

▼ The subject of a sentence is usually a noun or a pronoun. Nouns name persons, places, and things. Nouns can be common (general) or proper (particular). Proper nouns are always capitalized.

▼ Pronouns are used to replace nouns in order to avoid repetition.

▼ Subject nouns often are confused with the nouns in prepositional phrases.

▼ To help identify the subject in a sentence, cross out prepositional phrases.

▼ There are three types of verbs you should become familiar with: action verbs, linking verbs, and helping verbs.

▼ Action verbs describe what the subject is doing.

▼ Linking verbs connect the subject with an idea that describes the subject.

▼ Helping verbs combine with a main verb to form a group of words called a verb phrase.

▼ The helping verb gives the main verb a specific time reference or meaning.

▼ In writing, time is called *tense*. Because tense is shown primarily through the verb, time is more accurately called *verb tense*. The three simplest forms of verb tense are past, present, and future.

▼ Subjects can be compound. A *compound subject* consists of two or more nouns or pronouns connected by *and, or, either/or,* or *neither/nor*.

▼ Verbs can be compound. A *compound verb* consists of more than one verb. With few exceptions, compound verbs are connected by the conjunction *and*.

▼ Sentence fragments occur when the subject, verb, or sufficient meaning are missing from the sentence. Correct by adding a subject, a verb, or adding additional information to create sufficient meaning.

Visit *The Write Start* Online!

For additional practice with the materials found in this chapter, visit our Website at:

http://www.ablongman.com/checkett

The Website also features additional readings, quizzes, writing activities, and Internet links, as well as a bulletin board and interactive chat.

For More Practice with Your Grammar and Writing Skills

For further exercises designed to improve your writing and grammar skills, use the Writer's ToolKit Plus CD-ROM included with this text. The toolkit provides a wealth of computerized tutorials and practice activities.

4

Linking Independent Clauses Using the Comma and Coordinators

You Need to Know

Before reading this chapter, you need to know the following about simple sentences:

- A simple sentence contains a subject, verb, and has sufficient meaning.
- A simple sentence contains one independent clause.
- Action verbs describe what the subject is doing.
- Linking verbs connect the subject with an idea that describes the subject.
- Helping verbs combine with the main verb and give the main verb time reference or meaning.
- Verbs express tense (time)—either past, present, or future.
- Subjects and verbs can be compound.

Students needing help with these concepts should review Chapter 3.

Coordinating Conjunctions

Simple sentences are the basis for most writing; however, writing only with simple sentences can lead to dull writing, and complex ideas often need a more complex sentence format for developed expression. For the sake of variety and developed ideas, a writer connects one simple sentence to another simple sentence by **using a comma (,)** and one of the following **coordinating conjunctions: B**ut, **O**r, **Y**et, **F**or, **A**nd, **N**or, **S**o. We remember the coordinating conjunctions by **BOYFANS** (taken from the first letter of each word). The mnemonic BOYFANS exists only to link simple sentences together to create *compound sentences*. A **compound sentence** consists of two simple sentences (two independent clauses) linked together with a coordinating conjunction and a comma.

The list below explains the meaning of each of the coordinating conjunctions in BOYFANS. They are not interchangeable. Note that the comma is placed before each coordinating conjunction to signal the start of the second complete sentence.

Using Coordinating Conjunctions

But—Use to connect two simple sentences that have contrasting meanings:

Jawan hit the ball, **but** *Christie caught the ball.*

Or—Use to combine two simple sentences that involve a choice:

Christie could have thrown the ball to Jose, **or** *she could have thrown it to home plate.*

Yet—Use to combine two simple sentences that have contrasting meanings:

Jawan hit the ball, **yet** *Christie caught the ball.*

For—Use to combine two simple sentences that involve a reason:

Malik tried to score from second base, **for** *there were already two outs.*

And—Use to combine two simple sentences that involve adding one idea to another:

Jason hit the ball, **and** *Latoya caught the ball.*

Nor—Use when the first simple sentence is in the negative and you want to combine it with another simple sentence:

Mark does not like striking out, **nor** *does Hakeem like sliding into a base.*

So—Use to combine two simple sentences that show a result:

Isabel scored a run, **so** *her team won the game.*

Instead of expressing ideas using all simple sentences, like this:

> Jawan hit the ball. Christie caught the ball. Christie could throw the ball to first base. She could throw the ball to third. Pang ran quickly to third base. Chinua tagged him out.

We can add variety and connect ideas, like this:

> Jawan hit the ball**, but** Christie caught the ball. Christie could throw the ball to first base**, or** she could throw the ball to third. Pang ran quickly to third base**, yet** Chinua tagged him out.

Notice that the coordinating conjunctions not only combine the shorter sentences into longer, more rhythmical ones, but they also help connect two different ideas, making them easier for the reader to understand.

PRACTICE 1

Practice *coordinating* using *conjunctions.* Combine the following pairs of simple sentences by using a comma and the BOYFANS in the parentheses ( ).

1. (but) Jawan hit the ball. Christie caught the ball.

_____

2. (or) Christie could throw the ball to first base. She could throw the ball to third.

_____

_____

3. (yet) Pang ran quickly to third base. Chinua tagged him out.

_____

4. (for) Jefferson struck out three times. The pitcher threw a wicked curve-ball.

_____

5. (and) Tom singled four times. Angie hit two home runs.

_____

6. (nor) Yoshi did not have a base on balls. Sarita did not bunt during the game.

_____

7. (so) Joe caused three errors. The other team scored five runs.

_____

Combine some more simple sentences, but this time you choose which BOY-FANS you think works the best. Try not to use the same coordinating conjunction twice. Choose from the list:

But **O**r **Y**et **F**or **A**nd **N**or **S**o

Examples: Mel wanted to go hiking. Shonda wanted to read a book.

Mel wanted to go hiking, but Shonda wanted to read a book.

1. Some friends wanted to go to the park. _____ Others wanted to go to the zoo.

2. Bicycling is good exercise. _____ Try to ride at least three times each week.

3. Salads are great tasting. _____ They are also healthy for you.

4. Morning is the best time to exercise. _____ There is less heat and humidity.

5. Genetics does not guarantee good health. _____ Eating only fruit is not the solution.

6. Fish is very tasty. _____ Too much sauce can mask its taste.

7. Broccoli is a tasty and nutritious choice. _____ You could also choose asparagus.

Try some more. Choose a different BOYFANS for each sentence, and remember to place a comma before each coordinating conjunction.

Examples: Flowers are very beautiful. Buying them can be expensive.

Flowers are very beautiful, but buying them can be expensive.

1. You can fly a jet to Chicago. You can ride a train.

_____

2. Reading a book can be exciting. Listening to music can be soothing.

_____

3. Good grades are important. Study hard and do your homework.

_____

4. The car did not get good gas mileage. It did not ride smoothly either.

_____

5. John did not like the restaurant. He continued eating there.

_____

6. Jenny enjoyed hiking. The woods were both beautiful and quiet.

_____

7. Snakes can make interesting pets. They can be dangerous.

_____

▼ PRACTICE 4

Combine the following ten simple sentences. You can try different combinations in the spaces between the sentences. Write your finished effort on the blank lines provided below the sentences. You should finish with five combined sentences instead of ten single sentences.

The camping trip was exciting.

The trip to the national forest took 13 hours.

Everyone was tired but happy when they arrived.

The cabins were rustic.

They had running water and electricity.

Dave did not bring mosquito repellant.

Juan did not bring extra blankets.

Everyone was hungry.

Pilar went to gather firewood.

The full moon emerged from the clouds later that evening.

Write your finished combined sentences below:

1. _____

2. _____

3. _____

4. _____

5. _____

PRACTICE 5

Try combining pairs of sentences with a variety of coordinating conjunctions. You can use the spaces between the sentences to try different BOYFANS. Write your finished sentences on the blank lines provided below the sentences. You should finish with seven combined sentences instead of 14 single sentences.

Maurice loved to fish.

He went to the lake as often as possible.

His girlfriend Liz did not like to fish.

She did find riding in the boat fun.

They both liked camping.

It was restful sitting around the campfire.

Liz enjoyed cooking the fish.

She took responsibility for packing the cooking equipment.

Cleaning fish was not her favorite activity.

She did not like the taste.

Sometimes Liz would sit in the boat and read.

She would also apply lotion and try tanning in the afternoon sun.

The ride back home was long.

Both Maurice and Liz could not wait to return.

Write your finished combined sentences below:

1. _____

2. _____

3. _____

4. _____

5. _____

6. _____

7. _____

Correcting Run-on and Comma Splice Sentences

Now that you have practiced combining simple sentences to create compound sentences, there are two pitfalls you should avoid: run-on sentences and comma splice sentences.

Run-on

A **run-on sentence** commonly occurs when two independent clauses (complete ideas) are combined without a comma and a coordinating conjunction.

Example

Joan rides the subway to work the bus is too slow.

This sentence announces two complete ideas:

Joan rides the subway to work—the bus is too slow.

There are two methods to correct a run-on sentence:

1. Create two separate sentences.

Joan rides the subway to work. The bus is too slow.

2. Use a comma and a coordinating conjunction (**b**ut, **o**r, **y**et, **f**or, **a**nd, **n**or, **s**o) to link the two ideas together to create a correctly punctuated compound sentence.

Joan rides the subway to work, **for** the bus is too slow.

Comma Splice

A **comma splice** sentence occurs when two independent clauses are joined with a comma but without a coordinating conjunction.

Example

Brian plays the cello, David plays the piano.

This sentence announces two complete ideas joined (or spliced together—hence the name comma splice) by only a comma.

Brian plays the cello , David plays the piano.

Correct the comma splice by adding a coordinating conjunction <u>after</u> the comma to create a correctly punctuated compound sentence.

Brian plays the cello, **and** David plays the piano.

▼ PRACTICE 6

Most of the following sentences contain run-on or comma splice errors. If you find a correct sentence, write **C** in the left-hand column. If the sentence contains a run-on or comma splice error, write either **RO** or **CS.** Then, correct the error using any of the techniques you have learned. Use all methods at least once.

Example: <u>RO</u> The space shuttle program has been very expensive it has also been very successful.

The space shuttle program has been very expensive, <u>but</u> it has also been very successful. (coordinating conjunction added)

1. _____ The shuttle is designed to carry large payloads, there are accommodations for up to seven crew members.

2. _____ The orbiter stage of the spacecraft has a lifetime of 100 missions, the winged orbiter can make unpowered landings on its return to earth.

3. _____ The shuttle is very flexible, for it can deploy and retrieve satellites.

4. _____ Its supporters saw it as a step to space exploration they passed legislation to fund the project.

5. _____ The first test flight occurred in 1981 various design problems surfaced.

6. _____ The first operational flight happened in 1982, two communication satellites were placed in orbit.

7. _____ The seventh mission was memorable, for its crew included the first U.S. female astronaut, Sally K. Ride.

8. _____ The program had many successes the program was in some trouble.

9. _____ The shuttle program has been lagging in its commercial plan, the military began absorbing most of the payload launches.

10. _____ Despite some setbacks, the U.S. government has not given up on the space shuttle program the program is still being funded.

PRACTICE 7

Most of the following sentences contain run-on or comma splice errors. If you find a correct sentence, write **C** in the left-hand column. If the sentence contains a run-on or comma splice error, write either **RO** or **CS**. Then, correct the error using any of the techniques you have learned. Use all methods at least once.

1. _____ The sun dominates our solar system its huge mass produces enormous gravitational force.

2. _____ Electromagnetic energy radiates from the sun's surface the energy supports all life on earth.

3. _____ The sun is actually quite close to the earth, stellar phenomena can be studied in great detail.

4. _____ Many ancient cultures worshiped the sun, and others recognized its importance in the cycle of life.

5. _____ Studying the sun has helped develop calendars solstices, equinoxes, and eclipses have also been studied for their own importance.

6. _____ In 1611, Galileo used a telescope to discover dark spots on the sun's surface, Chinese astronomers reported sunspots in 200 B.C.

7. _____ The discovery of sunspots changed science's view of the sun, for the sun finally was seen as a dynamic, evolving body.

8. _____ Progress in understanding the sun has continued, new scientific instruments have allowed new advances in observation.

9. _____ The coronagraph permits study of the solar corona without the assistance of an eclipse, the magnetograph measures magnetic-field strength over the solar surface.

10. _____ Interest in the sun has facilitated the discovery of new space instruments space telescopes and spectrographs sensitive to ultraviolet radiation revolutionized the study of the sun and outer space.

CHAPTER REVIEW

▼ Using coordinating conjunctions, combine simple sentences to create compound sentences. Remember the coordinating conjunctions by recalling BOYFANS—**B**ut, **O**r, **Y**et, **F**or, **A**nd, **N**or, **S**o.

▼ Each BOYFANS has its own meaning. They are not interchangeable.

But—use when contrasting meaning.

Or—use when there is a choice.

Yet—use when contrasting meaning.

For—use when there is a reason.

And—use when adding one idea to another.

Nor—use when the first simple sentence is in the negative.

So—use when a result is shown.

▼ A comma always precedes a coordinating conjunction when combining two simple sentences.

▼ Combining sentences helps connect ideas, adds sentence variety, and creates rhythm, which are important factors in making communications easier for the reader to understand.

▼ Correct run-on errors by either of two methods:

1. Create two separate sentences.
2. Add a comma and a coordinating conjunction to link the two independent clauses.

▼ Correct comma splice errors by adding a coordinating conjunction after the comma found between the two independent clauses.

Visit *The Write Start* Online!

For additional practice with the materials found in this chapter, visit our Website at:

http://www.ablongman.com/checkett

The Website also features additional readings, quizzes, writing activities, and Internet links, as well as a bulletin board and interactive chat.

For More Practice with Your Grammar and Writing Skills

For further exercises designed to improve your writing and grammar skills, use the Writer's ToolKit Plus CD-ROM included with this text. The toolkit provides a wealth of computerized tutorials and practice activities.

5 Combining Independent Clauses Using the Semicolon

Another method that a writer uses to combine simple sentences or independent clauses to create compound sentences is to use a **semicolon (;).** Keep in mind that a semicolon isn't a substitute for a comma; it's a substitute for a comma and a coordinating conjunction. Therefore, when using a semicolon, do not use a coordinating conjunction or a comma with it. Also, remember that the first word following the semicolon is *not* capitalized.

Proper Use

The anaconda is the world's largest snake; it can grow to 30 feet or more in length. ("size" is the relating idea)

Proper Use

The nurse measured the patient's blood pressure; she also took a blood sample. ("blood" is the relating idea)

Proper Use

The submarine dove to a depth of 300 fathoms; it hovered silently at that depth for two hours. ("depth" is the relating idea)

Do not combine sentences/independent clauses with a semicolon if the ideas are not closely related.

Improper Use

The bear rummaged through the camp food supply; some people believe in angels. (no relating idea)

Improper Use

Japan consists of four large islands; solar panels can generate electricity. (no relating idea)

Improper Use

Sundials are practical and decorative; snorkeling is a popular vacation pastime. (no relating idea)

When there is no relating idea between two simple sentences (independent clauses), as was the case in the three preceding examples, we cannot use a semicolon to combine them. Instead, we merely separate the two sentences with a period.

Examples

The bear rummaged through the camp food supply. Some people believe in angels.

Japan consists of four large islands. Solar panels can generate electricity.

Sundials are practical and decorative. Snorkeling is a popular vacation pastime.

The semicolon is used sparingly and only to connect very closely related ideas. The semicolon can add sentence variety to your writing, but don't overuse it.

PRACTICE 1

The following ten simple sentences describe a medical operation. Because all the sentences deal with a common theme, we can combine some of them using semicolons. Choose those pairs of sentences that have a related idea and combine them with a semicolon. Leave the unrelated sentences as single simple sentences. Remember that the first word in the independent clause after the semicolon is not capitalized. Write your finished sentences, both those you combined and those you did not, on the lines following the list of original sentences.

The surgical team prepared the operating room for the procedure.

The surgeon dressed in a green surgical gown.

She wore a protective cap covering her hair.

Bach's *Toccata and Fugue* was piped into the operating room during the operation.

It helped to maintain a relaxed atmosphere during the delicate procedure.

The operation was a success.

The patient experienced a quick recovery.

He was back at work in less than two weeks.

His insurance paid for the operation.

His family was happy to have him healthy again.

_____

_____

_____

_____

_____

_____

_____

_____

_____

_____

_____

▼ PRACTICE 2

Create compound sentences by adding a semicolon and an independent clause to the independent clauses below. Be certain that the independent clause you add has a relating idea that makes connecting the two ideas appropriate.

Example: The manager trained the crew each Friday _____

The manager trained the crew each Friday; the training was important.

1. The bakery held a sale once a week _____

_____

2. The airplane taxied down the runway _____

_____

3. The books were arranged neatly on the shelves _____

_____

4. Simone waxed the china cabinet _____

_____

5. A strange noise came from the attic _____

_____

6. A flock of geese flew over the field _____

_____

7. Ari seemed perplexed by the math problem _____

_____

8. The driver applied the car's emergency brake _____

_____

9. *Gunsmoke* was a popular television western for decades _____

_____

10. The bells in the town hall steeple chimed every evening _____

_____

▼
PRACTICE 3

For each of the following topics, create a compound sentence by supplying two independent clauses combined with a semicolon. Write your finished sentences on the lines provided below the list of topics.

    A favorite pet

    An exciting event

    A memorable person

    A meaningful place

    A fantastic meal

    A thoughtful gift

    An enjoyable hobby/pastime

    A disturbing dream

    A rewarding job

    A fantastic vacation/trip

1. _____

_____

2. _____

_____

3. _____

_____

4. _____

_____

5. _____

_____

6. _____

_____

7. _____

_____

8. _____

_____

9. _____

_____

10. _____

_____

CHAPTER REVIEW

▼ Combine simple sentences or independent clauses with a semicolon.
▼ Make sure the sentences or independent clauses have a related idea.
▼ Do not use a coordinating conjunction (BOYFANS) with the semicolon.
▼ The word following the semicolon is not capitalized.

Visit *The Write Start* Online!

For additional practice with the materials found in this chapter, visit our Website at:

http://www.ablongman.com/checkett

The Website also features additional readings, quizzes, writing activities, and Internet links, as well as a bulletin board and interactive chat.

For More Practice with Your Grammar and Writing Skills

For further exercises designed to improve your writing and grammar skills, use the Writer's ToolKit Plus CD-ROM included with this text. The toolkit provides a wealth of computerized tutorials and practice activities.

CHAPTER

6

Combining Independent Clauses Using the Adverbial Conjunction

In Chapter 4, we learned to combine independent clauses and simple sentences by using a comma and a coordinating conjunction, and in Chapter 5, we learned to do so using just a semicolon. These techniques allow a writer to create sentence variety and rhythm, and to establish connections between ideas that have a related idea.

Writers add more variety to their writing by combining independent clauses and simple sentences with the use of **adverbial conjunctions.** Adverbial conjunctions are joining words that help you move from one idea to the next by linking ideas even more forcefully.

Commonly Used Adverbial Conjunctions and Their Meanings

Conjunction	Meaning	Conjunction	Meaning
accordingly	since, so	*hence*	for this reason, from now
additionally	in addition	*however*	by contrast, in spite of
also	in addition	*incidentally*	by the way
anyway	nevertheless, whatever	*indeed*	in fact, undoubtedly
besides	also, in addition	*likewise*	in the same way, similarly
certainly	inescapable, sure	*meanwhile*	the time between events
consequently	as a result of	*moreover*	in addition, more, plus
finally	at the end	*nevertheless*	but, despite, in spite of, still
furthermore	in addition	*next*	after, afterward, since

(continued)

Conjunction	Meaning	Conjunction	Meaning
nonetheless	however, nevertheless	*then*	at that time, next in time
now	at present, immediately	*thereafter*	from then on
otherwise	under other circumstances	*therefore*	as a result, on account of
similarly	as, as if, like	*thus*	as a result, in this way
still	as before, now, yet	*undoubtedly*	certainly, indeed, truly

Notice that some, but not all, adverbial conjunctions have similar meanings and can be used interchangeably. Also, notice that when using adverbial conjunctions, you must precede them with a semicolon and follow them with a comma.

Examples

The team practiced in the morning; furthermore, they practiced again in the evening.

Aunt Louisa stopped at the bakery; meanwhile, her niece waited in the car.

Linking two independent clauses or simple sentences by using a semicolon is the least emphatic link because it merely shows that the two ideas are related somehow.

Example

Glenn's favorite pastime is listening to music; he doesn't play an instrument.

Using a comma and a coordinating conjunction is a more emphatic link because the choice of BOYFANS provides a clue as to the nature of the relationship.

Example

Glenn's favorite pastime is listening to music, but he doesn't play an instrument.

The adverbial conjunction, however, provides the most explicit and forceful link because the choice of adverbial conjunction tells you the nature of the relationship and also adds some perceived importance because of the dramatic pause.

> **Example**
>
> Glenn's favorite hobby is listening to music; <u>however</u>, he doesn't play an instrument.

PRACTICE 1

Add the adverbial conjunction that best expresses the appropriate relationship between the pairs of independent clauses that follow. Do not use the same adverbial conjunction twice.

Example: Sheila hit the ball; <u>however</u>, she was thrown out at first base.

1. The CAT scan discovered a tumor _____ it turned out to be benign.

2. Wrestling at the high school or college level is physically demanding _____ staying in shape is a necessity.

3. Jackie did not like writing essays _____ she worked hard and received an "A" in the class.

4. The dentist warned my children to floss after every meal _____ cavities and gum disease would surely develop over the next few years.

5. The vacationers didn't like the tour guide's itinerary _____ they rented a car, bought a guide book, and went their own way.

6. The crew chief made out the weekly shift schedule _____ she hired three evening workers.

7. The assistant unloaded the cases of soda _____ his boss settled the account with the café's owner.

PRACTICE 2

Read the following five independent clauses carefully. In the spaces provided, add an adverbial conjunction and an appropriately related second independent clause. Be sure that the second independent clause in each of the five resulting compound sentences clearly relates to the first, and that you use the correct adverbial conjunction to show this relationship. Also, be sure to use correct punctuation. Don't use the same adverbial conjunction more than once.

Example: The falling leaves covered the ground_____

_____ .

The falling leaves covered the ground**; consequently,** the golfers had a difficult time finding their golf balls.

1. The volunteer dug the irrigation ditch for the village _____

_____

2. A puppy is cute and cuddly _____

_____

3. Speedboats are fast and exciting _____

_____

4. My boyfriend does not enjoy the ballet _____

_____

5. Purchasing a computer is important _____

_____

▼
PRACTICE 3

Write five compound sentences, each having two related independent clauses. Use a different adverbial conjunction in each sentence to clarify the relationship existing between the two clauses. Do not use the same adverbial conjunction twice.

1. _____

_____

2. _____

_____

3. _____

_____

4. _____

_____

5. _____

_____

▰▰▰ **CHAPTER REVIEW** ▰▰▰

> ▼ Combine simple sentences or independent clauses using an adverbial conjunction. Remember to precede the adverbial conjunction with a semicolon and follow it with a comma.
> ▼ The word following the comma is not capitalized.
> ▼ Make certain the adverbial conjunction you choose clarifies the nature of the relationship between the two independent clauses or simple sentences.

Putting It All Together

▰ **PRACTICE 4**

Combine the following pairs of independent clauses using one of the three methods you have learned in Chapters 4, 5, and 6: a semicolon, a coordinating conjunction (BOYFANS) preceded by a comma, or an adverbial conjunction preceded by a semicolon and followed by a comma. Place your choices in the spaces provided.

1. Abstract art uses form having little direct reference to external or perceived reality _____ it is normally synonymous with various types of twentieth century avant-garde art.

2. The term *abstract* also refers to images that have been abstracted or derived from nature _____ the images have been considerably altered or have been simplified to their basic geometric or biomorphic forms.

3. The term *nonobjective* has been abandoned by most critics _____ now they have supplanted it with the term *abstract.*

4. Abstract expressionism appeared in the mid-twentieth century _____ it was primarily concerned with expression through line and color.

5. The artist was interested in expressing emotional reaction to the world _____ objective experiences and situations were seen as less interesting.

6. The movement was part of the organic, emotional, expressionistic approach to art _____ it was developed to contrast with the geometrically structural, rationalistic approach of the cubists.

7. The roots of abstract expressionism can be found in the works of Kandinsky, Ernst, Duchamp, Chagall, and Tanguy _____ they inspired a blossoming of abstract expressionism among American painters in the 1950s.

8. The abstract movement centered in New York City _____ this core of American painters was dubbed the New York school.

9. The New York school included many now-famous artists _____ Pollock, de Kooning, Kline, and Rothko were the most famous American artists.

10. Abstract expression also flourished in Europe _____ the Tachism school emphasized patches of color while the *art informal* school rejected formal structure.

▼ PRACTICE 5

Combine the following pairs of independent clauses using one of the methods you learned in Chapters 4, 5, and 6: a semicolon, a coordinating conjunction (BOYFANS) preceded by a comma, or an adverbial conjunction preceded by a semicolon and followed with a comma. Place your choices in the spaces provided.

1. The moon is a natural satellite of the earth _____ the name moon is sometimes applied to the satellites of other planets in the solar system.

2. The moon's diameter is about 2160 miles _____ while this is a large distance, it is only about one-fourth that of earth.

3. The moon's volume is about one-fiftieth that of earth _____ the mass of the earth is 81 times greater than the mass of the moon.

4. The moon has no free water and no atmosphere _____ no weather exists to change its surface topography.

5. The moon orbits the earth at an average distance of 238,000 miles _____ it completes one revolution about the earth every 27 days, 7 hours, 43 minutes, and 11.5 seconds.

6. At any one time, an observer can see only 50 percent of the moon's entire surface _____ an additional 9 percent can be seen around the apparent edge because of the relative motion called libration.

7. Libration is caused by slightly different angles of view from the earth _____ different relative positions of the moon influence our "true" perception of it.

8. The moon shows progressively different phases as it moves along its orbit _____ half the moon is always in sunlight, just as half the earth has day while the other half has night.

9. In the phase called the new moon, the face is completely in shadow _____ about a week later, the moon is in first quarter, resembling a luminous half-circle.

10. Another week later, the full moon shows its fully lighted surface _____ a week afterward, in its last quarter, the moon appears as a half-circle once again.

Visit *The Write Start* Online!

For additional practice with the materials found in this chapter, visit our Website at:

http://www.ablongman.com/checkett

The Website also features additional readings, quizzes, writing activities, and Internet links, as well as a bulletin board and interactive chat.

For More Practice with Your Grammar and Writing Skills

For further exercises designed to improve your writing and grammar skills, use the Writer's ToolKit Plus CD-ROM included with this text. The toolkit provides a wealth of computerized tutorials and practice activities.

7 Adding a List

So far, we have been combining independent clauses and simple sentences to add sentence variety, and rhythm, and to connect related ideas. Sometimes a simple sentence or a combination of two simple sentences isn't sufficient to express your thoughts as a writer. Often, you will need to add information to clarify or expand on your ideas. Another way to add variety to your writing is to use **lists**. Not only can lists vary your writing, they also can add necessary information to explain, clarify, or illustrate one of your ideas.

Example
Charles went to the mall to shop.

This sentence does not clarify what it was that Charles bought.

Example
Charles went to the mall and purchased a <u>CD, a shirt, and sunglasses.</u>
      ↑
     the list

By using a list, what Charles bought at the mall is illustrated.

A **series** can consist of single words (nouns, adjectives, verbs, adverbs) or phrases.

Examples
Nouns: The pizza consists of <u>cheese, sausage, green onions, and mushrooms.</u>
Adjectives: The <u>large, powerful, and majestic</u> lion sleeps 16 hours a day.
Verbs: The athlete <u>walks, jogs, runs, and sprints</u> during practice.
Adverbs: The sea otter swims <u>swiftly, smoothly, and playfully.</u>
Phrases: The cruise ship offers extravagant meals <u>in the morning, in the afternoon, in the evening, and after midnight.</u>

For definitions and examples of adjectives and adverbs, see The Writer's Resources, Parts of Speech, Adjectives, Adverbs (pages 301, 302).

Punctuating and Placing the List

The list can be added at the beginning, middle, or at the end of the sentence.

> **Examples**
> *Beginning*: <u>Cheese, wine, and fruit</u> were served at the picnic.
> *Middle*: The hosts served <u>cheese, wine, and fruit</u> at the picnic.
> *End*: The food served at the picnic included <u>cheese, wine, and fruit.</u>

Notice the use of commas in our examples. In lists with three or more items, you need to separate each item from the other items with a comma. In lists with only two items, you do not need to use a comma. Instead, you can separate the two items with the word *and*.

> **Examples**
> *Two-item series*: The taxicab stopped <u>and</u> started. (no commas)
> *Three-or-more-item series*: The taxicab <u>stopped, started, and sped away.</u>

▼ PRACTICE 1

Underline the series in each sentence, and punctuate it correctly. If you think the sentence is correct, write a **C** in front of the sentence's number.

Example: The Super Bowl Football game included <u>four touchdown passes, three extra-points failing, and a parachutist landing at midfield.</u>

1. They ordered steak potatoes and asparagus at dinner.

2. The three cats hid under the table in the closet and in the basement during the thunderstorm.

3. The weather consisted of rain and sleet.

4. King Albert Queen Lucinda and Prince Arn rode inside a golden carriage.

5. The garden consisted of tulips crocuses and jonquils during the three months of spring.

6. The groups of high school seniors corporate executives and international chefs toured Paris for three days.

7. The fog blanketed the fields in the morning during the afternoon and after evening.

8. Talent and poise are ingredients for a successful career in business.

9. The orchestra's violins cellos and violas answered the woodwinds during the second movement.

10. The trapeze artist soared over the crowd performed a loop and swung upside down.

PRACTICE 2

Add a list to complete each of the following incomplete sentences. Punctuate correctly.

1. _____

_____ made the workers thirsty.

2. The dolphins _____

_____.

3. The hosts and their guest followed dinner _____

_____.

4. The entire choir _____

_____ prior to the concert.

5. Justin's favorite rides at the amusement park were _____

_____.

6. The carpenter _____

_____ to complete the project.

7. The cowboy won the rodeo by _____

_____.

8. The chef prepared_____

_____ for his customers.

9. _____

_____ made the farmer successful.

10. The early morning hours are the teacher's favorite time for _____

_____.

Write three different sentences, each containing three or more items in a list. Place the list at the beginning of one sentence, in the middle of one sentence, and at the end of one sentence. Punctuate each sentence correctly.

1. _____

_____

2. _____

_____

3. _____

_____

Parallelism in a Series

As we have seen, lists can be made up of nouns, adjectives, verbs, adverbs, and phrases. Any items work well in the list *as long as every item in the list is the same type of word or phrase*. This is known as **parallelism.**

Mixing different categories of words or phrases in the same list makes the sentence hard to read and understand, and it also violates the rule of parallelism.

> **Example**
> The birds are finches, under a tree, and yellow.

In this example, a noun, a prepositional phrase, and an adjective have been mixed inappropriately as the items in the list. See how confusing this sentence is. It also sounds choppy. Additionally, the reader might be confused as to which item is yellow—the finch or the tree. Parallel lists read smoothly, and rhythmically, and they clarify content.

> **Examples**
>
> At the supermarket, Sarina purchased bread, butter, and milk. (nouns)
>
> The garden was colorful, fragrant, and beautiful. (adjectives)
>
> Frank swims, bicycles, and runs every day for triathlon practice. (verbs)
>
> The gymnast vaulted athletically, aggressively, and purposefully. (adverbs)
>
> Chin looked for the passport in the dresser, on the counter, and under the newspaper. (prepositional phrases, beginning with *in, on,* and *under*)

▼ PRACTICE 4

Add a three-item list to complete each of the sentences below. Be certain that each list is parallel and achieves clear content and consistent rhythm.

Make one list of only nouns, one of adjectives, one of verbs, one of adverbs, and one of phrases.

1. My favorite music groups are _____, _____, and _____.

2. The ice-cream sundae was _____, _____, and _____.

3. When Shaunista was a teenager, she would hide her diary _____, _____, and _____.

4. The air show audience was fascinated by the experimental airplane's _____, _____, and _____ shape.

5. The space shuttle roared _____, _____, and _____ into the clouds over Cape Kennedy.

▼ PRACTICE 5

For each of the topics listed below, write a sentence that includes a list. Be certain that each list is parallel. Make one list of only nouns, one of adjectives, one of verbs, one of adverbs, and one of phrases. Punctuate correctly.

1. Library— _____

_____

2. Weather— _____

_____

3. Car— _____

_____

4. Dating— _____

_____

5. Sky-diving— _____

_____

CHAPTER REVIEW

▼ A list of words and phrases can be added to a sentence to explain, clarify, or illustrate a basic idea.

▼ In a two-item list, the word _and_ separates the items in the list, and no comma is used.

▼ In a three-item list, the items in the list are separated by a comma.

▼ The list can be added at the beginning, middle, or at the end of the sentence.

▼ Do not mix categories of words (nouns, adjectives, verbs, adverbs) and different kinds of phrases in a list. Items in a list must be parallel for clear meaning and consistent rhythm.

Visit _The Write Start_ Online!

For additional practice with the materials found in this chapter, visit our Website at:

http://www.ablongman.com/checkett

The Website also features additional readings, quizzes, writing activities, and Internet links, as well as a bulletin board and interactive chat.

For More Practice with Your Grammar and Writing Skills

For further exercises designed to improve your writing and grammar skills, use the Writer's ToolKit Plus CD-ROM included with this text. The toolkit provides a wealth of computerized tutorials and practice activities.

8 Adding a Colon for Variety

To add sentence variety and to emphasize particular information, you can use a colon. A colon looks like one period above another period (:). Use a colon to do the following:

▼ To introduce a list
▼ When telling time
▼ For the salutation of a business letter
▼ To separate the titles and subtitles of a book

1. Use a colon after an independent clause to introduce a list.

> **Examples**
>
> Preparing a soufflé requires four ingredients: <u>milk, eggs, butter, and cheese.</u>
>
> The pharmacy technician ordered popular items sold most often: <u>aspirin, gauze, bandages, and antacid.</u>

Note: Do not use a colon before a list if the list immediately follows a verb or a preposition.

> **Examples**
>
> The most popular condiments <u>are</u>: catsup, mustard, and mayonnaise. (omit colon after verb)
>
> You will find the cats hiding <u>under</u>: the house, the porch, the tool shed. (omit colon after preposition)

It is best only to use a colon after an independent clause.

> **Examples**
>
> The following are the most popular condiments: <u>catsup, mustard, and mayonnaise.</u>
>
> The cats were found in the following places: <u>under the house, under the porch, and under the tool shed.</u>

2. Use a colon when telling time.

> **Examples**
> The train arrived at 4:15 P.M.
> My 2:30 P.M. doctor's appointment was changed to 5:00 P.M.

3. Use a colon for the salutation of a business letter.

> **Examples**
> Dear Mrs. Hilliard:
> To Whom It May Concern:
> Sirs:

4. Use a colon to separate the titles and subtitles of a book.

> **Examples**
> *Accounting in Context: A Business Handbook*
> *Writing Made Easy: A Plain Language Rhetoric*
> *Washington: The First Leader of the Nation*

PRACTICE 1

Add colons to introduce lists, to tell time, and to separate titles and subtitles of books in the following sentences.

1. The teacher taught using a variety of methods lecturing, using an overhead projector, and by in-class group projects.

2. Jerry enjoyed many activities while vacationing boating, fishing, and hiking.

3. The Concorde jetliner left Paris at 605 P.M. instead of its scheduled time of 550 P.M.

4. The librarian reshelved the book left on her desk *Retire Early How to Make Money in Real Estate Foreclosures.*

5. The two movies had different start times *The Front* at 440, and *Godzilla* at 455.

6. The office workers ate lunch in a variety of places in the employee lounge, on the roof, and out by the lake.

7. Sheila enjoyed reading the new book about food shopping *Using Coupons Free Meals for Your Family.*

8. Joaquin used three types of peppers to add color to his special salsa red, yellow, and green.

9. HOMES is a mnemonic device to help people remember the names of the five Great Lakes Huron, Ontario, Michigan, Erie, and Superior.

10. The children enjoyed the party because of the food hot dogs, hamburgers, and chips.

Correct the colon errors in the following sentences. You will have to rewrite some of the sentences to do so. Put the rewritten sentences on the lines provided.

1. The two falcons: found a tree, gathered twigs, and built a nest.

_____

_____

2. My bus left the station at 515, instead of 615 as written in the schedule.

_____

_____

3. The surgical team had a good reputation because: they were up on the latest techniques and had worked together for four years.

_____

_____

4. The Liberian flag is: red, white, and blue.

_____

_____

5. The book was titled *The Stock Market An Investor's Guide.*

_____

_____

6. The man's hidden desires turned out to be: baseball, baseball, and baseball.

_____

_____

7. The plane: could not take off: the engine wasn't powerful enough to handle the load.

_____

_____

8. The book was titled _Towards Better Scoring on the SAT An Exercise Booklet._

_____

_____

9. Amelia was in a hurry because her date was at 700 P.M., and it was already 645 P.M.

_____

_____

10. The children's favorite schoolyard activities were: the merry-go-round, the jungle-gym, and hopscotch.

_____

_____

▼ PRACTICE 3

Write three sentences using the colon to introduce a list, to include a time, and to illustrate a book title and subtitle.

1. _____

_____

2. _____

_____

3. _____

_____

CHAPTER REVIEW

▼ Use a colon after an independent clause to introduce a list.
▼ Do not use a colon before a list if the list immediately follows a verb or a preposition.

▼ Use a colon when telling time.
▼ Use a colon for the salutation of a business letter.
▼ Use a colon to separate the titles and subtitles of a book.

Visit *The Write Start* Online!

For additional practice with the materials found in this chapter, visit our Website at:

http://www.ablongman.com/checkett

The Website also features additional readings, quizzes, writing activities, and Internet links, as well as a bulletin board and interactive chat.

For More Practice with Your Grammar and Writing Skills

For further exercises designed to improve your writing and grammar skills, use the Writer's ToolKit Plus CD-ROM included with this text. The toolkit provides a wealth of computerized tutorials and practice activities.

9 The Dependent Clause

In Chapter 4, we learned to link ideas using the coordinating conjunctions: *for, and, nor, but, or, yet, so.* We called these compound sentences. Another method to connect ideas is to use **subordinating conjunctions.** Sentences with subordinating conjunctions are called **complex sentences.**

Commonly Used Subordinating Conjunctions

after	if	when
although	since	whenever
as	though	wherever
because	unless	whether
before	until	while

Subordinating conjunctions are used to join independent clauses just as coordinating conjunctions are. However, coordinating conjunctions give the same emphasis to both clauses while subordinating conjunctions de-emphasize one clause by turning it into a **dependent clause** (a process called **subordination**).

Independent versus Dependent Clauses

As we have already learned, an independent clause (a clause that can stand alone as a simple sentence) must have a subject, a verb, and complete meaning. A **dependent clause** also has a subject and a verb, but it does not have sufficient meaning allowing it to stand alone. It is dependent on an independent clause to complete its meaning. When using a subordinating conjunction to combine clauses, we actually start out with two independent clauses, each of which can stand on its own but is related to the other.

Example
The ship returned to port. Its propeller was broken.

As two independent clauses, the information in each clause is considered of equal value or importance. In reality, however, the first clause is considered the more important piece of information. It is more important to know that the ship had to return to port. Why it had to return is of secondary importance.

To let the reader know which clause is of primary importance, the writer can make one of the independent clauses a dependent clause by adding a subordinating conjunction to the front of the clause.

Here is the Less Important Independent Clause
Its propeller was broken.

Next, this independent clause is changed to a dependent clause by adding the appropriate subordinating conjunction.

Example
Because its propeller was broken.

Notice that this clause no longer can stand on its own because it does not have sufficient meaning. It is dependent on the independent clause for its complete meaning.

If left alone to stand as a sentence, this dependent clause would be a sentence fragment.

Here is the Complete Sentence
The ship returned to port *because* its propeller was broken.

(independent clause)(subordinating conjunction)(dependent clause)

Subordination, then, is a process for making one idea less, or below, in value or importance than another idea. Subordination is commonly done when there are two independent clauses, and the writer decides that one main idea is actually more important or needs more emphasis than the other main idea.

PRACTICE 1

In the following sentences, underline the independent clause once, the dependent clause twice, and circle the subordinating conjunction.

Example: The crowd raced for their cars (after) the football game was over.

1. Gas prices increase during the summer because many people drive on their vacations.

2. Although the Congress consists of the House and Senate, they are distinctly different legislative bodies.

3. Golfers can play all day and night in Finland since the sun never sets.

4. The teenagers partied each day while their parents were away.

5. Before an earthquake sends tremors through the ground, some scientists believe animals can somehow sense it is going to happen.

6. The amateur hoopsters loved to travel first class as if they were a professional team.

7. Until their economy failed, the Russians were considered a world power.

8. Whether she spoke with royalty or peasants, Mother Teresa was always humble.

9. The students had a study session every Sunday evening unless there was a good concert at the student center.

10. Whenever the cartoonist finished a week's worth of strips, she rewarded herself with four cookies and a cold glass of milk.

PRACTICE 2

Read each of the following sentences for its meaning. Then, fill in the blank space with the subordinating conjunction that best expresses the relationship between the two ideas.

1. The butcher sliced 50 pounds of roast beef each morning _____ the deli down the street sold it all during lunch.

2. _____ the blackjack player had a good hand, he pulled on his left earlobe.

3. The cruise ship passengers stayed out on deck _____ the breeze became too strong and too chilly.

4. _____ the United States purchased Alaska from the Soviet Union, it became known as "Seward's Folly."

5. His parents have to have the cracked windshield fixed _____ he can take the driver's test tomorrow.

6. _____ the ozone layer is protected, harmful radiation will cause more skin cancer.

7. _____ the bullet train gained speed, the passengers became more nervous.

8. _____ some workers sliced the lettuce from their stalks, others placed the heads into cardboard boxes.

9. The wine had to be decanted _____ the waiter served it to the guests.

10. The pear tree lost a limb _____ the wind blew over 40 miles per hour.

Punctuating Dependent Clauses

You may have noticed in the previous practice exercises that when combining sentences with subordinating conjunctions, some of the newly created dependent clauses use a comma and others do not. This depends on whether or not the dependent clause precedes the independent clause or comes after it.

If the dependent clause comes before the independent clause, a comma follows the dependent clause.

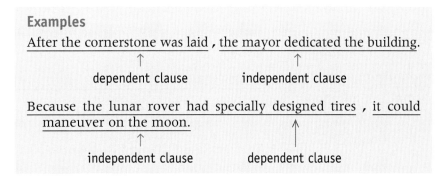

Examples

After the cornerstone was laid , the mayor dedicated the building.
          ↑   ↑
    dependent clause   independent clause

Because the lunar rover had specially designed tires , it could maneuver on the moon.
          ↑   ↑
   independent clause   dependent clause

If the dependent clause follows the independent clause, a comma is not used.

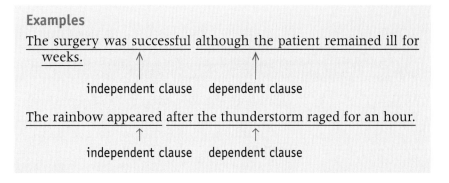

Examples

The surgery was successful although the patient remained ill for weeks.
          ↑   ↑
   independent clause   dependent clause

The rainbow appeared after the thunderstorm raged for an hour.
          ↑   ↑
   independent clause   dependent clause

▼ PRACTICE 3

Combine the following pairs of sentences. In each pair, change the first independent clause to a dependent clause by placing the appropriate subordinating conjunction in front of it. Punctuate correctly.

Example: The man at the front door was a stranger. Tajel did not let him in.
Because the man at the front door was a stranger, Tajel did not let him in.

1. She was from a desert region of Nevada. Her desire was to be a ski instructor.

   _____

   _____

2. Jennifer's test scores were very high. She was accepted at 12 universities.

   _____

   _____

3. The Oscars ceremony was completed. The stars drove off in their limousines.

   _____

   _____

4. The NATO peacekeeping force accomplished its goal. The fighting would cease.

   _____

   _____

5. The restaurant changed its menu to all Tex-Mex. Sales skyrocketed.

   _____

   _____

▼ PRACTICE 4

Combine the following pairs of sentences. In each pair, change the second independent clause to a dependent clause by adding the appropriate subordinating conjunction to the front of it. Remember, do not use a comma.

Example: The wolves howled across the valley. They wanted the pack to hunt. The wolves howled across the valley whenever they wanted the pack to hunt.

1. Winnie couldn't help diagnosing everyone in her family. She had become a doctor.

   _____

   _____

2. The alligator is essentially solitary. The piranha lives in schools.

_____

_____

3. The movie studio head threw an expensive party. His movies were a box office success.

_____

_____

4. Corporate headquarters never ordered extra parts. The factory produced more VCRs.

_____

_____

5. The game can never begin. The National Anthem is sung.

_____

_____

PRACTICE 5

Using the pairs of topics below, create six subordinated sentences. Three of the sentences should have dependent clauses at the beginning, and the other three should end with dependent clauses. Punctuate correctly.

1. Hit/Catch— _____

_____

2. Cook/Eat— _____

_____

3. Work/Promotion— _____

_____

4. Vote/Elect— _____

_____

5. Success/Luck— _____

_____

6. Driving/Accidents— _____

_____

CHAPTER REVIEW

▼ You can combine sentences by using a subordinating conjunction and changing one independent clause to a dependent clause.

▼ When the dependent clause comes before the independent clause, you need to follow the dependent clause with a comma.

▼ When the dependent clause comes after the independent clause, you do not need to use a comma.

Visit *The Write Start* Online!

For additional practice with the materials found in this chapter, visit our Website at:

http://www.ablongman.com/checkett

The Website also features additional readings, quizzes, writing activities, and Internet links, as well as a bulletin board and interactive chat.

For More Practice with Your Grammar and Writing Skills

For further exercises designed to improve your writing and grammar skills, use the Writer's ToolKit Plus CD-ROM included with this text. The toolkit provides a wealth of computerized tutorials and practice activities.

CHAPTER

10 The Introductory Phrase

As we have seen in other chapters, there are many methods writers use to add more information to a simple sentence or independent clause. One good method for adding information or clarifying the main idea in an independent clause—as well as adding variety to your writing—is to start the sentence with an **introductory phrase.** The introductory phrase (or phrases—it can be more than one) is separated from the independent clause by a comma.

Examples

At the beginning of the tournament, the team played rather poorly.

Because of the weight loss program, Lee's cholesterol was reduced.

At the barn, the workers made a plan for harvesting all 500 acres of wheat.

When driving across the country, Rosita always has the radio turned to the "Salsa" station.

PRACTICE 1

Underline the introductory phrase, or phrases, in the following sentences, and place a comma between it and the main clause.

Examples: To the Navy Seals, the insurmountable obstacle was just another challenge to overcome.

On the stove in the kitchen, a small egg timer rang its warning.

1. On an African safari the tourist group saw giraffes, lions, and elephants.

2. At first I did not see the need to know CPR for my job as a lifeguard.

3. Made of thick steel the frying pan looked like it would last forever.

4. More often the traffic is heavier in the evening than in the morning.

5. To most surfers around the world the fear of shark attack is of little concern.

6. All in all it was a very profitable day selling pennants outside the stadium.

7. For the very first time in the company's history its stock price went down.

8. Being thin and tall the model easily fit into all the designer's latest gowns.

9. As worn and rundown as the town itself the old feed store was a symbol of the town's decay as a business center.

10. Whether guilty or not the defendant seemed believable when testifying.

▼ PRACTICE 2

Underline the introductory phrase, or phrases, in the following sentences, and place a comma between it and the main clause.

1. After the matinee showing the tour bus left Las Vegas and headed for Reno.

2. Because of psoriasis the best swimmer on the team has to miss the meet.

3. On most sunny days the students gathered in the quadrangle to read and visit.

4. Inside the hull a ton of grain awaited transfer to the trucks waiting on the road.

5. Over the mountains the highway trailed away like a giant black snake.

6. Around the dance club and near the alley five low riders gleamed hauntingly.

7. Under the viaduct a homeless person had established living quarters.

8. Through the looking glass in the famous story Alice found her Wonderland.

9. As lava eventually cools more living space is realized.

10. In the Galápagos Islands off of western South America Darwin made important discoveries that helped him create his version of evolution.

Introductory Phrase Variety

The introductory phrase is used best when it contains information that helps explain or clarify the subject or the main idea in the independent clause. This information can help define the "who, what, where, when, why, and how" of the main idea.

Examples

Who Being *Chuck Norris*, he could do his own martial arts stunts for the show.

As *King of England*, Henry the Eighth had the power to create his own church.

What Because of the *snow*, school was cancelled for an entire week.

After the *party*, four garbage bags were needed to haul out all the trash.

Where In *India*, they use tusked elephants like we use forklift trucks.

At the *Smithsonian Institute*, historical artifacts are on display.

When In the *spring*, crocuses and tulips bloom even when there is still snow.

Each *morning*, the newspaper was flung into the bushes near the porch.

Why With *little fuel* in the tank, the barbeque grill wouldn't ignite.

Because of the *hurricane threat*, all boats were moored in the harbor.

How By *twisting* his body to the left, the electrician squeezed through the shaft.

After *adjusting the carburetor*, the dragster won its next heat.

PRACTICE 3

Add an introductory phrase, or phrases, to each independent clause in the following sentences. Punctuate correctly. In the parenthesis provided after each sentence, indicate how the introductory phrase helps to explain or clarify the independent clause by writing in the appropriate label: **who, what, where, when, why,** or **how.**

Example: _____ the contestants could not answer.

<u>After the buzzer sounded</u>, the contestants could not answer. (Why)

1. _____ the plane returned to the airport.

(   )

2. _____ fishing became a favorite pastime.

(   )

3. _____ the clouds darkened and the rain came pounding down on the village. (   )

4. _____ the two teams shook hands and went to the locker room. (   )

5. _____ losing to her opponent was especially painful. (   )

6. _____ Denise decided the Mediterranean cruise was much too expensive. (   )

7. _____ they needed to buy extra ice and fans. (   )

8. _____ Lonnie jumped right back up into the saddle. (   )

9. _____ three hundred geese landed on the small pond. (   )

10. _____ all three intersections were blocked by the train. (   )

Special effects, properties, and relationships that exist about and between people and events also can be clarified by using introductory phrases.

Examples	
Description	Being 6 feet 6 inches tall and weighing 260 pounds, the freshman football player was selected by the coaching staff to be one of the starting defensive ends.
	By expanding and fluttering beautifully colored tail feathers, the male peacock hopes to attract a mate.
Cause and effect	Because of the low voter turnout, the party in power retained its majority.
	Caused by too many people using major appliances, the brownouts continued throughout the night and into the next day.
Definition	Having four sides of the same length, the square is one of the basic geometric designs used in architecture.
	By crying and throwing toys, the child hoped his tantrum would force his parents to let him watch more cartoons.
Comparison	By acting rather than complaining, the newest employee was promoted before those with more seniority.

(continued)

	After the conservatives won and the liberals lost, the school board voted to accept the new budget for the upcoming fiscal year.
Process	By calculating the jet stream position and isobar readings, the meteorologist put together her forecast.
	By counting deposits against expenditures, the bank teller balanced the cash drawer.
Persuasion	With skyrocketing tuition and cost of living increases, parents should start college funds for their children before they're born!
	As the IRS is increasing its tax rate on earnings, donating to charity is becoming a more attractive method of reducing taxable income.

▼ PRACTICE 4

In the parentheses provided after each sentence, indicate how the introductory phrase helps to explain or clarify the independent clause by writing in the appropriate label: **description, cause and effect, definition, comparison, process,** or **persuasion.** Do not write in the same label twice.

1. As interest rates on loans and credit cards climb, it would be wise to

consolidate all bills into one payment to a single lending company.

( )

2. With snowcapped peaks and thick cloud cover, the Himalayas offer some

of the world's most spectacular scenery. ( )

3. By using sonar and dazzling speed, dolphins hunt successfully in groups

and as individuals. ( )

4. In foggy conditions or bright sunlight, driving lights have reduced the

number of automobile collisions. ( )

5. Because of not recruiting younger members, the gang eventually became

too old and too small to scare anyone. ( )

6. Consisting of a compartment for air and a breathing tube, the aqua lung

has revolutionized undersea exploration. ( )

▼ PRACTICE 5

Write five of your own sentences using an introductory clause in front of the independent clause. Punctuate correctly. In the parentheses provided following each sentence, write in the label that best describes how the introductory phrase is helping to explain or clarify the independent clause. Use any of the labels you have studied, but don't use the same label twice.

1. _____

_____

_____

(   )

2. _____

_____

_____

(   )

3. _____

_____

_____

(   )

4. _____

_____

_____

(   )

5. _____

_____

_____

(   )

CHAPTER REVIEW

▼ Use an introductory phrase, or phrases, to add information or to clarify or explain the basic idea in an independent clause.

▼ Introductory phrases can explain or clarify properties or special relationships of and between persons and events, such as who, what, where, when, why, and how.

▼ Introductory phrases also can help explain or clarify properties or special relationships of and between persons and events, such as description, definition, cause and effect, comparison, process, and persuasion.

▼ Separate the introductory phrase, or phrases, from the independent clause with a comma.

Visit *The Write Start* Online!

For additional practice with the materials found in this chapter, visit our Website at:

http://www.ablongman.com/checkett

The Website also features additional readings, quizzes, writing activities, and Internet links, as well as a bulletin board and interactive chat.

For More Practice with Your Grammar and Writing Skills

For further exercises designed to improve your writing and grammar skills, use the Writer's ToolKit Plus CD-ROM included with this text. The toolkit provides a wealth of computerized tutorials and practice activities.

11 Starting a Sentence with an Introductory Word

Another method that writers use to add variety and rhythm to their writing is to begin a sentence with an **introductory word,** also called a **sentence modifier.** Although this technique is not used to combine sentences, it is important, nonetheless.

> **Examples**
>
> <u>Yes</u>, I will be going to the show.
>
> <u>Well</u>, I might buy a motorcycle instead of a car.
>
> <u>Obviously</u>, Einstein was an intelligent person by any standard.

Punctuating the Introductory Word

Notice that the introductory words in the examples above are followed by a comma just as we saw in Chapter 9 when using the introductory dependent clause before the main clause and in Chapter 10 when using the introductory phrase.

When to Use Introductory Words

Introductory words are most often used to create sentence variety and rhythm, but they also can add useful information to a sentence.

Commonly Used Introductory Words	
Ah	No
Certainly	Oh
Hmmm	Sure, surely
However	Typically
Names of people and pets	Well
Nevertheless	Yes
Nonetheless	

Use the one-word modifier for the following five reasons:

1. To introduce an affirmative or negative reply

> <u>Yes</u>, the team has won three games in a row.
> <u>No</u>, I don't think I will be majoring in Refuse Disposal
> Management.

2. To address someone by name

> <u>Lennox</u>, bring the newspaper into the dining room.
> <u>Henrietta</u>, please come to the dinner table.

3. To express surprise or wonderment

> <u>Oh</u>, what a gigantic cake!
> <u>Ah</u>, I never suspected that the butler did it!

4. To express a contrast

> <u>However</u>, the business picked up during the next quarter.
> <u>Nevertheless</u>, I will continue to support the school board's
> decision.

5. To express a contemplative pause

> <u>Well</u>, I was actually thinking about buying a different model of car.
> <u>Hmmm</u>, that doesn't sound like something that would
> interest me.

▼ PRACTICE 1

Underline the introductory word in each of the following sentences. Punctuate correctly.

1. No taking the driver's exam is not possible until Monday morning.

2. Ah that picture of the Orion Nebula is amazing.

3. Nevertheless we are spending a full week in Toronto.

4. Eugenia don't drive over the speed limit tonight.

5. Yes the mechanic says he can fix the radiator.

6. However the other team has a better pitching staff.

7. Hmmm I can't decide on sausage or pepperoni on my pizza.

8. Oh I think that news is fantastic.

9. Well I might go hang gliding if the weather conditions are good.

10. Mischa don't leave your dirty clothes on the floor.

▼ PRACTICE 2

Underline the introductory word in each of the following sentences. Punctuate correctly. In the parentheses following each sentence, identify one of the five reasons for using the introductory word you have learned: **affirmative or negative reply, address by name, surprise or wonderment, contrast, or contemplative pause.**

Example: <u>Ah</u>, that's the biggest hamburger I've ever seen! (surprise or wonderment)

1. Germaine please turn the air conditioning down.

(_____)

2. Nevertheless the new supermarket will be built where the current children's amusement park is located. (_____)

3. No qualifying for the Olympic track team is based on how you do during the tryout meet next month. (_____)

4. Ah this apple strudel is the best I've ever eaten.

(_____)

5. Hmmm I'm not sure I want to be away from my pets that long.

(_____)

6. However the rain washed away the topsoil as well as the grass seed.

(_____)

7. Yes the German Shepherd is a great guard dog.

(_____)

8. Well I might take History if it satisfies a graduation requirement.

(_____)

9. Oh the budget is already 20 percent over projected costs.

(_____)

10. Leonardo don't play with your food. (_____)

Not all single words can be used as one-word modifiers. For example, subordinating conjunctions (see Chapter 9) cannot be used as introductory words. These words must be part of a dependent clause and cannot be separated from the clause by a comma.

> **Examples**
>
> **(Independent clause)** The coroner examined the body thoroughly. He released the finding to the press.
>
> **(Made into a dependent clause)** After the coroner examined the body thoroughly, he released the findings to the press.
>
> **(Incorrect use of the subordinating conjunction)** After, the coroner examined the body thoroughly, he released the findings to the press.
>
> **(Correct use of a one-word modifier)** Typically, the coroner examined the body before releasing the findings to the press.

PRACTICE 3

Choose appropriate one-word modifiers from the examples given in this chapter and place them in front of the sentences below. Do not use the same modifier more than once. Punctuate correctly.

_____ the law will be carried out under the watchful eye of the police.

_____ that is something I will have to think about long and hard.

_____ Mark McGwire will hit at least three home runs tonight.

_____ the nuclear reactor is functioning at 100 percent capacity.

_____ the committee will make a decision in lieu of the president's vote.

_____ go to the store and buy bread and milk.

_____ that behavior is not acceptable at any time.

_____ now that's what I call a gourmet meal.

PRACTICE 4

Create sentences using the one-word modifiers from the examples given in this chapter. Do not use the same modifier more than once. Punctuate correctly.

1. _____

2. _____

3. _____

4. _____

5. _____

6. _____

7. _____

8. _____

CHAPTER REVIEW

Use a one-word modifier for the following reasons:

▼ To introduce an affirmative or negative reply
▼ Addressing someone by name
▼ Exclamations of surprise or wonderment
▼ Expressing a contrast
▼ A contemplative pause
▼ Do not confuse subordinating conjunctions, or dependent words, with one-word modifiers. Subordinating conjunctions are placed at the beginning of an independent clause to change it to a dependent clause, and no punctuation is used. (Refer to Chapter 9 for a list of subordinating conjunctions.)

Visit *The Write Start* Online!

For additional practice with the materials found in this chapter, visit our Website at:

http://www.ablongman.com/checkett

The Website also features additional readings, quizzes, writing activities, and Internet links, as well as a bulletin board and interactive chat.

For More Practice with Your Grammar and Writing Skills

For further exercises designed to improve your writing and grammar skills, use the Writer's ToolKit Plus CD-ROM included with this text. The toolkit provides a wealth of computerized tutorials and practice activities.

12 Adding Interrupters to the Sentence

Simple sentences are very good for conveying simple, straightforward ideas. Sometimes, though, reading several simple sentences in a row can be dull. Variety always makes writing more interesting, and a different method of adding variety is using interrupters. Some books also call this extra information "transitional expressions," or "parenthetical expressions," or "parenthetical information" because it can be placed in parentheses ( ). Most often, however, interrupters are preceded and followed by commas.

Interrupters are single words, phrases, or clauses often interrupting the flow of the basic clause.

Examples of Single-Word Interrupters

The exam, however, came to an end.

The opera diva, undoubtedly, could hold a single note for a long time.

The scientists, therefore, had a different reaction to the new discovery.

Examples of Phrase Interrupters

The coach, on the other hand, was not pleased with the team's performance.

The entire town, for instance, stopped watching television for a week.

The Southern writer William Faulkner, from Mississippi, wrote "The Bear."

Notice that interrupters most often are placed in between the subject and verb of the main clause. For further discussion of clause interrupters, see The Writer's Resources, Restrictive and Nonrestrictive Clauses (page 327).

Commonly Used Interrupters

Single Words	Phrases
also	as a matter of fact
besides	as a result
certainly	at last
consequently	believe me
eventually	by the way
finally	for example
furthermore	for instance
however	in fact
incidentally	on the other hand
likewise	to tell the truth
meanwhile	
naturally	
nevertheless	
subsequently	
therefore	
undoubtedly	
unfortunately	

Interrupters can be necessary or not necessary to the basic understanding of the main clause. If the interrupter is not necessary to understand the main clause, place commas around it. If the interrupter is necessary to understand the main clause, do not place commas around it.

Examples

The student, with a shocked expression, read the favorable comments on his paper. (unnecessary prepositional phrase—commas needed)

The boy with the red hair was the one riding the bike. (necessary phrase—commas not needed)

The surgeon, consequently, ordered more blood for the operation. (unnecessary single word—commas needed)

The student with the highest grades won the scholarship. (necessary prepositional phrase—commas not needed)

The boss, satisfied with employee morale, cancelled the company picnic. (unnecessary phrase—commas needed)

PRACTICE 1

In the following sentences, use commas to set off the single-word interrupters from the basic idea of the sentence. First, identifying the subject and the verb may help you select the interrupter.

1. Today, the United States and Japan however are considered allies.

2. So, World War II naturally is an event discussed to this day.

3. The United States and Japan unfortunately both were after dominance in the Far East.

4. Poor relations meanwhile developed between the two powers.

5. The two nations subsequently could not come to common agreement.

6. The Empire of Japan therefore attacked Pearl Harbor.

7. Although isolationist, the Congress nevertheless voted for a Declaration of War.

8. The United States consequently entered World War II on December 8, 1941.

9. The war however had begun in Europe in September of 1939.

10. The United States eventually would fight a war on two fronts: Asia and Europe.

11. After six years, the Allies finally defeated the Axis powers.

▼
PRACTICE 2

In the following sentences, use commas to set off the phrase interrupters from the basic idea of the sentence. First, identifying the subject and the verb may help you select the interrupter.

1. Robert Frost for instance is one of America's most beloved poets.

2. Frost in fact was from the New England region of the country.

3. The poet by the way was funny, witty, and enjoyed poking fun at himself and others.

4. His poetry on the other hand often dealt with death and alienation.

5. "Desert Places" for example is concerned with loneliness.

6. Frost as a matter of fact achieved his first success while living in England.

7. The poet as a result returned to America where his success continued.

8. Robert Frost at last had attained the status of a major poet worldwide.

▼
PRACTICE 3

After reading each of the following sentences, decide if the interrupters are unnecessary or necessary. Punctuate correctly.

1. Our solar system the only planetary system known to exist consists of nine major planets.

2. The nine planets commonly grouped into the inner and outer planets vary significantly in composition.

3. The inner planets of Mercury, Venus, Earth, and Mars are composed primarily of rock and iron.

4. The outer planets Jupiter, Saturn, Uranus, Neptune, and Pluto are much larger and consist mainly of gas and ice.

5. Mercury not only is nearest the sun but orbits the sun most quickly.

6. The morning star Venus is next closest to the medium sized star.

7. The earth known for a myriad of life forms is the only planet known to have abundant liquid water and oxygen.

8. Mars by the way once had water on its surface.

9. Jupiter's mass of 317 times that of earth makes it the largest of the planets.

10. Pluto incidentally is so distant from the sun and so cold that methane freezes on its surface.

▼ **PRACTICE 4**

Write a sentence for each of the following topics. From the list of Commonly Used Interrupters, provide an appropriate interrupter in each sentence. Do not use the same word or phrase twice. Punctuate correctly.

1. School _____

_____

2. Speeding _____

_____

3. Voting _____

_____

4. War _____

_____

5. Flowers _____

_____

6. Breakfast _____

_____

7. Math _____

_____

8. Cooking _____

_____

9. Pets _____

_____

10. Money _____

_____

▼ **PRACTICE 5**

Write a sentence for each of the following topics. From the list of Commonly Used Interrupters, provide an appropriate interrupter in each sentence. Do not use the same word or phrase twice. Punctuate correctly.

1. Automobiles _____

_____

2. Dating _____

_____

3. Vitamins _____

_____

4. Hobbies _____

_____

5. Sports _____

_____

6. Friends _____

_____

7. Art _____

_____

8. Computers _____

_____

9. Humor _____

_____

10. Clothes _____

_____

CHAPTER REVIEW

▼ Interrupters are single words, phrases, or clauses often interrupting the flow of the sentence.

▼ Interrupters most often are placed between the subject and the verb.

▼ Interrupters can be necessary or unnecessary to the basic understanding of the sentence.

▼ If the interrupter is unnecessary to the basic understanding of the sentence, place commas on either side of it.

▼ If the interrupter is necessary to the basic understanding of the sentence, do not place commas around it.

Putting It All Together: Sentence Combining to Improve Paragraph Style

Combine the following groups of simple sentences using a combination of sentence combining strategies (coordination, subordination, insertion of words and phrases). Omit repeated words, phrases, and unnecessary pronouns.

These exercises are taken from paragraphs from the professional essays in the "Additional Readings" section at the back of this book. When you have finished combining each group of sentences, you may compare your answer to the paragraph as written by the original author. A sample exercise has been done for you.

Sample Exercise

1. This happened several summers ago.
2. It was on one of those August evenings.
3. The evenings are endless.
4. The sun is hanging suspended.
5. The sun is above the horizon.
6. I made up my mind.
7. I decided to become beautiful.

Student Paragraph

On an August evening several summers ago, I decided to become beautiful. It was one of those endless evenings when the sun was hanging suspended above the horizon.

Original Paragraph as Written by Author

Several summers ago, on one of those endless August evenings when the sun hangs suspended just above the horizon, I made up my mind to become beautiful. (Grace Suh, "The Eye of the Beholder, paragraph 1)

Notice that both paragraphs are better written than if the original sentences had been organized into a paragraph.

The professional paragraph is somewhat better organized than the student example because the most important information (the decision to become beautiful) is contained in the independent clause while the less important information is subordinated in a series of introductory phrases and a dependent clause (Several summers ago) and (on one of those endless August evenings) and (when the sun hangs suspended just above the horizon).

In other words, it is more important to leave the readers with the idea of "becoming beautiful" than it is to let them know what type of evening it was.

PRACTICE 6

1. The following sentences come from the essay "The Mute Sense" by Diana Ackerman, paragraph 8. Combine each group of sentences into one sentence. Then, combine these sentences into one paragraph. Compare your answer to the author's paragraph at the back of the book.

1.1 I leaned against the flank of a boulder.
1.2 The flank was cool.
1.3 I fanned myself with my hat.

2.1 I could hear the drill of a woodpecker.
2.2 The sound was far away.
2.3 The drill was staccato.
2.4 The woodpecker was a Nutall's woodpecker.

_____

_____

_____

_____

_____

2. The following sentences are taken from "The Roommate's Death" by Jan Harold Brunvand, paragraph 5. Combine each group of sentences into one sentence. Then, combine these sentences into one paragraph.

1.1 The night was windy.
1.2 The night was especially dark.
1.3 Rain was threatening.

2.1 All went well for the girls.
2.2 The girls read stories aloud.
2.3 The girls read stories to the three little boys.
2.4 The girls were sitting for the three little boys.
2.5 The girls had no problem putting the boys to bed.
2.6 The boys were put to bed in the upstairs bedroom.

3.1 The boys were put to bed.
3.2 The girls settled down to watch television.

_____

_____

_____

_____

_____

3. The following sentences are taken from "The Eye of the Beholder" by Grace Suh, paragraph 26. Combine each group of sentences into one sentence. Then, combine these sentences into one paragraph.

1.1 I bought the skincare system.
1.2 I bought the foundation.
1.3 I bought the blush.
1.4 I bought the lipliner.
1.5 I bought the lipstick.

1.6 I bought the primer.
1.7 I bought the eyeliner.
1.8 I bought the eyeshadows.
1.9 The eyeshadows came in four colors.

2.1 The stuff filled a bag.
2.2 The bag was the size of a shoe box.

3.1 There was a cost.
3.2 The cost was a lot.

4.1 Estee handed me my receipt.
4.2 She handed it to me with a flourish.

5. I told her, "Thank you."

_____

_____

_____

_____

_____

4. The following sentences are taken from "The Culture of Violence" by Myriam Miedzian, paragraph 17. Combine each group of sentences into one sentence. Then, combine those sentences into one paragraph.

1.1 Our young boys watch TV.
1.2 They spend about twenty-eight hours a week watching TV.

2.1 They have seen an average of twenty-six thousand TV murders.
2.2 This is by the time they are eighteen.
2.3 These figures are an average.
2.4 The majority of murders are committed by men.
2.5 The majority is vast.

_____

_____

_____

_____

_____

5. The following sentences are taken from "Cyberspace: If You Don't Love It, Leave It" by Esther Dyson, paragraph 7. Combine each group of sentences into one sentence. Then, combine each group of sentences into one paragraph.

1.1 We should put this plainly.
1.2 Cyberspace is a destination.

1.3 The destination is voluntary.
1.4 This is reality.
1.5 This is many destinations.

2.1 You don't just get "onto the Net."
2.2 You have to go someplace.
2.3 The place is particular.

3.1 This has a meaning.
3.2 This meaning is that people can choose where to go.
3.3 This means that people can choose what to see.

4.1 Yes, the community has standards.
4.2 The standards must be enforced.
4.3 The standards should by set by cyberspace communities themselves.
4.4 The standards should not be set by courts.
4.5 The standards should not be set by politicians in Washington.

5.1 What we need is not Government control.
5.2 The control is over all these electronic communites.
5.3 We need self rule.

_____

_____

_____

_____

_____

Visit *The Write Start* Online!

For additional practice with the materials found in this chapter, visit our Website at:

http://www.ablongman.com/checkett

The Website also features additional readings, quizzes, writing activities, and Internet links, as well as a bulletin board and interactive chat.

For More Practice with Your Grammar and Writing Skills

For further exercises designed to improve your writing and grammar skills, use the Writer's ToolKit Plus CD-ROM included with this text. The toolkit provides a wealth of computerized tutorials and practice activities.

PART 2

Writing Effective Paragraphs

Prewriting Activities

We will explore a variety of techniques that you can use to develop specific details for writing assignments. Later in this chapter, the technique of *questioning* (asking the questions *who, what, when, where, why,* or *how* of the topic) is introduced. The development of a topic is influenced by the **purpose** of the assignment, as well as the **audience.** Often, more than one method of expanding a topic or developing details is necessary for writers. The techniques of **listing, clustering, cubing,** and **cross-examination** are summarized here. Writers should experiment with many of these techniques (and any others suggested by your writing teachers) in order to overcome writer's block.

Listing

For this strategy, write the topic at the top of a blank sheet of paper (or at the top of your computer screen). Then quickly list any idea that pops into your head. This is a form of free association; do not edit, correct, or revise. A list on the topic of musicianship may look like this

Musicianship			
performance	attention	strings	practice
anxiety	phrasing	cello	technique
concerts	dynamics	violin	emotion
conductors	interpretation	flutes	control
rehearsal	crescendo	brass	tension
orchestra	audience	oboes	tone
solo	musicians	percussion	intonation

Keep writing for ten minutes to inspire more thoughts. The act of writing actually helps thinking processes for many people. Next, look at your list and see which topics are related (such as technique, control, practice, interpretation, and dynamics). After you have chosen several ideas on your list that would best develop your topic, group them in the correct order (time/space, most to least important, and so on). This last step also helps you formally out-line your topic.

Clustering (Mind Mapping)

This technique is similar to listing but is less structured. Write your topic in the center of a piece of paper. Place related ideas in nearby circles, then keep connecting the circles with lines, grouping those ideas that seem to be related. Note the following diagram on the topic of violence.

After studying the diagram or map, select the cluster of ideas that best develops the topic or thesis statement you have chosen. Further clustering on these selected terms may help expand your options. Additionally, you may wish to try another method of prewriting at this point.

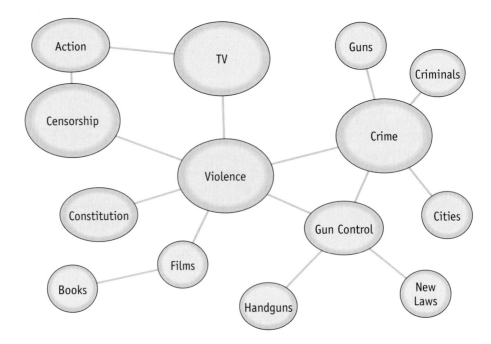

PRACTICE: CLUSTERING (Mapping)

Choose one of the following topics, and write it in the center of a piece of paper. Then, cluster your ideas around it.

A favorite holiday
The color red
The future
A dream
A best/worst boss
A hero

Cubing

Another type of brainstorming uses a cube to generate new approaches to a topic. Imagine a six-sided cube with the following questions on each side:

Describe the topic: What does the subject look like? What is the size, color, shape, texture, smell, sound, and so forth? Which details are unique?

Compare or contrast it: What is your subject like? How does it differ from similar subjects? Give details.

Free-associate it: What does your subject remind you of? What further ideas do you think of?

Analyze it: What are the parts of the subject? How does each part function? How are the parts connected? What is the significance of this subject?

Argue for or against it: What are the arguments for or against your topic? What are the advantages and disadvantages?

Apply it: How can the subject be used?

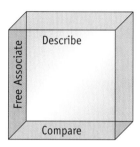
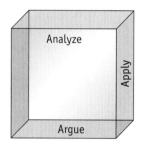

Approach your topic from each of the above six perspectives, freewriting your answers as with the techniques of listing or clustering and giving yourself 10 to 15 minutes to explore each idea. Do not worry about correctness at this point. Review your responses and see if any are suited to your assignment or inspire your ideas for the writing assignment.

Cross-Examination

This approach can be used with a partner or individually. It is a variation of the questioning form that is introduced in Chapter 13. The questions can be grouped depending on the type of essay assigned or depending on the type of essay you would like to write. Interview yourself or your partner regarding your topic.

Definition
1. How is the topic/subject defined or explained by the dictionary or encyclopedia?
2. How do most people define the topic informally?
3. How do I define the subject?
4. What is the history, origin, or background of the topic?
5. What are some examples of the topic?

Relationship
1. What is the cause of the topic/subject?
2. To what larger group or category does the subject belong?
3. What are the values or goals of the subject?
4. What are the effects of the subject?

Comparison and Contrast
1. What is the topic/subject similar to?
2. What is the topic different from?
3. What is the subject better than?
4. What is the subject worse than?
5. What is the subject opposite to?

Testimony
1. What do people say about the topic/subject?
2. What authorities exist on this topic?
3. Has anything been written on this subject?
4. What are the important statistics?
5. Is there any further research on the topic?
6. Have I had any personal experience on this topic?

Circumstance
1. Is this subject/topic possible?
2. Is the subject impossible?
3. When has this subject happened before?
4. What might prevent it from happening?
5. Why might it happen again?
6. Who or what is associated with the topic?

Not all of these questions will apply to every topic. Choose the questions that help develop your topic most thoroughly.

CHAPTER 13

The Paragraph

In the preceding chapters, you have been practicing the basic sentences that allow for communicating information with focus, variety, and rhythm. Sentences are good for conveying short pieces of information, but for longer, more developed ideas, a longer format is necessary.

The next five chapters will help you in discovering, understanding, and writing the basic paragraph. A paragraph can be a complete piece of writing by itself; most often, however, paragraphs are grouped together in longer pieces of writings, for example, essays, letters, reports, research papers, and chapters in a book or novel.

Many of the elements in longer pieces of writing are found in the paragraph, so it is a good model to use before learning to write longer pieces.

A **paragraph** is a group of sentences concerned with developing or expressing a single **topic** (one main idea). In fact, what you are reading right now is a paragraph. It is developing the concept of the paragraph! Generally, paragraphs can be as long as you want them to be, although most are usually 4 to 15 sentences in length. The key to writing a good paragraph is to make it long enough to develop the topic and no longer. This paragraph is between 4 and 15 sentences in length, and it is describing the elements that make up the paragraph.

There are two basic types of sentences in a paragraph: the **topic sentence** and **support sentences.** The topic sentence tells the reader what the main idea, or topic, of the paragraph is. Although there is no set place in the paragraph for the topic sentence, making the topic sentence the first sentence in the paragraph will make organizing and developing the topic easier. The topic sentence is followed by support sentences that explain, clarify, and define the topic by using specific detail. Support sentences should demonstrate a variety of styles to show the relationship between the various pieces of information and to create rhythm (see Chapters 3 through 12). Exhibit 13–1 summarizes the elements and characteristics of a paragraph.

1. A topic sentence announces one main idea (the topic).
2. Support sentences use specific detail to develop the main idea.
3. Sentence variety connects related ideas and adds rhythm.

Exhibit 13–1

Let's look at the characteristics of a basic paragraph. Specific points are illustrated in the bulleted comments following the paragraph.

> ### Example Paragraph
>
> Sophocles, the Greek dramatist, was greatly admired for his tragedies. *Oedipus* was his most famous tragedy, and Aristotle praised it as the finest example of dramatic irony. Sophocles wrote over 130 plays. Even though he was so prolific, his plays won over 20 first prizes at drama festivals.

▼ The first sentence is the topic sentence, and it announces the topic (Sophocles) and the **controlling idea** (which also contains the writer's attitude toward the topic: that Sophocles *was greatly admired* for his tragedies).

▼ The following three support sentences develop the controlling idea by (1) naming his most famous tragedy, and by explaining why it was praised by a famous critic; (2) giving the vast number of plays he wrote; and (3) giving the number of times his plays were rewarded.

▼ The sentences also exhibit variety. The first sentence contains extra information, between the commas. The second sentence is coordinated with the coordinating conjunction *and*. The third sentence is a simple sentence. The fourth sentence is subordinated by using an introductory dependent clause preceding the independent clause.

The Topic Sentence

The topic sentence has two parts: the **topic/subject** and the **controlling idea.** The topic is the subject of the paragraph. The controlling idea states what the writer will be developing about the subject of the paragraph, and it contains the writer's attitude toward the subject. The controlling idea limits what you can say about the topic subject so that you don't stray to other subjects or ideas.

> ### Example
>
> In a movie, music often enhances a romantic atmosphere.

The subject is "music." The controlling idea is "often enhances a romantic atmosphere." The attitude is "often enhances."

In a paragraph with this topic sentence, the controlling idea about the music is that it is romantic. The writer cannot talk about other aspects of the movie, such as violence, comedy, production costs, advertising, or attendance figures. The controlling idea forces the writer to talk only about those features of the music that developed the romantic aspects of the movie.

Let's look at another topic sentence.

> ### Example
>
> The Marshall Plan brought economic relief to Europe.

The subject is "the Marshall Plan." The controlling idea is that it "brought economic relief to Europe." In a paragraph with this topic sentence, the writer cannot write about European art, pollution, hunting, or vegetation. The writer must focus on economic factors that became successful because of the Marshall Plan.

Topic sentences missing a controlling idea lack focus and specific direction. Without a controlling idea, the writer's attitude about the subject can be unclear.

> **Examples**
>
> Soccer is a popular high school sport. (incomplete controlling idea—popular is an attitude only)
>
> Michael Jordan was a basketball player. (no controlling idea—this is simply a statement of fact)
>
> Soccer is a popular high school sport because it is relatively inexpensive to fund. (controlling idea: *cheap funding* makes soccer popular—the attitude)
>
> Michael Jordan's diverse skills made him an exciting basketball player. (controlling idea: Jordan is exciting because of *diverse skills*—"exciting" is the attitude)

▼ **PRACTICE 1**

In the following sentences, circle the topic/subject, and underline the controlling idea.

Example: (Swiss watches) are popular because of the fine craftmanship with which they are made.

1. Mud-slinging and personal attacks turn off some people when it comes to politics.

2. Many students dislike high school because of social cliques and favoritism for some students.

3. Families can help children by being a support system for all their activities.

4. A hobby can assist people in easing the stresses of everyday life.

5. The movie was a success because of the script, the acting, and the special effects.

6. Vacation expenses can be reduced by purchasing a good travel book.

7. The depletion of the ozone layer might cause global warming and an increase in skin cancers.

8. Many current fads are driven by how the rich and famous are portrayed in the media.

9. Helping others can make almost any profession a rewarding experience.

10. Laws are effective only if they are enforced fairly and equitably.

In the following sentences, circle the topic/subject, and underline the controlling idea.

1. Exercising can be more enjoyable if done in a group.

2. The fence was built to keep the coyotes away from the livestock.

3. The band played an extra hour because their fans wouldn't let them off the stage.

4. Great teamwork has made the United States' women's soccer team an international success.

5. Pizza is a best selling fast food because of the variety of toppings available.

6. Versatility and size make the laptop computer a good business tool for travelers.

7. Learning about long-term investing can help people have a happier retirement experience.

8. The Spanish Inquisition impaired scientific thought for decades.

9. Technology has as many drawbacks as it does advantages.

10. A quiet place with good lighting can help students study more effectively.

The following sentences are inadequate as topic sentences because they lack a complete controlling idea. Turn them into topic sentences by adding a controlling idea to each.

1. The Final Four basketball tournament is exciting.

_____

_____

2. Dining out is enjoyable.

_____

_____

3. I attend college.

_____

_____

4. Live theater is dramatic.

_____

_____

5. My clothes are stylish.

_____

_____

6. I drive a Volvo.

_____

_____

7. Dr. Jonas Salk created a vaccine to combat polio.

_____

_____

8. Many new stadiums are being built with old stadium features.

_____

_____

9. Museums house many beautiful sculptures.

_____

_____

10. The final days of the Vietnam War were hectic.

_____

_____

▼ PRACTICE 4

Write topic sentences for the following subjects. Don't forget to add the controlling idea.

1. Nuclear energy _____

_____

2. Presidential elections _____

_____

3. Rock music _____

_____

4. Jogging _____

_____

5. Farming _____

_____

6. Science fiction _____

_____

7. Classical music _____

_____

8. Tornadoes _____

_____

9. Vacationing _____

_____

10. Clothes _____

_____

Support Sentences

Support sentences follow the topic sentence and develop the subject using specific examples, details, and facts. These support ideas must be consistent with the controlling idea. In other words, the controlling idea unifies the paragraph by determining the kind of support ideas you can use in the support sentences.

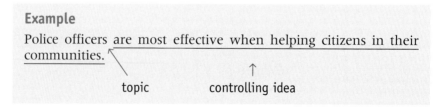

> **Example**
> Police officers are most effective when helping citizens in their communities.
>
>   topic   controlling idea

Support sentences for this topic sentence would focus on *what* police officers do to help citizens and might include such activities as

    a. finding lost/stolen property
    b. solving crimes
    c. preventing crimes

Six Important Support Questions

When writing a story, reporters ask six questions. The answers provide the focus that allows them to select the details, facts, and examples to develop the story with specific information. The six questions are **who, what, where, when, why,** and **how.**

After you have selected, or have been given, the topic you are to write about, decide on the controlling idea. To do this, choose which of the following reporter's questions allows you to write about the topic with the desired focus.

For instance, your topic is an *important event.* In the support sentences, you could focus on

Who?

Who started the event?

Who attended/witnessed/participated in the event?

Who was affected by the event?

What?

What was the event?

What happened before/during/after the event?

What was special about the event?

Where?

Where did the event occur?

Did the location affect the event in any way?

Did the location have historical significance?

When?

When did the event occur (A.M./P.M., day, month, year)?

Did the time frame add any special significance to the event?

Did the event coincide with a historically significant time?

Why?

Why did the event occur?

Why was the event important?

How?

How did the event happen?

How was the event funded?

How was the event advertised?

You can add your own focus to these questions if other ideas come to you. There is no need to limit yourself to the questions presented in the list.

Examples

1. Reading can help people become better educated.

2. Reading is best done in a quiet, secluded place.

3. Anyone interested in becoming a better writer should read as much as possible.

Although the topic subject of each sentence, *reading*, is the same, the focus of the controlling idea is different. In sentence 1, the focus is on *what* reading can do for people (educate them); in sentence 2, the focus is on *where* reading is best accomplished (in a quiet, secluded place); and in sentence 3, the focus is on *who* (anyone interested in becoming a writer).

Creating the Working Outline

Before you begin writing, you may want to sketch out the major ideas that will appear in your paragraph. This can help you discover whether or not you have a topic, controlling idea, and support ideas that work together for proper development. To create a **working outline,** list your topic, controlling idea, and support ideas in a ladderlike list.

> **Example**
> Topic: Dieting
> Controlling idea: Can cause harmful effects
> Support ideas: anorexia/bulimia
>   malnutrition
>   psychological problems

In this paragraph, the harmful effects of dieting are discussed. This topic is developed and supported by using anorexia/bulimia, heart disease, and psychological problems as the negative outcomes that dieting can produce. The finished paragraph might look like this:

> Dieting can cause many harmful effects. It can lead to a potentially deadly eating disorder called anorexia/bulimia. This disorder is characterized by eating binges followed by self-induced vomiting or laxative abuse. Because the body is not ingesting the proper amounts of nutrients, malnutrition often occurs. Of course, physical problems are not the only negative effects caused by dieting. Stress and a poor self-image can lead to self-destructive psychological states requiring long-term medical help. The safest and most effective method to lose weight is eating balanced meals combined with a consistent exercise program.

PRACTICE 5

To practice creating *working outlines*, add a controlling idea for each of the subjects listed below. Then, using the six reporter's questions, list three specific details that develop the controlling idea. Try to use all six of the reporter's questions. After you are finished, you will have a list of all the basic ideas that will go into the paragraph. This is called a *working outline* because the paragraph is still unfinished.

1. The *Star Wars* movies

Controlling idea: _____

a. _____

b. _____

c. _____

2. The United Nations

Controlling idea: _____

a. _____

b. _____

c. _____

3. Computers

Controlling idea: _____

a. _____

b. _____

c. _____

4. Abraham Lincoln

Controlling idea: _____

a. _____

b. _____

c. _____

5. Exercising

Controlling idea: _____

a. _____

b. _____

c. _____

6. Investments

Controlling idea: _____

a. _____

b. _____

c. _____

7. Violence

Controlling idea: _____

a. _____

b. _____

c. _____

8. Course scheduling

Controlling idea: _____

a. _____

b. _____

c. _____

9. Recycling

Controlling idea: _____

a. _____

b. _____

c. _____

10. Vacations

Controlling idea: _____

a. _____

b. _____

c. _____

The First Draft

To write your first draft of any one paragraph, combine the topic and the controlling idea listed in your working outline to create the topic sentence. Then, write a sentence for each of the specific detail ideas. These will be your support sentences used to develop the topic sentence. When you match your topic sentence with your support sentences, you'll have a **first draft,** or **rough draft,** paragraph.

Example

Topic: Civil War

Controlling idea (Reporter's question—Who?): Leaders having an impact on war.

A. Lincoln   B. Grant   C. Lee

Rough Draft Paragraph

The Civil War had three great leaders. President Lincoln believed that all men should be free. General Grant enjoyed drinking whiskey and smoking cigars. General Lee symbolized the belief that an aristocratic class should govern men of unequal status.

▼ **PRACTICE 6**

On separate sheets of paper, using the ten examples you have created in Practice 5, turn each example into a short paragraph of four sentences.

Revising the Rough Draft

No one—not even professional writers—creates a perfect paragraph in the first draft. There are always some rough spots to smooth out—why else do you think the first draft is called the rough draft? To improve what you wrote in your rough draft, you must revise.

As you revise, answer these four questions:

▼ Is the topic subject clear?
▼ Will the controlling idea develop the subject adequately?
▼ Do my support sentences consist of specific facts, details, and examples?
▼ Is there sentence variety?

Let's look at our rough draft from the previous example and ask our four revision questions.

Example

(A) The Civil War had three great leaders. (B) President Lincoln believed that all men should be free. (C) General Grant enjoyed drinking whiskey and smoking cigars. (D) General Lee symbolized the belief that an aristocratic class should govern men of unequal status.

---

1. **Is the topic subject clear?** The topic subject is clear: Civil War leaders.
2. **Will the controlling idea develop the subject adequately?** There is no controlling idea that clarifies how the subject will be developed. The topic sentence is simply a statement of fact.
   Revised topic sentence with controlling idea: Three great leaders embodied the ideals of the North and South during the Civil War. (Now, the controlling idea clarifies that it is the beliefs of the three leaders that will be discussed.)
3. **Do my support sentences consist of specific facts, details, and examples?** Support sentences (B) and (D) consist of details that support the

controlling idea. However, sentence (C) does not. General Grant's enjoying whiskey and cigars does not explain how his beliefs symbolized the North's beliefs.

Revised support sentence: General Grant believed that all men should determine their own destiny. (This rewrite clarifies Grant's belief and mirrors Lincoln's belief as stated in sentence (B).

4. **Is there sentence variety?** All the sentences in the paragraph are simple sentences. Although these sentences are grammatically correct, they don't add rhythm or help to link the ideas they express.

Revised sentences demonstrating variety: (A) Three great leaders embodied the ideals of the North and South during the Civil War. (B) While President Lincoln detested the thought of war, he believed that all men should be free. (C) General Grant shared Lincoln's belief, for he believed that all men should determine their own destiny. (D) General Lee symbolized the belief that an aristocratic class should govern men of unequal status.

The Final Draft

Three great leaders embodied the ideals of the North and South during the Civil War. While President Lincoln detested the thought of war, he believed that all men should be free. General Grant shared Lincoln's belief, for he believed that all men should determine their own destiny. General Lee symbolized the belief that an aristocratic class should govern men of unequal status.

In this revision the information is presented more clearly, and the rhythm moves the reading along smoothly and quickly. This is a sign of mature, controlled writing.

▼ PRACTICE 7

On separate sheets of paper, revise the rough draft paragraphs you wrote in Practice 6.

Proofreading: The Final Step

After revising your rough draft into a final draft, there is still one last step you should accomplish before submitting your work.

You should always take time to make sure that your work does not have errors that will detract from its presentation. A great idea, one that professional writers use, is to have someone else read your finished writing. Sometimes, it is easier for someone else to see errors and inconsistencies than it is for the writer. Ultimately, the errors in your writing are your responsibility to find and correct. Typically, you should look for the following types of errors:

a. Sentence fragments; see Chapter 3 for a review of correcting sentence fragments.
b. Run-on sentences and comma splice sentences; see Chapter 4 for a review of correcting run-on and comma splice sentences. Use your computer's *grammarcheck* function to help you correct errors as you find them.
c. Spelling; use both your computer's *spellcheck* function and a dictionary to help you correct errors as you find them. Remember, *spellcheck* does not correct for meaning. If you use *lien* instead of *lean*, *spellcheck* will not correct the error because *lien* is spelled correctly even though it is not the word the writer meant to use.

PRACTICE 8

Find and correct sentence fragments in the following paragraph. Neatly write your corrections in the text.

Facing the Night

I was 8 years old the first time I had the biggest scare of my life. The thought of sleeping in the basement all by myself was frightening. I'll never forget that night. My brother at the house of his best friend, and that left me in the "dungeon" all by myself. At first, didn't think it would be that bad. Then, night came. There I was, lying in my bed in darkness, where I could not my hand in front of my face. Soon, could hear every sound a dark, large, haunted and gloomy house makes. As my eyes adjusted to the darkness, enough light shining through the basement window to let me see all the scary monsters on the wall. Quickly, I pulled the covers over my head and started to pray for sunlight. After a few minutes I heard a noise, so the covers from my head only to see my brother standing in the doorway. His best friend was sick, so he had to come home. What a relief!

PRACTICE 9

Find and correct sentence fragments in the following paragraph. Neatly write your corrections in the text.

My Baby Brother

Nothing changed my life like the birth of my second brother. In July of 1999, my 32-year-old mother; announced she was pregnant. My brother Ryan and I thrilled by the thought of a baby; however, at the time we didn't realize what actually having a new member of the family involved. Didn't know about all the crying sessions or diaper changes. Soon afterwards, the newness of the baby and things started to get back to a routine. Went back to work, Ryan began staying after school for basketball practice. As for me, my life drastically. I became my mother's full-time baby-sitter.

Find and correct the run-on sentence errors in the following paragraph. Neatly write your corrections in the text.

My Happiest Moment

The happiest moment of my life was the day I was married. The day started out a blustery 32 degrees. The sun was shining it looked to be a great day. First, we began decorating the hall, blowing up balloons and arranging tables my fiancée took his buddies to play a chilly round of golf. Next, the bridesmaids headed off to the beauty salon to get their hair and nails done to perfection. Time was moving very quickly there were still many projects that needed to be attended to before the wedding could begin. Finally, people began to arrive at the church they were wearing their finest dresses and suits. The ceremony was beautiful everything had fallen into place. The hardest part was over we would be heading for the reception to party away the tensions of the all the hard work and worry that had gone into the planning. Before the night ended, my new husband and I made a toast we thanked each and every person for helping to make this a beautiful day that we would never forget.

Find and correct the run-on sentences in the following paragraph. Neatly write your corrections in the text.

Mr. Unusual

Dennis Rodman, looming over the world at 6'8", may be the most unusual looking person in America. As a star player in the NBA, he stands out like a garish, neon sign Rodman is widely acknowledged for his outlandish behavior as well as his looks. He has been suspended many times for abusing officials with offensive language and starting fights has been almost a monthly occurrence during games. Rodman is very outgoing the rumors about his nightlife are legend Madonna was even seen with him in on several occasions. On the street, you might see him dressed in anything from a full length mink coat or a wedding dress! Rodman loves the attention and he loves making millions of dollars each year as an NBA player and celebrity.

PRACTICE 12

Find and correct the comma splice errors in the following paragraph. Neatly write your corrections in the text.

The Journey's End

It was early June, the sun was bright but not blistering on my face. The silent motion of the pedals of my bike moved me closer to my destination. It had been two months since my last visit with Bev, her usual shining face grew grim as she saw me approach. Her tone was one of concern, "Have you spoken to your mother today?" I was startled. She continued, "Your grandmother is in the hospital." I rushed home and called mother, she told me that grandmother was very ill, and I couldn't visit her without being accompanied by her. I refused to wait, I couldn't let my grandmother lay in a cold, indifferent room without being by her side, we were close as mother and daughter.

PRACTICE 13

Find and correct the comma splice errors in the following paragraph. Neatly write your corrections in the text.

The Dilemma of Modern Progress

Despite senseless tragedies and horrors, well-documented in history books, the twentieth century has been a time of continuing progression for humanity. Many wonderful advances, commonplace today, would have been beyond even the most imaginative of nineteenth century dreamers, there appears to be no slow down to this trend, moreover, new ideas are now being developed at an ever-increasing pace. Although most would agree these accomplishments are desirable, many so-called "time savers" can have us chasing our own tails, modern technology often produces more inconvenience than convenience because of our lack of understanding of the full scope of the impact that our inventions have on us.

Find and correct the spelling errors in the following paragraph. Neatly write your corrections in the text.

Deserted Waters

A place I find sothing is a desserted picnic area next to the river near Old Town. Standing under the roof of a small pavilion, I can look out over the dirty ruhsing water of the Mississippi River. I can hear the water craxsh as it hits the rocks with every wave. Surrounding me on the cracked concrete are half a dozen old, warpped picnic talbles. I can hear birds singing above as they guard their nests hiding in the beams. On my left stand shabby homes that once were vibrant mansions. The stairs ledding up to the front doors are missing, and the glass in the windows has been rplaced with boreds. There is a lifeless playground, grass growing over the rusting equipment, behind me. The seen may look depressing, but it is a beautifull place where I can relax.

Find and correct the spelling errors in the following paragraph. Neatly write your corrections in the text.

The Sound of Music

How does the music we listen too broden our minds? Music an make people happy, sad, mello, or even overjoyed. The words to a song tell a story; therefore, the outcome of a great storey means a great song to the artist and listener. Music fills our lives; we hear it in doctors' offices, elevaters, and every time we turn the ignition key in our car. The music can be rock, soul, classicall, bluegrass, our country and wesstern. Whatever your taste, there is a style of music that will touch your heart and you soul.

PRACTICE 16

The following paragraphs contain sentence fragment, run-on, comma splice, and spelling errors. Correct as many of the errors as you can find. Neatly write your corrections in the text.

The Staff of Life

Bread is called "the Staff of Life" and the foodstuff is the most universal food known to man. Primiative man took centuries to discover how to identify seeds and how to grow them and adapt them to local enviroments.

Oats, barley, rye, and wheat breads are made threw the process of applying heat to a mixture of flower, grain, yeast, and water three kinds of bread were the first foods made by baking, flat bread, yeast bread, and quick bread are the three kinds, consequently, causing a surplus of food in homes. Bread sonn became a favorite food item to eat with all meals and they were a tasty and newtrisious treat.

Soon, bread production mover from the home to commercial bussiness, therefore, the amount of bread produced rose dramatically the numbers of loafs produced was staggering, it was an enormous boom. In the 1940s, newtrients and vitamens were added into commercial baking; reducing various deseases around the wrld. When bread is served in restarants, most loaves are not baked on the premises the bread is baked at a commercial bakary. With the amount of bread being eaten, is justified in beign called "the staff of life."

PRACTICE 17

The following paragraphs contain sentence fragment, run-on, comma splice, and spelling errors. Correct as many of the errors as you can find. Neatly write your corrections in the text.

Viva Las Vegas!

The trip my family tood to Las Vegas was one of the best times of my life, the plain landed, and my family and I stepped off into the cool night air of Las Vegas the gambling capitol of the world. Our baggage was picked up first, it seemed to take forever. Then, we took a cab to the most exotic hotel casino we had ever seen. The hotel casino; a giant castle, was called the Excalibur. In the front of the hotel, was a fire-breathing dragon during the evening, its mouth blew a flame that must have been 20 feet long.

The next day, we awoke to the beautiful dessert sun. After eating a huge breakfast. My sister and I went for a swim, and took in some of the attractions like the Treasure Island Casino Ship show. Which was a virtual reality ride. We also went to Circus-Circus and watched the acrobates high above the casino floor they did have a net but it was still exciting. After a delicious dinner, we saw a show starring Bette Midler it was so funny and entertaining. It was the perfect end to a perfect day. Which I will be looking forward to taking agan some day, I just hope it is with my family again.

CHAPTER REVIEW

▼ Write a topic sentence with a clear topic subject and a controlling idea by which the subject can be developed.
▼ Choose the focus for the support details by using the six reporter's questions: who, what, where, when, why, and how.
▼ Write as many support sentences as are required to develop the topic. Be certain they contain specific facts, details, and examples.
▼ Check for sentence variety that clarifies relationships and adds rhythm.
▼ Revise when necessary, looking for paragraph unity.
▼ Proofread for grammar and spelling errors.
▼ Check for paper presentation: tears, creases, and smudges.

Additional Writing Assignments

The following paragraph writing assignments will help you practice the techniques you have learned in this chapter. Use the seven steps in the chapter review as you do your work.

As you write each paragraph, use the reporter's question in the parenthesis as your focus. Remember to revise and proofread each paragraph.

1. (*Who?*) Describe a person. This can be a person you know, such as a parent, sibling, relative, friend, teacher, co-worker, or a historical person with whom you are familiar. In your topic sentence, name the person, and write a controlling idea you wish to develop in the support sentences.

2. (*What?*) Describe an event. This can be an event from your own life, such as a religious ceremony, a birthday/graduation party, an operation, or a historical event with which you are familiar. In the topic sentence, name the event, and write a controlling idea you wish to develop in the support sentence.

3. (*Where?*) Describe a location. This can be a place that you know, such as your room, house, school, workplace, or a historical location with which you are familiar. In your topic sentence, name the location, and write a controlling idea you wish to develop in the support sentences.

4. (*When?*) Describe an important time. This can be a time in your life, such as your childhood, or teenage years, or a well-known time in history with which you are familiar. In your topic sentence, name the time frame, and write a controlling idea you wish to develop in the support sentences.

5. (*Why?*) Describe why something happened. This can be something that happened to you, someone you know, or the reason something happened in history. In your topic sentence, name the reason, and write a controlling idea you wish to develop in the support sentences.

6. (*How?*) Describe how something occurs or is done. This can be something you have accomplished or were witness to or how something happened historically. In your topic sentence, name the process, and write a controlling idea you wish to develop in the support sentences.

Writing Opportunities

Home

You want your sister, who lives across town, to accompany you on a shopping trip to a mall. Your sister doesn't like malls because she thinks they are too boring because all they have are women's clothing shops. In one of your monthly letters, you include a paragraph convincing her of why she should meet you at the brand new mall that has just opened near your neighborhood.

School

Your Intro to Sociology professor wants you to visit a shopping mall and write one paragraph about the type of people who might be attracted by the different types of shops and services the mall offers.

Work

The owners of a shopping mall have hired the advertising agency you work for to attract customers to its newest mall. Write one paragraph of text to accompany the photograph above that will appear in a brochure advertising the grand opening of the mall.

Visit *The Write Start* Online!

For additional practice with the materials found in this chapter, visit our Website at:

http://www.ablongman.com/checkett

The Website also features additional readings, quizzes, writing activities, and Internet links, as well as a bulletin board and interactive chat.

For More Practice with Your Grammar and Writing Skills

For further exercises designed to improve your writing and grammar skills, use the Writer's ToolKit Plus CD-ROM included with this text. The toolkit provides a wealth of computerized tutorials and practice activities.

CHAPTER 14

Description

All paragraphs build on a topic. One way to build on a topic is by describing it in detail. Effective **description** creates images in the reader's mind by using specific details. Like a painter using color on a canvas, the writer uses words (the color) to create pictures in the reader's mind (the canvas).

Instead of merely writing

> The clouds flew by overhead.

A writer using good description might write

> The billowing clouds, like delicious mounds of white, mashed potatoes, floated lazily by overhead as if they hadn't a care in the world.

The specific details help develop the word-painting that describes persons, places, things, and emotions. At times, writers want their meaning to convey a feeling of sadness. At other times, they might want to evoke a feeling of happiness, or frustration, or hope or sarcasm. Effective description adds clarity, depth, and feeling to your writing.

Types of Description

There are two types of description: **objective** and **subjective.**

Objective description relies on factual detail without much embellishment.

> **Example**
>
> The snowman consisted of three round balls stacked one on top of the other. It stood 5 feet high. Its eyes were round stones, with a carrot serving as a nose. A baseball cap sat atop its head.

From this objective description, it is difficult to recognize what emotion or impression the writer wants us to feel.

In contrast, subjective description creates an easily identifiable emotion or impression.

> **Example**
> The snowman's body consisted of three <u>plump</u> balls of <u>fluffy</u>, <u>white snow</u> stacked like an <u>ice-cream cone</u>. Its eyes were <u>made</u> from <u>brightly colored</u> stones, with a <u>squiggly</u>, <u>pigtail</u>, orange <u>carrot</u> serving as a nose. A <u>fuzzy</u>, red baseball cap with a <u>crooked</u> bill sat <u>cockeyed</u> on his head.

From this subjective description, it is clear that the writer wants the snowman to evoke a funny or happy emotion. Objective description describes what the writer actually sees. Subjective description describes how the writer feels.

Dominant Impressions

When writing descriptively, the content of your writing will be clearer and more enjoyable if you focus on just one **dominant impression.** When writing a descriptive paragraph, each support sentence should build on the dominant impression you created in the topic sentence. Adding descriptive detail helps writers achieve these dominant impressions. Writers convey the dominant impression to the reader by a word or phrase in the topic sentence of a paragraph and then support this word or phrase throughout the paragraph by using specific detail.

> (No dominant impression) The sky was filled with dark, brooding clouds, and slivers of bright sunlight glistened toward the ground.

In this paragraph, the reader will not know the writer's intention. Is the writer trying to convey a negative or a positive mood?

> (Dominant impression) The sky was filled with dark, brooding clouds, and horrible flashes of lightning sent ugly scars across the horizon.

In this paragraph, the negative dominant impression is clear. Remember, the dominant impression is the overall feeling or emotional response that you want your reader to take away from your description. The words you choose to make your dominant impression should be specific enough to be easily understood; they should not be vague.

For example, the word "nice" has no specific meaning because it can mean almost anything. Nice can mean friendly, or pretty, or neat, or clean.

Examples

Topic sentences without dominant impressions:

>Melody was a model.

>It was evening in St. Louis.

>The ball game was played.

>The diamond necklace lay on the dresser.

Topic sentences with a dominant impression:

>Melody was a glamorous model.

>The evening in St. Louis was dreary.

>The ball game was exciting.

>The dazzling, diamond necklace lay on the dresser.

Tip: A useful book to help you select better dominant impression words is a *thesaurus*. This is a reference book that contains lists of synonyms, homonyms, and antonyms for almost any word you can think of. You can find inexpensive paperbacks at any bookstore.

Sensory Images

Description creates images. It can tell the reader what a person, a place, or a thing

▼ Looks like
▼ Feels like
▼ Smells like
▼ Sounds like
▼ Tastes like

These **sensory images** are based on the five senses we are all familiar with: sight, touch, smell, sound, and taste. By using sensory images, writers can draw a more fully developed picture of what they are describing. Good description actually causes readers to remember similar persons, places, or things from their own experience. This personal interaction between the reader and the writing is a wonderful and powerful process.

Examples

Sight

>a. Nondescriptive: The model walked down the runway wearing a dress.

>b. Descriptive: The spaghetti-thin fashion model slinked down the long runway wearing a shining, cherry-red dress.

Touch

>a. Nondescriptive: The new bedsheets were uncomfortable.

>b. Descriptive: The new, stiff bedsheets felt like sandpaper scraping against my skin.

Smell

>a. Nondescriptive: Fred's car trunk smelled awful.

>b. Descriptive: Fred's car trunk smelled like a gym locker stuffed with rotten eggs.

Sound

    a. Nondescriptive: The band was loud.

    b. Descriptive: The band's ear-splitting punk music was loud enough to make your teeth vibrate.

Taste

    a. Nondescriptive: The bread tasted old.

    b. Descriptive: The bread tasted musty, like some moldy cheese I remember eating at my grandmother's house last year.

▼ PRACTICE 1

In the blank spaces below, rewrite the nondescriptive sentences by using various sensory images.

1. Nondescriptive: The boy's clothes didn't fit properly.

    Sight: _____

_____

2. Nondescriptive: The car was not in good shape.

    Sight: _____

_____

3. Nondescriptive: The tree bark felt rough.

    Touch: _____

_____

4. Nondescriptive: The baby's skin was soft.

    Touch: _____

_____

5. Nondescriptive: The odor of Fred's gym shoes was awful.

    Smell: _____

_____

6. Nondescriptive: The perfume smelled good.

    Smell: _____

_____

7. Nondescriptive: My younger brother was loud.

    Sound: _____

_____

8. Nondescriptive: The storm made a lot of noise.

Sound: _____

_____

9. Nondescriptive: The breakfast pastries tasted good.

Taste: _____

_____

10. Nondescriptive: The fancy dinner was delicious.

Taste: _____

_____

Comparisons

Another device that writers use to describe something is **comparison,** also known as **figurative language.** Comparisons to well-known or everyday objects or images provide descriptions that readers can immediately recognize. Many writers find comparison the easiest descriptive tool because comparisons allow writers to provide clear ideas to the reader by tapping into images and emotions that the reader has already experienced. The three most effective figurative language devices are

▼ Simile
▼ Metaphor
▼ Personification

Simile

A **simile** is a comparison using either *like* or *as* to show a similarity between two different things. Notice how similar the words "simile" and "similarity" are.

> **Examples**
> My boss roars <u>like</u> a lion at his employees.
> The fog was <u>like</u> a blanket covering the city, so you couldn't see a thing.
> The runner was fast <u>as</u> a cheetah, and he won the race.
> The searchlight shined brightly <u>as</u> the sun, blocking our vision.

Metaphor

A **metaphor** is a stronger comparison between two things without using *like* or *as*. The implication is that one thing "is" the same as the other.

> **Examples**
> My boss <u>is</u> a lion, roaring at all his employees.
> The fog <u>was</u> a blanket covering the city, covering all the buildings and trees.

Personification

In **personification,** the writer gives human emotions or characteristics to animals, objects, or even ideas.

Examples

The tree howled in the wind.

Love danced in their eyes.

The bear cheated his rivals out of their food.

The house's windows winked at the passersby.

The car rested in the driveway after the long drive home.

PRACTICE 2

In the spaces below, create comparisons between the two objects in the parentheses using the figurative language device marked in boldface.

Example: (simile—raindrops/ball-bearings) The raindrops sounded **like** steel ball-bearings smashing into the roof with a metallic bang!

1. (**simile**—lake/glass) _____

    _____

2. (**simile**—mansion/monster) _____

    _____

3. (**metaphor**—airplane/bird) _____

    _____

4. (**metaphor**—car/tiger) _____

    _____

5. (**personification**—wind/caring person) _____

    _____

6. (**personification**—stuffed animal/jolly person) _____

    _____

PRACTICE 3

In the space to the right, replace the underlined, vague dominant impression word in the sentence with a more specific and descriptive word or phrase.

Example **Vague:** The wedding dress was beautiful.
            Specific: The wedding dress was dazzling.

1. The haunted house was <u>scary</u>.   Specific: _____

2. The thick, woolen blanket felt <u>nice</u>.   Specific: _____

3. My Uncle Jacob is <u>fun</u>.   Specific: _____

4. The bowl of chili tasted <u>hot</u>.   Specific: _____

5. Fiona's ballet practice was <u>good</u>.   Specific: _____

6. The actor's performance was <u>bad</u>.   Specific: _____

7. The band's music was <u>loud</u>.   Specific: _____

8. The dorm room was <u>messy</u>.   Specific: _____

9. The aquarium decorations were <u>pretty</u>.   Specific: _____

10. The chocolate mousse was <u>rich</u>.   Specific: _____

PRACTICE 4

The following paragraph is taken from a descriptive essay, "Halloween Havoc," by student writer Erin Nelson. The paragraph is jam-packed with expressive description that brings the special evening to life!

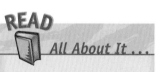

READ
All About It . . .

To read the full essay from which this paragraph is excerpted, see page 395.

The spooky old houses come to life at night with gruesome decorations. With grotesque carved faces, the jack-o'-lanterns give off an eerie glow. Tombstones line the sidewalk, like a long narrow graveyard; beware of the bloody hand reaching out to grab intruders. Bats as black as the night sky fly in quick circles, darting in the air, and a black cat with razor sharp fangs crosses the path of unseen, terrified prey. The ghosts and the goblins sneak around monster-like trees, ready to snatch their next victim.

Descriptive Technique Questions

1. What is the topic?

   _____

   _____

2. What do you think is the dominant impression Nelson is attempting to describe?

   _____

   _____

3. Underline any figurative language techniques you find. How do they enhance the dominant impression?

_____

_____

_____

PRACTICE 5

In this paragraph taken from a descriptive essay, "New York—The Big Apple," by student writer Amber Barton, the cosmopolitan environs of New York City are compared to the rural area of Missouri in which she grew up.

> The sights of New York City bombard the senses; rural Missouri soothes them. From the Twin Towers to the subway system, the sights and sounds of New York City invigorate the spirit. The vision of Lady Liberty standing proudly in the East River with Ellis Island, its now silent companion, evokes pride in its visitors. The rich hills and valleys of rural Missouri are lovely, yet they pale in comparison to the stark beauty of New York skyscrapers. A traveler would have to visit more than once to be able to take in all the diverse sights New York City has to offer.

Descriptive Technique Questions

1. What is the topic?

_____

2. What do you think is the dominant impression Barton is trying to describe?

_____

3. Underline any figurative language techniques you find. How do they enhance the dominant impression?

_____

_____

PRACTICE 6

The following paragraph uses sensory images and figurative language to clarify and support the topic sentences. In this paragraph from the essay "The Mute Sense" from Diane Ackerman's 1990 book _The Natural History of the Senses,_ the writer piles one descriptive device upon another until a full picture emerges. The first sentence in the paragraph is the topic sentence.

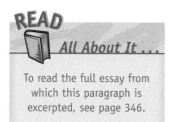

To read the full essay from which this paragraph is excerpted, see page 346.

Nothing is more memorable than a smell. One scent can be unexpected, momentary, and fleeting, yet conjure up a childhood summer beside a lake in the Poconos, when wild blueberry bushes teemed with succulent fruit, and the opposite sex was as mysterious as space travel; another, hours of passion on a moonlit beach in Florida, while the night-blooming cereus drenched the air with thick curds of perfume and high sphinx moths visited the cereus in a loud purr of wings; a third, a family dinner of pot roast, noodle pudding, and sweet potatoes, during a myrtle-mad August in a midwestern town, when both of one's parents were alive. Smells detonate softly in our memory like poignant land mines, hidden under the weedy mass of many years and experiences. Hit a tripwire of smell, and memories explode all at once. A complex vision leaps out of the undergrowth.

Descriptive Technique Questions

1. What is the topic?

_____

2. What do you think is the dominant impression Ackerman is attempting to describe?

_____

3. Ackerman uses two similes. Can you identify them?

_____

_____

4. Is the tone of the essay more objective or subjective? Cite examples of both.

_____

_____

_____

_____

_____

_____

5. Ackerman uses very active verbs, such as "teemed," "drenched," "detonate," "explode," and "leap." How are these action words effective in supporting and clarifying the dominant impression Ackerman wants to give the reader?

_____

_____

_____

6. Can you identify the transitional words and phrases that help connect information and add rhythm to the sentences.

_____

_____

A Ten-Step Process for Writing the Descriptive Paragraph

Experienced writers often follow a step-by-step process that helps them write effectively. As you develop as a writer, you will undoubtedly create your own process. In the meantime, this set of easy-to-follow guidelines will help you write an effective descriptive paragraph.

Writing the Descriptive Paragraph

1. Choose a topic. The topic should be a person, place, or thing (an idea, event, or situation).
2. Think about the topic, and choose the dominant impression (the overall feeling) you want your reader to experience.
3. Write a topic sentence with the dominant impression word included.
4. Make a list of the details you want to include in the paragraph that will support and clarify the dominant impression.
5. Put each of the details into a separate sentence.
6. Rewrite the sentences. Use sensory details and figurative language to create descriptive images.
7. Be certain that the sensory images and figurative devices support the dominant impression.
8. Proofread for punctuation errors, sentence fragments, and run-on sentences.
9. If possible, have another person read the paragraph. Ask him or her to point out any errors or unclear ideas. Rewrite, if necessary.
10. Prepare your finished product for presentation to your instructor.

Example of the Ten-Step Process at Work

1. Topic: A person you have observed.
2. Dominant impression: joy
3. The man was **joyful** when he learned he had the winning lotto number.
4. Details: *facial expressions* (eyes and mouth); *mannerisms* (hand gestures and body language); *clothing* (style, color, accessories); *speech* (expressions and loudness).
5. a. The man smiled and his eyes lit up.
   b. He held his arms over his head and danced all around the store.
   c. He was wearing a yellow shirt, white pants, and a gold necklace matching the three gold diamond rings on each hand.
   d. He yelled and screamed about how happy he was to be a millionaire.

First Draft of Paragraph

The man smiled, and his eyes lit up. He held his arms over his head and danced around the store. He was wearing a yellow shirt, white pants, and a gold necklace matching three gold diamond rings on each hand. He yelled and screamed about how happy he was to be a millionaire.

6. Rewrites:
   a. The man's smile flashed like a beam of light, and his eyes twinkled.

      (simile)   (sight)

   b. He waved his shaking arms over his head as he danced around the store

      (sight) (sight)

      like a statue made from Jell-O that had suddenly come to life.

      (simile)

   c. He wore a bright-yellow, satin shirt and gleaming white slacks

      (sight) (touch)   (sight)

      accented by a shining gold necklace matching three sparkling

      (sight)   (sight)

      diamond rings on each hand.

   d. The jewelry seemed to cry out, "I'm rich! I'm a millionaire!"

      (personification)

7. Does the following list support the dominant impression of **joy?** Yes!!

flashed like a beam of light	satin
twinkled	gleaming white
waved	shining
shaking	sparkling
like a statue made from Jell-O	jewelry seemed to cry out "I'm rich …"
bright-yellow	

8. Proofread the paragraph.
9. Have someone else read the paragraph and make comments.
10. Rewrite the paragraph.

Final Draft of the Paragraph

The man's smile flashed like a beam of light, and his eyes twinkled. He waved his shaking arms over his head as he danced around the store like a statue made from Jell-O that had suddenly come to life. He wore a bright-yellow, satin shirt and gleaming white slacks accented by a shining gold necklace matching three sparkling diamond rings on each hand. The jewelry seemed to cry out, "I'm rich! I'm a millionaire!"

Now, compare this final paragraph to the original, and you can see how much more effective the final paragraph is. The dominant impression is clear, and the support sentences clearly describe the dominant impression.

▼ **PRACTICE 7**

In this exercise you try the step-by-step process described above. Using the ten steps, write one descriptive paragraph each for a person, place, and thing that you know very well. If you want to be adventurous, you can create a person from your own imagination. In other words, have some fun with it!

Person

Possible persons:

    a. An actor/actress
    b. An athlete
    c. An entertainer
    d. A relative
    e. A historical figure
    f. A circus performer
    g. A science fiction character
    h. A bodybuilder
    i. A movie monster
    j. A nurse

1. Choose a topic: _____

2. Dominant impression: _____

3. Write a topic sentence with the dominant impression word included:

_____

_____

4. Choose three or four details that support the dominant impression:

    a. _____

    b. _____

    c. _____

    d. _____

5. Put each detail into a separate sentence:

a. _____

_____

b. _____

_____

c. _____

_____

d. _____

_____

6. Rewrite the sentences creating descriptive images by using sensory details and by using figurative language techniques you have practiced.

a. _____

_____

b. _____

_____

c. _____

_____

d. _____

_____

Put these sentences into paragraph form with the topic sentence first.

_____

_____

_____

_____

_____

_____

7. Check to make sure the descriptive images support the dominant impression by making a list of the sensory details and figurative devices. Then evaluate the effectiveness of your images.

Dominant impression: _____

List of descriptive images: _____

_____

_____

_____

_____

_____

8. Now, proofread your paragraph looking for punctuation errors, sentence fragments, run-on sentences, and spelling errors.

9. If possible, have another person read the paragraph. Ask them to point out any errors or unclear ideas. Rewrite, if necessary.

10. Write your final paragraph version:

_____

_____

_____

_____

_____

_____

Place

Using the ten steps you have practiced, write a paragraph describing a place. Possible places:

a. An amusement park
b. A restaurant
c. A doctor's office
d. A rural setting
e. The zoo

f. The circus
g. A nightclub
h. A library
i. A grocery store
j. A business office

Thing

(Remember, a thing can be an idea, event, or situation.)
Using the ten steps you have practiced, write a descriptive paragraph for a thing.
Possible things:

a. The atmosphere at a concert
b. A job interview
c. A romantic date
d. Oppression
e. A time of day

f. Christmas morning
g. A graduation ceremony
h. A wedding
i. A car wreck
j. Freedom

CHAPTER REVIEW

▼ Effective description creates images by using specific details.
▼ There are two types of description: objective and subjective.
▼ In descriptive writing, the topic is most clearly defined by creating one dominant impression.
▼ Effective description can be achieved through sensory images, based on the five senses: sight, touch, smell, sound, and taste.
▼ Figurative language also can help create effective description through the use of simile, metaphor, and personification.

Writing Opportunities

Home

You are traveling through the West on summer vacation with your family. You are using a camcorder to record the memorable sites you see, and you've also decided to keep a journal of the sites you experience to supplement the visual images. You spot an old barn set against the backdrop of the Rockies. Write a paragraph in your journal to describe the scene you have captured with your camcorder.

School

Your Geography instructor has given each member of the class a picture of an old barn set against the Rocky Mountains. Your assignment is to write a paragraph describing one prominent feature of the picture explaining how it reflects the spirit of the people who might live in the area.

Work

A mineral mining company wants to strip-mine the area in the photograph on page 145. A government committee is considering whether or not to comply with their request. As an employee with the Department of the Interior, you have been given the task of writing a descriptive paragraph to help your agency's director convince the committee not to vote in favor of the project.

Visit *The Write Start* Online!

For additional practice with the materials found in this chapter, visit our Website at:

http://www.ablongman.com/checkett

The Website also features additional readings, quizzes, writing activities, and Internet links, as well as a bulletin board and interactive chat.

For More Practice with Your Grammar and Writing Skills

For further exercises designed to improve your writing and grammar skills, use the Writer's ToolKit Plus CD-ROM included with this text. The toolkit provides a wealth of computerized tutorials and practice activities.

CHAPTER

15

Narration

Writers use paragraphs to develop or express a main idea or topic. One way of doing so is through **narration.** Narration is simply the telling of a story, either to entertain or inform a reader. The stories in narrative paragraphs either can be fictional (made up) or nonfiction (the retelling of an incident that actually happened). What's important, though, is that the stories develop the topic of the paragraph.

The elements of a narrative paragraph are the same as those in any other type of paragraph:

▼ A topic sentence announcing the subject and controlling idea
▼ Support sentences using specific detail to develop the subject
▼ Sentence variety that connects related ideas and adds rhythm

The Point of the Story

There must be a point to every story; otherwise, no one will be interested in reading it. Therefore, every narrative paragraph you write must have a clear point or purpose. That purpose should always be to develop the topic and controlling idea of the paragraph. This might seem like an obvious and easy point to follow in a paragraph, but too many writers lose sight of it. The best way to get to the point of the story is to examine the topic sentence and see what makes it interesting to the reader. That will be the point of the story.

Exhibit 15–1 provides an example of a topic sentence for a narrative paragraph. The subject, controlling idea, and the point of the story are listed.

Example

When my mother had hip surgery, I assumed responsibility for running the household.

> Subject: Running the household
>
> Controlling idea: Assuming responsibility for running the household
>
> Point of the story: Acting responsibly in a time of need

Exhibit 15–1

147

In the following topic sentences, underline the subject once, the controlling idea twice, and, in your own words, summarize what you think the point of the story is in the space provided.

1. I studied day and night for two weeks and passed all my exams with A grades.

Point of the story: _____

_____

2. I voted for the challenger even though he was behind in all the polls.

Point of the story: _____

_____

3. Although my first camping trip was not at all what I expected, I eventually had a good time.

Point of the story: _____

_____

4. I relied on my parents' advice when I bought my first car.

Point of the story: _____

_____

5. I read three fashion magazines before I went shopping for winter clothing.

Point of the story: _____

_____

Write your own narrative topic sentences for the topics listed below. After you have finished, underline the topic once, the controlling idea twice, and, in your own words, summarize the point of your story in the space provided.

1. Topic: Driving _____

_____

Point of the story: _____

2. Topic: Working at a job _____

_____

Point of the story: _____

3. Topic: A hospital experience _____

_____

Point of the story: _____

4. Topic: Television _____

_____

Point of the story: _____

5. Topic: Video games _____

_____

Point of the story: _____

Developing the Narrative Paragraph

Once you've chosen the subject, controlling idea, and the point of the story, you must decide on how to develop the subject. What details, facts, and examples will be chosen to develop the story and get the point of the story across? The easiest way to develop a subject and maintain focus is to use the six reporter's questions: who, what, where, when, why, and how. (See Chapter 13, The Paragraph, for a broader discussion of the six reporter's questions.)

For the topic sentence example in Exhibit 15–1 presented earlier, the developing focus could be any of the following.

Examples

Who?   Who assumed responsibility for running the household? (As the topic sentence states, the writer did.)

What?   What household activities had to be done? (This might be a list of activities, such as paying bills, food shopping, cooking, cleaning, and babysitting.)

Where? Where were the activities finished? (The household has been identified.)

When?   When were the activities completed? (The period encompassing the hospital stay and the convalescence time.)

Why?   Why did the household activities have to be assumed? (Because the mother was in the hospital.)

How?   How were the activities completed? (Did the writer use any special appliances to help out with the chores, or to do the chores in a particular order each day?)

From the list above, *who, where,* and *why* are obvious and probably do not need to be developed. The important features to develop would be *what* (what activities had to be done), *when* (how long did it take), or *how* (how were the activities taken care of). (For additional discussion of the importance of detail, see Chapter 14, Description.)

Model Paragraphs

The following are examples of paragraphs developed for the topic sentence in Exhibit 15–1 using different focus questions.

1. *Focus*: **What**—all the household chores and activities that needed to be done.

> When my mother had hip surgery, I assumed responsibility for running the household. First, I had to take care of a stack of bills for the month. After that, I planned a menu for the week, and I went to the supermarket to buy food. In addition to cooking daily meals, I prepared some meals in advance; afterward, I placed them in the freezer. I tried to clean part of the house each day, so I wouldn't have an overwhelming job on the weekend. Besides all of these chores, I had to take care of my younger sister and brother. Although I was very nervous at the thought of shouldering all these responsibilities, I was up to the challenge.

In this paragraph, the topic is developed using those activities that support the *what* focus question: paying bills, food shopping, cooking, cleaning, and baby-sitting. The list of chores is linked by the use of words and phrases that order the events: "first," "after that," and "in addition." Instead of a choppy list, the paragraph reads smoothly and rhythmically.

2. *Focus*: **When**—The period when the writer's mother was in the hospital, and the period when the mother was home recuperating but unable to help.

> When my mother had hip surgery, I assumed responsibility for running the household. The total time period for my running the house was four weeks. First, my mother had to stay in the hospital for an entire week; afterward, she came home, but she had to stay in bed for another week. Finally, when she could get out of bed, I had to be at her side to help her on short exercise walks. This lasted for two more weeks. All the while, I still had to do all the household chores by myself. After the four weeks had passed, my mother made me a special dinner, and she thanked me for being so mature in running the house. It was a proud day for the both of us.

Notice that this paragraph uses "time" words and phrases to facilitate the development supporting the *when* focus question: "when," "time period," "four weeks," "entire week," "afterward," "another week," "two more weeks," "all the while," and "four weeks had passed." Also, notice the order of events is chronologically sound: the mother is in the hospital, then comes home, convalesces at home in bed, and, finally, gets out of bed to exercise.

3. *Focus*: **How**—How the chores were taken care of.

> When my mother had hip surgery, I assumed responsibility for running the household. I knew that I could not take care of everything, so I enlisted some help. My brother and sister were very young, so my Aunt Jessie came every other evening to help babysit; consequently, I could do laundry and prepare some meals for the following week. My neighbor and best friend, Celeste, also helped with food shopping and yard work. After my mother came home from the hospital, there was even more to do. So, every Saturday, I paid a maid service to come in and clean the house. When my mother finally was able to get up and around, we went for a walk, and she had tears in her eyes when she told me how proud she was of how I had handled all the responsibilities.

This paragraph develops the focus question *how* by describing how the chores were completed (the writer enlisted friends and relatives to help out): Aunt Jessie (babysitting), friend and neighbor Celeste (food shopping and yard work), and a maid service (housecleaning). Notice that this focus also could satisfy the *who* question. Often, one focus helps in developing ideas that are relevant to another focus.

The important aspect to remember is that each paragraph develops the same topic, yet parts of the topic are developed using information that places emphasis on a different aspect of the situation.

Time

Because narrative paragraphs relate a story, you have to present events in the proper order. That way, the reader can stay focused on the events without being confused about when things happened. To keep track of time and show readers the correct sequence of events, you need to use **transitional expressions.**

Commonly Used Transitional Expressions		
after	first	soon
afterward	last(ly)	then
as	later	third
as soon as	meanwhile	upon
before	next	when
during	now	while
finally	second	

Exhibit 15–2

Transitional expressions are simply words and phrases that indicate when one event happened in relation to another.

The following paragraph is taken from a narrative essay, "Shattered Sanctuary," by student Stephanie Higgs. Underline the transitional expressions. Discuss how they help add rhythm and move the story from idea to idea smoothly.

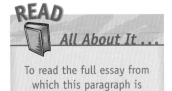

READ
All About It . . .

To read the full essay from which this paragraph is excerpted, see page 397.

Thunderstorms the previous night had settled into a steady, rhythmic rain shower by daylight. After finally getting the last child out the door and onto the school bus around 7:00 A.M., I was alone in the house following my predictable routine. First, I had put the dogs in the garage by 7:45 A.M. because I was leaving the house for a college art history class. Then, I heard the scraping of the vinyl floor trim on the French door against the ceramic floor tiles. Now, much like the sound of nails on a chalkboard, it is forever recorded in my memory coming back during waking and sleeping hours alike, to torture me. It makes no difference whether the door is actually opening or not because my mind will always believe that it is. Next, I remember calling out down the hallway to the kitchen, "What did you forget?" I guessed my husband had forgotten some important papers he needed for a meeting he had scheduled in Hazelwood that morning. As I rounded the corner, what I saw made fear rise in my throat like green bile forced up from the pit of my stomach. As soon as I saw them, panic increased my heart rate, bringing it to ear-shattering crescendos until I thought I would go deaf or explode. Incapacitating shock and disbelief bordering on denial paralyzed my entire body as I stared at two masked black men wielding knives standing in my kitchen breakfast room and heading straight toward me.

The following paragraph is taken from a narrative essay, "Small Town Views," by student writer Matt Grant. Underline the transitional expressions. Discuss how they help add rhythm and move the story from idea to idea smoothly.

At first, the town of Sault Ste. Marie appeared large. A drive down the main four-lane road through town revealed several restaurants, stores, and businesses. Even though only a few streets intersected the main road, the town seemed to sprawl before me. During my drive down Main Street, a fairly new Wal-Mart stood out as one of the larger buildings. As soon as I passed through town, on top of a large, grassy hill, Lake Superior State College stood facing the divided highway that passed by town. Sitting on the hill, the college seemed to appear larger and more majestic to cars passing by on the highway. Finally, the Soo Locks controlled the north end of town, policing Lake Freighter traffic on the Saint Marys River. Yet, something was missing; the town was as quiet as night.

▼
PRACTICE 5

The following paragraph's topic is *how* the Spanish-American War began. The sentences are out of chronological sequence. In their current order, the ideas are not developed coherently, and the information is difficult to understand. On a separate sheet of paper, rewrite the paragraph by reordering the sentences in proper time sequence, using transitional expressions from Exhibit 15–2 to help establish the proper order, link the ideas, and add rhythm.

This savage warfare frightened Americans, but the United States did not intervene. The Cubans reverted to destroying their land to cause the Spanish to leave. In the year 1898, America declared war on Spain. The Spanish Army, which was commanded by General Valeriano Wyler, began capturing Cuban citizens and placing them in concentration camps. The war was an overwhelming victory for America and also for Cuba. The rebellion that arose in 1895 was the most devastating. Cubans had, for many years, attempted to overthrow Spanish rule. But, how the war actually began was the most interesting part of history. Thousands of Cubans died of disease and malnutrition.

Following are six writing exercises for narrative paragraphs. Each exercise will give you the development focus (who, what, where, when, why, and how) and a topic idea on which to write. Supply a topic for each of the focus questions. Next, complete a controlling idea for the topic you have selected. Then summarize, in your own words, what the point of the story will be. Afterward, write a topic sentence using the elements you have created. Finally, create support sentences that develop, explain, support, and clarify the point of the story.

1. (*Who?*) Personal heroes: either people you know or persons from history

    a. Topic: _____

    b. Controlling idea: _____

    c. Point of the story: _____

    d. Topic sentence: _____

    _____

    e. Development sentences: _____

    _____

    _____

    _____

    _____

    _____

2. (*What?*) An important decision you made that affected your life

    a. Topic: _____

    b. Controlling idea: _____

    c. Point of the story: _____

    d. Topic sentence: _____

    _____

    e. Development sentences: _____

    _____

    _____

    _____

    _____

3. (*Where?*) A place that is meaningful in your life

    a. Topic: _____

    b. Controlling idea: _____

    c. Point of the story: _____

    d. Topic sentence: _____

    _____

    e. Development sentences: _____

    _____

    _____

    _____

    _____

    _____

4. (*When?*) An important time in your life

    a. Topic: _____

    b. Controlling idea: _____

    c. Point of the story: _____

    d. Topic sentence: _____

    _____

    e. Development sentences: _____

    _____

    _____

    _____

    _____

    _____

5. (*Why?*) Why you are looking forward to the future

    a. Topic: _____

    b. Controlling idea: _____

    c. Point of the story: _____

    d. Topic sentence: _____

    _____

    e. Development sentences: _____

    _____

    _____

    _____

    _____

    _____

6. (*How?*) How a task was completed

    a. Topic: _____

    b. Controlling idea: _____

    c. Point of the story: _____

    d. Topic sentence: _____

    _____

    e. Development sentences: _____

    _____

    _____

    _____

    _____

    _____

▼ PRACTICE 7

The following is a narrative paragraph taken from a chapter in a book titled, *The Vanishing Hitchhiker: American Urban Legends and Their Meaning* (1981) by Jan Harold Brunvand, a folklorist and professor of English at the University of Utah. Brunvand has gathered examples of contemporary storytelling—strange, scary, funny, macabre, and embarrassing tales storytellers relate as true accounts of real-life experience. This excerpt is from an urban legend called "The Roommate's Death."

READ
All About It . . .

To read the full essay from which this paragraph is excerpted, see page 347.

It was not long before the telephone rang. Linda answered the telephone, only to hear the heavy breathing of the caller on the other end. She attempted to elicit a response from the caller but he merely hung up. Thinking little of it and not wanting to panic Sharon, Linda went back to watching her television program, remarking that the caller had dialed a wrong number. Upon receiving the second call at which time the caller first engaged in a bit of heavy breathing and then instructed them to check on the children, the two girls became frightened and decided to call the operator for assistance. The operator instructed the girls to keep the caller on the line as long as possible should he call again so that she might be able to trace the call. The operator would check back with them.

Questions for Discussion

1. How does Brunvand order the events? Point out words and phrases that help the reader recognize the order of events as they occur.

_____

_____

_____

_____

_____

_____

2. What is the primary focus of the paragraph: who, what, where, when, why, or how?

_____

_____

Suggestions for Writing

1. Rewrite the paragraph using appropriate transitional expressions from Exhibit 15–2. Reread both versions. Which reads more smoothly and rhythmically?

2. Rewrite the paragraph using a different focus than the one you selected for the answer to Question 2 in Questions for Discussion above.

▼ PRACTICE 8

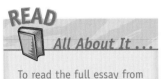

READ
All About It . . .

To read the full essay from
which this paragraph is
excerpted, see page 351.

The following is a paragraph taken from a narrative essay by Grace Suh. Suh
works in academic publishing and as a poetry editor of the _Asian Pacific American Journal._ In this piece, Suh writes about her visit to a makeup counter in
search of the transformation promised by the "priestesses of beauty."

And so, in an unusual exertion of will, I resolved to fight back against
the forces of entropy. I envisioned it as reclamation work, like scything down
a lawn that has grown into meadow, or restoring a damaged fresco. For the
first time in ages, I felt elated and hopeful. I nearly sprinted into the nearby
Nieman Marcus. As I entered the cool, hushed, dimly lit first floor and saw
the gleaming counters lined with vials of magical balm, the priestesses of
beauty in their sacred smocks, and the glossy photographic icons of the goddesses themselves—Paulina, Linda, Cindy, Vendella—in a wild, reckless burst
of inspiration I thought to myself, Heck, why just okay? Why not BEAUTIFUL?

Questions for Discussion

1. How does Suh order the events? Point out words and phrases that help
the reader recognize the order of events as they occur?

_____

_____

_____

_____

_____

_____

2. What is the primary focus of the paragraph: who, what, where, when,
why, or how?

_____

_____

Suggestions for Writing

1. Visit a cosmetics counter at a large department store. Take notes about the
products and displays that you see there. How did the advertisements and
the arrangements of the products induce you to "become beautiful" by
using them? Did the salespeople themselves seem to conform to a particular ideal of beauty? Write a report about your findings and read it to your

class. Afterward, discuss the similarities and differences between the various reports made by members of your class.

2. Write an essay describing a time in which you made yourself look different than you normally do (this could be for a prom, wedding, or other special occasion). Did you act differently than you normally act? Did other people treat you differently? Was the experience enjoyable or not?

Other Paragraph Topics

A funny incident	Watching a scary movie
A first date	A family argument
An employment interview	Preparing for an important exam
An embarrassing moment	Taking on a huge responsibility
A tense athletic event	Your first day on a new job

CHAPTER REVIEW

▼ Narration is the telling of a story, either to entertain or inform a reader.

▼ Narrative stories either can be fictional (made up) or nonfiction (the retelling of an incident that actually happened).

▼ There must be a point to every story; otherwise, no one will be interested in reading it.

▼ Use the six reporter's questions (who?, what?, where?, when?, why?, and how?) to develop your story.

▼ Transitional expressions help develop the order of events that unfold in your story.

Writing Opportunities

Home

You are looking through a family photo album when you come upon a picture of your son when he was little. The picture brings back a flood of memories. You pick up a pen and write a paragraph beneath the photograph that tells a brief story about why he was walking down the road alone.

School

The photographs taken by you and your fellow art students are going on display in the Fine Arts Building. You have been asked to choose someone else's picture and write a one-paragraph story about its subject matter. Your story will be typed on a card and affixed to the wall beneath the photo.

Work

You work for a movie studio that is going to release a new movie. The picture of the little boy on the road is going to be the advertising poster that will appear in movie theaters throughout the country. Write a one-paragraph "press release" detailing what the movie is about.

Visit *The Write Start* Online!

For additional practice with the materials found in this chapter, visit our Website at:

http://www.ablongman.com/checkett

The Website also features additional readings, quizzes, writing activities, and Internet links, as well as a bulletin board and interactive chat.

For More Practice with Your Grammar and Writing Skills

For further exercises designed to improve your writing and grammar skills, use the Writer's ToolKit Plus CD-ROM included with this text. The toolkit provides a wealth of computerized tutorials and practice activities.

CHAPTER

16 Using Examples

One of the most popular and effective methods for developing a topic is through the use of examples. The **example paragraph** can develop a topic quickly and clearly and help hold the reader's attention. Maybe you've heard a friend say, "My job is terrible." Your thought might be to question why your friend feels this way: "What makes the job so terrible? What does your friend have to do that makes the job so terrible?" Your friend might respond with specific examples: the boss is a tyrant, working several hours after closing is a frequent demand, and the pay is low without any benefits. By recounting several examples, your friend supports and clarifies the general critical view of the job experience.

Detailed examples are used to convince, clarify, illustrate, or make concrete a general idea about the subject. For instance, the following subjects are accompanied by a list of examples that might be used to develop the subject in the paragraph.

Topic	Examples
Cars	Honda, Chrysler, Fiat
Wines	Bordeaux, Riesling, Merlot
Presidents	Washington, Lincoln, Truman
Houses	ranch, split-level, Tudor
Cheeses	gouda, mozzarella, cheddar

The Topic Sentence

The following is a topic sentence for an example paragraph. The subject, controlling idea, developing focus, and developing examples are given. (See Chapter 13 for clarification of the developing ideas of *who, what, where, when, why,* and *how.*)

Example

Topic sentence: <u>President Roosevelt was a successful leader during World War II despite overcoming many obstacles.</u>

Subject: <u>Franklin D. Roosevelt</u>

Controlling idea: <u>Overcoming adversity</u>

Developing focus: <u>What</u>

Developing examples: <u>isolationists</u>

<u>Congress</u>

<u>illness</u>

Finished Paragraph

President Roosevelt was a successful leader during World War II despite overcoming many obstacles. For example, the American people were overwhelmingly isolationist, not wanting to go through the horrors that they remembered from World War I. Another example of overcoming hurdles was Congress's passing of a number of neutrality laws intended to prevent America from entering the war in Europe. Personal problems also had to be overcome. For instance, Roosevelt had to deal with poliomyelitis, a disease he had contracted in 1921. Eventually, Roosevelt's ideas won out when Congress passed his lend-lease legislation after Germany's defeat of France in 1940.

Each example helps to clarify, explain, and develop the controlling idea that President Roosevelt overcame adversity to be successful. Also, the transitional expressions help to connect related ideas and add rhythm to the writing. In the example paragraph above, transitional expressions, such as "for example," "another example," "for instance," and "eventually," are also used to announce to the reader that an example is forthcoming. Use transitional expressions in your example paragraph so that the examples don't appear merely as a list. Examples should act in unison to develop the subject in the topic sentence.

Transitional Expressions for Example Paragraphs	
a case in point is _____	for example
another example of _____	for instance
another instance of _____	to illustrate
another illustration of _____	specifically

Exhibit 16–1

PRACTICE 1

The following is an example paragraph written by a student. Read the paragraph, and check to see if it has all the elements for an example paragraph:

1. Topic sentence with controlling idea

2. A development focus

3. Three or four development ideas

4. Transitional expressions

In the spaces provided after the paragraph, write in the elements that you have found.

In this paragraph from an example essay, "A Stroke of Bad Luck," by Margaret Ewart, she relates how taking care of her father after his having a stroke affected her life.

> Shortly after I started taking care of my father, I came to realize that there was never any time for myself, much less my family. I rarely ever have the time to play with my children, help my daughter with her schoolwork, or spend time with my husband. My father requires a tremendous amount of my time, which prevents me from being a mother as well as being a wife. Most of the time I feel as if I am missing out on a great deal of my children's lives due to the fact that I have become a primary care giver. I have felt like a prisoner in my own home since the stroke. I have a great fear of leaving my home in the event that he may need me. My husband tries to take me out for dinner and a movie to give me some sense of relief from all of the stress, but I always decline. I would never be able to live with myself if something were to happen to my father and I weren't at home to receive his call for help. Because I have become a recluse, our vacations are spent at home sitting by the phone. With the fear of leaving the house because of my new responsibilities, family members are reluctant to make plans with me due to the fact that I always have to decline. They began to treat me differently as well as see me as a different person.

Topic: _____

Controlling idea: _____

Development focus: _____

Development ideas: _____

_____

_____

_____

Transitional expressions: _____

_____

_____

_____

▼ **PRACTICE 2**

The following is an example paragraph written by a student. Read the paragraph, and check to see if it has all the elements for an example paragraph.

1. Topic sentence with controlling idea

2. A development focus

3. Three or four development ideas

4. Transitional expressions

In the spaces provided after the paragraph, write in the elements that you have found.

In this paragraph from an example essay, "Seaside Sensation," by Lora Smith, she recounts how the atmosphere in a seafood restaurant captures the "seaman's life."

The atmosphere in Crabby's Crab Shack, in Cherry Grove, North Carolina, exudes the seaman's life from top to bottom and everywhere in between. For example, walking on the crunchy peanut shells strewn all over the floor simulates the creaking deck of a ship. Another example of the "sea" décor can be found on the walls, for they are lined with hunks of driftwood, fishing poles, mounted sailfish and marlin, and paintings of seascapes and sailing vessels from around the world. To illustrate the completeness of the setting, the patrons only have to look up! Specifically, the ceiling has been hung with fishing nets interlaced with twinkling Christmas lights. When the restaurant is darkened, it's as if you are gazing up into the vast, star filled sky as seen from the deck of a ship. At Crabby's Crab Shack, the only thing missing is the gentle rocking of the sea.

Topic: _____

Controlling idea: _____

Development focus: _____

Development ideas: _____

_____

_____

_____

Transitional expressions: _____

_____

_____

_____

PRACTICE 3

For each of the following topics, choose a controlling idea and write a topic sentence. Afterward, choose a development focus (*who, what, where, when, why,* or *how*) and list three development examples. Do not use the same development focus idea more than once.

> **Example**
> Subject: Bad eating habits
> Controlling idea: Cause illnesses
> Topic sentence: Poor eating habits can cause many serious illnesses.
> Development focus: What
> Development examples: anorexia/bulimia
> diabetes
> osteoporosis

1. Topic: Favorite Rock Groups

Controlling idea: _____

Topic sentence: _____

_____

Development focus: _____

Development examples: _____

_____

_____

2. Topic: <u>Vacation Locales</u>

Controlling idea: _____

Topic sentence: _____

_____

Development focus: _____

Development examples: _____

_____

_____

3. Topic: <u>Video Games</u>

Controlling idea: _____

Topic sentence: _____

_____

Development focus: _____

Development examples: _____

_____

_____

4. Topic: <u>College Courses</u>

Controlling idea: _____

Topic sentence: _____

_____

Development focus: _____

Development examples: _____

_____

_____

5. Topic: <u>Job Hunting</u>

Controlling idea: _____

Topic sentence: _____

_____

Development focus: _____

Development examples: _____

_____

_____

6. Topic: <u>Studying</u>

Controlling idea: _____

Topic sentence: _____

_____

Development focus: _____

Development examples: _____

_____

_____

▼ **PRACTICE 4**

Complete this exercise on separate sheets of paper. Using the topic sentences, controlling ideas, development focuses, and development examples from Practice 3, write paragraphs for each subject. Use transitional expressions from Exhibit 16–1 to announce examples and create rhythm.

Example

Subject: <u>Bad eating habits</u>
Controlling idea: <u>Cause illnesses</u>
Topic sentence: <u>Poor eating habits can cause many serious illnesses.</u>
Development focus: <u>What</u>
Development examples: <u>anorexia/bulimia</u>
                    <u>diabetes</u>
                    <u>osteoporosis</u>

Finished Paragraph

    Poor eating habits can cause many serious illnesses. For example, because many young girls are pressured to try to emulate fashion models, their lives are threatened by becoming anorexic and bulimic. It is not only young people who are threatened by eating-related diseases; for instance, both young adults and older adults can develop diabetes from unhealthy diets. Senior citizens are not exempt from such problems either. Specifically, osteoporosis can often afflict the elderly after many years of poor eating habits and diets. In order to combat these diseases, eat a well-balanced diet, and don't snack on unhealthy foods between meals.

Using One Extended Example

Sometimes, you might want to use only one more detailed example to develop the topic rather than using many shorter examples. This type of longer, more detailed example, is called an **extended example.**

For instance, you might want to discuss how children's television programming can help educate preschool children. Instead of discussing many different programs, you could decide to focus on one program that is particularly effective. Choosing the most successful and popular program would be a good choice because your readers have most likely heard of it and would be more willing to accept what you have to say.

> **Example**
>
> Sesame Street continues to help preschool children learn to enjoy learning as well as to get a head start on their education. For instance, basic math processes, such as adding and subtracting, usually are illustrated with everyday objects, such as pieces of pie and fruit, for these are objects with which the toddlers are familiar. Another instance of blending instruction into the entertainment occurs at the beginning of each broadcast. Instead of advertising sponsoring the show, the shows are "sponsored" by a different number and letter of the alphabet each day. The letter and number are integrated into the many sketches that pop up throughout the program. For example, Count Count, the vampire, will count bats, spiders, and lightning bolts, always emphasizing the "sponsoring" number. Another example occurs when a spelling game emphasizes words that contain the "sponsoring" letter. By mixing educational information with entertaining characters and skits, Sesame Street has helped millions of young boys and girls see learning as both fun and useful.

Notice, however, that whether many examples or one example is used, the same elements are used in the paragraph:

Subject: <u>Children's educational television</u>
Controlling idea: <u>Helps children enjoy learning and learn some basics</u>
Topic sentence: <u>*Sesame Street* continues to help preschool children learn to enjoy learning as well as to get a head start on their education.</u>
Development focus: <u>What</u>
Development example: *Sesame Street*

Also notice that transitional expressions are used to announce examples and keep the number of examples from appearing merely as a list.

PRACTICE 5

On separate sheets of paper, write an **extended example** paragraph for each of the following topic sentences. The controlling idea has been included. Choose a developing focus (who, what, where, when, why, or how) and a development example that will develop the subject. Do not choose the same development focus question more than once. Don't forget to use transitional expressions.

1. Fear of flying has prevented me from visiting foreign countries.

2. Success means making many sacrifices.

3. Advertisements are often very misleading.

4. Today's athletes are better than those of the past.

5. College is much more difficult than high school.

6. Being a good son/daughter requires assuming responsibilities.

PRACTICE 6

To read the full essay from which this paragraph is excerpted, see page 354.

In the following paragraph, taken from an essay titled "The Culture of Violence," by professional writer Myriam Miedzian, the author relates how cultures influence the behavior of children. Answer the questions following the paragraph.

Every child in the world is born into a particular culture and "from the moment of his birth the customs into which he is born shape his experience and behaviour," we are told by anthropologist Ruth Benedict.[1] Throughout history people have known this intuitively, and so they have been careful to acculturate their children from the youngest age into a pattern of behavior that is acceptable to the group. We have in our own society some very clear and simple examples: Christian groups like the Hutterites and the Amish, or Jewish groups like the Hasidim want their children to grow up to be devoted primarily to religious rather than material values, to be sexually modest and completely chaste before marriage. They share a strong sense of community and commitment to taking responsibility for the well-being of all their members. Among the Hutterites and Amish there is a strong emphasis on non-violence. None of these groups allows their children to participate in the mainstream culture.

Questions for Discussion

1. What specific examples does Miedzian use to help support her idea that culture influences children's behavior?

_____

_____

_____

2. Why don't the specific groups Miedzian mentions allow their children to mix with the mainstream culture?

_____

_____

3. Does the author use many transitional expressions? If so, point them out, and explain why they help connect ideas and add rhythm. Could the author have used more? Point out where in the paragraph she could have used additional ones and how they would have helped the paragraph.

_____

_____

_____

_____

PRACTICE 7

The following is a paragraph taken from an essay titled "Heroine Worship: The Age of the Female Icon," by professional writer Holly Brubach. In the essay, Brubach examines the rise of women as icons and role models in our starstruck culture. Answer the questions following the paragraph.

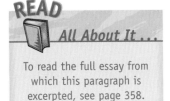

READ
All About It . . .

To read the full essay from which this paragraph is excerpted, see page 358.

An icon is a human sound bite, an individual reduced to a name, a face and an idea: Dale Evans, the compassionate cowgirl. In some cases, just the name and an idea suffice. Few people would recognize Helen Keller in a photograph, but her name has become synonymous with being blind and deaf to such an extent that she has inspired an entire category of jokes. Greta Garbo has gone down in collective memory as an exalted enigma with a slogan about being alone. Asking a man if that's a gun in his pocket is all it takes to invoke Mae West. Catherine Deneuve's face, pictured on a stamp, is the emblem of France. Virginia Woolf has her own T-shirt. Naomi Campbell has her own doll. Celebrity being the engine that drives our culture, these women have been taken up by the media and made famous, packaged as commodities and marketed to a public eager for novelty and easily bored. . . .

Questions for Discussion

1. What specific examples does Brubach use to help support her ideas about role models?

_____

_____

_____

_____

2. How have these various female icons become famous in our culture?

_____

_____

_____

_____

3. Does the author use transitional expressions? If so, point them out, and explain why they help connect ideas and add rhythm. Could the author have used more? Point out where in the paragraph she could have used additional ones and how they would have helped the paragraph.

_____

_____

_____

_____

_____

_____

CHAPTER REVIEW

▼ Examples can develop a topic quickly and clearly and help hold the reader's attention.
▼ Transitional expressions can help connect examples, so they do not appear as a list.
▼ Sometimes, it is better to use one detailed, extended example rather than many shorter ones.

Writing Opportunities

Home

You have recently remarried, and the number of children in the family has doubled. Now there are four sons to add to your four daughters. To give this large and hungry new brood some breakfast variety, you travel to the nearest supermarket and make a one-paragraph inventory of the cereal possibilities, remembering that your children range in ages from five to sixteen years old, and their preferences are based on a number of different criteria: cartoon figures on the box, sugar content, numbers of colors, calories, or vitamin content.

School

Your Advertising & Marketing 205 professor wants you to go to the supermarket and write one paragraph detailing the various types of breakfast cereals and for what age group you think each is targeted based on the information on the box.

Work

Your boss at the consumer health agency you work for is going to appear on a television show to talk about nutrition and breakfast cereals. So that she'll have some facts to use, she wants you to write one paragraph giving examples of a variety of breakfast cereals pointing out their good and bad nutritional qualities.

Visit *The Write Start* Online!

For additional practice with the materials found in this chapter, visit our Website at:

http://www.ablongman.com/checkett

The Website also features additional readings, quizzes, writing activities, and Internet links, as well as a bulletin board and interactive chat.

For More Practice with Your Grammar and Writing Skills

For further exercises designed to improve your writing and grammar skills, use the Writer's ToolKit Plus CD-ROM included with this text. The toolkit provides a wealth of computerized tutorials and practice activities.

17 Classification

Some subjects about which you will be asked to write a paragraph are very complicated or contain many parts. A simple explanation or description of these subjects often is not enough for your readers to understand them fully. How, then, do you get your point across? Sometimes, you need to break a larger point into smaller points so you can explain it in your writing. **Classification** is the process of separating out smaller points from a larger concept and separating these smaller points into easily recognized groups. These groups can be based on color, shape, kind, or any other type of category that readers will understand easily.

For instance, if you were asked to write a paragraph about William Shakespeare, you could classify his writing into sonnets, histories, comedies, tragedies, dark comedies, and romances. Classifying his writing into smaller categories makes it easier to make a point about some aspect of his writing. Classifying can focus your writing into a specific area. For example, you could discuss his use of iambic pentameter in the sonnets as opposed to some of the plays.

Breaking Down a Topic

The same subject can be classified in a variety of ways. Whales can be classified as humpback, right, sperm, blue, sei, and pilot, among others. Food can be separated into meat, dairy, vegetables, fruits, and grains; trees into deciduous and coniferous; and music into soul, rock, alternative, jazz, classical, swing, and so on. It is important, however, to keep the units of classification of the same type.

Example

Dress slacks might be classified according to fabric: cotton, twill, wool. Adding a category of *price range* would be inappropriate. Price does not belong with fabric.

PRACTICE 1

Look at each of the following groups of items. Circle the letter of the item that does not belong with the other members of the group.

Example

Shoes

a. wingtip

b. athletic

(c.) blue

d. high heel

The *color* blue does not belong with the types of *shoes*.

1. Highways

    a. one-lane

    b. two-line

    c. tollway

    d. four-lane

2. Fruit

    a. apples

    b. yellow

    c. pears

    d. grapes

3. Houses

    a. split-level

    b. ranch

    c. colonial

    d. brick

4. Money

    a. lira

    b. coins

    c. rupee

    d. yen

5. Politicians

    a. mayors

    b. senators

    c. lobbyists

    d. representatives

6. Boats

    a. yachts

    b. motorized

    c. schooners

    d. sloops

PRACTICE 2

Look at each of the following groups of items. Circle the letter of the item that does not belong with the other members of the group.

1. Musicals

    a. *Phantom of the Opera*

    b. *Evita*

    c. *Cabaret*

    d. *To Kill a Mockingbird*

2. Sports

    a. tennis

    b. workout

    c. football

    d. racquetball

3. Trees

    a. elm

    b. leaves

    c. oak

    d. Douglas fir

5. Oceans

    a. Atlantic

    b. Michigan

    c. Indian

    d. Pacific

4. Nations

    a. Russia

    b. Australia

    c. Canada

    d. California

6. Medical personnel

    a. nurse

    b. surgeon

    c. anesthetist

    d. accountant

The Topic Sentence

The classification paragraph begins with a topic sentence that clearly states the subject, how the subject will be divided, and why classifying the subject is important.

Example

To study the geologic evolution of the Earth more easily, rocks can be classified as igneous, sedimentary, and metamorphic.

Subject: Rocks.

Categories: Igneous, sedimentary, metamorphic

Controlling idea: To learn about the formation of the Earth.

The entire paragraph might look like this:

> To study the geologic evolution of the Earth more easily, rocks can be classified as igneous, sedimentary, and metamorphic. The first type, igneous rock, is formed when a molten mass of rock (magma) from deep within the earth rises and fills in cracks close to the surface of the earth through a volcano. Magma cools rapidly and usually forms into a fine-grained, glasslike rock. Sedimentary rocks, the second category, are formed when other rocks disintegrate, and the particles from these rocks usually are carried by water into larger bodies of water where they settle on the bottom and form layers of rocks. Shale and sandstone are common sedimentary rocks. The last type, metamorphic rock, can be traced to a parent igneous or sedimentary rock and is formed through heat and pressure. For instance, the metamorphic rock slate is formed when shale is pressurized, over time, in a low-temperature environment.

▼ Into what categories does the writer classify the subject?
Igneous, sedimentary, and metamorphic

▼ What does the writer say about the first category?
Igneous rock is formed by volcanic magma cooling near the earth's surface.

▼ What is said about the second category?
Sedimentary rock is formed from the particles of other rocks.

▼ When classifying, using examples is an excellent method of achieving clarity. What example of a sedimentary rock does the writer use?
Shale

▼ What information does the writer state about the third category?
Metamorphic rock is formed from other rocks by heat and pressure.

▼ What example is given to clarify the information?
Slate is formed from shale.

Note that the only categories of rocks discussed in the paragraph are those mentioned in the topic sentence. No new topics or subtopics can be added.

Transitional Expressions: Linking Your Classifications

In classification paragraphs, transitional expressions help link your categories together so that they don't simply appear as a list. Transitional expressions also help focus the reader's attention on the variety of categories, types, kinds, and divisions.

Transitional Expressions for Classification

The first type	can be categorized	the first kind	the first division
The second type	can be classified	the second kind	the second division
The last type	can be divided	the next kind	the final division

PRACTICE 3

List the transitional expressions you find in the example paragraph regarding types of rocks.

_____

_____

_____

PRACTICE 4

Groups can be classified in more than one way. Buildings, for example, can be classified by the activity that goes on in them (medical, office, school), or by the material out of which they are constructed (brick, stucco, wood). Think of three ways to classify each of the following groups:

Example

Friends
a. to whom you can tell any secret
b. who are "fair weather"
c. who are only "social"

1. Animals

a. _____

b. _____

c. _____

2. Military personnel

a. _____

b. _____

c. _____

3. Water

a. _____

b. _____

c. _____

4. Dresses

a. _____

b. _____

c. _____

5. Fans

a. _____

b. _____

c. _____

PRACTICE 5

For the following groups, separate each into similar units of classification. Afterward, write a topic sentence for each one.

Example

Group: Oil paints

Unit of classification: <u>Color</u>

Categories: <u>Sunset red, forest green, sky blue</u>

Topic Sentence: <u>Because landscape painters want to capture nature realistically, oil paints come in a variety of colors, including sunset red, forest green, and sky blue.</u>

1. Group: Relatives

Unit of classification: _____

Categories: _____

Topic Sentence: _____

_____

2. Group: Birds

Unit of classification: _____

Categories: _____

Topic Sentence: _____

_____

3. Group: Restaurants

Unit of classification: _____

Categories: _____

Topic Sentence: _____

_____

PRACTICE 6

On a separate sheet of paper, write a paragraph for each of the topic sentences you have written for Practice 5. Use examples to help in classifying the groups you chose. Don't forget to use transitional phrases to connect ideas and to add rhythm.

PRACTICE 7

In the following paragraph taken from a classification essay titled "Michelangelo Madness," student writer Martin Brink takes a humorous look at tools used by homeowners. The tools are not classified by how helpful they are in making tasks easier but how they promote Murphy's Law by making any project frustrating and even dangerous.

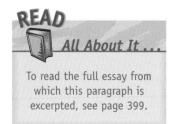

To read the full essay from which this paragraph is excerpted, see page 399.

A good rule of thumb (red and swollen by now) to follow is that any tools powered by fossil fuels—weed whackers, lawn mowers, edgers, and snow blowers—are temperamental by design. These helpful devices (a.k.a. "accidents waiting to happen") have starter cords to assist in starting the engine. According to the manual, the happy homeowner should pull the starter cord three or four times to prime the engine with gas. The manufacturer calls this activity "pre-ignition" because on the fifth pull, the engine is supposed to hum into full force. This activity should really be called "aerobic exercise" because the only thing demonstrating full force is the red-faced homeowner who is approaching unconsciousness after pulling on the starter cord fifty-seven times without so much as a puff of exhaust.

Classification Technique Questions

1. How does the writer classify power tools that use fossil fuels?

   _____

   _____

2. What do you think is the reaction the writer wants to get from his audience?

   _____

   _____

   _____

   _____

3. What examples does the writer give for the tools that use fossil fuels? Does this make the essay more effective? Why or why not?

   _____

   _____

   _____

   _____

4. What other examples can you think of that might fit into the category?

_____

_____

5. Does the writer use any transitional devices to connect ideas and to add rhythm? If not, would the paragraph have been more effective if the writer had done so? Where in the paragraph would you suggest using a few?

_____

_____

PRACTICE 8

In this paragraph taken from a classification essay titled "Who Else Is Going to Do It?" student writer Nicholas Wade extols the virtues of blue-collar workers. According to Wade, these talented construction workers provide places to work and live while experiencing many dangers on the job.

Pile drivers, carpenters, and millwrights are the dedicated blue-collar workers in the honorable field of construction. The first type of worker, the pile driver, lays the foundation for massive buildings. Unfortunately, working with heavy concrete pilings is a risky job, and many pile drivers have lost their lives performing this task. The second kind of blue-collar worker is the carpenter. They stand the walls, supply the roof, and prepare the interior. Carpenters often suffer aching joints and other early signs of aging. The last category of worker is the millwright. Millwrights install the machinery in office buildings and factories. Working with such heavy equipment is dangerous and often leads to serious injury.

Classification Technique Questions
1. What do you think is the writer's purpose in writing this paragraph?

_____

_____

_____

2. How does the writer categorize blue-collar workers? What do the categories have in common?

_____

_____

3. Can you think of other categories of blue-collar workers? Is there a dangerous aspect to their jobs?

_____

_____

4. Identify any transitional devices the writer has used. How do they add to the effectiveness of the paragraph?

_____

_____

_____

_____

5. Does the writer's word choice support the serious tone? Point out some examples.

_____

_____

_____

_____

PRACTICE 9

In this paragraph taken from a classification essay titled "The Plot Against People," by professional writer Russell Baker, inanimate objects are classified as things that break, get lost, and not work—on purpose! Although short in length, Baker packs the paragraph with many examples to support his contention that inanimate objects can confound unsuspecting humans at any moment.

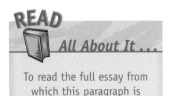

To read the full essay from which this paragraph is excerpted, see page 362.

It is not uncommon for a pair of pliers to climb all the way from the cellar to the attic in its single-minded determination to raise its owner's blood pressure. Keys have been known to burrow three feet under mattresses. Women's purses, despite their great weight, frequently travel through six or seven rooms to find hiding space under a couch.

Classification Technique Questions

1. Personification (giving human qualities to nonhuman things) is a figurative language technique that writers use to enhance their writing. Point out some examples of personification in the paragraph. How do they enhance the tone (serious, humorous, sarcastic, ironic) of the paragraph?

_____

_____

_____

2. How does word choice support the tone of the paragraph? Give examples.

_____

_____

_____

3. What other inanimate objects can you think of, and how do they confound you?

_____

_____

4. The paragraph is short. Would the paragraph have been more effective if Baker had developed each item more fully? Explain.

_____

_____

_____

5. What do you think is Baker's purpose in writing this essay?

_____

_____

_____

_____

Suggestions for Writing

1. Using one of your answers from Question 3 in the classification technique questions above, write a paragraph about some inanimate object that confounds or frustrates you.

2. With some of your classmates, write a paragraph about an inanimate object that confounds or frustrates a group or groups of people.

PRACTICE 10

In this paragraph taken from a classification essay titled "Relatively Speaking," by sociology teacher Jan Borst, the definition of family is explored. In an age of so many divorces and remarriages, the traditional family is undergoing fundamental changes. Borst raises some serious issues that such families confront including what to call people and what their responsibilities are in the new "unconventional" families. The paragraph attempts to define Borst's daughter's new marriage consisting of her new husband's daughter and her two daughters.

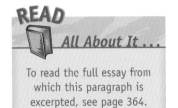

READ
All About It . . .

To read the full essay from which this paragraph is excerpted, see page 364.

Questions arise as to who is family. Will our daughter's new family be a family of four, made up of those who live in the house? Or a family of five—the four plus the child who visits on weekends? In their home, who is the real parent? Who sets the rules? When does the mother relinquish some of her parenting role to her husband? When does the stepparent step in; when does he or she back off? How much time should the visiting child spend alone with her father and how much time with her new family?

Classification Technique Questions

1. How does Borst classify her daughter's new family?

_____

_____

_____

_____

_____

2. What problems are suggested by the categories?

_____

_____

3. What problems will they have in deciding how to name or identify their relationships?

_____

_____

4. Borst poses questions about her daughter's situation. Why is this more effective than supplying her own answers?

_____

_____

_____

5. Do you know of anyone who has gone through this same dilemma? What were some of their problems and solutions?

_____

_____

Suggestions for Writing

1. In her paragraph, Borst mentions that her daughter's family will have three children, including one who stays only on the weekends. Write a paragraph classifying some of the problems other family members will have in trying to include this girl as a full-fledged member of the family.
2. Multiracial families are becoming more common. What kinds of issues similar to Borst's daughter's do they have to face? Write a paragraph classifying these issues. If you can suggest some solutions, do so.

Other Paragraph Topics

1. Fans at a sporting event
2. Bosses
3. Athletic shoes
4. Sit-coms
5. Clothes
6. Dates you've had
7. People you've worked with
8. Successes or failures
9. Movies
10. Problems you face as a new student or employee

CHAPTER REVIEW

▼ Large or complicated subjects can be made more manageable and easier to understand by classifying them into smaller units: types, kinds, categories, or divisions.

▼ It is important to classify a group into smaller units of the same type.

▼ Classification paragraphs begin with a topic sentence that clearly states the subject, how the subject will be divided, and why classifying the subject is important.

▼ In classification paragraphs, transitional expressions focus on categories, types, kinds, and divisions. Transitional expressions connect ideas and add rhythm to the writing.

Writing Opportunities

Home

For your visit to your child's "Parent's Day" at school, you've been asked by the teacher to talk about the various types of jobs at the company where you are employed. You decide to bring the two photographs above accompanied by a written paragraph classifying the various categories that the workers in the photographs represent.

School

Your Business 333 professor has given you an assignment to create your own manufacturing company. Your first task is to write a paragraph that both identifies the product you will be making and the types of workers necessary to make and bring your product to market.

Work

As the Personnel Director of your company, the president has instructed you, because of declining profits, to downsize the number of employees by ten percent in each job classification. You decide that your first step is to write a paragraph classifying the job categories in each of the three divisions of the company.

Visit *The Write Start* Online!

For additional practice with the materials found in this chapter, visit our Website at:

http://www.ablongman.com/checkett

The Website also features additional readings, quizzes, writing activities, and Internet links, as well as a bulletin board and interactive chat.

For More Practice with Your Grammar and Writing Skills

For further exercises designed to improve your writing and grammar skills, use the Writer's ToolKit Plus CD-ROM included with this text. The toolkit provides a wealth of computerized tutorials and practice activities.

18 Process

Have you ever had to explain to a friend how to perform a specific task? Perhaps you had to explain how to play a video game or how to work a certain piece of electronics. Think about how you would give that explanation in writing. You would have to provide a step-by-step account. Now, consider how such an account might apply to your writing for school or work. Sometimes, you might be called on to explain how you performed a certain science experiment, how a certain historical event came to pass, or how a meeting with a client was conducted. All of these writing situations involve a process.

Process explains the steps necessary to complete a procedure, an operation, or an event. Process is an important method when you are asked to develop ideas in areas such as science, history, sports, medicine, and business. For example, you may be asked to explain how stars are born and how they eventually die; or, you may be asked to write about the events that led to World War II; or, you may have to give a report illustrating how to assemble a piece of machinery.

Types of Process

There are two kinds of process descriptions: **directional** and **informational.** *Directional* process explains to the reader how to do something: how to bake a cake, how to tune a car engine, or how to write a process essay. The goal of directional process is to enable the reader to be able to do something or to duplicate some process after they have completed following the directions.

Informational process explains to the reader how something was made or how an event occurred, or how something works: how a treaty between two countries was finalized, how the Panama Canal was built, or how an industrial laser is used in medical procedures. Readers are not expected to be able to actually repeat or duplicate the process explained, but they should be able to understand the process.

PRACTICE 1

In the space provided to the left, identify each topic as directional **(D)** or informational **(I)**.

1. _____ How to install gas logs in a fireplace

2. _____ How Dr. Jonas Salk developed the polio vaccine

3. _____ How to balance a checkbook

4. _____ How the automobile was developed by Henry Ford

5. _____ How lightning forms

6. _____ How to sew a dress from a pattern

7. _____ How to build a brick barbecue

8. _____ How to read the stock market page

9. _____ How to begin a hobby

10. _____ How the Spanish Inquisition occurred

PRACTICE 2

In the space provided to the left, identify each topic as directional **(D)** or informational **(I)**.

1. _____ How to study for an exam

2. _____ How to be a friend

3. _____ How to send e-mail using a computer

4. _____ How to repair a clock

5. _____ How the War of the Roses occurred

6. _____ How to fill out a job application

7. _____ How to register to vote

8. _____ How to plan for a vacation

9. _____ How to make a quiche

10. _____ How photosynthesis works

Organizing the Process Paragraph

Both directional and informational process paragraphs are developed according to the order in which the steps of the process occurred. Adhering to chronological order avoids confusion. For example, in describing how to change a tire, the instructions would not occur as suggested by the list on the left; rather, they would follow the chronological steps as listed on the right:

1. Replace the hubcap	**1.** Remove the hubcap
2. Replace lug nuts and tighten	**2.** Unscrew and remove lug nuts
3. Replace with spare tire	**3.** Remove flat tire
4. Unscrew and remove lug nuts	**4.** Replace with spare tire
5. Remove flat tire	**5.** Replace lug nuts and tighten
6. Remove the hubcap	**6.** Replace the hubcap

▼ **PRACTICE 3**

Here are two lists of steps for process paragraphs. They are not in chronological order. Number the steps in the proper order in the spaces provided to the left. If you find any steps that should not be included, cross them out.

1. Sending an e-mail using a computer is an easy method of communication.

_____ Move the cursor to the text box and begin composing your message.

_____ Finally, click on the "send" icon.

_____ Move your cursor to the "subject" icon, and type in a subject word or phrase.

_____ Press the number lock key.

_____ First, click on the "Compose Message" icon.

2. Alice became a good student through hard work and sticking to a schedule.

_____ Each evening, she studied between 7 and 10 o'clock.

_____ During class, she always took notes.

_____ She spent many hours drinking coffee in the Student Center.

_____ In the morning before class, she looked over her notes from the day before.

_____ After class each day, she did research in the library for one hour.

▼ **PRACTICE 4**

Here are two lists of steps for process paragraphs. They are not in chronological order. Number the steps in the proper order in the spaces provided to the left. If you find any steps that should not be included, cross them out.

1. How pearls are created is both a fascinating and unusual process.

_____ The particle acts as an irritant.

_____ Pearls are produced inside certain bivalve mollusks, such as an oyster.

_____ A small particle, like a grain of sand, lodges in the mollusk's soft tissue.

_____ Either spherical or irregular pearls are formed depending on the shape of the particle.

_____ Pearl coloration varies widely, the most prized shades being white, black, rose, and cream.

_____ The irritant becomes coated with layer upon layer of lustrous nacre.

2. While stopping smoking is difficult, it can be achieved by breaking some old habits and by establishing some new ones.

_____ Treat yourself to a thick, rich, strawberry milkshake.

_____ Instead of smoking while talking on the telephone, twirl a pencil with your fingers. Pretend it's the cigarette you normally hold when on the phone.

_____ Instead of having a cigarette the first thing in the morning, go for a brisk walk around the neighborhood.

_____ After lunch, suck on a piece of hard candy instead of having a smoke.

_____ Begin by making a list of when and where it is that you normally smoke.

_____ If all else fails, see your doctor about wearing a nicotine patch.

_____ Finally, before you retire to bed, do 50 pushups and eat a piece of fruit.

_____ On the way to work, keep your mind off having a cigarette and use the tape deck or CD to learn a new language.

Transitional Expressions: Connecting the Steps

Now that you have the steps of your process in the correct order, you have to connect them in your paragraph so that they follow each other chronologically. Transitional expressions are extremely helpful in connecting these steps.

Commonly Used Transitional Expressions for Process			
afterward	before	initially	to begin
as	begin by	later	until
as soon as	during	meanwhile	upon
at first	finally	next	when
at last	first, second, third, etc.	now	while
at this point	following	then	

The Topic Sentence

Now that you have smooth transitions between the steps of the process, you are ready to put the paragraph together. Both directional and informational paragraphs begin with a topic sentence that clearly states what the reader should be able to do or understand after reading the steps of the process and why the process is important.

Example

Learning to make a budget, looking for discount packages, and calling hotels for advanced reservations can make vacationing more enjoyable.

The entire paragraph might read:

Learning to make a budget, looking for discount packages, and calling hotels for advanced reservations can make vacationing more enjoyable. Setting a budget helps you plan your trip and save money. First, decide how much money is available, and base your trip around places that fit your budget. Overestimating on food and souvenirs is a good idea. Remember to keep the other family members informed on the budget when it is set. Discount packages are popular and can save you big bucks. Begin by stopping by a travel agency for brochures and catalogs. Most agencies can provide information on inexpensive and fun places to go. Next, check out the Internet. Many discount programs can be found in only a few minutes, and sometimes you can participate in an auction and bid on the package that fits your budget. Finally, call hotels in the area where you are planning to stay. Many resort hotels have their own special packages for families. Find out what type of "rainy day" facilities they have, such as indoor pools, spas, fitness centers, and game rooms. After making a reservation, be sure to get a confirmation number so that you can check to be assured that you have the rooms you want for the time period you planned for.

PRACTICE 5

Answer the following questions about the preceding paragraph.

1. What process does the paragraph explain?

_____

_____

2. Is this process paragraph intended to be directional or informational?

_____

3. How many steps are there in the process? Name them.

_____

_____

4. Identify the transitional expressions in the paragraph. How do they help organize the information chronologically?

_____

_____

_____

PRACTICE 6

In the following paragraph taken from a process essay titled "How to be Successful at Kicking the Smoking Habit," student writer Stephanie Higgs outlines the many reasons why people begin smoking before tackling the daunting procedure to end the habit.

People smoke for many reasons; therefore, it is important for smokers to identify the reasons why they smoke. Analyzing the origin of the habit is the first positive step toward kicking the habit. For most people, smoking is a learned behavior; consequently, smokers tend to come from families where one or more of their parents were smokers. The majority of them are anxious people who started smoking because it seemed to provide a temporary release from current or future distress and uncertainties. Some tobacco users started smoking to be cool and to fit in with the crowd; likewise, others started smoking because they enjoyed the taste of tobacco after trying it. While others did not necessarily enjoy the act of smoking, they felt addicted to the nicotine and needed to continue to satisfy their cravings. Now, with the origin of the habit exposed, the smoker is empowered with the knowledge of why he or she smokes and each can seek out healthier alternatives to satisfying needs.

Process Technique Questions

1. What is the process that is being explained?

   _____

2. Is the paragraph intended to be directional or informational?

   _____

3. How many steps or reasons are discussed?

   _____

   _____

   _____

4. Identify any transitional expressions that are used. Do they help organize the information chronologically?

   _____

   _____

5. What transitional expressions would be more effective, and where would you place them in the paragraph?

   _____

   _____

   _____

▼ PRACTICE 7

In this paragraph taken from a process essay titled "A Step-by-Step Guide to Photography," student writer Stephanie Weidemann clarifies the steps necessary to produce visually effective prints.

A photographer must set the scene, correctly develop the negative, and creatively enlarge the print to achieve a worthwhile photograph. First, using a grey card, measure the light that the camera is reading from the scene. Adjust the aperture so that the light meter is floating in the center of its scale; this insures the picture will not be under or over exposed. Next, great care must be given when developing the negative. No light must ever reach the negative during the developing process. In complete darkness, the film is loaded onto a developing reel and placed into a series of chemical liquids that develop and fix the negative. After this, the negative is enlarged. The process is achieved by first placing the negative into an enlarger, followed by shining a light through the negative onto resin coated paper. By manipulating the amount of light and time, the photographer can create a variety of special effects. The paper is then run through another series of chemical liquid baths and then allowed to dry.

Process Technique Questions

1. What process is being explained in the paragraph?

   _____

2. Is the paragraph intending the process to be directional or informational?

   _____

3. How many steps are explained?

   _____

   _____

4. Identify any transitional expressions that are used. Do they help organize the information chronologically?

   _____

   _____

   _____

5. Would other transitional expressions be more effective? Which ones would you add, and where would you place them?

   _____

   _____

   _____

In this paragraph from an essay titled "Give Juggling a Hand!" professional mathematicians Joe Buhler and Ron Graham give a particularly compact explanation of an intriguing activity. It reflects the authors' enjoyment of juggling as well as their expertise. By providing some historical background, clear directions, and interesting explanations, the writers make the activity seem as enjoyable to readers as it is to them.

READ
All About It . . .

To read the full essay from which this paragraph is excerpted, see page 366.

The Cascade. Here, each ball travels from one hand to the other and back again, following a looping path that looks like a figure eight lying on its side. The juggler starts with two balls in his right hand, using a scooping motion and releasing a ball when his throwing hand is level with his navel. As the first ball reaches its highest point, the other hand scoops and releases a second ball, and as that one reaches *its* apogee, he throws the third. Skilled jugglers can keep three, five, or even seven balls going in a cascade, but never four or six. With an even number, balls collide at the intersection of the figure eight.

Process Technique Questions

1. What is the specific process that the paragraph explains?

_____

2. Is the paragraph intending the process to be directional or informational?

_____

3. How many steps are explained?

_____

_____

_____

4. Identify any transitional expressions that are used. Do they help to organize the steps in the proper order?

_____

_____

5. Would other transitional expressions be more effective? Which ones would you add, and where would you place them?

_____

_____

_____

Suggestions for Writing

1. Physical activities can be difficult or challenging, but so can mental, social, or artistic activities. Think of activities you undertake with some success that others might find difficult, and list as many as you can. From the list, choose several that you are interested in writing about. Note which ones you might be able to explain in ways that will intrigue readers and teach them something useful. Choose one as the topic for a process paragraph, and write about it.

2. Many sports and hobbies can seem difficult or mystifying. Drawing on Buhler and Graham's paragraph as a model, create a set of directions to simplify a seemingly challenging, dangerous, or mysterious sport or activity. Write a paragraph describing your process.

▼ PRACTICE 9

In this paragraph taken from an essay titled "We Build Excitement," Professor James B. Twitchell talks about the process by which advertising became part of our culture and now serves as a primary force in shaping our culture, our perceptions, and our values. The paragraph makes use of many examples in its analysis of the process advertising uses to attach to itself cultural importance.

To read the full essay from which this paragraph is excerpted, see page 369.

Start the day with breakfast. What's on the cereal box but the Ninja Turtles, Batman, or the Addams Family? Characters real or imagined once sold cereal; now they *are* the cereal. Once Wild Bill Hickock, Bob Mathias, Huckleberry Hound, and Yogi Bear touted Sugar Pops or Wheaties. Now the sugar gobs reappear every six months, renamed to cross-promote some event. When the most recent Robin Hood movie was released, a Prince of Thieves Cereal appeared on grocery shelves. Alas, the movie did not show Mr. Hood starting the day with his own brand. But Kellogg has tried for this brass ring of promotion anyway. It has marketed cereal with Jerry Seinfeld and Jay Leno on the boxes and then gone on to buy commercial time on their network, NBC. It is of some comfort that while cereals sporting Barbie and Donkey Kong have gone stale on the shelves, the redoubtable Fred Flintstone and his Flintstones cereal survive.

Process Technique Questions

1. What is the specific process the paragraph explains?

_____

_____

2. Is the paragraph intending the process to be directional or informational?

_____

3. How many steps are explained?

_____

_____

4. Identify any transitional expressions that are used. Do they help to organize the steps in the proper order?

_____

_____

_____

5. Would other transitional expressions be more effective? Which ones would you add, and where would you place them?

_____

_____

_____

Suggestions for Writing

1. Twitchell's paragraph is filled with details and brief examples. Use a similar strategy in a paragraph of your own, perhaps exploring some other feature of contemporary life such as the attention paid to sports and sports heroes, popular magazines or novels, or the way television news programs operate.

2. Drawing on "We Build Excitement" as a model, create a paragraph of your own showing how the contemporary form of some activity or process (fishing, basketball, clothing design and manufacture, for example) differs from earlier forms.

Other Paragraph Topics

1. How to plan an exercise program
2. How to plan a budget
3. How a specific historical event occurred
4. How to prepare a specific meal
5. How to prepare a report
6. How a camera works
7. How stars form (and/or die)

8. How to plan a health food diet
9. How legislation becomes a bill
10. How to repair an appliance (lamp, toaster, radio, etc.)

CHAPTER REVIEW

▼ A process explains the steps necessary to complete a procedure, an operation, or an event.
▼ There are two kinds of process descriptions: directional and informational.
▼ Directional process explains to the reader how to do something. The goal of directional process is to enable the reader to be able to do something or to duplicate some process after they have completed following the directions.
▼ Informational process explains to the reader how something was made, how an event occurred, or how something works. Readers are not expected to be able to actually repeat or duplicate the process explained, but they should be able to understand the process.
▼ Because process paragraphs are organized chronologically, transitional expressions help connect ideas in proper order and add rhythm to the writing.
▼ Both directional and informational process paragraphs begin with a topic sentence that clearly states what the reader should be able to do or understand after reading the steps of the process and why the process is important.

Writing Opportunities

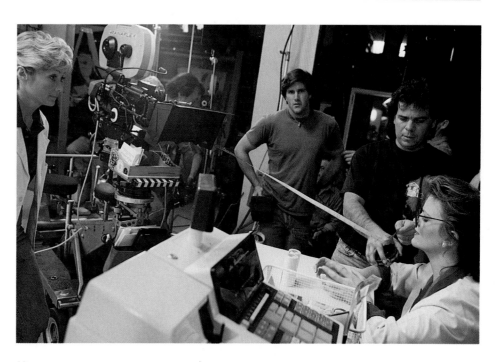

Home

You and your spouse want to film your daughter's college graduation ceremony and the reception and party at your home afterwards. Additionally, your two youngest children want to be a part of the "crew." Write a paragraph describing the process that the four of you will follow to do a good job of filming the events.

School

The Student Senate at your school wants to make a short video to be shown at Freshman Orientation in hopes of inducing more students to become active in campus organizations. You have been chosen to direct the shoot. Write a paragraph explaining to the Student Senate the process that you want to follow to make the video.

Work

The CEO of a new computer software company has hired your Public Relations company to make a video to introduce their new product line. The CEO wants to be filmed sitting at her desk as she introduces the company and its products to the consumer. Before you and your crew arrive at the company offices, you will need for her to make certain arrangements to make the shoot successful and less time-consuming. Write a paragraph to the CEO explaining to her the process she will need to accomplish prior to your arriving for the shoot.

Visit *The Write Start* Online!

For additional practice with the materials found in this chapter, visit our Website at:

http://www.ablongman.com/checkett

The Website also features additional readings, quizzes, writing activities, and Internet links, as well as a bulletin board and interactive chat.

For More Practice with Your Grammar and Writing Skills

For further exercises designed to improve your writing and grammar skills, use the Writer's ToolKit Plus CD-ROM included with this text. The toolkit provides a wealth of computerized tutorials and practice activities.

CHAPTER

19

Comparison and Contrast

Often in your writing you will need to discuss an object, idea, or item not in terms of its own features, but in terms of how it relates to another object, idea, or item. This type of writing can be a challenge because it forces you to think about each item on its own, as well as about the ways in which the items relate to one another. Are they alike? Are they different? How? Although you will often need to compare and contrast several items at one time in your writing, this chapter focuses on comparing and contrasting just two items, for the sake of simplicity.

Deciding to Compare or to Contrast

The two main tools you use in this type of writing are **comparison and contrast.** When you compare things, you are looking for similarities. When you contrast things, you are looking for differences. For example, consider two shirts. In comparing them, you might notice that they are both white, both have collars, and both have buttons. When contrasting them, you might notice that they are made of different materials, that only one has buttons on the collar, and that one is a dress shirt and one is a casual shirt. Comparison and contrast, therefore, assists the reader in understanding one person, place, feeling, idea, or object in relation to another.

PRACTICE 1

Look at the following pairs of topics. Decide whether it would be better to compare or contrast each pair.

	Compare	Contrast
1. My friends Bob and Carl	_____	_____
2. Antarctica and the Sahara Desert	_____	_____
3. Concrete and rubber	_____	_____

201

	Compare	Contrast
4. Beef and fish	_____	_____
5. Internet search engines Yahoo and Webcrawler	_____	_____
6. Idaho and Yukon Gold potatoes	_____	_____
7. A French and California wine	_____	_____
8. Nurses and doctors	_____	_____
9. Jogging and walking	_____	_____
10. Apples and oranges	_____	_____

▾ **PRACTICE 2**

Look at the following pairs of topics. Decide whether it would be better to compare or contrast each pair.

	Compare	Contrast
1. Board games Monopoly and Careers	_____	_____
2. Attorney and judge	_____	_____
3. Movie star and rock star	_____	_____
4. Swimming in a pool or a lake	_____	_____
5. Oral exam and essay exam	_____	_____
6. Coin collecting and stamp collecting	_____	_____
7. Canada and the United States	_____	_____
8. Soccer and rugby	_____	_____
9. Running shoes and walking shoes	_____	_____
10. Chicago and New York style pizza	_____	_____

The Topic Sentence

The comparison/contrast paragraph begins with a topic sentence that clearly states the two items being compared or contrasted and why comparing or contrasting them is important. Here is an example of a topic sentence for a comparison/contrast paragraph.

> When choosing between ice hockey and roller hockey for your child's participation, cost is usually the deciding factor.

This topic sentence clearly states the two items for comparison: Ice hockey and roller hockey. "Cost" is the factor mentioned that indicates that the writer is going to compare ice hockey and roller hockey.

The entire paragraph might look like this:

> When choosing between ice hockey and roller hockey for your child's participation, cost is usually the deciding factor. When playing roller hockey in small in-house leagues, the average cost is $75. If children show talent, they may play for a "select" tournament team, and the average cost will skyrocket to $300. Equipment for roller hockey, although expensive, is necessary for protection against injury. Well-padded, durable skates can cost an average of $200; helmets, on average, cost $50; and knee pads, girdle, and pants can cost $150. This brings the average cost total to $475 for an in-house league and $750 for a select tournament team. Ice hockey is considerably more expensive than roller hockey because more equipment is required. Playing ice hockey in an in-house league costs an average of $350, and playing for a select tournament team can cost $600. As with roller hockey equipment, ice hockey equipment is not inexpensive. In addition, ice hockey requires shoulder pads while roller hockey does not. The pads can cost upward of $75. Also, ice hockey requires a thicker, heavier stick than does roller hockey that can cost $90 to $100. Ice hockey skates, as compared to roller hockey skates, have an average cost of $300; helmets, knee pads, girdle, and pants can cost $200 to $350. The total average cost for playing in an in-house league is $900 to $1200.

PRACTICE 3

Compose both a comparison and a contrast topic sentence for the pairs of items listed below.

Example

Topic: Two Friends

a. Julio and Angelina have very different study habits. (Contrast)

b. Aretha and Maurice have similar exercise routines. (Comparison)

1. Two Musical Groups

a. _____

b. _____

2. Two Restaurants

a. _____

b. _____

3. Two School Courses

a. _____

b. _____

▼
PRACTICE 4

Compose both a comparison and a contrast topic sentence for the pairs of items listed below.

1. Two Vacations Spots/Resorts

a. _____

b. _____

2. Two Bosses

a. _____

b. _____

3. Two Types/Styles of Clothes

a. _____

b. _____

Organizing Comparisons and Contrasts

Once you know what comparisons and contrasts you are going to use, you need to organize your thoughts and decide how to present them. There are two commonly used organizational plans for comparison and contrast paragraphs: **block** and **point-by-point.** The block method presents information about one item first, then uses this information for comparison or contrast when presenting information about the second item in the second half of the paragraph. The point-by-point method presents the information about both items together, creating an ongoing series of comparisons and contrast.

In the preceding paragraph about ice hockey and roller hockey, the **block method** is used. Notice that the cost elements of roller hockey are discussed in the first half of the paragraph (without mention of ice hockey). Afterward, the same elements in regard to ice hockey are discussed in the second half of the paragraph. However, this time, as each item in regard to ice hockey is mentioned, reference is made to roller hockey, as well. In this way, the comparison between the elements is continually made. If not, then the two halves of the paragraph would seem disconnected, and the comparison would not exist.

The **block method** is illustrated in this manner:

Thesis: When choosing between ice hockey and roller hockey for your child's participation, cost is usually the deciding factor.

1. Roller hockey
    a. In-house league fee
    b. Select tournament team fee
    c. Cost of skates
    d. Cost of helmet
    e. Cost of pads, girdle, pants

2. Ice hockey
    a. In-house league fee
    b. Select tournament team fee
    c. Cost of skates
    d. Cost of helmet
    e. Cost of pads, girdle, pants

Remember, when using the block method, you discuss all the factors in the first item of comparison in the first part of the paragraph without mentioning the second item in the comparison. Then, in the second half of the paragraph, discuss each point regarding the second item in the comparison, remembering to make reference to each item that was mentioned in the first half of the paragraph. This will connect the two items of the comparison so that the paragraph will not seem to be about two items that have nothing to do with one another.

When using the **point-by-point method,** each point concerning each item in the comparison is followed by the similar point in regard to the second item in the comparison. The point-by-point method is illustrated in this manner:

Thesis: When deciding on ice hockey or roller hockey for your child's participation, cost is usually the deciding factor.

First Point:
    a. Roller hockey in-league fee
    b. Ice hockey in-league fee

Second Point:
    a. Roller hockey select tournament team
    b. Ice hockey select tournament team

Third Point:
    a. Roller hockey skates
    b. Ice hockey skates

Fourth Point:
    a. Roller hockey helmets
    b. Ice hockey helmets

Fifth Point:
    a. Roller hockey pads, girdle, pants
    b. Ice hockey pads, girdle, pants

Using the point-by-point method, the same paragraph might be written like this:

> When choosing between ice hockey and roller hockey for your child's participation, cost is usually the deciding factor. When playing roller hockey in small in-house leagues, the average cost is $75. On the other hand, playing ice hockey in an in-house league costs an average of $350. If children show talent, they may play for a "select" tournament team, and the average roller hockey team cost will skyrocket to $300, whereas, on a select ice hockey tournament team, the costs can soar to $600. Equipment for roller hockey, although expensive, is necessary for protection against injury. Well-padded, durable skates can cost an average of $200, while ice hockey skates, as compared to roller hockey skates, have an average cost of $300 and up. In roller hockey, helmets, on average, cost $50. Similarly, ice hockey helmets cost about $50 to $60. Knee pads, girdle, and pants, for roller hockey, can cost $150. However, ice hockey knee pads, girdle, and pants can cost $200 to $350. In addition, ice hockey requires shoulder pads, while roller hockey does not. The pads can cost upward of $75. Also, ice hockey requires a thicker, heavier stick than does roller hockey, and the stick can cost $90 to $100. In conclusion, the average cost for playing in a roller hockey in-house league comes to $475, and the cost is $900 to $1200 for playing in an ice hockey in-house league. While the cost for playing for a roller hockey select tournament team can rise to $750, playing for an ice hockey select team can be as much as $1400.

Notice that in the point-by-point method each item in the elements to be compared is developed in the same order. It is important to keep the order consistent to avoid confusion.

Transitional Expressions: Connecting Your Comparisons and Contrasts

Transitional expressions are important because they stress either comparison or contrast, depending on the type of paragraph you are writing.

Transitional Expressions Showing Contrast

although	nevertheless
but	on the contrary
despite	on the other hand
different from	otherwise
even though	still
except for	though
however	whereas
in contrast	while
instead	yet

Transitional Expressions Showing Comparison

again	in addition
and	in the same way
also	like
as well as	likewise
both	neither
each	similar to
equally	similarly
furthermore	so
just as	the same
just like	too

PRACTICE 5

The following paragraph is difficult to understand because of a lack of transitional expressions that stress *contrast*. On separate paper, add proper transitional expressions that show contrast. To achieve variety, do not use the same transitional expression more than once.

The United States has many historical places of interest. They are more modern than those in Mexico. The Statue of Liberty is not even a century old. The pyramids found in Tenochtitlán are at least a millennium old. Another historic place to visit in the United States is Philadelphia where many of the events of the American Revolution occurred. It is over two hundred years old. Guanajuato, in Mexico, is historic because many historical events of the Mexican Revolution happened there. The city itself is historic. Walking down Guanajuato's streets is just like going back in time. The houses and roads are four and five hundred years old. Many of the houses have been ravaged by time, and the ancient roads polished shiny by the winds of time.

PRACTICE 6

The following paragraph is difficult to understand because of a lack of transitional expressions that stress *comparison*. On separate paper, add proper transitional expressions that show comparison. To achieve variety, do not use the same transitional expression more than once.

The occupations of cosmetologist and nurse may seem very different, but they share many common attributes. The cosmetologist makes the client's appearance better by using the proper grooming techniques. The nurse uses the latest medical procedures when treating a patient. A cosmetologist's client often feels depressed or anxious about his or her appearance. By using the coloring products appropriate to the client's complexion and age, the cosmetologist can change a person's appearance dramatically, making people feel good about themselves once again. The nurse makes the patient feel better by administering the proper medications or exercise appropriate for the patient's problem and age group. Both the cosmetologist and the nurse make the people in their care feel better about themselves.

PRACTICE 7

In the following paragraph taken from an essay titled "'The Jury' Is In!" student writer Carol Hoxworth contrasts two novels by popular writer John Grisham. Hoxworth focuses on character development as a crucial difference between the two stories.

In *The Runaway Jury*, the character development is superb because Grisham alludes to certain aspects of the characters' personalities throughout the development of the plot. One of the strong points of this novel is being fed only enough information about them at the crucial time; therefore, a desire is created within the reader to know each character more intimately and how they will relate to the rest of the story. In contrast, *The Testament* has a glaring lack of character development from the very beginning of the novel. There is some confusion in the first few chapters as to who the main characters are. Instead of revealing the nature of each personality throughout the book, the reader is given bland, generic, and brief descriptions of them. There also seems to be an overabundance of characters that truly are not necessary to the development and enrichment of the

plot, so the desire to know the characters better and to see how the plot

relates to them is not achieved.

Contrast Technique Questions

1. What is the writer contrasting in the paragraph? Is there a topic sentence that clearly states the items for contrast? If not, write one for the paragraph.

_____

_____

2. What organizational pattern does the writer use, point-by-point or block?

_____

3. How does the writer make a smooth transition to the second part of the paragraph?

_____

_____

_____

4. Does the writer use enough specific examples to develop and clarify the contrast?

_____

_____

_____

▼ PRACTICE 8

In the following paragraph taken from an essay titled "Commercial vs. Residential Real Estate," student writer Nancy Smith compares two aspects of her job that on the surface might seem quite different but, in reality, are very similar.

Marketing costs for commercial real estate are paid for by the com-

pany; similarly, in residential real estate, costs are usually picked up by the

company, as well. Like residential real estate, commercial real estate sends

out thousands of flyers advertising property for lease or sale. For example, both commercial and residential agents mail advertising brochures to area residents and other agents announcing available properties. Both commercial and residential agents can act alone or share commissions with other agents when a property is sold, rented, or leased.

Comparison Technique Questions

1. What is the writer comparing in the paragraph? Is there a topic sentence that clearly states the items for comparison? If not, write one for the paragraph.

_____

_____

_____

2. What organizational pattern does the writer use, point-by-point or block?

_____

3. How does the writer transition smoothly so that the points do not seem like merely a list of items strung together?

_____

_____

_____

4. Does the writer use enough specific examples to develop and clarify the comparison?

_____

_____

_____

▼
PRACTICE 9

In this paragraph taken from an essay titled "Grant and Lee: A Study in Contrasts," by professional historian Bruce Catton, the author focuses on the differences that the two great generals embodied for their sides during the Civil War. However, Catton does, on occasion, comment on the similarities existing between the two leaders.

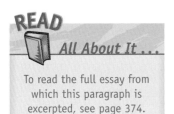

To read the full essay from which this paragraph is excerpted, see page 374.

Lastly, and perhaps greatest of all, there was the ability, at the end, to turn quickly from war to peace once the fighting was over. Out of the way these two men behaved at Appomattox came the possibility of a peace of reconciliation. It was a possibility not wholly realized, in the years to come, but which did, in the end, help the two sections to become one nation again . . . after a war whose bitterness might have seemed to make such a reunion wholly impossible. No part of either man's life became him more than the part he played in their brief meeting in the McLean house at Appomattox. Their behavior there put all succeeding generations of Americans in their debt. Two great Americans, Grant and Lee—very different, yet under every-thing very much alike. Their encounter at Appomattox was one of the great moments of American history.

Comparison Technique Questions

1. What is the writer comparing in the paragraph? Is there a topic sentence that clearly states the items for comparison. If not, write one for the paragraph.

_____

_____

_____

_____

_____

2. What organizational pattern does the writer use, point-by-point or block?

_____

3. Point out transitional expressions the writer uses to connect ideas and to add rhythm. Are there any that the writer could have used to achieve smooth transitions? If so, which ones and where would they be placed for greatest effectiveness?

_____

_____

_____

4. Does the writer use enough specific examples to develop the comparison?

_____

_____

_____

Suggestions for Writing

1. Write a paragraph comparing two moral, social, economic, or political disagreements that have been or might become conflicts.

2. Write a paragraph on why the two items you chose in Question 1 are so difficult to resolve. Concentrate on explaining, not taking either side or trying to persuade the reader to adopt a particular solution.

▼ PRACTICE 10

In this paragraph taken from an essay titled "Hasta la Vista, Arnold," by professional writer Margaret Talbot, she suggests that recent movies have signaled a shift toward female action heroes. This trend might reveal changing cultural attitudes; however, she worries that this trend might also reinforce stereotypes.

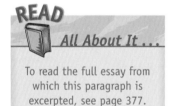

READ
All About It . . .

To read the full essay from which this paragraph is excerpted, see page 377.

For actresses, the new availability of action roles is a boon, but not an unmitigated one. Action movies propel a few of them into the salary stratosphere as nothing else can. They still don't occupy the same gilded bracket as, say, Schwarzenegger, Stallone, or—God help us—Jim Carrey, all of whom make $20 million a film. But Sandra Bullock did take home $12.5 million for _Speed 2: Cruise Control,_ and Sigourney Weaver got $11 million for _Alien Resurrection._ On the other hand, the roles can be, well, a bit robotic. Elizabeth Hurley had fun playing a jokey action heroine in silver lamé boots but says she's not especially eager to sign up for a lot of rock-'em-sock-'em blockbusters. "I really prefer to do a scene that you can get your teeth into, rather than just waiting around for things to blow up. Action films can be a little tedious." Minnie Driver agrees. In _The Flood,_ she plays, of all things, a church restorer who manages to save her work and her town from rising waters and marauding robbers. She says she liked playing a character who was "definitely not a damsel in distress," and she's encouraged by the prospect of more parts for "women who can be strong across the board without being bitches." Still, Driver says she "wouldn't necessarily do another action thriller," because she's "interested in movies that are more about character. Though I have to say that if it involved somebody more like Sigourney Weaver's character in the *Alien* movies, I'd make an exception. That role, and Sigourney in it, has such grace and passion. It's never cheesy." Weaver herself worries that action movies may not embrace women who, like Ripley, project a sinewy tenacity rather than something more traditionally feminine. "The important thing in introducing new female action heroes," Weaver says, is that they don't try to make us too glamorous, put us all in see-through uniforms or something."

Contrast Technique Questions

1. Is there a topic sentence that clearly states the items being contrasted? If not, write a topic sentence for the paragraph.

_____

_____

_____

2. What organizational pattern does the writer use, point-by-point or block?

_____

3. Does the writer use a transitional expression to smoothly move from point to point? If not, which ones would you choose, and where would you place them?

_____

_____

4. In the paragraph, the writer notes Sigourney Weaver's worry that Hollywood will not "embrace women who . . . project a sinewy tenacity rather than something more traditionally feminine." What is Weaver worried about? What exactly is being contrasted here?

_____

_____

Suggestions for Writing

1. Write a paragraph contrasting some recent action movies starring women with those mentioned in the paragraph you have just read. Do they support or differ from what the writer suggests about female heroes?

2. Write a paragraph focusing on this question: How do action movies define the difference between masculine and feminine. What, then, do action movies say about the traditional characteristics of gender division?

Other Paragraph Topics

Compare or contrast:

1. Two pieces of art
2. Your mother and your father
3. Two magazines
4. A former attitude about a social or political belief and how you feel about it now
5. Two schools you have attended
6. Two bosses or co-workers
7. A widely held belief and its real meaning
8. Two places you have lived (a city, or house, or country)
9. Two forms of government (local, city, state, or country)
10. Two novels

CHAPTER REVIEW

▼ Comparison and contrast assists the reader in understanding one person, place, feeling, idea, or object in relation to another.

▼ When comparing, you are looking for similarities.

▼ When contrasting, you are looking for differences.

▼ There are two commonly used organizational patterns for comparison and contrast paragraphs: point-by-point and block.

▼ In comparison and contrast paragraphs, transitional expressions are important because they stress either comparison or contrast, depending on the type of paragraph you are writing.

▼ Comparison and contrast paragraphs begin with a topic sentence that clearly states the two items being compared or contrasted and why comparing or contrasting them is important.

Writing Opportunities

Home

The Community Council in your town has decided to raise funds by publishing and selling a book of recipes from local townspeople. As you are known as the best dessert maker in the community, the committee has asked you to write a paragraph comparing the variety of uses of the blueberry versus the strawberry.

School

For your final exam in Home Economics 314, you had to make one dessert using blueberries and one dessert using strawberries. Additionally, you were instructed to write a paragraph comparing the two efforts.

Work

As Communications Director for the National Association of Fruit Growers, your current challenge is to put together a brochure extolling the virtues of people including a variety of fruits in their daily diet. Research indicates that most people only think of blueberries and strawberries as dessert fruits. Write a paragraph that makes a case for the blueberry and the strawberry as an "anytime food" when compared to apples, bananas, and oranges.

Visit *The Write Start* Online!

For additional practice with the materials found in this chapter, visit our Website at:

http://www.ablongman.com/checkett

The Website also features additional readings, quizzes, writing activities, and Internet links, as well as a bulletin board and interactive chat.

For More Practice with Your Grammar and Writing Skills

For further exercises designed to improve your writing and grammar skills, use the Writer's ToolKit Plus CD-ROM included with this text. The toolkit provides a wealth of computerized tutorials and practice activities.

20 ▼ Definition

Often, when writing, the writer uses words, terms, or concepts that his or her audience may not fully understand. To explain clearly what these words and terms mean is to **define** them.

For example, you might use a term such as *quasar*, a star-like object that emits powerful blue light and often radio waves; or, you might use *griffin*, a fabulous, mythological beast with the head and wings of an eagle and the body of a lion.

Simple Definitions

Simple definitions are basic one- or two-sentence definitions, such as those you might find in a dictionary. There are three types of simple definitions:

1. **Synonym definition** defines a word by supplying another simpler word that means the same thing. For example, *ubiquitous* means *everywhere*; *cacophony* means *noisy*.
2. **Class definition** defines by placing a word or term in a broad group or class that readers will readily understand, and then provides a specific detail that differentiates the original word or term from other members of that class. For example, a *convertible* is a *car* with a *top that goes up and down*. In this definition, *convertible* is the term being defined. It is put into a class of similar things (cars), and then it is distinguished from other cars, such as sedans, because it has a top that goes up and down.
3. **Definition by negation** begins by saying what a given word or term is not before saying what the word or term actually is. For example: A bagel isn't just a doughnut-shaped piece of bread. It's actually a unique type of bread that's boiled before it's baked.

Definition is important because clear communication depends on clear understanding. Precise language is essential if you are to understand what someone else means. The same word can have multiple meanings, so it is essential that you define those kinds of terms for your reader.

Use a synonym definition to define each of the following terms.

Example: Chagrined: <u>To be chagrined is to be embarrassed.</u>

  1. Dichotomy:_____

  2. Blunder: _____

  3. Literal: _____

  4. Rustic: _____

  5. Malevolent: _____

Using a class definition, define the following terms.

Example: Martini: <u>A martini is a cocktail made with gin and vermouth.</u>

  1. Robin: _____

_____

  2. Banana: _____

_____

  3. Shark: _____

_____

  4. Dictionary: _____

_____

  5. Prude: _____

_____

For each of the following terms, write a definition by negation.

Example: Hero: <u>A hero is not just someone performing an act of bravery; it is also someone taking care of his or her daily responsibilities.</u>

  1. Moral (to be): _____

_____

2. Freedom: _____

_____

3. Knowledgeable (to be): _____

_____

4. Grades: _____

_____

5. A job: _____

_____

Extended Definition

Sometimes, terms such as *self-esteem, love, free speech,* and *macroeconomics* can require much more developed definitions if they are to be fully understood. A simple, one-sentence dictionary definition may not suffice. Instead, you may need to use an entire paragraph to define such terms adequately. This longer type of definition is called an **extended definition.** Extended definition can be accomplished by means of any of the **modes of development:** description, example, comparison and contrast, process, and so forth.

To help define your term, you might

a. describe some of its parts or elements
b. explain its process
c. compare and/or contrast it to other like terms
d. give some examples
e. explain what it is not

You may use one of these modes to develop your definition, or you may use as many modes in the paragraph as you find necessary. For example, if you were writing an extended definition paragraph for the term *soul music,* you might choose one or several of the following strategies:

▼ Compare or contrast soul music to other kinds of music, such as blues, alternative rock, and jazz.
▼ State some examples of well-known soul hits.
▼ Describe its parts: lyrics, themes, musical motifs.

A simple definition for *soul music* might be "music relating to or characteristic of African American culture." This definition does not give the reader the full flavor of just how soul music represents a part of the American culture. An extended definition might expand on this idea:

> Soul music is a combination and merging of gospel and blues, two African American musical styles. While blues praised the worldly desires of the flesh, gospel extolled the virtues of spiritualism. This opposition of themes was melded into wide ranging and extremely diverse style, full of passion, pride, and optimism mixed with the historical emotion of pain and discrimination.

Whatever concept you are defining, use only those modes and strategies that are necessary to define the concept fully. Do not use techniques solely for the sake of variety.

The Topic Sentence of an Extended Definition

The definition paragraph begins with a topic sentence that clearly states the term(s) being defined, the mode of development that will be used to define the term(s), and why defining the term is important. Because there are many different reasons for supplying a reader with a definition, and because there are many different types of terms you might want or need to define in your writing, your topic sentence must clarify why you're defining a given term. For example, are you defining:

▼ A specialized term that is unfamiliar to most people, such as *lasik eye surgery* or *superstring theory*
▼ An abstract term that can have a variety of meanings, such as *freedom*, or *indifference*
▼ A concept that is often misunderstood, such as *liberalism* or *Generation X*
▼ A new slang or cultural term, such as *extreme sport* or *anime*

Here is an example of a topic sentence for a definition paragraph about being a high school freshman:

> Entering new surroundings, being harassed by upper class-men, and having four long years of school ahead of you make being a high school freshman a dreadful experience.

The entire paragraph might look like this:

> Entering new surroundings, being harassed by upperclass-men, and having four long years of school ahead of you make being a freshman a dreadful experience. Freshmen become very confused when rushed to find classes in a labyrinth of unfamiliar hallways. They act like mice attempting to find their way through a complicated maze. Additionally, harassment by upperclassmen makes running the maze even more of a challenge. Veteran students play pranks on the unsuspecting newcomers, such as asking them for elevator and hall passes. Finally, being a freshman means having four more years of headaches. Just because you are new, teachers will have little leniency in regard to the quantity of homework given and the quality of the homework returned. All three factors contribute to the realization that being a high school freshman is a dreadful existence.

In this paragraph, the term being defined is "high school freshman," and the mode of development is by example and description, using typical events that happen to freshmen.

▼ PRACTICE 4

Write a topic sentence for each of the definitions you wrote for Practice 3.

1. Moral (to be):

_____

_____

2. Freedom:

_____

_____

3. Knowledgeable (to be):

_____

_____

4. Grades:

_____

_____

5. A job:

_____

_____

▼ PRACTICE 5

In the following paragraph taken from an essay titled "My Hot Flathead," student writer Trevor Campbell defines a specific type of automobile engine not only by its design and horsepower output but through its cultural importance.

After World War II, countless GI's returned home with extra money to spend. Almost overnight, custom shops sprung up in southern California catering to the Flathead owner. The Flathead-powered Ford was cheap and plentiful, making this motor a prime candidate to customize. Within a few years, the Ford Flathead V-8 became the popular choice among custom builders; this power plant combined with a light-bodied chassis was considered a winning combination at the dragstrip. Success is often copied, a circumstance which, in turn, further established the Flathead presence.

Definition Technique Questions

1. Does this paragraph have a topic sentence that states the term to be defined? If not, how does the writer introduce the term?

_____

_____

_____

2. What is the mode of development for the paragraph?

_____

_____

_____

3. In what larger class of items would you put the Flathead powered Ford?

_____

4. What made the Flathead engine so popular?

_____

_____

_____

▼ PRACTICE 6

In this paragraph taken from an essay titled "The Perfect Store," student writer Jeanette Weiland defines the perfect store in terms of pricing. According to Weiland, low price is important, but there are also other aspects of pricing that put the customer in a buying mood.

While shopping at a perfect store, customers are generally sold products at an inexpensive price. Shoppers are typically offered items that are clearly marked with price tags on each separate package. This allows customers to rapidly and easily choose the product that gives them the best buy. There aren't any reasons to look for the price on the store shelf and then have to worry about whether or not the item matches the price tag. A perfect store does not only honor its own sales coupons, but it also accepts other department store advertised prices and coupons. This gives the customers the convenience of shopping at one store instead of having to go to two or three. No matter what store they are shopping at, these pricing policies offer shoppers an opportunity to receive the best possible price.

Definition Technique Questions

1. Does this paragraph have a topic sentence stating the term to be defined? What is the mode of development?

_____

_____

2. How many different pricing policies does the writer mention?

_____

_____

_____

3. In which sentence does the writer define by negation? Point out what it is that the perfect store not only does not do, but also what it does do for its customers.

_____

_____

_____

PRACTICE 7

READ
All About It . . .

To read the full essay from which this paragraph is excerpted, see page 381.

In this paragraph from an essay titled "Discrimination Is a Virtue," professional writer Robert Keith Miller takes a deep and thoughtful look at the meaning of the often-misused word *discrimination*. Miller points out that the overuse, misuse, and misunderstanding of this word is so widespread that most people have probably never thought about its true meaning. This improper use of the term carries with it negative social consequences.

We have a word in English which means "the ability to tell differences." That word is *discrimination*. But within the last 30 years, this word has been so frequently misused that an entire generation has grown up believing that "discrimination" means "racism." People are always proclaiming that "discrimination" is something that should be done away with. Should

that ever happen, it would prove to be our undoing.

Definition Technique Questions

1. The *denotative* meaning of a term is its direct, definite, and easily understood meaning, while its *connotative* meaning are those ideas that are suggested by the word in addition to its essential meaning. In the paragraph,
   what is *discrimination*'s denotative meaning and what is its connotative
   meaning.

   _____

   _____

2. Miller suggests that doing away with "discrimination" would have awful
   consequences for all of us. What are some of the consequences you can
   think of?

   _____

   _____

   _____

3. Miller suggests, then, that discrimination, when properly defined, is beneficial for society. How can discrimination be a positive force?

   _____

   _____

   _____

Suggestions for Writing

1. Think of two words that you are apt to confuse, such as *lay/lie; there/their;
   leave/let; bring/take;* and *scratch/itch.* Check out the correct use of the words
   and then write a paragraph defining them. Your topic sentence is ready-
   made: The two words are commonly confused.
2. Slang has become more and more a part of everyday speech, and much of
   it is specialized, used by a particular group. Select a slang word that you
   or your friends use and define it, explaining both how it is used and misused or misunderstood by those outside of your group.

PRACTICE 8

In this paragraph taken from an essay titled "Style in Revolt: Revolting Style,"
college lecturer Dick Hebdige examines the political and cultural importance
of the British punk movement. Hebdige focuses on punk's use of style as a tool
of disruption and revolt.

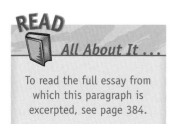

To read the full essay from which this paragraph is excerpted, see page 384.

Objects borrowed from the most sordid of contexts found a place in the punks' ensembles: lavatory chains were draped in graceful arcs across chests encased in plastic bin-liners. Safety pins were taken out of their domestic "utility" context and worn as gruesome ornaments through the cheek, ear or lip. "Cheap" trashy fabrics (PVC, plastic, lurex, etc.) in vulgar designs (e.g., mock leopard skin) and "nasty" colours, long discarded by the quality end of the fashion industry as obsolete kitsch, were salvaged by the punks and turned into garments (fly boy drainpipes, "common" mini-skirts) which offered self-conscious commentaries on the notions of modernity and taste. Conventional ideas of prettiness were jettisoned along with the traditional feminine lore of cosmetics. Contrary to the advice of every woman's magazine, make-up for both boys and girls was worn to be seen. Faces became abstract portraits: sharply observed and meticulously executed studies in alienation. Hair was obviously dyed (hay yellow, jet black, or bright orange with tufts of green or bleached in question marks), and T-shirts and trousers told the story of their own construction with multiple zips and outside seams clearly displayed.

Definition Technique Questions

1. What would you say is Hebdige's attitude toward the punk movement? Point to passages that best convey that attitude.

_____

_____

_____

_____

2. Hebdige's paragraph is primarily about the British punk movement. Is there a mainstream culture, a minority culture, a subculture, or several variations of those in your own community? How do you recognize each? What of Hebdige's discussion might seem to apply to the way these different groups express themselves?

_____

_____

_____

3. Point out some examples that the author uses to support and develop his definition of the punk movement.

_____

_____

_____

Suggestions for Writing

1. Hebdige explains how punks use common objects or forms of dress in new ways. Write a paragraph on how a group that you know about uses objects or styles in ways that depart from their originally intended uses.

2. Write a paragraph that defines how a group or an individual in your school or local community uses style of dress as part of its group identity.

Other Paragraph Topics

1. Success or failure
2. A misused or misunderstood term, such as feminism, racism, euthanasia
3. A good or poor roommate
4. A technical or medical term
5. A fanatic
6. A new form of art or music
7. A good or bad teacher, parent, or friend
8. A good or bad movie or concert
9. Heroism or cowardice
10. A sports term

CHAPTER REVIEW

▼ Clearly explaining a word, term, or concept that a reader might not fully understand in your writing is known as defining.

▼ There are many types of definitions. Some short, dictionary-type definitions are synonym definitions, class definitions, and definition by negation.

▼ Some terms and concepts require more than a short, one-sentence definition. You may need to use an entire paragraph to define them adequately. This is called an extended definition.

▼ Extended definition can be accomplished by means of any of the modes of development: description, example, comparison and contrast, process, and so forth.

▼ Definition paragraphs begin with a topic sentence that clearly states the term being defined, the mode of development, and why defining the term is important.

Writing Opportunities

Home

You want to hang a print of Magritte's painting in your family room. You are talking about the painting's content by e-mail with your spouse who is away on a long business trip. Your spouse is unsure about hanging the painting because the content sounds so unusual. So, you send him a scanned copy of the painting with an accompanying paragraph defining what you think the content means.

School

Your Psych 205 professor comes into class one day and displays a slide of Magritte's painting on the overhead. He directs you to write a paragraph defining what you think the artist is like by the contents of the painting. He also instructs that you can, if you like, define by negation—pointing out what you think the artist would not be like based on the painting's contents.

Work

As a new, summer tour guide at the Art Museum, you find out that your job will include giving brief talks about a variety of paintings. Your schedule indicates that your first stop will be Magritte's surreal painting. Write a paragraph that you will memorize to help you define surrealism for your tour group.

Visit *The Write Start* Online!

For additional practice with the materials found in this chapter, visit our Website at:

http://www.ablongman.com/checkett

The Website also features additional readings, quizzes, writing activities, and Internet links, as well as a bulletin board and interactive chat.

For More Practice with Your Grammar and Writing Skills

For further exercises designed to improve your writing and grammar skills, use the Writer's ToolKit Plus CD-ROM included with this text. The toolkit provides a wealth of computerized tutorials and practice activities.

21

Persuasion (Including Cause and Effect)

When writers use persuasion, they are trying to convince someone else that their point of view or belief is correct. Persuasion can be *informal*, *semiformal*, or *formal*. Think of informal persuasion as verbally convincing someone else of your point of view, for example, when you and your friends or members of your family try to convince each other about opinions on issues ranging from which college basketball team should be number one or which fast food restaurant has the best pizza. Commercials on radio and television also are types of informal persuasion. So are public service advertisements for nonprofit organizations and most political advertisements.

Formal persuasion is usually called argumentation. This type of persuasion requires not only arguing for your own beliefs but also arguing directly against someone else's beliefs. Argumentation uses evidence from secondary sources (information often found in the library) that are cited by using a formal documentation process (MLA or APA, for example). Research papers, analytical essays, and certain business reports fall into this category.

However, in this chapter, we are interested in a semiformal type of persuasion that falls somewhere in between the two mentioned above. Persuasion requires a bit more logical thought and organization than that expressed around the kitchen table in informal arguing but not quite the rigid requirements that occur with the inclusion of quotes and the accompanying documentation needed in formal argumentation.

Persuasion is one of the most common writing demands in school. Students are required to argue for and against ideas in quizzes, papers, and examinations. Therefore, learning the fundamentals of the **persuasive paragraph** is one of the most important skills a student writer can learn.

Building the Persuasive Paragraph

The **topic sentence** states the writer's conclusion or point of view about a particular topic. The writer's conclusion can be for or against (pro or con) the idea concerning the topic. Therefore, the topic sentence is the key to a successfully persuasive paragraph. The verbs used in a persuasive topic sentence are most often *should/should not* or *must/must not*.

Examples

The pending legislation on the right for citizens to carry concealed handguns should be defeated.

This paragraph will argue against (con) citizens having the right to carry concealed handguns.

Employers should provide day care for their employees.

This paragraph will argue for (pro) companies providing day care for the children of their employees.

Euthanasia should be legalized because of our constitutional rights of personal freedom.

This paragraph will argue for (pro) physician assisted suicide.

Athletics should not receive more funding than academics.

This paragraph will argue against (con) sports receiving more money than academics.

▼ PRACTICE 1

For the ten topics listed below, write either a pro (for) topic sentence or a con (against) topic sentence. Try to write five sentences pro and five con.

1. Topic: Instant replay in sports

_____

_____

2. Topic: Mandatory drug testing in schools/workplace

_____

_____

3. Topic: A federally regulated Internet

_____

_____

4. Topic: National ban on smoking

_____

_____

5. Topic: Reinstitution of the military draft

_____

_____

CHAPTER

6. Topic: Elderly drivers

_____

_____

7. Topic: Interstate highway speed limits

_____

_____

8. Topic: Paying college athletes

_____

_____

9. Topic: Boom boxes on public transportation

_____

_____

10. Topic: Clubs/organizations excluding certain groups for membership on the basis of race, religion, or ethnic origin

_____

_____

▼ PRACTICE 2

In this paragraph from a persuasive essay titled, "Nuke Nuclear Energy," by student writer Danny Butler, the author's argument is concerned with the nuclear fuel industry.

Because of waste management problems, the nuclear fuel industry must not be revived. Many researchers see nuclear energy as the source of power for the future because it can greatly lessen the consumption of other fuels. A typical nuclear reactor can produce many times more energy than plants using other materials such as fossil fuels. Although this new form of energy can help to preserve diminishing resources, it leads to a new problem of waste management. The fission of radioactive materials causes leftover wastes that can remain radioactive for many years. Waste management has already become a problem that will have to be faced by generations to come; we must decide which is more important, a new energy source, or the survival of life on Earth.

Technique Questions

1. Identify the topic sentence. Does it clearly state whether the author is for or against the topic?

_____

_____

2. Do the support sentences support the writer's position?

_____

_____

_____

3. Point out any sentences that are simply informational and that do not support the author's position.

_____

_____

PRACTICE 3

In this paragraph from a persuasive essay titled, "The Revolt of the Black Bourgeoisie," by professional writer Leonce Gaiter, the author confronts stereotypical thinking.

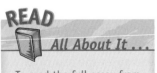

To read the full essay from which this paragraph is excerpted, see page 389.

Yes, there are the beginnings of a new candor about our culture, but the question remains, How did one segment of the African-American community come to represent the whole? First, black society itself placed emphasis on that lower caste. This made sense because historically that's where the vast majority of us were placed; it's where American society and its laws were designed to keep us. Yet although doors have opened to us over the past 20 years, it is still commonplace for black leaders to insist on our community's uniform need for social welfare programs, inner-city services, job skills training, etc. Through such calls, what has passed for a black political agenda has been furthered only superficially; while affirmative action measures have forced an otherwise unwilling majority to open some doors for the black middle class, social welfare and Great Society-style programs aimed at the black lower class have shown few positive results.

Technique Questions

1. What is a "stereotype"?

_____

_____

2. How does the use of stereotype hurt successful African-Americans?

_____

_____

_____

3. Whom does Gaiter blame for this stereotypical thinking?

_____

_____

The Pro/Con List

Once you have decided on the topic, it is vital that you know the major argument points on either side of the issue whether or not you know which side you are going to take. For example, if the topic is nuclear energy, list as many points for either side that you can think of.

Topic: Nuclear Energy	
Pro (For) List	**Con (Against) List**
Cheaper fuel costs	Radioactive waste
Less dependence on foreign oil	Causes unemployment in traditional fossil fuels industry
Creates high-tech jobs	Nuclear accidents
Saves natural resources	Nuclear weapons proliferation
Ensures strong nuclear arsenal	Environmental pollution

Once you have listed as many points as you can think of, consider the points on both sides of the argument, and choose the side you wish to argue for. Decide which points you will use in your paragraph to support your topic.

▼
PRACTICE 4

Create a pro/con list for each of the following topics. Think of as many items for each list as you can.

1. Topic: Sex education should be taught in elementary school.

Pro	Con
_____	_____
_____	_____
_____	_____
_____	_____
_____	_____

2. Topic: Women in the military should be allowed to fight as infantry soldiers.

Pro	Con
_____	_____
_____	_____
_____	_____
_____	_____
_____	_____

3. Topic: The drinking age should be reduced to 18 years of age.

Pro	Con
_____	_____
_____	_____
_____	_____
_____	_____
_____	_____

4. Topic: The English language should be America's official language.

<table>
<tr><th>Pro</th><th>Con</th></tr>
<tr><td>_____</td><td>_____</td></tr>
<tr><td>_____</td><td>_____</td></tr>
<tr><td>_____</td><td>_____</td></tr>
<tr><td>_____</td><td>_____</td></tr>
<tr><td>_____</td><td>_____</td></tr>
<tr><td>_____</td><td>_____</td></tr>
</table>

5. Topic: The government should provide health insurance for all citizens.

<table>
<tr><th>Pro</th><th>Con</th></tr>
<tr><td>_____</td><td>_____</td></tr>
<tr><td>_____</td><td>_____</td></tr>
<tr><td>_____</td><td>_____</td></tr>
<tr><td>_____</td><td>_____</td></tr>
<tr><td>_____</td><td>_____</td></tr>
<tr><td>_____</td><td>_____</td></tr>
</table>

Support in Persuasion Paragraphs

Persuasion paragraphs need to demonstrate the different types of support used to convince readers. These include *answering the opposition, referring to an authority, predicting consequences, presenting facts,* and *giving examples.* Although you probably will never use all of them in one paragraph, you will use them when you write persuasively.

1. **Answering the opposition:** At times, the best way to persuade your reader is to respond to an opponent's point. This also shows your reader that you are aware of your opponent's side of the issue, not just your own.
2. **Referring to an authority:** An authority is a person or a group that is considered an expert on the subject under discussion and will give an unbiased opinion.
3. **Predicting consequences:** Predicting consequences can help your reader agree with your point of view and disagree with your opponent's.
4. **Facts:** Facts are those things that actually exist or have existed, such as people, places, things, and events. A *fact* differs from an *opinion* in a quite significant way. An opinion is how we think about, or interpret, facts. For instance, it is a fact that the United States Congress removed our currency

from the gold standard in 1978. That fact cannot be argued. However, whether or not you think it was a good idea to remove the gold standard is your opinion, and that can be argued. Whether your *opinion*, or your opponent's *opinion*, is the more persuasive, the *fact* remains that the gold standard was removed in 1978.

5. **Examples:** Good examples can develop an idea quickly and clearly and help convince your reader of your point of view. Examples also are used to clarify, illustrate, or make concrete a general idea about the subject. Therefore, be certain that your examples support your position or convincingly argue against your opponent's position.

▼ **PRACTICE 5**

Write an **F** for *fact* or an **O** for *opinion* in the space to the left of each item in the following list.

_____ There are nine known planets in our solar system.

_____ The Congress of the United States consists of the Senate and the House of Representatives.

_____ I am 6 feet tall.

_____ Wolves make great pets.

_____ Water freezes at 32 degrees Fahrenheit and 0 degrees Celsius.

_____ I am the greatest basketball player in my state.

_____ Hurricanes are more destructive than tornadoes.

_____ Laughter is the best medicine.

_____ Pastrami is better sandwich meat than ham.

_____ Neil Armstrong was the first man on the moon.

▼ **PRACTICE 6**

In this paragraph, taken from a persuasive essay titled, "Cyberspace: If You Don't Love It, Leave It," by Esther Dyson, the author attempts to persuade the reader that cyberspace communities evolve and take on the characteristics of earthly communities.

READ
All About It . . .

To read the full essay from which this paragraph is excerpted, see page 392.

Cyberspace communities evolve just the way terrestrial communities

do: People with like-minded interests band together. Every cyberspace com-

munity has its own character. Overall, the communities on Compuserve tend to

be more techy or professional; those on America Online, affluent young singles; Prodigy, family oriented. Then there are independents like Echo, a hip,

downtown New York service, or Women's Wire, targeted to women who want to

avoid the male culture prevalent elsewhere on the Net. There's SurfWatch, a

new program allowing access only to locations deemed suitable for children.

On the Internet itself, there are lots of passionate noncommercial discussion

groups on topics ranging from Hungarian politics (Hungary-Online) to copy-

right law.

Technique Questions

1. Dyson compares the cyberspace community to a real earthly community. List the issues a real community faces. Are these the same issues that exist in a cybercommunity? Discuss their similarities and differences. What issues are unique to each?

_____

_____

_____

2. Point out sentences in which Dyson uses opinion and those in which she uses facts to support her topic. Which does she use more frequently, fact or opinion? How convincing is her support evidence?

_____

_____

_____

PRACTICE 7

In the following persuasive paragraph, taken from an essay titled "Don't Give Up the Right to Carry," by student writer Tim Schuette, the author tries to persuade his audience that giving citizens the right to carry concealed guns will reduce the crime rate.

The opposition is worried that the crime rate will increase overall with

a concealed weapon law. However, after passing concealed weapon laws, states

have seen a decrease in crime. John Lott, who has never been a member of the

National Rifle Association (N.R.A.), is an economist at the University of

Chicago. Lott examined gun laws and crime in 3,054 U.S. counties. He found

that "not only did violent crime drop after states relaxed concealed weapon laws, but . . . after five years murder was down 15%, rape 9%." If Missouri residents could carry a concealed weapon, crime would likely decrease.

Technique Questions

1. The writer does not state his attitude (pro or con) about the topic directly in a topic sentence. State in your own words what you think the author's attitude is about the topic.

_____

_____

_____

2. How convincing are the support points that the writer makes? How many of the types of support does the writer use? How convincing are the support points that the writer makes? Do quotes and statistics seem more convincing than opinion?

_____

_____

_____

Organization Patterns

Once you have made your pro/con list and have chosen the type of evidence you want to use to support your topic, you will need to organize your paragraph for an effective presentation. There is no defined pattern that a writer has to use when writing persuasively. However, several patterns logically come to mind that will organize your points into a convincing persuasive paragraph.

Pattern 1: Using only support points that argue for your point of view (only pro-list items if you are arguing for a point of view, or using only con-list items if you are arguing against a point of view).

Pattern 2: Stating only your opposition's support points (either pro or con) and arguing against them.

Pattern 3: Alternating use of support points for your side of the argument and listing your opponent's points and arguing against them. This is a hybrid of patterns 1 and 2.

Once the organization pattern has been chosen, select several points from the appropriate list or lists and write sentences for each. Arrange the sentences according to the organization pattern you have chosen.

The following are three persuasive paragraph examples using the pro/con list on page 233. Each paragraph is organized according to one of the three patterns you have studied.

Pattern 1 Persuasive Paragraph: Against Nuclear Energy (Con-List Items)

Topic Sentence
Con Item

Con Item

Conclusion
Con Item

Con Item

Example

Fact
Consequence
Conclusion

Conclusion

Nuclear energy should not be restored because of radioactive waste disposal problems and the possibility of a nuclear reactor accident. One of the problems with nuclear energy is waste management. Radioactive waste can remain dangerous for thousands of years; therefore, safe disposal sites must meet rigid safety standards to keep the public safe. Sites must be deep in the ground to shield the public from possible radiation exposure, and the sites must be immune to earthquake damage. Such sites are hard to find and expensive to maintain. In addition to the waste disposal problem, nuclear accidents pose a real danger to people living near nuclear reactors. In 1986, in the Ukrainian town of Chernobyl, a nuclear reactor accident put thousands at risk of radioactive poisoning. A radiation cloud spread over northern Europe and Great Britain. Thirty-one Soviet citizens died, and over 100,000 had to be evacuated from surrounding areas. The dangers involved in the long term control and management of such a volatile substance as radioactive materials make it a very risky proposition. Until more trustworthy safeguards can be developed in both the operation and waste disposal of radioactive substances, nuclear energy should remain a thing of the past.

Pattern 2 Persuasive Paragraph: Arguing Against the Opposition (Pro-List Items)

Topic Sentence
Opposition/Argument

Answering Opposition
Using a Fact
Consequence
Opposition/Argument

Answering Opposition (Fact)

Possible Consequence

Possible Consequence

Conclusion

Despite the possible benefits to society, nuclear energy should not be restored as a fuel source. Many scientists and researchers claim nuclear energy is desirable as an energy source because it creates enormous amounts of power from small resources. While this may be true, there are other costs that outweigh the purely monetary. In 1986, in the Ukrainian town of Chernobyl, a nuclear reactor accident killed 31 Soviet citizens and caused 100,000 people to be evacuated. A radioactive cloud covered much of northern Europe and Great Britain. Military leaders in Washington, D.C. state that a nuclear energy industry will also ensure a continuous source of radioactive material necessary to maintain our nuclear weapons arsenal for the defense of the nation. However, every year there are reports of nuclear byproducts missing from government inventories. Enemies of the United States could use this material to build nuclear weapons with which to threaten us. Also, the plans for building, running, and producing nuclear reactors for energy could be used to produce materials for making nuclear weapons and might be stolen and used by unfriendly nations. The potential for disaster far outweighs the potential benefits coming from a nuclear energy industry. Nuclear energy is not a safe or practical energy source.

Pattern 3 Persuasive Paragraph: Alternating Your Points with Arguing Against the Opposition's Points (Pro- and Con-List Items)

Topic Sentence
Con Item
Con Item
Conclusion

Opposition/Argument

Answering Opposition
Uusing a Fact

Consequences

Opinion
Answering Opposition (Fact)

Possible Consequence
Opposition/Argument

Answering Opposition (Opinion)

Conclusion

Despite the possible benefits to society, nuclear energy should not be restored as a fuel source. One of the problems with nuclear energy is waste management. Radioactive waste can remain dangerous for thousands of years; therefore, safe deposit sites must meet rigid safety standards to keep the public safe. Sites must be deep in the ground to shield the public from possible radiation exposure, and the sites must be immune to earthquake damage. Many scientists and researchers claim nuclear energy is desirable as an energy source because it creates enormous amounts of power from small resources. While this may be true, there are other costs that outweigh the purely monetary. In 1986, in the Ukrainian town of Chernobyl, a nuclear reactor accident killed 31 Soviet citizens and caused 100,000 people to be evacuated. A radioactive cloud covered much of northern Europe and Great Britain. Nuclear weapons proliferation is another problem if nuclear energy production is increased. Every year there are reports of nuclear byproducts missing from government inventories. Enemies of the United States could use this material to build nuclear weapons with which to threaten our security. Economists like to say that increasing the nuclear energy industry will create more high tech jobs, but the same industry will cause widespread unemployment in traditional fossil fuel industries like coal, oil, and gas. The potential for both disaster and a negative impact on the economy should convince lawmakers to prohibit the return of nuclear energy as a fuel source.

PRACTICE 8

On separate sheets of paper, write a persuasive paragraph for three of the topics below using a separate organization pattern for each. Write your completed draft on the lines provided.

Topics

The academic year should/should not be extended to 12 months with 2 weeks vacation every 3 months.

Tobacco and alcohol advertising should/should not be regulated.

Young people should/should not be given college tuition money for public service because soldiers are for military service.

All guns should/should not be licensed and registered with the authorities.

Prayer should/should not be allowed in public schools.

Welfare recipients should/should not have to have a job to receive benefits.

Grades should/should not be abolished as the method for judging student performance.

Marijuana should/should not be legalized for medical use.

All coursework should/should not transfer to any other college in the country.

Same-sex couples should/should not be allowed to legally marry.

Persuasive Paragraph—Pattern 1

_____

_____

_____

_____

_____

_____

_____

_____

_____

Persuasive Paragraph—Pattern 2

_____

_____

_____

_____

_____

_____

_____

_____

_____

Persuasive Paragraph—Pattern 3

_____

_____

_____

_____

_____

_____

_____

_____

_____

_____

▼ PRACTICE 9

Transitional expressions are useful in connecting related ideas and for adding rhythm to the paragraph so that it reads more smoothly. Rewrite the three persuasive paragraphs from Practice 8 using transitional expressions from the following list as appropriate.

Transitional Expressions for Persuasive Writing		
Answering the Opposition and Referring to Authority	**Predicting Consequences and Stating Conclusions**	**Facts and Examples**
according to...	consequently	another...
although	in conclusion	because
nevertheless	therefore	finally
of course	thus	first
on the other hand		for
others may say...		last
		next
		second
		since
		third

Pattern 1 Rewrite

_____

_____

_____

_____

_____

_____

_____

_____

_____

Pattern 2 Rewrite

_____

_____

_____

_____

_____

_____

_____

_____

_____

Pattern 3 Rewrite

_____

_____

_____

_____

_____

_____

_____

_____

_____

Suggested Writing Topics

1. Mandatory drug testing should/should not be allowed at schools.
2. Instant replay should/should not be used in all professional sports.
3. Controversial organizations (Communist Party, Ku Klux Klan) should/should not be allowed to advertise in campus publications.
4. Birth control products should/should not be distributed to any person wanting them.
5. Women should/should not be allowed to be combat soldiers in the military services.
6. Affirmative action should/should not be implemented for college enrollment.
7. The legal drinking age should/should not be eighteen years of age.
8. Marijuana should/should not be legalized for medical purposes.
9. English should/should not be legally designated as the official language of the United States.
10. Health insurance should/should not be made available for all citizens of the United States.

Persuasive Logic: Cause and Effect Reasoning

Often, when attempting to persuade someone about a belief or point of view you hold, you are also trying to convince them by pointing out special relationships that different things or events share. In persuasion, **cause/effect** reasoning can be a powerful tool in convincing your reader that your point of view is both logical and reasonable.

Cause/effect development explains the reasons behind *why* something occurs: **cause** analysis develops *why* something happens, and **effect** analysis explains *the results and consequences* stemming from the causes. These are called **causal relationships,** and they help us understand why things happen in the world around us and the possible consequences that may occur in the future.

For example, a writer might ask the question, "Why did President Clinton lie to the American public?" as a way of finding out the possible causes of this problem. (*Possible causes:* he didn't define his actions with Monica Lewinsky as "having sex"; he didn't want the First Lady, Hillary Rodham Clinton, to find out about his relationship with Ms. Lewinsky; he did not want to be embarrassed publicly in the press; he didn't want history to focus on this aspect of his presidency.) The writer also might ask, "What will happen because President Clinton lied to the American public?" as a way of figuring out the possible events that might occur in the future stemming from the lying. (*Possible effects:* he might be impeached for "high crimes and misdemeanors"; history books might focus on this aspect of his presidency rather than his successes with domestic and foreign affairs; the Democratic Party might find it harder to get legislation passed through Congress; Democratic candidates might find it difficult to get elected or re-elected to office.)

Obviously, the search for cause/effect answers can be a complex undertaking. More than one explanation can be found and, often, all the answers fit. This can be helpful in achieving thorough development of the issue. In persuasion, thoroughly developing your point of view can help you persuade your reader that your side of the issue has been both logically and reasonably stated.

Causal Chains

Whether you are focusing on cause or effect, it is helpful, before you begin writing, to develop a **causal chain.** A causal chain demonstrates the chain of events that can develop between things and can help clarify the relationships that exist between them, as well.

Example

CAUSES		EFFECTS
Too many unpaid bills	can lead to	increased physical tension.
Increased physical tension	can lead to	severe headaches.
Severe headaches	can lead to	nausea and loss of appetite.
Nausea and loss of appetite	can lead to	physical and mental fatigue.
Physical and mental fatigue	can lead to	health problems.

In the example above, notice how an effect can become a cause for the next effect, and so on. Things and events do not exist in a vacuum isolated from the other things and events around them. Yes, we can focus on cause, and we can focus on effect, but for your insights to be most persuasive, it will be helpful during your argument to share with the reader the knowledge you have learned from the causal chain.

Once a reader knows *why* something has happened and the consequences that might occur, they are much more receptive to accept your persuasive conclusions about the topic. In other words, they are clear as to why you feel the way you do, and "understanding" an issue is often half the battle to "accepting" the arguer's ideas concerning the issue.

Problems to Avoid

When using cause and effect reasoning, do not confuse **chronological sequence** and **coincidence** with true cause and effect relationships.

In chronological sequence, do not assume that because one event follows another in time that the first event causes the second to occur.

> **Example**
>
> After I attend a movie, I read in the paper several days later that another movie star has died. Therefore, my going to the movies causes actors to die. (There are literally thousands of movie stars spanning decades of time. One movie star is likely to die on almost any day of the week and, because they are famous, their passing also is likely to be reported in newspapers. So the chances of a movie star's death being reported at about the same time as you do anything, not just attending a movie, is a likely occurrence.)

With coincidence, do not assume that because one thing occurs that it is the cause for another thing that occurs, that a cause and effect relationship exists between them.

> **Example**
>
> Every time a black cat crosses my path, something bad happens to me. (Bad things indeed may happen to you, but the proverbial "black cat," as a cause of bad luck, is a superstition that has no basis in reality. Your "bad luck" is probably due to your not being properly prepared for the events in your life or possibly just being at the wrong place at the wrong time—chance occurrence.)

Transitional Expressions for Cause/Effect Writing

There are several transitional expressions you will find useful when writing about causes or effects.

Cause	Effect
because	as a consequence of
causes, caused by	as a result (of)
the reason…	consequently
since	then
	therefore

The Topic Sentence in a Cause/Effect Paragraph

After choosing your subject and figuring out some ideas using one or more of the prewriting techniques you have learned, you will need to decide whether you are going to focus on causes or effects. The topic sentence will announce your purpose to the reader, and it will clarify the paragraph's development.

Examples

Focus on Causes:

Proper nutrition, regular exercise, and a positive attitude can lead to a long, healthful life. (This essay will develop *proper nutrition, regular exercise, and a positive attitude* in the body paragraphs to show how each "causes" a *long, healthful life.*)

Focus on Effects:

A long, healthful life can increase earnings potential, intelligence levels, and an active retirement period. (This essay will develop *earnings potential, intelligence levels, and an active retirement period* as "effects" or "results" of a *long, healthful life.*)

▼ PRACTICE 10

This practice will help you develop a paragraph that focuses on causes.

1. Pick one of the following topics: divorce; poor job performance; disinterest in politics.

2. List as many causes of your topic choice as you can think of.

a. _____

b. _____

c. _____

d. _____

e. _____

3. If any of the causes in your list are merely chronological or coincidental, draw a line through them.

4. Write a topic sentence that focuses on causes.

_____

_____

5. Write a sentence for each of the remaining causes in your list.

_____

_____

_____

_____

_____

_____

6. On a separate sheet of paper, rewrite your sentences into paragraph form.

PRACTICE 11

This practice will help you develop a paragraph that focuses on effects.

1. Pick one of the following topics: drug abuse; dieting; organizational skills.

2. List as many effects of your topic choice as you can think of.

a. _____

b. _____

c. _____

d. _____

e. _____

3. If any of the effects in your list are merely chronological or coincidental, draw a line through them.

4. Write a topic sentence that focuses on effects.

_____

_____

5. Write a sentence for each of the remaining effects in your list.

_____

_____

_____

_____

_____

_____

6. On a separate sheet of paper, rewrite your sentences into paragraph form.

Suggested Writing Topics for Cause

1. The causes of drug abuse
2. The causes of the increasing high school dropout rate
3. The causes of test anxiety
4. The causes of high taxation
5. The causes of road rage
6. The causes of divorce

7. The causes of spousal abuse
8. The causes of a high teen pregnancy rate
9. The causes of low unemployment
10. The causes of high prison populations

Suggested Writing Topics for Effect

1. The effects of prejudice
2. The effects of pollution
3. The effects of a school grading system
4. The effects of over-prescribing antibiotics
5. The effects of high speed limits
6. The effects of high interest rates
7. The effects of international trade agreements
8. The effects of alcohol abuse
9. The effects of a tornado
10. The effects of a large corporation leaving a small town

CHAPTER REVIEW

▼ Writers use persuasion to try to convince others that their point of view is correct.

▼ Persuasion can be informal, semiformal, or very formal.

▼ The topic sentence in a persuasive paragraph states the writer's conclusion or point of view about a particular topic.

▼ Answering the opposition, referring to an authority, predicting consequences, facts, and examples are types of evidence.

▼ A fact differs from an opinion. An opinion is how we think about, or interpret, facts.

▼ To present a persuasive paragraph convincingly, the ideas must be organized into a pattern that offers the evidence and ideas in an effective manner.

▼ Cause and effect reasoning can be a powerful tool in convincing your reader that your point of view is both logical and reasonable.

▼ Cause analysis explains the reasons *why* something occurs.

▼ Effect analysis explains *the results and consequences* stemming from causes.

▼ Transitional expressions help organize and connect ideas. They also add rhythm to writing so it reads more smoothly.

Writing Opportunities

Home

The factory near your home has been releasing foul-smelling clouds of smoke for nearly three months. You have phoned City Hall on several occasions to complain, but nothing has been done. In an attempt to persuade the mayor of your city to look into the air pollution caused by the factory, write one paragraph detailing the problems associated with the factory's smokestacks.

School

Your Biology 101 professor's assignment sheet states that each student must find a potential source of pollution (air, water, or land) in the local community, and write a one-paragraph report detailing the potential hazardous conditions. The report should try to persuade people in the community that action needs to take place to correct the problem. You decide to write about the fumes coming from the smokestacks at the local chemical factory just outside of town.

Work

You work for the Environmental Protection Agency (EPA). Write a one-paragraph report convincing your boss to bring action against the factory in the photograph for violation of air pollution standards.

Visit *The Write Start* Online!

For additional practice with the materials found in this chapter, visit our Website at:

http://www.ablongman.com/checkett

The Website also features additional readings, quizzes, writing activities, and Internet links, as well as a bulletin board and interactive chat.

For More Practice with Your Grammar and Writing Skills

For further exercises designed to improve your writing and grammar skills, use the Writer's ToolKit Plus CD-ROM included with this text. The toolkit provides a wealth of computerized tutorials and practice activities.

Writing Effective Essays

Writing effective paragraphs is very useful when it comes to memos, short-answer exams, and brief writing assignments, but many business reports and longer college writing assignments require multiple paragraphs to explain many ideas.

Just as we joined together sentences to form a paragraph, we can join together paragraphs into a longer piece of writing called an *essay*.

CHAPTER 22

The Essay

Business and academic writing often requires considerable length to fully express a variety of complex ideas. Length in academic writing, in particular, often demands two to three pages in the form of an essay.

An **essay** is a written composition made up of a number of paragraphs that develop a particular subject. Therefore, an essay can be developed using the same methods demonstrated in the preceding chapters dealing with writing single paragraphs. Many of the same writing techniques are used in the essay as we used in learning to write the different kinds of paragraphs presented in Part 2 of this text.

Although an essay can have any number of paragraphs, we will use a five-paragraph model to introduce the basic elements of the essay.

The Five-Paragraph Essay

Almost all essays should have a **title.** The title should piqué the reader's interest. It should be a catchy or dramatic phrase, usually two to six words; longer titles can become wordy and cumbersome to read. If you can't come up with something clever or dramatic, pick several of the key words from your thesis sentence and use them. It's a good idea to wait until your essay is finished before you create the title. That way you give yourself enough time to fully understand the point of your essay and come up with the most appropriate title.

When writing your title, do the following:

1. Capitalize all words except articles (a, an, the) and prepositions (of, on, to, in).
2. Center the title on the page and leave two spaces between it and the introductory paragraph.

Do not put quotation marks on either side of the title, and do not underline it.

Most essays begin with the **introductory paragraph.** Its purpose is to introduce the reader to the topic of the essay. The paragraph consists of *introductory sentences* and the *thesis sentence.*

After the introductory paragraph comes the **body paragraphs.** Their purpose is to develop, support, and explain the topic idea stated in the thesis sentence. Body paragraphs consist of a *topic sentence* followed by *support sentences.*

The essay ends with the **concluding paragraph.** Its purpose is to bring the essay to a conclusion that gives the reader a sense of completeness. The most common methods for concluding the essay are emphasizing one of the following: *a call to action, a warning, a prediction,* or an *evaluation* of the important points.

The Introductory Paragraph

The purpose of the **introductory paragraph** is to introduce the reader to the topic of the essay. This is accomplished through a series of introductory sentences followed by the thesis sentence.

The Thesis Sentence

The most important element in an essay is the **thesis sentence** because it sets the tone for the entire essay. It states what the writer is going to explain, clarify, argue for/against about the topic/subject. It is usually placed as the last sentence in the introductory paragraph. The thesis sentence is a roadmap for the entire essay.

▼ It announces the overall topic/subject.
▼ It states the writer's attitude toward the subject.
▼ It outlines the organizational structure of the entire essay.
▼ It limits the scope of the essay using an essay map.
▼ It is not expressed as a fact.
▼ It expresses the topic as an opinion that can be discussed.
▼ It is never expressed as a question.

The writer's **attitude** is simply how the writer feels about the topic at hand. The verb in the topic sentence usually starts to express the writer's attitude about the subject. For example, the verbs *are/are not, is/is not, should/should not,* and *can/can not,* begin to tell you how the writer feels about the subject. Perhaps, the topic is good citizenship, and the writer feels that reading a newspaper each day will make people better informed about community affairs, thus making them good citizens. The verb and the wording after the verb finishes expressing the writer's attitude. So, the verb "will make," when tied to the idea of "good citizen," expresses the writer's attitude that "reading a newspaper" will make people good citizens. As a writer, your attitude can not only express why the subject is important to you but also why you think the subject should be important to the reader.

Examples

In the following sentences, the attitudes are italicized.

1. Breakfast *is the most important* meal of the day.
2. *Psycho is a scary* movie because of the shower scene.
3. Vitamin supplements *can help* you feel more energized.
4. Vitamins *have no* role in whether or not you feel more energized.
5. Ford *makes better* trucks than Chevrolet.

Essay Map

Because you are learning to write an essay with three development paragraphs, the three-item essay map located in the thesis sentence will both organize and limit your essay's topic discussion. Each of the three essay map items will become the topic for each of the three development paragraphs. To do this most effectively, this chapter demonstrates and uses the thesis sentence containing the three **essay map** items. The essay map automatically organizes the essay for you and limits its scope.

> ### Examples
>
> In the following sentences, the essay map is italicized.
>
> **1.** To be safe during a tornado alert, people should *go to the basement, hide inside an interior room closet,* or *get underneath a heavy piece of furniture.*
> **2.** *Intelligence, dedication,* and *hard work* are necessary ingredients for a successful career.
> **3.** Because of an *excessive military budget, poor farming methods,* and *insufficient international trade strategies,* Communism was a failure in Russia.

PRACTICE 1

Rewrite the following thesis sentences if the essay map items do not explain, clarify, or support the writer's attitude about the topic. If the essay map does explain, clarify, or support the writer's attitude about the topic, write **correct** in the space provided.

Example: Thesis Sentence: *St. Louis is an exciting city to visit because of clouds, elm trees, and cats.*

Topic: St. Louis

Attitude: An **exciting** city to visit

Why: Clouds, elm trees, cats (the three-item essay map)

Problem: The three essay map items are not exciting reasons to visit the city.

Rewrite: St. Louis is an exciting city to visit because of the fantastic array of restaurants, the tremendous number of cultural attractions, and the dazzling scenery.

In this rewritten thesis sentence, the essay map items better explain why the city is exciting to visit. Additionally, the writer has chosen descriptive adjectives that also support the "exciting" attitude—*fantastic, tremendous,* and *dazzling.*

1. A vegetarian diet is healthier than one with meat because of temperature, salt, and water retention.

   _____

   _____

   _____

2. Expanding your vocabulary, learning about new places, and developing a better writing style makes reading a valuable activity.

   _____

   _____

   _____

3. Weekly household chores help children learn math, tuna salad, and opera houses.

   _____

   _____

   _____

4. Cultural awareness, civic responsibility, and volunteerism make coin collecting an interesting hobby.

   _____

   _____

   _____

5. Maintaining a successful professional sports career is difficult because of talented newcomers, the constant travel, and the aging process.

   _____

   _____

   _____

Putting It All Together

It is vital that your thesis sentence be constructed properly. Without a good thesis sentence, the essay cannot succeed. To check your thesis sentence, ask this question:

Do the **essay map items** explain or support why the writer has chosen the **attitude** about the **topic?**

Examples

Poor	Voting and military service are important activities for all citizens. (two topics, no essay map)
Better	Voting is an important responsibility for all citizens. (one topic and clear attitude, no essay map)
Good	Voting is an important responsibility for all citizens because it gives people a voice in how the government is run, removes ineffective politicians from office, and influences political decision making. (one topic, clear attitude, three-item essay map)
Poor	Many students work while going to school. (statement of fact, no attitude, no essay map)
Better	Working, while going to school, can teach students valuable lessons. (one topic, clear attitude, no essay map)
Good	Working, while going to school, can teach students responsibility, organizational skills, and teamwork. (one topic, clear attitude, three-item essay map)
Poor	Are regular automobile oil changes really necessary? (question—not a clear opinion, no essay map)
Better	Regular oil changes can keep a car running better. (one topic, a clearly stated opinion, no essay map)
Good	Regular oil changes can keep a car running more efficiently, improve gas mileage, and reduce long-term maintenance costs. (one topic, clear attitude, three-item essay map)

▼ PRACTICE 2

In each of the following thesis sentences, underline the topic once, circle the attitude, and underline the essay map twice. On the line provided, indicate if any element is missing.

1. Broccoli and oranges are good sources for vitamins.

_____

2. Playmaking, speed, and bench-clearing brawls make ice hockey an exciting sport.

_____

3. The Rolex is considered by many as a better wristwatch than the Breitling.

_____

4. College students go to class, study, and write papers.

_____

5. Laptop computers are good buys because of portability.

_____

6. Solar power should be a governmental priority because of diminishing fossil fuels, environmental pollution, and skyrocketing costs.

_____

7. Bungee jumping is a dangerous activity.

_____

8. The St. Louis Rams, Green Bay Packers, and Pittsburgh Steelers are football teams.

_____

9. Are savings bonds better investment instruments than annuities because of interest, safety, and liquidity?

_____

10. Humor, social satire, and musicality, have made the Beatles popular long after their breakup as a rock group.

_____

PRACTICE 3

From Practice 2, rewrite those sentences that do not meet the necessary criteria for an effective thesis sentence. Number your finished sentences.

_____

_____

_____

_____

_____

_____

_____

_____

_____

_____

_____

▼ **PRACTICE 4**

Write thesis sentences for the following topics. Use the criteria for writing an effective thesis sentence that you have studied.

1. A movie you have seen

_____

_____

2. A social issue you are interested in

_____

_____

3. A job you have or would like to have

_____

_____

4. A famous person you admire

_____

_____

5. A piece of artwork you like

_____

_____

Introductory Sentences

In the introductory paragraph, the thesis sentence is introduced by **introductory sentences.** The introductory sentences should catch the reader's attention and clarify your tone (humorous, serious, or satiric). Some effective techniques for introducing the thesis sentence are as follows:

▼ *Shocking statistics or statements*

> One of every four babies born in America is born out of wedlock. Fifty percent of teenage deaths involves alcohol. More Americans die and are injured in automobile accidents than from all diseases combined. It's time something is done about these national tragedies. (*Place thesis sentence here*)

▼ *A series of questions*

> Tired of the same old political promises? Are the current politicians in Washington, D.C. not representing your concerns? Are you thinking about not voting in the upcoming elections? Maybe you simply need to find a new direction. *(Place thesis sentence here)*

▼ *A common problem or misconception*

> Most people think welfare only goes to poor people living in the inner city. They believe that welfare recipients have no job and are hopelessly lazy, and that welfare recipients are poorly educated and lack skills necessary to hold a job. What you don't realize about welfare and who gets it may shock you. *(Place thesis sentence here)*

▼ PRACTICE 5

Write introductory sentences for each of the following thesis sentences. Try to create at least three sentences that lead logically to the thesis sentence.

1. Expanding your vocabulary, learning about new places, and developing a better writing style make reading a valuable activity.

_____

_____

_____

_____

_____

2. Solar power should be a governmental priority because of diminishing fossil fuels, environmental pollution, and skyrocketing costs.

_____

_____

_____

_____

_____

_____

3. Maintaining a successful professional sports career is difficult because of talented newcomers, the constant travel, and the aging process.

_____

_____

_____

_____

_____

The Body Paragraphs

The **body paragraphs** get their organization from the three-item essay map located in the thesis sentence. Each topic for each body paragraph is taken from the essay map in the thesis sentence. There are two types of sentences in the body paragraph: the *topic sentence* and *support sentences*.

The Topic Sentence

The **topic sentence** tells the reader what the main idea, or topic, of the paragraph is. Although there is no set place in the paragraph for the topic sentence, making the topic sentence the first sentence in the paragraph will make organizing and developing the topic easier.

The topic sentence has two parts: the *topic/subject* and the *controlling idea*. The **topic** is the subject of the paragraph taken from the essay map in the thesis sentence. The **controlling idea** states what the writer will be developing about the subject of the paragraph. The controlling idea limits what you can say about the subject so that you don't stray to other subject areas.

Topic sentences missing a controlling idea lack focus and specific direction. Without a controlling idea, the writer's attitude about the subject can be unclear.

> **Examples**
>
> Soccer is a popular high school sport. (no controlling idea—popular is too ambiguous)
>
> Michael Jordan was a popular basketball player. (no controlling idea—simply a statement of fact)
>
> Soccer is a popular high school sport because it is relatively inexpensive to fund. (controlling idea: cheap funding makes soccer popular)
>
> Michael Jordan's diverse skills made him an exciting basketball player. (controlling idea: Jordan is exciting because of diverse skills.)

Support Sentences

Support sentences follow the topic sentence and develop the subject using specific examples, details, and facts. These support ideas must be consistent with the controlling idea. In other words, the controlling idea unifies the paragraph by determining the kind of support ideas you can use in the support sentences.

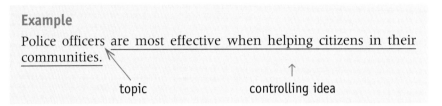

Example

Police officers are most effective when helping citizens in their communities.

topic   controlling idea

Support sentences for this topic sentence would focus on *what* police officers do to help citizens and might include such activities as

    a. finding lost/stolen property
    b. solving crimes
    c. preventing crimes

Six Important Support Questions

When writing a story, reporters ask six questions. The answers provide the focus that allows them to select the details, facts, and examples to develop the story with specific information. The six questions are *who, what, where, when, why,* and *how.*

After you have selected, or have been given, the topic you are to write about, decide on the controlling idea. To do this, choose which of the following reporter's questions allows you to write about the topic with the desired focus.

For instance, your topic is An Important Event. In the support sentences, you could focus on

Who?	Who started the event?
	Who attended/witnessed/participated in the event?
	Who was affected by the event?
What?	What was the event?
	What happened before/during/after the event?
	What was special about the event?
Where?	Where did the event occur?
	Did the location affect the event in any way?
	Did the location have historical significance?
When?	When did the event occur (A.M./P.M., day, month, year)?
	Did the time frame add any special significance to the event?
	Did the event coincide with a historically significant time?
Why?	Why did the event occur?
	Why was the event important?
How?	How did the event happen?
	How was the event funded?
	How was the event advertised?

You can add your own focus to these questions if other ideas come to you. There is no need to limit yourself to the list above.

> **Examples**
> **1.** Reading can help people become better educated.
> **2.** Reading is best done in a quiet, secluded place.
> **3.** Anyone interested in becoming a better writer should read as much as possible.

Although the topic subject of each sentence, Reading, is the same, the focus of the controlling idea is different. In sentence 1, the focus is on *what* reading can do for people (educate them); in sentence 2, the focus is on *where* reading is best accomplished (in a quiet, secluded place); and, in sentence 3, the focus is on *who* (anyone interested in becoming a writer).

For a more developed discussion of body paragraphs and outlining, see Chapter 13.

The Concluding Paragraph

An essay should not suddenly stop after you have finished discussing the last body paragraph topic. You should leave your reader with a feeling of completion. Use the concluding paragraph to emphasize why your essay is important. The **concluding paragraph** can help convince your reader that your ideas are valid. The concluding paragraph should not introduce new points; developing new points is the function of the body paragraphs. However, the concluding paragraph should give the points you have made a dramatic purpose. Also, it is not necessary to restate the thesis sentence and essay-map items at the end of your essay unless you are doing a longer paper. In a short, five-paragraph essay, the reader is not likely to forget three points.

Just as there were several introductory techniques you could use in the introductory paragraph, there also are several concluding techniques that you can use in the concluding paragraph. These include:

▼ Call to action
▼ Warning
▼ Prediction
▼ Evaluation

Call to Action
You are actually asking the reader to take action, to do something.

> **Example**
> New subdivisions are necessary to house the burgeoning population in our suburbs, but the wholesale destruction of mature trees simply to make building easier is not an acceptable construction practice. <u>Call your local alderperson, and complain about this anti-environmental practice.</u> It takes 20 to 30 years for a sapling to mature into a fully foliaged shade tree.

Warning

You are warning the reader that there is the possibility of something adverse happening.

> **Example**
>
> Buying products and services on the Internet is becoming commonplace. The amount of money being spent online is doubling every year. The main reason for the Internet's popularity for consumers is convenience. However, be careful when giving out credit card numbers on the Internet. <u>Unauthorized use of credit cards is a growing problem for Internet shoppers.</u> Make sure that the online business you are dealing with has a secure server for credit information. Your economic security is at stake.

Prediction

You "look into the future," so to speak, and predict outcomes stemming from the topic.

> **Example**
>
> The new suburban vans are becoming bigger every year. They look like off-road vehicles with glandular problems. The extra roominess inside the vans are great for large families, hauling Little League teams, and traveling with lots of luggage. But the larger vehicles are hard to handle, and their greater bumper height and extra weight make for more damage to regular-sized cars when accidents occur. <u>Because of the proliferation of these monster-vans, insurance rates will surely rise in the near future.</u> Suburban van manufacturers should begin to study ways to counter this potential negative impact on all drivers.

Evaluation

You summarize the importance of the overall topic.

> **Example**
>
> Studying plants in the Amazon rainforest has had and will continue to have many benefits for society. <u>New drugs to combat disease are an important result of these studies. Additionally, new antibiotics are needed to replace those that bacteria have become resistant to because of overuse.</u> Synthetic derivatives also can be developed from studying the new drugs. The Amazon rainforest is a valuable resource for all the world.

Sample Student Essay

The following is a student essay demonstrating all the elements of an effectively written essay that you have learned in this chapter. The key elements and concepts are noted in the margin and underlined in the text of the essay.

In this essay, student writer Nancy Smith relates the emotionally devastating effects of finding out that her 3-year old son has cancer, followed by the equally disturbing period of surgery and treatment.

The Ravages of Childhood Cancer

Shocking Statistic

Shocking Statement

Introductory Paragraph

Thesis Sentence with Three-Item Essay Map "Terrifying" Is the Attitude Controlling Idea: "What"

Topic Sentence: "Diagnosis"

Support Sentences: The Ordeal of the Diagnostic Procedure

Topic Sentence: "Surgery"

Body Paragraphs #1, #2, #3

Support Sentences: Emphasis on "Time"

Topic Sentence: "Treatment"

Support Sentences: The Difficulty of Treatment

Call to Action Concluding Paragraph

Prediction

Nearly one-third of all children diagnosed as having a childhood malignancy die. This number strikes fear into the heart of any parent unfortunate enough to have to face such awful news about their child. Most everyone has been a patient in a hospital, but a grave uncertainty about leaving alive is not a common experience. Being told, "If there is a type of cancer to have, this is the kind," is of little comfort. The "C" word is frightening in any context. Diagnosis, surgery, and treatment are terrifying experiences for the family of a child having cancer.

We had taken him to Cardinal Glennon Children's Hospital for testing to find out a diagnosis. When he had not felt good over the past month, cancer was not even a remote thought in any of our minds. Apparently, it was for the doctors. Nurses tried five times before successfully finding a vein that would hold the IV tube. Derek cried out of pain and fear. I could feel myself becoming nauseous as I tried to comfort him. Next, we moved to the ultrasound room where Derek, exhausted from the IV ordeal, slept soundly. The doctor inspected the screen. Yes! There it was. A tumor the size of a quarter. Wilms tumor, otherwise known as cancer of the kidney, was Derek's diagnosis.

As the day of the surgery arrived, the family gathered at the hospital. We were told the operation to remove the tumor and infected kidney would take two to three hours. Although sedated, Derek looked at me longingly through frightened eyes. I was surrounded by my entire family, but I never felt more vulnerable. Three hours passed, then four, with no word. My hand trembled uncontrollably as I tried to sip from my coffee cup; I could not stop the tears welling in my eyes. Finally, after five hours, the surgeon entered the waiting room and told us the results. He was fairly certain they had gotten all of the tumor. If all went well, Derek would start chemotherapy and be released from the hospital in two weeks.

Derek's treatment consisted of six radiation therapy sessions and chemotherapy spread over a one and a half year period. The radiation came first—once a day for six consecutive days. The procedure only lasted a few minutes; however, thirty minutes after the session Derek would vomit every fifteen minutes for hours. His little body would convulse like a dying snake's. His little voice split the air with terrifying screams. The chemotherapy started early and lasted all day. The medicine was administered through a port-catheter in his chest. After the chemo was injected, Derek would be sick for days.

It's been five years since the operation, and there has been no sign of a tumor on his remaining kidney. The prognosis is good. Doctors and scientists still do not know all the causes of the various forms of cancer. Research is needed at all levels, so give generously to the Cancer Foundation. Someone once said that a statistic is a victim without the tears. Your continued support of cancer research will help eliminate future statistics.

Sample Student Essay

In the following essay, student writer Rebecca Eisenbath revisits a horrendous time in our history—the genocide of six million people based on their race, religion, or nationality at the hands of Adolf Hitler and the Nazis before and during World War II.

First, read the essay. Then, answer the questions following the essay.

The Holocaust: The Ashes Remain

Most people know that World War II began in September of 1939 when Germany invaded Poland. But the year 1933 may not ring any bells; however, the event that began that year surely would: the beginning of the Holocaust. Over the next decade, six million people would be exterminated in what became euphemistically known as "the Final Solution." The Holocaust remains one of the most devastating events in human history due to its horrendous policies, numbers of victims, and the terrible effect it continues to have on the survivors and the people around the world.

Germany's horrendous policies led to the decision to commit genocide. Hitler and his followers believed their Aryan race was the only one that deserved to rule other "inferior" races, and they made slave laborers of those different than themselves. They blamed the Jews for their economic problems, so Reinhard Heydrich, the Chief of Reich Security, thought up the idea of mass extermination in prisoner camps. This policy came to be known as the "Final Solution." All Jews had to wear an identification badge or armband emblazoned with a yellow Star of David. They either were herded into traincars and taken to the extermination camps, or they were imprisoned in ghettos and killed by bands of SS military units.

The Holocaust also was alarming because of the numbers and types of people it claimed. The total death toll was over six million. Although they are the most written about because of the sheer numbers that were killed, the "Final Solution" did not stop with the Jews. Catholics, Poles, Czechs, Gypsies, homosexuals, and even the mentally ill were shot, gassed, poisoned, and tortured until merciful death came.

Near the end of the war, when the Allies overran German held countries, they liberated the concentration camps. What they found inside, emaciated prisoners, huge ovens filled with human bones, and mass graves overflowing with bodies, devastated many of the liberators. Many of these men had to undergo years of psychological treatment to deal with the horrors of the camps. The Jewish survivors were sent to Palestine after the war to try and rebuild their lives. Three years later, the State of Israel was recognized by the United Nations. The survivors of the Holocaust, although never forgetting their pain (how could they with camp numbers tattooed on their forearms?), never lost hope.

Even today, the world cannot escape what happened so many decades ago. In 1993, two museums commemorating the Holocaust were dedicated in the United States. Yet, the practice of genocide still exists as wars rage in parts of Asia, Africa, and Europe. Nations must learn from the past or, as we are seeing today, we will be doomed to repeat it. Be an advocate for peace, and let your congresspersons know how you want them to act.

Questions

1. What type of introductory technique does the writer use?

_____

2. Write the thesis sentence on the line below.

_____

_____

_____

3. Identify the topic in the thesis sentence.

_____

4. Identify the attitude.

_____

5. What are the three essay-map items?

_____

_____

6. Write the three topic sentences of the three body paragraphs on the lines below. Underline the topic in each sentence.

_____

_____

_____

_____

7. Choose the method by which the writer develops the topic in each of the body paragraphs: who, what, where, when, why, or how?

Body paragraph 1 _____

Body paragraph 2 _____

Body paragraph 3 _____

8. What technique(s) does the writer use in the concluding paragraph?

_____

_____

PRACTICE 7

Sample Student Essay

In the following essay, student writer Tim Schuette explores why exercising properly can be a benefit to your health.

First, read the essay. Then, answer the questions following the essay.

Effective Exercising

Are you overweight? After cutting the grass, are you exhausted? Are you unable to keep up with your friends or your children? Would you like to feel younger? Exercising the upper body, abdominal, and leg muscles correctly is important for proper functioning.

The most important muscles to exercise in the upper body are the triceps, biceps, and pectorals. The triceps and biceps, located in the upper arm, work as a team so that your arm can flex at the elbow. Exercising only one or the other of these muscles can reduce flexibility and can facilitate injuries like "tennis elbow." When you exercise the chest, you need to use an equal amount of weight in each hand and do the exact number of repetitions so that neither right nor left pectoral muscle will dominate the other. When this happens, "pulled" muscle injuries occur more often. The upper body muscles will work freely and efficiently when exercised proportionately.

The abdominal muscles are significant because they support the entire body. Therefore, you need them to simply sit upright in a chair. The abdominals consist of eight separate muscles that must be exercised for total effectiveness. The upper and lower muscles, known as the "six pack," are located from navel to chest, and they support your body front to back. The oblique muscles are located on either side of the "six pack" and assist in supporting the body when bending left or right. If your back is constantly hurting or you simply want to lose that "spare tire," then exercising the abdominals is essential.

The three major muscles in the legs give you the ability to stand, walk, run, and jump. The rectus femoris and the semitendinous are located in the upper leg. The gastrocnemius better known as the calf muscle, is located in the lower leg. The upper leg muscles make the leg bend at the knee, and the lower leg muscles make the foot moveable. If the muscles are worked unevenly, they can become damaged; additionally, injured or weakened leg muscles can cause shin splints and hip problems. Also, the leg muscles must be exercised properly when you are younger, so that more problems won't occur as you get older.

No single muscle works by itself; therefore, it is important to exercise all your muscles and their group partners evenly. If your muscles are worked correctly, you will lose weight, have more energy, and feel younger. A total workout only takes about thirty minutes, three times per week. Exercise regularly. Your body deserves it!

Questions

1. What type of introductory paragraph technique does the writer use?

_____

2. Write the thesis sentence on the line below.

_____

_____

3. Identify the topic in the thesis sentence.

_____

4. Identify the attitude.

_____

5. What are the three essay-map items?

_____

_____

_____

6. Write the three topic sentences of the three body paragraphs on the lines below. Underline the topic in each sentence.

_____

_____

_____

_____

7. Choose the method by which the writer develops the topic in each of the body paragraphs: who, what, where, when, why, and how.

Body paragraph 1 _____

Body paragraph 2 _____

Body paragraph 3 _____

8. What technique(s) does the writer use in the concluding paragraph?

_____

_____

CHAPTER REVIEW

▼ An essay consists of a number of paragraphs that develop a particular topic.
▼ Almost all essays should have a title.
▼ Most essays begin with an introductory paragraph. Its purpose is to introduce the reader to the topic of the essay.
▼ The introductory paragraph consists of introductory sentences and the thesis sentence.
▼ The thesis sentence names the topic of the essay, gives the writer's attitude toward the topic, and organizes the body paragraphs through the use of an essay map.
▼ The essay-map items become the topics for the body paragraphs.

▼ Introductory sentences introduce the thesis by piquing the reader's interest through using a shocking statistic or statement, a series of questions, or by stating a common problem or misconception.

▼ Body paragraphs develop, support, and explain the topic idea stated in the thesis.

▼ Body paragraphs consist of topic sentences and support sentences.

▼ Topic sentences have two parts: the topic/subject and the controlling idea.

▼ The controlling idea unifies the paragraph by determining the kind of support ideas the writer can use in the support sentences.

▼ To support and develop the body paragraphs, the six reporter's questions can be used: who, what, where, when, why, and how.

▼ The essay ends with a concluding paragraph. Its purpose is to bring the essay to a conclusion that gives the reader a sense of completeness.

▼ The most common methods for concluding the essay are to emphasize one of the following: a call to action, a warning, a prediction, or an evaluation of the important points.

Writing Opportunities

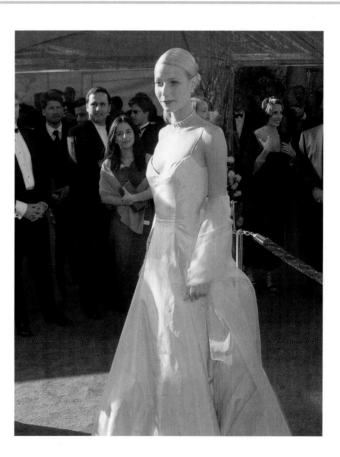

Home

You convince your spouse to take you to your 25th high school reunion. It's a formal affair, strictly tuxedos and gowns. From 7 in the evening until 2 in the morning, you and your old classmates dance to the music popular the year you graduated and reminisce about the good old days at Smarmy High. When you return home, you are so excited about what you have witnessed that you decide to write about the experience and send copies to all your friends and relatives around the country. In hopes of organizing the vast amount of details in your mind, and remembering your writing class from college, you decide to write a five-paragraph essay using the thesis sentence with three-item essay map.

School

You are a reporter for your school newspaper. Your editor wants a five-paragraph column detailing the major events at the year's biggest campus social activity, the Homecoming Formal Dance. You decide to make the Homecoming Queen the focus of your story.

Work

As a freelance writer, you'll take any assignment as long as the money is right or the subject interests you. For the right price, the editor of a popular national magazine, concerned with "the rich and famous," has convinced you to write a five-paragraph article about the movie industry's Academy Awards Ceremony. You decide that the focus of your article will be the crowds, the parade of stars, and the unfolding pageantry.

Visit *The Write Start* Online!

For additional practice with the materials found in this chapter, visit our Website at:

http://www.ablongman.com/checkett

The Website also features additional readings, quizzes, writing activities, and Internet links, as well as a bulletin board and interactive chat.

For More Practice with Your Grammar and Writing Skills

For further exercises designed to improve your writing and grammar skills, use the Writer's ToolKit Plus CD-ROM included with this text. The toolkit provides a wealth of computerized tutorials and practice activities.

The Writer's Resources

PARTS OF SPEECH

Nouns

Nouns are words that stand for people, places, or things. They can be singular or plural.

Nouns	Singular	Plural
Person	man	men
	woman	women
	child	children
Place	cave	caves
	beach	beaches
	forest	forests
	yard	yards
	mountain	mountains
Thing	ring	rings
	computer	computers
	discussion	discussions
	truth	truths
	sport	sports
	idea	ideas
	vacation	vacations
	conversation	conversations

To **form the plural of most nouns,** you simply add an *–s* or *–es* to the end of the word. However, there are some exceptions:

1. Nouns ending in *–f* or *–ve* form the plural by adding *–ves*:

half	halves
shelf	shelves

2. Hyphenated nouns (names that are formed by joining several short words with hyphens "-") form plurals by adding *–s* or *–es* to the main word in the phrase:

mother-in-law	mothers-in-law
sergeant-at-arms	sergeants-at-arms

3. Some nouns form plurals in other ways, such as by changing the spelling of the plural form. These are sometimes called irregular forms of plural nouns:

foot	feet
child	children

criterion	criteria
woman	women
man	men

4. Other nouns do not change at all when forming the plural. These exceptions must simply be memorized:

fish	fish
deer	deer
shrimp	shrimp

Nouns can also be classified as *proper* and *common*. **Proper nouns** are the specific names or titles of people, places, or things, and they are capitalized. **Common nouns** are general terms for people, places, or things, and they are not capitalized.

Common Nouns	Proper Nouns
singer	Sheryl Crow
beach	Corona Del Mar
magazine	*Time*
student	Julianne

PRACTICE EXERCISE: NOUNS

Underline the nouns in the following sentences

Example: The <u>family</u> travels to the <u>mountains</u> every <u>weekend</u>.

1. They pack up the family van, drive two hours, and arrive at the small cabin in Big Bear Lake.

2. The weekend is spent relaxing in the fresh air.

3. The four children spend their time hiking, skiing, swimming, or reading, depending on the season.

4. The parents try to relax as they do the yardwork, repair the cabin, and prepare meals for the children.

5. When they get home, the kids are relaxed but the parents are exhausted.

Pronouns

A **pronoun** is a word that takes the place of, or refers to, nouns. The word or words that the pronoun refers to are known as the **antecedent(s)** of the pronoun.

> **Example**
>
> Fariba said that she did not understand the question. (she is the pronoun, and Fariba is its antecedent)

Pronouns can be divided into several categories. The most common categories are *personal pronouns, relative pronouns, demonstrative pronouns, indefinite pronouns,* and *reflexive pronouns.*

Personal Pronouns

Personal pronouns are those that refer to a person *(I/me, you, he/him, she/her, it, we/us,* and *they/them). Personal pronouns* are divided into three forms, depending on how they are used in a sentence. These forms are **subjective** (pronoun used as a subject), **objective** (pronoun used as an object), or **possessive** (the pronoun indicates possession/ownership).

Subjective Pronouns

	Singular	Plural
1st person	I	we
2nd person	you	you
3rd person	he, she, it	they

Objective Pronouns

	Singular	Plural
1st person	me	us
2nd person	you	you
3rd person	him, her, it	them

Possessive Pronouns

	Singular	Plural
1st person	my (mine)	our (ours)
2nd person	your (yours)	your (yours)
3rd person	his (his)	their (theirs)
	her (hers)	
	its (its)	

The following examples demonstrate the uses of these three types of personal pronouns:

I frequently listen to music when I drive. (subjective pronoun; the pronoun is used as a subject)

They enjoy decorating their home. (subjective pronoun)

Dave is starting to annoy you. (objective pronoun; the pronoun is the object of the sentence)

He gave the same gift to him. (objective pronoun)

That is my sweater. (possessive pronoun; the pronoun shows ownership or possession)

He borrowed her keys. (possessive pronoun)

▼ PRACTICE EXERCISE: PERSONAL PRONOUNS

In the following sentences, underline subjective pronouns once, objective pronouns twice, and possessive pronouns three times. Some sentences may contain more than one type.

1. He came home from work.

2. His new car was covered with oak leaves.

3. As she walked to the water cooler, her shoe came off and slid under a desk.

4. They decided that not participating in the parade was a better decision for them.

5. It will not be as surprising to you after they explain the rules.

6. Would you like to eat at your place or ours?

7. We sold their horses for them while they were in Europe.

8. It was never my intention to buy his car for you.

9. It's never a good idea to put all of your investments into one stock.

10. I thought the best plan for you would be to go with them to the game.

Relative Pronouns

Relative pronouns are those pronouns used to introduce a qualifying or explanatory clause.

Relative Pronouns	
who	Used as a subject in reference to people
whom	Used as an object in reference to people
which	Used as a subject in reference to things
that	Used as a subject in reference to people or things
whoever	Used as a subject in reference to an uncertain number of people
whichever	Used as a subject in reference to an uncertain number of things

The following examples illustrate the use of relative pronouns:

Who made the phone call? (*Who* is used as the subject)

The phone call was made by *whom?* (*Whom* is used as the object)

Which movie shall we watch tonight? (*Which* is used as a subject referring to things)

I don't like *that!* (*That* is used as the object referring to a thing)

▼
PRACTICE EXERCISE: RELATIVE PRONOUNS

Choose the correct relative pronoun in the following sentences.

Example: The scientist <u>who</u> is studying AIDS received a grant.

1. _____ field of study has he chosen as a major?

2. For _____ did he buy this bicycle?

3. _____ wants to go to the concert may go.

4. The biology lab _____ I attend is three hours long.

5. He did not know _____ the performance had been cancelled.

Demonstrative Pronouns

These pronouns are used to point out or specify certain people, places, or things.

Demonstrative Pronouns		
	Singular	**Plural**
	this	these
	that	those

Indefinite Pronouns

These pronouns do not refer to a specific person; they refer to general or indeterminate people, places, or things.

Indefinite Pronouns

These pronouns do not refer to a specfic person.

Singular

everyone	someone	anyone	no one
everybody	somebody	anybody	nobody
everything	something	anything	nothing
each	another	either	neither

Singular or Plural

all	more	none
any	most	some

Plural

both	few	many	several

Reflexive Pronouns

The reflexive form adds –*self* or –*selves* to the pronoun and is used to indicate action performed to or on the antecedent.

Reflexive Pronouns

		Singular	**Plural**
1st person	(I)	myself	(we) ourselves
2nd person	(you)	yourself	(you) yourselves
3rd person	(he)	himself	(they) themselves
	(she)	herself	
	(it)	itself	

The following examples illustrate the use of the reflexive pronoun:

We gave *ourselves* a party to celebrate the end of the school year.
Vinh found *himself* in an impossible situation.

The reflexive pronoun form can also be used to intensify meaning. When a reflexive pronoun is used this way it is called an **intensifier.**

The instructor *herself* found the concepts confusing.
Raoul *himself* had made the engine.

▼
PRACTICE EXERCISE: DEMONSTRATIVE AND REFLEXIVE PRONOUNS

In the following sentences, draw a line through the incorrect pronoun, and write in the correct form.

1. Them tennis shoes belong to the team.

2. Those pie will be eaten after the dance.

3. Every Thursday, we treat ourself to a root beer float for lunch.

4. After I considered all my options, this are the ones I chose to use.

5. I bought a new shirt for himself.

Pronoun-Antecedent Agreement

It is important that pronouns agree with their antecedents. For example, the singular antecedent *everyone* must be used with the singular pronouns *he* or *she*.

The following examples illustrate sentences in which pronouns agree with the antecedent:

> If *someone* works late at night, *he* or *she* may not be able to concentrate in class the next morning.
>
> Or
>
> When Adam works late at night, *he* is not able to concentrate in class the next morning.
>
> *Each* ticket holder stood in line waiting for *his* or *her* refund.
>
> *Many* were angry that *their* efforts had not been rewarded.

▼
PRACTICE EXERCISE 1: PRONOUN-ANTECEDENT AGREEMENT

Fill in the blanks with the correct pronouns. Underline the antecedent of each pronoun.

Example: All <u>students</u> must do _____**their**_____ assigned reading before class.

1. Each soccer player gave _____ best effort in the world cup match.

2. Jennifer referred to recent local social conflict in _____ history project.

3. Anyone can learn to dance if _____ has a patient instructor.

4. Someone left _____ clothes all over the locker room.

5. The managers want us to attend _____ sales meeting next week.

6. Although the average consumer wants the best price, _____ may not shop carefully enough to find one.

7. Lana and Patricia gave _____ opinions to Alicia.

8. The creative writing students turned in _____ portfolios.

9. She grows tomatoes and green beans; _____ taste best fresh from the garden.

10. _____ is going to the dance with _____ date.

PRACTICE EXERCISE 2: PRONOUN-ANTECEDENT AGREEMENT

Correct any errors in pronoun reference in the sentences below. Put a **C** in the blank if the sentence has no error in pronoun reference.

                                        its
Example: _____ The business has ~~their~~ problems.

1. _____ The jury delayed their verdict.

2. _____ Mr. Billings' class is planning for its field trip to the science center.

3. _____ The crowd roared their approval as the ball dropped in Times Square.

4. _____ The group of friends have continued to share their lives over many years.

5. _____ The family did not take their annual vacation to the beach this year.

6. _____ The soccer team is at their best during challenging tournaments.

7. _____ The faculty of the college argued over their grading policies all semester.

8. _____ The orchestra performed the difficult symphony as well as they could.

9. _____ Our committee changes their decision every month.

10. _____ The student council is working on an award banquet for

its members.

PRACTICE EXERCISE 3: PRONOUN USE

Correct the following paragraphs for pronoun use. The first sentence has been done for you. The correct answer is in parentheses. Some sentences will be correct. (The following paragraphs are from a student essay, "A Stroke of Bad Luck" by Margaret Ewart.)

On August 25, 1997, I received a phone call that changed the lives of ~~anyone~~ (everyone) in my family. My father had a stroke while traveling from North Carolina to Mississippi. After the detailed phone conversation about my father's condition, I realized that as a supportive and caring daughter, one needed to be at my father's side. Looking at my frail father, partially paralyzed and unable to take care of his own personal needs, I became aware that you had to take care of him throughout the rest of his life. Making the decision to become a primary care giver affected my family by the changes in a father-daughter role, and the loss of family time, which resulted in new attitudes among all family members.

PRACTICE EXERCISE 4: PRONOUN USE

Correct the following paragraphs for pronoun use. The first one has been done for you.

Shortly after I started taking care of my father, I came to realize that there was never any time for ~~me~~ (myself), much less my family. I rarely ever have the time to play with my children, help my daughter with her (correct) school work or spend time with my husband. My father requires a tremendous amount of my time, which prevents me from being a mother as well as being a wife. Most of the time I feel as if I am missing out on a great deal of mine children's lives, due to the fact that I have become a primary care giver. I have felt like a prisoner in our own home since the stroke. My husband and I have a great fear of leaving my home in the event that he may need us. My husband tries to take me out for dinner and a movie to give me some sense of relief from all of the stress, but I always decline. Due to her fear of leaving the house because of my new responsibilities, family members are reluctant to make plans with me. They have begun to treat me differently and to see me as a different person.

PRACTICE EXERCISE 5: PRONOUN USE

Edit the following (concluding) paragraph for pronoun usage. The first sentence has been done for you.

As each day brings new obstacles and solutions, you (I) have overcome almost anyone (every one) of them. What was once a difficult situation has become part of everyday life for them. In the midst of taking care of my father, I have realized that you can't help him unless I can help oneself. I was becoming extremely exhausted trying to take care of anything, and I was losing myself. Finally, I realized that I didn't need to be around my father that much, and you could do something to better oneself. Going back to school was the first thing that had come into my mind, and I said, "Why not?" So I enrolled in school. I have made a special schedule for my family, my father my school, and most importantly, myself. Emotionally, I am the happiest that I have ever been in my life, which reflects on any member of your family.

Verbs E S L

A **verb** is a word indicating action, feeling, or being. Verbs can be divided into three classes: action verbs, linking verbs, and helping verbs (see Chapter 3). Additionally the form of the verbs can indicate the time of the action: **present, past,** or **future** (also known as **tense).** Each of these tenses has many forms that we use everyday.

The most commonly used tenses are **simple present** and **simple past:**

Present Tense

Verbs in the Simple Present Tense

Sample verb: think

	Singular		**Plural**
1st person	I	think	we think
2nd person	you	think	you think
3rd person	he*		they think
	she }	thinks	
	it		

*Use an –s or –es ending on the verb when the subject is *he, she,* or *it,* or the equivalent.

Past Tense

Regular Verbs

Regular verbs are those verbs that form the past tense by adding –*ed* or –*d*. The **simple past tense** is used to refer to an action that began and ended at one time period in the past.

Past Tense of Regular Verbs

Sample verb: dance

Singular		**Plural**
1st person	(I) danced	(we) danced
2nd person	(you) danced	(you) danced
3rd person	(he, she, it) danced	(they) danced

In addition to simple forms, there are other present and past verb forms. The following table illustrates the most commonly used verb tenses. Each tense expresses a specific time or duration. Students for whom English is a foreign language need to practice the use of each tense in spoken and written English.

Common Verb Tenses in English
Sample verb: talk

Tense	Sample Sentence
Present	I talk.
Present continuous	I am talking.
Present perfect	I have talked.
Present perfect continuous	I have been talking.
Past	I talked.
Past perfect	I had talked.
Past perfect continuous	I had been talking.
Future	I will talk.
Future continuous	I will be talking.
Future perfect	I will have talked.
Future perfect continuous	I will have been talking.

Irregular Verbs

Many irregular verbs (more than 100 in English) do not form the past tense by adding –*ed*, or –*d*. Some verbs do not change form at all, or they form the past tense by changing the spelling of the entire word (*stem-changing verbs*). The following table lists the most commonly used irregular verbs.

An Alphabetical List of Irregular Verbs

Simple Form	Simple Past	Past Participle
arise	arose	arisen
be	was, were	been
bear	bore	borne/born
beat	beat	beaten/beat
become	became	become
begin	began	begun
bend	bent	bent
bet	bet	bet*
bid	bid	bid
bind	bound	bound
bite	bit	bitten
bleed	bled	bled
blow	blew	blown
break	broke	broken
breed	bred	bred
bring	brought	brought
broadcast	broadcast	broadcast
build	built	built
burst	burst	burst
buy	bought	bought

---

*See page 290.

Simple Form	Simple Past	Past Participle
cast	cast	cast
catch	caught	caught
choose	chose	chosen
cling	clung	clung
come	came	come
cost	cost	cost
creep	crept	crept
cut	cut	cut
deal	dealt	dealt
dig	dug	dug
do	did	done
draw	drew	drawn
eat	ate	eaten
fall	fell	fallen
feed	fed	fed
feel	felt	felt
fight	fought	fought
find	found	found
fit	fit	fit*
flee	fled	fled
fling	flung	flung
fly	flew	flown
forbid	forbade	forbidden
forecast	forecast	forecast
forget	forgot	forgotten
forgive	forgave	forgiven
forsake	forsook	forsaken
freeze	froze	frozen
get	got	gotten*
give	gave	given
go	went	gone
grind	ground	ground
grow	grew	grown
hang	hung	hung
have	had	had
hear	heard	heard
hide	hid	hidden
hit	hit	hit
hold	held	held
hurt	hurt	hurt
keep	kept	kept
know	knew	known

*See page 290.

Simple Form	Simple Past	Past Participle
lay	laid	laid
lead	led	led
leave	left	left
lend	lent	lent
let	let	let
lie	lay	lain
light	lit/lighted	lit/lighted
lose	lost	lost
make	made	made
mean	meant	meant
meet	met	met
mislay	mislaid	mislaid
mistake	mistook	mistaken
pay	paid	paid
put	put	put
quit	quit	quit*
read	read	read
rid	rid	rid
ride	rode	ridden
ring	rang	rung
rise	rose	risen
run	ran	run
say	said	said
see	saw	seen
seek	sought	sought
sell	sold	sold
send	sent	sent
set	set	set
shake	shook	shaken
shed	shed	shed
shine	shone/shined	shone/shined
shoot	shot	shot
show	showed	shown/showed
shrink	shrank/shrunk	shrunk
shut	shut	shut
sing	sang	sung
sit	sat	sat
sleep	slept	slept
slide	slid	slid
slit	slit	slit
speak	spoke	spoken
speed	sped/speeded	sped/speeded

*See page 290.

Simple Form	Simple Past	Past Participle
spend	spent	spent
spin	spun	spun
spit	spit/spat	spit/spat
split	split	split
spread	spread	spread
spring	sprang/sprung	sprung
stand	stood	stood
steal	stole	stolen
stick	stuck	stuck
sting	stung	stung
stink	stank/stunk	stunk
strive	strove	striven
strike	struck	struck/stricken
string	strung	strung
swear	swore	sworn
sweep	swept	swept
swim	swam	swum
swing	swung	swung
take	took	taken
teach	taught	taught
tear	tore	torn
tell	told	told
think	thought	thought
throw	threw	thrown
thrust	thrust	thrust
understand	understood	understood
undertake	undertook	undertaken
upset	upset	upset
wake	woke/waked	woke/waked
wear	wore	worn
weave	wove	woven
weep	wept	wept
win	won	won
wind	wound	wound
withdraw	withdrew	withdrawn
wring	wrung	wrung
write	wrote	written

*The following are some differences in verb forms between American English and British English.

American	British
bet-bet-bet	*bet-bet-bet* OR *bet-betted-betted*
fit-fit-fit	*fit-fitted-fitted*
get-got-gotten	*get-got-got*
quit-quit-quit	*quit-quitted-quitted*

> **American:** *burn, dream, kneel, lean, leap, learn, smell, spell, spill, spoil* are usually regular: *burned, dreamed, kneeled, leaned, leaped, etc.*
>
> **British:** simple past and past principle forms of these verbs can be regular but more commonly end with *-t: burnt, dreamt, knelt, leant, leapt, learnt, smelt, spelt, spilt, spoilt.*
>
> *Source:* Azar, Betty S., *Understanding and Using English Grammar,* Volume A. Second edition. Englewood Cliffs, New Jersey: Prentice Hall Regents. 18–19.

The Verb *Be*

Because the verb *be* is used so often, as a helping verb, linking verb, as well as to form verb tense, it is useful to see how irregular the form is.

To Be (Infinitive form)

	Present Tense		Past Tense	
	Singular	**Plural**	**Singular**	**Plural**
1st person	I **am**	We **are**	I **was**	We **were**
2nd person	You **are**	You **are**	You **were**	You **were**
3rd person	He, she, it, **is**	They **are**	He, she, it **was**	They **were**

Some irregular verbs do not follow the stem-changing pattern:

Irregular Verbs That Do Not Change Their Form
(All end in *–t* or *–d*)

Present Form	Past Form	Past Participle
bet	bet	bet
cost	cost	cost
cut	cut	cut
fit	fit	fit
hit	hit	hit
hurt	hurt	hurt
quit	quit	quit
spread	spread	spread

▼
PRACTICE EXERCISE: CHOOSING THE CORRECT VERB FORM

Supply the past form of the past tense or the participle in the following sentences.

Example: (sing) For her recital, the soprano <u>sang</u> a variety of arias.

1. (go) Yesterday we _____ to the beach.

2. (go) All summer we have _____ to beaches on the coast.

3. (ride) We _____ the waves with boogie boards for hours in the morning.

4. (blow) The wind _____ violently all afternoon.

5. (lose) We _____ our umbrella and all of our towels.

6. (leave) We _____ the beach after searching up and down the shore for our belongings.

7. (swim) Normally, we have _____ all afternoon during a beach outing.

8. (drive) Yesterday, we _____ home, exhausted and windblown, but ready to return today.

9. (be) Why _____ you absent for three weeks?

10. (lie) The book _____ on the desk yesterday.

Additional Practice for Complex Verb Forms

Present Perfect/Past Perfect

How to form the present/past perfect:

Present perfect tense:	*has* or *have* + past participle of the main verb
	Has talked (singular)
	Have talked (plural)
Past perfect tense:	*had* + past participle of the main verb
	Had talked (singular and plural)

When to Use the Present/Past Perfect Tenses

The **present perfect tense** is used to describe an action that started in the past and continues to the present time. It can also be used to describe an action that has recently taken place or an action in which the exact past time is indefinite.

Julia has played with the symphony for five years.

This sentence means that Julia began playing with the orchestra five years ago and is still playing with the symphony today.

Asim has traveled to Pakistan several times recently.

This sentence indicates no specific time for the travel mentioned. If the specific time were to be emphasized, the simple past would have been used.

Asim traveled to Pakistan last December.

The **past perfect tense** is used to describe an action that occurred in the past before another point in time in the past or before another past activity.

Julia <u>had played</u> with the symphony for five years before she retired.

This sentence means that Julia played in the symphony for five years, and then she retired. All of this activity took place in the past.

▼ PRACTICE EXERCISE: USING THE PRESENT AND PAST PERFECT TENSES

Fill in each of the blanks in the following sentences with the correct form of the perfect tense for the verb given.

Example: He <u>said</u> that Jon <u>had reported</u> the results of the experiment to the rest of the class.

1. (charm)   Salzburg _____ tourists for many years.

2. (told, visit) Jill _____ us that she _____ Salzburg

with a group of students before graduating from college.

3. (tour)   The group of students _____ France and Italy as

well.

4. (travel, end) They later _____ to Prague and Berlin before the

Cold War _____ .

5. (attend)   Frequently, alumni from the group _____ reunions

to share memories of a fantastic trip.

Forming the Passive Verb

The **passive voice** is chosen when the actor of the sentence is not important or when the writer wishes to avoid naming the subject.

In the passive voice, the object of an active verb becomes the subject of the passive verb. The form of the verb becomes *be* + **past participle.**

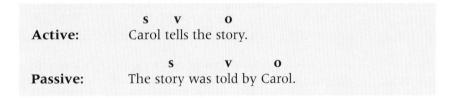

	s	**v**	**o**
Active:	Carol	tells	the story.

	s	**v**	**o**
Passive:	The story	was told	by Carol.

Use of the Active Voice Compared with the Passive Voice

In the **active voice** the subject of the sentence does the acting (action verb/transitive verb).

In the **passive voice** the subject is acted upon.

The students finished the project. (subject is *students*; active verb is *finished*)

The project was finished by the students. (subject is *project* [acted upon by the students]; passive verb is *was finished*)

Most writing is done in the active voice for direct, concise expression. The following list shows the conversion of the active to the passive for the important verb tenses:

	Active	Passive
Present	Carol tells the story.	The story is told by Carol.
Present continuous	Carol is telling the story.	The story is being told by Carol.
Present perfect	Carol has told the story.	The story has been told by Carol.
Simple past	Carol told the story.	The story was told by Carol.
Past progressive	Carol was telling the story.	The story was being told by Carol.
Past perfect	Carol had told the story.	The story had been told by Carol.
Future	Carol will tell the story.	The story will be told by Carol.
Future continuous	Carol will be telling the story.	The story is going to be told by Carol.
Future perfect	Carol will have told the story.	The story will have been told by Carol.

Going to is often used instead of *will*.

PRACTICE EXERCISE: ACTIVE VERBS (VOICE)

The following sentences are written in the passive voice. Rewrite each in the active voice.

1. The car was fixed by the mechanic.

_____

2. The wedding will be planned by the fiancée and her mother.

_____

3. The test is given by the instructor.

_____

4. The plans for the house had been created by the architect.

_____

5. The sermon was delivered by the pastor.

_____

▼ PRACTICE EXERCISE: PASSIVE VERBS (VOICE)

The following sentences are written in the active voice. Rewrite each in the passive voice.

1. Josh ate the strawberry shortcake.

_____

2. Congress voted to increase Social Security payments.

_____

3. The doctors isolated the virus causing the disease.

_____

4. The youngest player won the chess tournament.

_____

5. The skiers chose the hardest, steepest run.

_____

▼ PRACTICE EXERCISE 1: USING THE CORRECT VERB FORM AND TENSE

Underline all the verbs in the following paragraph. Change the tense of the paragraph from past to present. Additional changes in the paragraph may be necessary as well.

Time stood still as I tried to reconcile in my mind what was happening in my cheery breakfast nook on that dreary Tuesday morning in September of 1998: a traumatic event happened there; consequently, my life has been changed forever. Before this event, I felt snug and secure in my roomy, comfortable two story home, peacefully nestled on three gently rolling acres where my loyal and intimidating German shepherds were on patrol, in a private neighborhood near suburban St. Louis. Two young men and their decision to invade my home took all of that away from me.

▼ PRACTICE EXERCISE 2: USING THE CORRECT VERB FORM AND TENSE

In the following paragraph, supply the correct form/tense of the verb in the spaces provided. The first sentence has been done for you. Be careful to use the perfect tenses when appropriate.

Perceptions of a small town all too often <u>are</u> (to be) the same.

Moviemakers _____ (to create) the ideal vision of what a rural

American town should _____ (to look like), and society

_____ (to believe) what moviemakers create. I _____

(to live) in a large town most of my life; my experience with small towns only

_____ (to involve) driving through them on vacation. What I

_____ (to see) during my trips _____ (to give) me the

same perception as most of society. My limited views would soon

_____ (to be) expanded when my first experience away from

home _____ (to land) me in a small Michigan town, on the U.S.-

Canada border.

Subject-Verb Agreement

Subjects and verbs in the present tense (as well as in the past and future) should agree in number. Thus, singular subjects require verbs with singular endings, and plural subjects require verbs with plural endings. The following sentences illustrate correct subject-verb agreement:

> The *woman* (singular subject) *takes* (singular verb form) a cab.
> The *men* (plural subject) *take* (plural verb form) a cab.

▼ PRACTICE EXERCISE 1: SUBJECT-VERB AGREEMENT

In each of the following sentences, choose the correct form of the verb in the parenthesis. First, underline the subject and decide whether it is singular or plural. Next, underline the verb form that correctly agrees with the subject.

Example: <u>He</u> always (carry, <u>carries</u>) a credit card in his wallet.

1. They (work, works) at the factory on the north side of town.

2. The group (walk, walks) in the mall every morning.

3. The senate (vote, votes) on legislation.

4. He (eat, eats) at the diner every Thursday after work.

5. The boy (run, runs) to the schoolyard to play basketball.

6. She (look, looks) like a skilled basketball player.

7. The team (eat, eats) steak and potatoes prior to each game.

8. The band (play, plays) at a local club every Friday.

9. His class (meet, meets) three times per week.

10. People (vote, votes) every four years in the presidential election.

▼ PRACTICE EXERCISE 2: SUBJECT-VERB AGREEMENT

Find and correct the errors in subject-verb agreement in the following paragraph. First, underline the subject in each sentence. Next, find the verb and correct those verbs that do not agree with the subject. The first sentence has been done for you.

The spooky old <u>houses</u> ~~comes~~ to life at night with gruesome decorations. With grotesque carved faces, the Jack-O-Lanterns gives off an eerie glow. Tombstones line the sidewalk; beware of the bloody hands, for they may grab intruders. Bats as black as the night sky flies around in the air, and a black cat with razor-sharp fangs cross the path of terrified prey. The ghosts and the goblins sneaks around monster-like trees, ready to grab their next victim with ease.

Compound Subject-Verb Agreement

In a sentence there may be more than one subject **(compound subject),** and the verb form chosen must agree in tense and number with the subjects.

Usually, if the compound subjects are connected by *and,* the verb is usually plural.

> Fredric and Elise *are* working together on the project.

However, if the compound subjects are thought of as a unit, a singular verb is used.

> Macaroni and cheese *is* a favorite dish for children.

If the compound subject is connected with the *either/or, neither/nor, not only/but also,* correlative conjunctions, the verb must agree with the following rules:

If both subjects are singular, the verb is singular.

> Either Fredric or Elise *is* going to turn in the project to the boss.

If both subjects are plural, the verb is plural.

> The violins and cellos *need* to rehearse their parts with the conductor.

If one subject is singular and the other is plural, the verb agrees with the subject closest to the verb.

> My sisters or my friend plans all my formal gatherings.

▼ PRACTICE EXERCISE 1: SUBJECT-VERB AGREEMENT WITH COMPOUND SUBJECT

Circle the correct verb in each sentence.

Example: During the summer, parents and children ((look), looks) forward to vacation.

1. At the high school, students and a teacher (work, works) on a project in archeology.

2. The committee and the administrators (plan, plans) the social activities for the year.

3. Both the lack of exercise and eating too much rich food can (cause/causes) serious health problems.

4. Whining, begging, and nagging (indicate, indicates) a lack of problem-solving skills.

5. Television and junk food (is, are) a bad diet combination.

6. Peanut butter and jelly (is, are) his favorite sandwich.

7. His mother and father, on the other hand, often (enjoy, enjoys) going out to the show.

8. Not only children but also adults (need, needs) to be aware of the level of violence in the media.

9. My co-workers or my supervisor (are, is) going to advise me.

10. A banana or raisins (make, makes) a high-energy snack.

PRACTICE EXERCISE 2: SUBJECT-VERB AGREEMENT WITH COMPOUND SUBJECT

In each sentence put two lines under the verb that agrees with the subject.

Example: The adults and children in the family often (selects, <u>select</u>) a Mexican restaurant for dinner.

1. Rice, refried beans, and corn cakes (accompany, accompanies) the serving of enchiladas.

2. Either flour tortillas or fried tortillas (come, comes) with dinner.

3. Flan, fried ice cream, or pastry (is, are) served as dessert.

4. In American restaurants, hot dogs or hamburgers (seem, seems) to be a favorite lunch.

5. French fries or, in some cases, hash browns (complement, complements) the burgers.

6. Either catsup, mustard, or both, (add, adds) to the uniquely American flavor.

7. As a beverage, a soda or a shake (complete, completes) the order.

8. Neither Wendy's nor Burger King (deserve, deserves) the reputation of McDonald's.

9. Often, McDonald's, Wendy's, and Burger King (compete, competes) for business at the same intersection.

10. Enchiladas as well as burgers for dinner (have, has) been known to ruin many diets!

PRACTICE EXERCISE 3: SUBJECT-VERB AGREEMENT

Edit the following paragraph for subject-verb agreement. (The first sentence has been done for you.) Some sentences may be correct. The following paragraphs are taken from a student essay, "Nuke Nuclear Energy" by Danny Butler.)

The question of nuclear energy ~~are~~ (is) a debate that has caused protests and conflicts since its discovery. Nuclear energy have the potential to be a remarkably effective energy source. Using the products of fission (the splitting of atoms to create energy) military experts has used nuclear energy for the manufacturing of defense weapons. Resources such as wood, oil, coal, and other fossil fuels can be preserved with the use of nuclear energy to produce power. Despite the possible benefits to society, nuclear energy are extremely dangerous due to the possibility of explosion causing mass pollution, creation of nuclear weapons, and production of radioactive waste.

PRACTICE EXERCISE 4: SUBJECT-VERB AGREEMENT

Edit the following paragraph for subject-verb agreement. The first sentence has been done for you.

Several military and political leaders have suggested that nuclear energy can greatly ~~contributes~~ (contribute) to world peace by allowing for countries to have nuclear defense systems. According to this theory, when an aggressive nation launch a nuclear attack, the opposing nation will always have time to counterattack, thus creating a stalemate. Weapons of mass destruction created from nuclear energy has the potential to cause such severe damage that the entire planet could be affected. Scientists estimate that the nuclear explosions in a major nuclear war could kill 500 million people. But four billion more people could starve to death in the next century because of nuclear winter. Nuclear energy have the potential to cause irreversible damage to the Earth. Because this damage could possibly causes the extinction of all life, nuclear energy are not a safe and practical energy source.

PRACTICE EXERCISE 5: SUBJECT-VERB AGREEMENT

Edit the following (concluding) paragraph for subject-verb agreement. The first sentence has been done for you.

The debate over nuclear energy <u>are</u> (is) sure to be a very important topic in years to come. Standing up against using nuclear energy can possibly lead to the eventual abolishment of many nuclear weapons as well as the protection of the environment. Hopefully, we learns from our mistakes and not repeat the tragic catastrophes of such accidents as that in Chernobyl. By finding alternate sources of energy, we can solve the nuclear energy crisis and helps to save the resources for generations to come.

Adjectives E S L

An **adjective** is a word that modifies (or describes) a noun or pronoun. Although adjectives usually come before the nouns they describe, they can also follow the noun (in the predicate of the sentence).

> The *glistening* ocean sparkled in the sunset.
> The coffee tasted *hot*.

Adjectives can be **objective** (describing nouns with sensory details) or **subjective** (describing concepts, feelings, ideas in more general terms). Both are useful in good writing and enhance meaning, especially in combination.

Objective Adjectives	Subjective Adjectives
glowing	beautiful
crashing	harsh
stabbing	painful
twisted	ugly
strident	annoying
tender	loving

▼ PRACTICE EXERCISE: ADJECTIVES

Complete each of the following sentences with an appropriate adjective from the list below.

beautiful	painful	young	red	large
brilliant	stuffy	rusted	broken	creative

1. The _____ star shone brightly in the cold, night sky.

2. The actress was _____.

3. Hawks and eagles are _____ birds of prey.

4. The _____ metal on the rail of the shipwreck began to separate from the hull.

5. My dog had a _____ rash on his hind legs.

Adverbs

An **adverb** is a word that modifies (describes) a verb or an adjective. Often adverbs end in *–ly*. Another test to identify adverbs is to ask if it answers one of the questions *where, how,* or *when.* Adverbs describe the action of a passage; in some cases they refer to other adverbs to intensify meaning. As with adjectives, the careful use of effective adverbs can improve the style.

Lisa stormed *angrily* up the stairs. (modifies the verb)
He was *very* cold. (modifies the adjective)
The guests were *too* early to dinner. (modifies the adverb)

Commonly Used Adverbs

happily	harshly	quietly	sadly	rudely
softly	perfectly	poorly	politely	slowly
sadly	loudly	quickly	carefully	very

PRACTICE EXERCISE: ADVERBS

Complete each of the following sentences with an appropriate adverb from the list below.

softly	happily	loudly	menacingly	rudely	dangerously
honestly	perfectly	poorly	swiftly	carefully	

1. The bird chirped _____.

2. The intruder glared _____ at the inhabitants.

3. She sang _____ during the concert.

4. The school bus full of children rocked _____ back and forth.

5. The figure in the drawing was shaped _____.

Clauses and Phrases

Independent and Dependent Clauses

A **clause** is a group of related words containing both a subject and a verb. There are two types of clauses: *independent clauses* and *dependent clauses.* **Independent clauses** can stand alone as a complete sentence. A **dependent clause** (or subordinate clause) begins with subordinating words/conjunctions and cannot stand alone as a sentence (see Chapter 9 for more information on dependent clauses).

> **Examples**
>
> We went shopping during the holidays. *Independent clause*
>   (subject is *we*; verb is *went*)
>
> although we went shopping during the holidays *Dependent clause*
>   (subordinate conjunction is *although*; subject is *we*; verb is *went*)
>
> Carl and Louisa were often late to class. *Independent clause*
>   (subject is *Carl and Louisa*; verb is *were*)
>
> because Carl and Louisa were often late to class *Dependent clause*
>   (subordinate conjunction is *because*; subject is *Carl and Louisa*; verb is *were*)

Phrases

A **phrase** is a group of related words missing a subject, verb, or both subject and verb. Phrases are used in sentences to complete thoughts or add descriptive detail; they may be restrictive or nonrestrictive (See: Additional Punctuation Rules, Interrupters in a later section). To avoid problems with ambiguous meaning or errors in punctuation, phrases must be carefully placed next to the noun, verb, or other parts of speech to which the phrase refers.

There are several types of phrases used as modifiers in sentences: *prepositional phrases, participial phrases, gerund phrases, infinitive phrases,* and *absolute phrases.*

Commonly Used Phrases

Prepositional Phrase

Prepositions connect a noun or pronoun to the rest of the sentence, often showing location or time. A **prepositional phrase** contains the preposition (*in, on, over, before, after,* etc.) and its object. (See Additional Practice with Prepositions in the following section, and a list of prepositions on page 308.)

> **Examples**
>
> He waited *for the train*.
> The cat prefers to stay *in the house*.
> They enjoy going out *for pizza after the football games*.

Participial Phrase

A **participial phrase** is a group of words consisting of a participle and its completing words. All verbs have present participle and past participle forms.

> **Examples**
>
> *Staring at the blank computer screen*, Martin found himself unable to finish his essay. (present participle form)
>
> *Interrupted by the demands of her hungry two year old*, she could not finish reading the paper. (past participle form)
>
> *Walking down the hall*, he was hit by the door as it flew open at the end of class.
>
> *Bewildered by the question*, the student could not finish the test.

Gerund Phrase

A **gerund** is the *–ing* form of a verb that functions as a noun in the sentence. A **gerund phrase** includes a gerund and its complete words.

> **Examples**
>
> *Dancing* is her favorite activity. (*Dancing* functions as the subject of the sentence)
>
> *Writing a collection of poems* remains Sophia's secret hobby. (The gerund phrase functions as the subject of the sentence)
>
> Employees will not be paid without *completing the weekly projects*. (The gerund phrase functions as the object of the preposition *without*)

In some cases, the possessive form of a noun or pronoun precedes a gerund:

> **Examples**
>
> The parents were thrilled with *their son's removal of all tattoos*.
>
> *Her dancing in the moonlight* amazed the children.

Infinitive Phrase

An **infinitive phrase** is a group of words consisting of *to* plus a verb and its completing words. An infinitive phrase can function as a noun, adjective, or adverb.

> **Examples**
>
> *To read* is the best way to study grammar. (The infinitive phrase functions as a noun, the subject of the sentence)
>
> Disneyland is one of the best places *to visit while on vacation*. (The infinitive phrase functions as an adjective and modifies the noun *places*)
>
> Her daughter was too nervous *to play the piano in front of an audience*. (The infinitive phrase functions as an adverb, modifying the adjective *nervous*)

Absolute Phrase

An **absolute phrase** is a group of words consisting of a noun or pronoun and a participle (not the regular verb form) plus any other completing words. Absolute phrases modify the entire sentence and cannot be punctuated as a complete sentence.

Examples

Their project nearly completed, the painters began to clean their equipment. (notice the past participle *completed* used in the phrase)

The violinist, *her arms and shoulders aching with pain,* practiced long hours every night. (the present participle *aching* is used in this verb phrase)

PRACTICE EXERCISE: IDENTIFYING PHRASES AND CLAUSES

In the blank to the side of each group of words, write **IC** if the group is an independent clause, **DC** if the groups of words is a dependent clause, and **P** if the group of words is a phrase. If the group of words is a phrase, identify the type of phrase.

Example: P (prepositional) Under the floor.

1. _____ he was born near Los Angeles, California

2. _____ to purchase a new car

3. _____ until the day he died

4. _____ even if she used the material provided

5. _____ hidden in the loft

6. _____ playing badminton

7. _____ when the long winter finally ends

8. _____ the weather being harsh and changeable

9. _____ while she sat by the ashes of the fire

10. _____ to complete the assignment

PRACTICE EXERCISE: PLACEMENT OF MODIFYING PHRASES (MISPLACED AND DANGLING MODIFIERS)

Misplaced modifying phrases modify the wrong word in a sentence or are placed so that it is not clear which word is being described.

Example: Incorrect: The courier delivered the material to the vice president *in the red envelope.*

Correct: The courier delivered the material *in the red envelope* to the vice president.

Dangling modifying phrases do not seem to modify anything in the sentence, or they may appear to describe a word that makes no logical sense. Dangling modifiers usually occur at the beginning of the sentence. To correct the sentence, add the correct subject/verb to the phrase, **or** restructure the sentence for accurate meaning.

Example: Incorrect: *After painting the house,* the furniture was rearranged.

   Correct: *After painting the house,* we rearranged the furniture.

The sentences below have misplaced or dangling modifying phrases. Underline the misplaced/dangling phrases and rewrite the sentences so that the meaning is clear and accurate.

Example: David fed the birds <u>in his robe and slippers.</u>

   <u>In his robe and slippers</u>, David fed the birds.

1. The waiter swept the crumbs away from the couple on the tablecloth.

_____

_____

2. Walking down the hall, the door hit her in the face.

_____

_____

3. Working on his homework, the dog barked all evening.

_____

_____

4. The saleswoman sold the suit to the customer that needed mending.

_____

_____

5. We enjoyed the performance in the theater which we had paid twenty dollars to see.

_____

_____

6. Singing in the shower, the cat suddenly dashed across the room, and the dog began to howl.

_____

_____

7. The car is in the garage with two cartons of ice cream unlocked.

_____

_____

8. Wrapped up in a mummy costume, I enjoyed my son's preparations for Halloween.

_____

_____

9. While enjoying the family picnic, the table suddenly fell to the ground.

_____

_____

10. The teacher gave the students an essay exam which was unprepared.

_____

_____

Additional Practice with Prepositions

Prepositions and Prepositional Phrases

Common Prepositions

about	before	despite	of	to
above	behind	down	off	toward(s)
across	below	during	on	under
after	beneath	for	out	until
against	beside	from	over	up
along	besides	in	since	upon
among	between	into	through	with
around	beyond	like	throughout	within
at	by	near	till	without

          S   V

(a) The student studies ***in the library.***
                 PREP   O of PREP
                     (NOUN)

       S   V

(b) We enjoyed the party ***at your house.***
                PREP   O of PREP
                   (NOUN)

(c) We went **to the zoo in the afternoon.**
         (place)   (time)

(d) **In the afternoon,** we went to the zoo.

An important element of English sentences is the prepositional phrase. It consists of a preposition (**PREP**) and its object (**O**). The object of a preposition is a noun or pronoun.

In (a): ***in the library*** is a prepositional phrase.

In (c): In most English sentences "place" comes before "time."

In (d): Sometimes a preposition phrase comes at the beginning of a sentence.

▼ PRACTICE EXERCISE: PRACTICE WITH PREPOSITIONS

Find the subjects **(S)**, verbs **(V)**, objects **(O)**, and prepositional phrases **(PP)** in the following sentences.

                S   V   O   PP

Example: Jack put the letter in the mailbox.

1. The children walked to school.

2. Beethoven wrote nine symphonies.

3. Mary did her homework at the library.

4. Bells originated in Asia.

5. Chinese printers created the first paper money in the world.

Preposition Combinations

Here is a list of preposition combinations with adjectives and adverbs

Preposition Combinations with Adjectives and Verbs

A
be absent from
accuse of
be accustomed to
be aquainted with
be addicted to
be afraid of
agree with
be angry at, with
be annoyed with
apologize for
apply to, for
approve of
argue with, about
arrive in, at
be associated with
be aware of

B
believe in
blame for
be blessed with
be bored with

C
be capable of
care about, for
be cluttered with
be committed to
compare to, with
complain about
be composed of
be concerned about
be connected to
consist of
be content with
contribute to
be convinced of
be coordinated with
count (up)on
cover with
be crowded with

D
decide (up)on
be dedicated to
depend (up)on
be devoted to
be disappointed in, with
be discriminated against
distinguish from
be divorced from

be done with
dream of, about
be dressed in

E
be engaged to
be envious of
be equipped with
escape from
excel in
be excited about
excuse for
be exposed to

F
be faithful to
be familiar with
feel like
fight for
be filled with
be finished with
be fond of
forget about
forgive for
be friendly to, with
be furnished with

G
be grateful to, for
be guilty of

H
hide from
hope for

I
be innocent of
insist (up)on
be interested in
be involved in

J
be jealous of

K
be known for

L
be limited to
look forward to

M
be made of, from
be married to

O
object to
be opposed to

P
participate in
be patient with
be polite to
pray for

Preposition Combinations with Adjectives and Verbs
(*continued*)

	be prepared for		*be* scared of
	prevent from		stare at
	prohibit from		stop from
	protect from		subscribe to
	be provided with		substitute for
	be proud of		succeed in
	provide with	**T**	take advantage of
R	recover from		take care of
	be related to		*be* terrified of
	be revelant to		thank for
	rely (up)on		*be* tired of, from
	be remembered for	**U**	*be* upset with
	rescue from		*be* used to
	respond to	**V**	vote for
	be responsible for		
S	*be* satisfied with	**W**	*be* worried about

PRACTICE EXERCISE 1: PREPOSITION COMBINATIONS

Fill in the blanks with the correct preposition combination. The verb has been indicated. Supply the correct form of the verb to *be* (if necessary) and the preposition. The first one has been done for you.

1. Shirley (be absent) <u>was absent from</u> class last week.

2. The students (be accustomed) _____ (not) _____ writing in a foreign language.

3. The exam (be composed) _____ questions from the text as well as lecture material.

4. Deidre could not (decide) _____ which classes to take for next semester.

5. Paul and Stephanie (be devoted) _____ their daughter Lydia.

6. The family (be excited) _____ the upcoming reunion.

7. Ramon could not (forgive) _____ Teresa _____ taking his money.

8. The president will (be remembered) _____ the scandal with the intern.

9. The instructor (be satisfied) _____ the progress of her students.

10. Helen (be terrified) _____ the film *Psycho*.

Articles ⟁E S L⟁

Articles are a type of word that introduces a noun and indicates whether it is specific or countable. (Most frequently used articles are *a, an,* and *the.*)

Basic Article Usage

I. Using Articles: Generic Nouns

Ø means no article is used.

Singular Count Noun   (a) *A banana* is yellow.*

A speaker uses generic nouns to make generalizations. A generic noun represents a whole class of things; it is not a specific, real, concrete thing but rather a symbol of a whole group.

Plural Count Noun   (b) Ø *Bananas* are yellow.

In (a) and (b): The speaker is talking about any banana, all bananas, bananas in general. In (c), the speaker is talking about any and all fruit, fruit in general.

Noncount Noun   (c) Ø *Fruit* is good for you.

Notice that no article (Ø) is used to make generalizations with plural count nouns and noncount nouns, as in (b) and (c).

II. Using *A* or *Some*: Indefinite Nouns

Singular Count Noun   (d) I ate *a banana*.

Indefinite nouns are actual things (not symbols), but they are not specifically identified.

Plural Count Noun   (e) I ate *some bananas*.

In (d): The speaker is not referring to "this banana" or "that banana" or "the banana you gave me." The speaker is simply saying that s/he ate one banana. The listener does not know nor need to know which specific banana was eaten; it was simply one banana out of that whole group of things in this world called bananas.

Noncount Noun   (f) I ate *some fruit*.

In (e) and (f): *Some* is often used with indefinite plural count nouns and indefinite noncount nouns. In addition to *some*, a speaker might use **two, a few, several, a lot of,** *etc.*, with plural count nouns, or **a little, a lot of,** *etc.*, with noncount nouns.

*Usually **a/an** is used with a singular generic count noun:
Examples:
> **A window** *is made of glass.* **A doctor** *heals sick people. Parents must give* **a child** *love.* **A box** *has six sides.* **An apple** *can be red, green, or yellow.*

The is sometimes used with a singular generic count noun (not a plural generic count noun, not a generic noncount noun). Generic **"the"** is commonly used with, in particular:
(1) species of animals: **The whale** *is the largest mammal on earth*
> **The elephant** *is the largest land mammal*

(2) inventions: *Who invented* **the telephone?** **the wheel?** **the refrigerator?** **the airplane? The computer** *will play an increasingly large role in all our lives.*
(3) musical instruments: *I'd like to learn to play* **the piano.**
> *Do you play* **the guitar?**

III. Using *The:* Definite Nouns

Singular Count Noun   **(g)** Thank you for *the banana.*

A noun is definite when both the speaker and the listener are thinking about the same specific thing.

Plural Count Noun   **(h)** Thank you for *the bananas.*

In (g): The speaker uses *the* because the listener knows which specific banana the speaker is talking about, i.e., that particular banana which the listener gave to the speaker.

Noncount Noun   **(i)** Thank you for *the fruit.*

Notice that *the* is used with both singular and plural count nouns and with noncount nouns.

General Guidelines for Article Usage

(a) *The sun* is bright today.
   Please hand this book to *the teacher.*
   Please open *the door.*
   Jack is in *the kitchen.*

GUIDELINE: Use *the* when you know or assume that your listener is familiar with and thinking about the same specific thing or person you are talking about.

(b) Yesterday I saw *some dogs.*
   The dogs were chasing *a cat.*
   The cat was chasing *a mouse.*
   The mouse ran into *a hole.*
   The hole was very small.

GUIDELINE: Use *the* for the second mention of an indefinite noun*; in (b): first mention = *some dogs, a cat, a mouse, a hole*
second mention = *the dogs, the cat, the mouse, the hole*

(c) INCORRECT: *The apples are my favorite fruit.*

   CORRECT: *Apples* are my favorite fruit.

GUIDELINE: Do not use *the* with a plural count noun (e.g., *apples*) or a noncount noun (e.g., *gold*) when you are making a generalization.

(d) INCORRECT: *The gold is a metal.*

   CORRECT: *Gold* is a metal.

(e) INCORRECT: *I drove car.*

   CORRECT: I drove *a car.*
   I drove *the car.*
   I drove *that car.*
   I drove *his car.*

GUIDELINE: Do not use a singular count noun (e.g., *car*) without:
(1) an article (*a/an* or *the*); OR
(2) *this/that*; OR
(3) a possessive pronoun.

*The is not used for the second mention of a generic noun. COMPARE:
   (1) What color is *a banana* (generic noun)? *A banana* (generic noun) is yellow.
   (2) Tom offered me *a banana* (indefinite noun) or an apple. I chose *the banana* (definite noun).

▼ PRACTICE EXERCISE 1: ARTICLES

In the following dialogues, try to decide whether the speakers would probably use **a/an** or **the.**

1. A: I have ___**an**___ idea. Let's go on ___**a**___ picnic Saturday.

   B: Okay.

2. A: Did you have fun at ___the___ picnic yesterday?

B: Sure did. And you?

3. A: You'd better have _____ good reason for being late!

B: I do.

4. A: Did you think _____ reason Jack gave for being late was believable?

B: Not really.

5. A: Where's my blue shirt?

B: It's in _____ washing machine. You'll have to wear _____ different

shirt.

6. A: I wish we had _____ washing machine.

B: So do I. It would make it a lot easier to do our laundry.

7. A: What happened to your bicycle? _____ front wheel is bent.

B: I ran into _____ parked car when I swerved to avoid _____ big pot-

hole in the street.

A: Did you damage _____ car?

B: A little.

A: What did you do?

B: I left _____ note for _____ owner of _____ car.

A: What did you write on _____ note?

B: My name and address. I also wrote _____ apology.

8. A: Can you repair my car for me?

B: What's wrong with it?

A: _____ radiator has _____ leak, and one of _____ windshield

wipers doesn't work.

B: Can you show me where _____ leak is?

9. A: Have you seen my boots?

B: They're in _____ closet in _____ front hallway.

PRACTICE EXERCISE 2: ARTICLES

Complete the sentences with **a/an, the,** or **Ø.** (Ø means no article).

1. __Ø__ beef is a kind of __Ø__ meat.

2. __The__ beef we had for dinner last night was excellent.

3. Jack is wearing __a__ straw hat today.

4. Jack likes to wear _____ hats.

5. _____ hat is _____ article of clothing.

6. _____ hats are _____ articles of clothing.

7. _____ brown hat on that hook over there belongs to Mark.

8. Everyone has _____ problems in _____ life.

9. My grandfather had _____ long life.

10. That book is about _____ life of Helen Keller.

11. Tommy wants to be _____ engineer when he grows up.

12. The Brooklyn Bridge was designed by _____ engineer.

13. John Roebling is _____ name of _____ engineer who designed the
    Brooklyn Bridge. He died in 1869 from _____ infection. He died before
    _____ bridge was completed.

14. _____ people wear _____ jewelry to make themselves more attractive.

15. _____ jewelry Diana is wearing today is beautiful.

16. Mary is wearing _____ beautiful ring today. It is made of _____ gold
    and rubies. _____ gold in her ring was mined in Canada. _____ rubies
    came from Burma.

17. One of the first things you need to do when you move to _____ new
    city is to find _____ place to live. Most _____ newspapers carry
    _____ advertisements (called "want ads") for _____ apartments that
    are for rent. If you find _____ ad for _____ furnished apartment,
    _____ apartment will probably contain _____ stove and _____ re-
    frigerator. It will also probably have _____ furniture such as _____
    beds, _____ tables, _____ chairs, and maybe _____ sofa.

18. My wife and I have recently moved to this city. Since we're going to be here for only _____ short time, we're renting _____ furnished apartment. We decided that we didn't want to bring our own furniture with us. _____ apartment is in _____ good location, but that's about the only good thing I can say about it. Only one burner on _____ stove works. _____ refrigerator is noisy, and _____ refrigerator door won't stay closed unless we tape it shut. _____ bed sags in the middle and creaks. All of the rest of _____ furniture is old and decrepit too. Nevertheless, we're still enjoying living in this city. We may have to look for _____ another apartment, however.

ADDITIONAL PUNCTUATION RULES

Basic rules of punctuation and sentence structure are covered in Chapters 4–12.

Capitalization

1. Capitalize proper nouns, the names of people, places, and specific products.

> Fredric Chopin
> Sacramento, California
> German class
> Fords

2. Capitalize the days of the week, names of months, and the titles of holidays.

> Saturday, August 28,
> Friday the 13th
> Christmas holiday

3. Capitalize the first word of every sentence.

> The dog, cat, and birds all began to bark, growl, and chirp at once.

PRACTICE EXERCISE: CAPITALIZATION

Correct the capitalization errors in the following sentences.

1. Every friday, the sociology class met in the eisenhower library.

2. The rent-a-car company used fords, chevrolets, and buicks.

3. Julie's birthday fell on saturday, august 14.

4. ludwig van beethoven wrote nine symphonies.

5. In chicago, the sears tower is the tallest skyscraper.

Numbers

1. Numbers (instead of words) should be used for dates, street addresses, page numbers, telephone numbers, and time stated in terms of A.M. and P.M. (words are used with the phrase "o'clock").

> August 29, 1998
> 321 Walnut St.
> page 34
> 12:00 A.M. (Twelve o'clock)
> 922–8000

2. Use numbers for figures above 100 (although some authorities tell us to spell out numbers that can be expressed in one or two words).

> 1,000 pages to be completed
> Twenty-four hours
> $15.99 per ticket
> $20,000 or Twenty thousand dollars

3. Use numbers in a short passage in which several numbers are used.

> On the initial placement test, Julia scored 75, Celia scored 60, and Luis scored 85.

4. Never begin a sentence with a number.

> 25 students filled the course. (Incorrect)
> Twenty-five students filled the course. (Correct)

▼ PRACTICE EXERCISE: NUMBERS

Correct the number errors in the following sentences.

1. 45 truck drivers participated in the salary dispute talks.

2. Meldrick lives at forty-two seventy-two Main Street.

3. The contestant won thirty-seven dollars playing the lottery.

4. Tickets for the tour cost eight dollars.

5. The program began at ten-thirty, Eastern Standard Time.

The Apostrophe

The **apostrophe** is used to indicate contractions or possession/ownership.

1. Some words can be combined, usually in informal writing, by using an apostrophe. This is a contraction.

> *Isn't* this strange? (is + not)
> We *couldn't* drive any farther. (could + not)

2. Add an apostrophe plus *s* to a noun to indicate possession.

> *Anna's* papers were left in the office.

3. To a plural noun ending in *s*, add only an apostrophe to indicate possession.

> *Parents'* advice often is ignored

4. For some words, an apostrophe plus *s* should be added to a singular word ending in *s*. This is most often true for a proper name.

> The *Billings's* recipe book

5. Apostrophe plus *s* can be used to form the plurals of figures, letters, and words being treated as words in isolation. (It is also acceptable to leave out this apostrophe.)

> Many students are not satisfied with C's.
> The 1970's were confusing years.
> Don't use so many "okay's" when you speak.

PRACTICE EXERCISE 1: THE APOSTROPHE

Correct the following apostrophe errors in the following sentences.

1. The Smiths in this society are very difficult to track down individually.

2. December 31, 1999 was a very exciting New Years Eve!

3. Whose your favorite football team?

4. Your right!

5. If she wasnt on time, she shouldve been.

▼ PRACTICE EXERCISE 2: THE APOSTROPHE

Correct the apostrophe errors in the following sentences.

1. Whats his name?

2. The 1960s brought about changes in many institutions in our society.

3. In your essays, change the *a lots* to words such as *many* or *several*.

4. When you change batteries, align the *+s* and *−s* correctly.

5. Its not correct to omit necessary apostrophes.

6. Students questions are usually not frivolous.

7. The mans shoes were made of leather.

8. Mr. Lewis donation to the walkathon was very generous.

9. The families plans for a joint vacation were put on hold.

10. George and Shirleys relationship is very unpredictable.

▼ PRACTICE EXERCISE 3: THE APOSTROPHE

Correct the apostrophe/possessive errors in the following sentences. (Some sentences may be correct.)

1. The boss plan was to intimidate his employees.

2. The months work was destroyed by a computer virus.

3. Luis frequently asked his father-in-laws advice.

4. The ladies raincoats dripped in the hall closet.

5. The sisters reunion in San Antonio was a fantastic success.

6. The minivan is theirs; the Porsche is yours.

7. The suns rays began to filter through the clouds.

8. The shirts for the boys were destroyed in the washing machine.

9. Louisa is suffering from the terrible twos.

10. The class spirit improved after their papers were returned.

Quotation Marks

1. Use **quotation marks** to set apart written words or the spoken words in dialogue.

> My mother wrote, "We will be traveling in our Mobile Home."
>
> Jung said, "I need to change my grammar text."

2. Periods and commas are placed inside the quotation marks, whereas semi-colons and colons are placed outside the quotation marks. If the quoted material is a question, place the question mark inside the quotation marks. However, if the quoted material is part of a longer sentence that asks a question, put the question mark outside the quotation marks.

> "Do the bats fly at night?" he asked.
>
> Did I hear you ask, "Do the bats fly at night"?
>
> He politely remarked, "I would like tea"; however, his wife asked for coffee.
>
> In his short story "Hills Like White Elephants," the male character makes several references to a "simple operation" as a solution to an inconvenient pregnancy, as a way to convince his girlfriend that the operation posed no risk, and as a way to keep his life uncomplicated.

3. Use quotation marks to set apart titles of essays (except for the title of your own essay), articles in magazines, short stories, short poems, songs, and chapter headings.

> The class discussed "My Life on the Streets" for two days.
>
> "Music of the Night" is her favorite song in *Phantom of the Opera.*
>
> The poem "Fire and Ice" by Frost illustrates two types of anger and destruction.
>
> "Letters From a Birmingham Jail" is an essay that effectively illustrates argumentation.

4. Quotation marks or italics can be used to set apart a word, phrase, or letter being discussed.

> Do not follow the conjunction "although" with a comma.
>
> Descriptive words such as "brilliant," "glowing," and "illuminating" support the dominant impression of "light."

5. Uncommon names/nicknames and words used in irony or sarcasm should be surrounded by quotation marks.

> "Buzz" McCarthy prefers to shave his head.
>
> His crime of adultery almost made him "public enemy number one."

6. Single quotation marks should be used to indicate a quotation within a quotation.

> Tasha said, "My favorite song is 'Layla' performed by Eric Clapton."

PRACTICE EXERCISE 1: APOSTROPHE AND QUOTATION MARK

Correct the apostrophe and quotation mark errors in the following sentences.

1. My Uncle Silas wrote, I'll be in St. Louis on Wednesday evening.

2. Marks car was left in the parking lot overnight.

3. The winning dragster was driven by Bud The Snake Collins.

4. The Joness prize heifer won the Blue Ribbon at the county fair.

5. The short story Mrs. Garland's Garden appeared in *Horticulture* magazine.

6. Studying all night for the exam is not what I wanted to do.

7. Slang expressions, such as dissed and way cool, should not be used in formal writing.

8. The 1960s saw the rise of hippies and the counterculture in American society.

9. Marva said, "My favorite saying is P. T. Barnum's Never Give a Sucker an Even Break.

10. Lawyers legal advice is usually based on case law.

PRACTICE EXERCISE 2: PUNCTUATION PRACTICE

Add the correct punctuation to the following student paragraph (taken from a student essay "Don't Give Up the Right to Carry" by Tim Schuette).

proposition b will allow people twenty one or older who have never been convicted of a felony the ability to carry a concealed weapon if they pass a background check and 12 hour handgun safety course people opposed to proposition b believe criminals will have easier access to weapons the danger for police officers will greatly increase people will misuse the guns therefore the crime rate will increase vote yes for proposition b because criminals already have guns police support concealed weapons and the crime rate will decrease.

Parentheses

1. **Parentheses** are used to set off specific details giving additional information, explanations, or qualifications of the main idea in a sentence. This would include words, dates, or statements.

> Many students name famous athletes as heroes (Sammy Sosa, Mark McGwire, and Maurice Green, for example).
>
> *Tom Sawyer* (1876) is one of Mark Twain's most enduring works.

2. Notice that the period for the sentence is placed outside the parenthesis when the enclosed information occurs at the end of the sentence and is not a complete sentence itself. If the enclosed information is a complete sentence, the period is placed inside the parenthesis.

▼ PRACTICE EXERCISE 1: THE PARENTHESES

Insert parentheses when necessary in the following sentences. The first exercise has been done for you.

1. Three new students (Marta, Eric, and Elena) were admitted to the class.

2. The rich desserts Bavarian Chocolate Cake, Chocolate Cream Pie, and Peach Melba were added to the menu.

3. Johann Sebastian Bach 1685–1750 is the featured composer for tonight's concert.

4. The appendix pp. 300–385 provides additional exercises for the text.

5. They thought she died from the "joy that kills" Chopin 344.

6. Women were restricted by the social role required of wives in the Victorian Period 1837–1901.

7. The media television, magazines, newspapers, and radio play a crucial role in each election.

8. The four brothers Thomas, Robert, Steven, and John Corey have grown up with one sister Amy.

9. His explanation of the "silent phase" see page 646 in language learning is very helpful for new teachers.

10. Wolfgang Amadeus Mozart 1756–1791 composed his favorite piano concerto.

Brackets

1. **Brackets** are used in quoted material to set apart editorial explanations.

> The tenor sang "Angel of Music" [original version sung by Michael Crawford] for his encore.

2. Brackets are also used to indicate editorial corrections to quoted material. The word "sic" (which means "thus") placed next to an error in quoted material means that the mistake appeared in the original text and that it is not the writer's error.

> The dean wrote, "All faculty must teach sumer [sic] school."

PRACTICE EXERCISE: PARENTHESES AND BRACKETS

Add parentheses and brackets where appropriate in the following sentences.

1. World War II 1939–1945 was divided into two main theaters of conflict.

2. The historian wrote, "Napoleon was exiled to the Island of Elbi sic."

3. Many famous presidents Washington, Lincoln, and Roosevelt are quoted in speeches by political candidates.

4. The coach said, "The Fighting Irish Notre Dame will be a tough opponent next week."

5. The student wrote "I threw the paper on the grownd sic yesterday."

6. Brian analyzed the performance of the concerto by Dvorak as performed by Rostropovich.

7. The President stated, "She the Vice-President described the financial crisis."

8. The erratic weather rain, wind, and sudden snow storms in Missouri make it difficult to plan outdoor activities.

9. The reporter wrote "The sailors were innured sic in the explosion."

10. These popular shoes Reebok, Adidas, and Naturalizer were available in a variety of sizes.

The Dash

1. The dash is used to set apart parenthetical information that needs more emphasis than would be indicated by parentheses.

> Irina's new teacher—a dynamic sociology teacher—helped her to understand American society.

2. Use a dash before a statement that expands on or summarizes the preceding statement (this could also include ironic or humorous comments).

> He studied for the exam for two days—then fell asleep before he finished!

▼ PRACTICE EXERCISE 1: THE DASH

Add dashes to the following sentences.

1. Alexis Jordan and I do not believe this is an exaggeration is a genius.

2. She is running I think in the 10K race.

3. Anna-Lee and Jake have traveled to every state I am not kidding!

4. Marjo and Marc met Gayle and Larry in Denver Colorado for vacation luckily they all like mountains!

5. He turned in the financial report and I know this is true before the deadline.

6. Brenda indicated in fact she insisted that the patient see a specialist.

7. Sergei arrived so we were told an hour ago.

8. Every morning so he says Andrew runs 3 miles.

9. Is dinner if you can call it that ready?

10. Never and I mean never open an attachment on e-mail!

The Hyphen

1. Hyphens are used to join descriptive adjectives before a noun.

> A well-written play
> A forty-year-old woman

2. Do not use a hyphen when the adjective ends in –*ly*.

> A quickly changed opinion
> A beautifully designed home

3. Check the dictionary for compound words that always require a hyphen.

> Compound numbers (twenty-five, fifty-six)
> Good-for-nothing
> Father-in-law (mother-in-law, and so on)
> President-elect

4. Some words with prefixes use a hyphen; check your dictionary if you are unsure.

> Ex-husband
> Non-English-speaking
> All-American

5. Use a hyphen to separate syllables at the end of a line. Do not divide a one-syllable word.

> Do not forget to review dependent clauses and subordinate con-junctions.

▼ PRACTICE: HYPHENS

Add hyphens where needed in the following sentences. The first sentence is done for you.

1. My brother-in-law will leave for Florida next week.

2. The seventeen year old driver was nervous on the highway.

3. The old violin was a very well constructed instrument.

4. The scientist prefers up to date results.

5. She stared into the blue green water.

Underlining

1. The titles of books, magazines, journals, movies, works of art, television programs, CDs, plays, ships, airplanes, and trains should be underlined.

> <u>The Sun Also Rises</u>
> <u>Good Housekeeping</u>
> <u>The New York Times</u>
> <u>The Last Supper</u>
> <u>Tapestry</u>
> <u>Buffy the Vampire Slayer</u>
> <u>Queen Mary</u>

2. There are some exceptions to this rule: the Bible, titles of legal documents (including the U.S. Constitution), and the title of your own essay on your title page.

3. Also, underlining is equivalent to or a symbol for *italics*, which may be used instead of underlining.

PRACTICE EXERCISE: THE DASH, HYPHEN, AND UNDERLINING

Add dashes, hyphens, and underlining where needed in the following sentences.

1. The fifteen year old cat sat on top of the television most of the day and night.

2. In the event of a nuclear accident, it is important to listen for broadcasts about emergency procedures.

3. Jack Nicklaus the greatest golfer of all times also is a successful golf course designer.

4. Singer Bob Dylan also wrote a novel titled Tarantula.

5. Her son in law always dropped by on Saturday to mow the lawn.

6. Sela baked four dozen cookies for her younger sister's camping trip then it rained!

7. Dawson's Creek is a very popular television program for younger adults.

8. Jim Thorpe was the first All American of Native American extraction.

9. The long jump winner at the Senior Olympics was seventy two years old.

10. Jose's new wrestling coach a woman competed for four years at Dellwood College.

Interrupters: Restrictive and Nonrestrictive Clauses

1. Sentences may be interrupted by clauses or phrases that clarify or provide additional meaning. These clauses usually begin with the relative pronouns *who, whom, which,* or *that.* These are also known as **restrictive and nonrestrictive clauses.**

> They did not know the man *who was speaking.*
> Their dog, *which was barking all night,* annoyed the neighbors.

2. Restrictive clauses are essential to identify nouns or to complete the meaning. These clauses simply follow the nouns or ideas they are modifying. No commas are used to set off restrictive clauses.

> In the line, the young woman *who was wearing a red bandana and hoop earrings* needed a ticket. (This relative clause is essential to identify which woman needed a ticket)
> The film *showing at the Rialto* is very provocative. (This descriptive phrase is necessary to identify which film/theater is under discussion)

3. Nonrestrictive clauses are not essential to complete the meaning of the sentence. You can remove them from the sentence, and the basic meaning of the sentence will remain clear. Because they are nonessential, these clauses are always set off by commas.

> Linda and Burt, *who just returned from Alaska,* would go on another vacation tomorrow. (This relative clause is not essential because it just adds interesting details to the sentence; without it, the meaning of the sentence is still clear)
> The cockatiels, *chirping loudly to the music of the nearby television,* should live for up to twenty years. (This verb phrase is nonessential, supplying interesting details but not essential information)

4. Most clauses beginning with *that* are not set off with commas

> Where is the report that he left on the the desk this morning?

PRACTICE EXERCISE: PUNCTUATING RESTRICTIVE AND NONRESTRICTIVE MODIFIERS

Punctuate the phrases or clauses in the following sentences correctly, putting commas only around nonessential phrases and clauses.

1. A person who insists on piling papers on any available space can be difficult to live with.

2. Mrs. Collins who once dreamed of being an anthropologist now works at the local bookstore.

3. The Alamo the site of the famous battle is a popular tourist attraction in San Antonio.

4. Calculus 101 which is required for many majors is a very demanding course for most college freshmen.

5. He reminds me of my son who always enjoys a spirited discussion of film. (The answer differs, depending on the number of sons!)

6. Asim who took Composition 102 last semester passed the course even though English is not his first language.

7. The storm racing up the eastern seaboard threatened South Carolina with dangerous weather.

8. The class nodding and yawning woke up quickly when the teacher announced a pop-quiz.

9. Fariba who is from Iran enjoyed meeting Svetlana who is from Bulgaria.

10. Pet dogs that run away at any opportunity should be fenced.

WORDS AND MEANING E S L

Commonly Misspelled Words

The following is a list of words that are difficult to spell:

across	grammar	possible
address	height	prefer
answer	illegal	prejudice
argument	immediately	privilege
athlete	important	probably
beginning	integration	psychology
behavior	intelligent	pursue
calendar	interest	reference
career	interfere	rhythm
conscience	jewelry	ridiculous
crowded	judgment	separate
definite	knowledge	similar
describe	maintain	since
desperate	mathematics	speech
different	meant	strength
disappoint	necessary	success
disapprove	nervous	surprise
doesn't	occasion	taught
eighth	opinion	temperature
environment	particular	thorough
embarrass	optimist	thought
exaggerate	perform	tired
familiar	perhaps	until
finally	personnel	weight
government	possess	written

▼ PRACTICE EXERCISE: MISSPELLED WORDS

Circle the correctly spelled word in each of the following pairs.

1. arguement   argument

2. seperate   separate

3. judgement   judgment

4. privelege   privilege

5. writen   written

6. jewelery   jewelry

7. sucess   success

8. desparate   desperate

9. occasion   ocasion

10. embarass   embarrass

Words That Sound Alike

Many words in English are pronounced alike but are spelled very differently. These words need special study or memorization. The following list includes word pairs that pose problems for all writers.

Words	Definition	Example
Aural/oral		
aural	having to do with hearing	The doctor said that he needs testing for *aural* skills.
oral	having to do with speech/the mouth	He had to give an *oral* presentation.
Buy/by		
buy (verb)	to purchase	They *buy* shoes whenever there is a sale.
by (preposition)	past; near; not later than	The dog sits *by* the door.
Capital/capitol		
capital (adjective)	fatal; major	The class debated *capital* punishment. The college is making *capital* improvements.
capital (noun)	money; leading city	He invested his *capital* in the stock market. Sacramento is the *capital* of California.
capitol (noun)	a legislative building	The *capitol* building in Washington D.C. is often visited by tourists.
Complement/compliment		
complement (noun)	something that adds to or completes	The drapery *complements* the furniture.
compliment (verb)	to express praise or admiration	He rarely gives *compliments*.
Passed/past		
passed (verb)	to move ahead	The jeep *passed* the car on the highway.
past (noun)	time before present	The *past* haunted him.
past (preposition)	beyond	The boys ran *past* the graveyard.
past (adjective)	not current	The storms were dangerous this *past* year.

Plain/plane

plain (adjective)	clear; ordinary	The letter lay on the table in *plain* sight.
plain (noun)	flat land with few trees	Early settlers lived in sod homes on the *plains*.
plane	flat/level surface; aircraft; degree of development	As part of her geometry assignment she was told to plot a line through a *plane*. He was afraid of *planes*. They talk on different *planes*.

Presence/presents

presence	being present; a person's way of behavior	Her *presence* calmed the child. The president has a hypnotic *presence*.
Presents	gifts	Piles of *presents* were stacked under the Christmas tree.

Principal/principle

principal (adjective)	main; most important	The *principal* idea is truth. The *principal* violinist led the orchestra.
principal (noun)	the head administrator of a public elementary or high school; amount of money	The *principal* is rarely popular. The *principal* earns interest in the account.
principle (noun)	a comprehensive and fundamental law, doctrine; a primary source; an ingredient that exhibits or imports a characteristic quality	Faith is a complex *principle*.

Rain/reign/rein

rain	water falling to earth from clouds	The *rain* ended the drought.
reign	the time a king or queen rules	The *reign* of Queen Elizabeth II of England has been controversial.
rein	a strap attached to the bridle, used by the rider to control a horse	The young rider grabbed the *reins* in fear.

Sight/site/cite

sight	able to see; a view	Her *sight* was excellent. The pep assembly was a confusing *sight*.
site	a location	They visited the *site* of their new home.
cite	to quote as an expert in research	Always *cite* any outside sources used in your writing.

To/too/two

to (preposition)	toward a given direction	The students ran *to* class.
too (adverb)	very; also	The sale was *too* tempting. My friend bought a dress and shoes, *too*.
two	the number 2	He needs *two* cups of coffee in the morning.

Waist/waste

waist	the middle of the body and the part of clothing that covers this area	The *waist* of the suit fits too snugly.
waste (verb)	careless use	Don't *waste* your time in class.
waste (noun)	objects/concepts that are not used and discarded	Often, *waste* can be recycled.

Weather/whether

weather (noun)	conditions of the atmosphere	The *weather* in the midwest changes hourly.
whether (conjunction)	if this were the case	He does not know *whether* or not he will pass.

Whole/hole

whole	all; complete	She read the *whole* novel in one day.
hole	an opening	The mouse came through the *hole* in the wall.

Write/right/rite

write	to convey ideas using words; to create	The students will *write* several essays.
right	correct	She enjoys being *right*!
	conforming to morality, justice, or law	We all know the *right* thing to do.
	close to a conservative position	The president's position is shifting to the *right*.
rite	ritual; repeated ceremonial action	Getting a driver's license at age 16 is a *rite* of passage for teenagers in our society.

PRACTICE EXERCISE 1: FREQUENTLY CONFUSED WORDS

Underline the correct sound-alike word in the parentheses for the sentence's meaning.

1. The students were nervous because this was their first (aural/oral) exam.

2. The (capital/capitol) of Missouri is Jefferson City.

3. The school's (principle/principal) left for a week to attend an educational seminar.

4. The guests brought many (presents/presence) to the baby shower.

5. The dessert was rather (plane/plain) for such a fancy party.

6. The taxi drove (past/passed) the address where it was supposed to have stopped.

7. (To/Too) many travelers often causes congestion at airports over Thanksgiving.

8. The belt was too small for my (waist/waste).

9. The game would begin (whether/weather) or not all the team members arrived on time.

10. Because his mother was watching, Jeremy ate the (whole/hole) plate of spinach.

PRACTICE EXERCISE 2: FREQUENTLY CONFUSED WORDS

Underline the correct sound-alike words in the following sentences.

1. We should (buy/by) a new car before the old one falls completely apart.

2. His uncle cannot accept a (compliment/complement).

3. Students need to learn how to (site/cite) sources used in research.

4. Linda leads the horse while holding the (reins/reigns).

5. Natalie is a dramatic (presents/presence) when she enters a room.

6. Getting a driver's license is a (right/rite) of passage in the United States.

7. She jogs (two/to) miles before work every day.

8. James is the (principal/principle) cellist of the local symphony orchestra.

9. The young couple does not have much (capital/capitol) to invest.

10. The runner (passed/past) the walkers on the track.

Contractions That Sound Like Other Words

Another category of words which sound alike but are spelled differently are **contractions.** The following words are frequently punctuated/spelled incorrectly.

Contraction	Definition	Example
It's/its		
it's	contraction: it is	*It's* going to rain.
its	belonging to it	*Its* wings were broken.
They're/their/there		
they're	contraction: they are	*They're* ready for any adventure.
their	belonging to them	*Their* pets run their home.
there	at that place	The library is over *there*, not here.
We're/were/where		
we're	contraction: we are	*We're* going to the beach for vacation.
were	verb/past tense of *are*	We *were* ready for a week.
where	in which location?	*Where* is the map?
Who's/whose		
who's	contraction: who is	*Who's* going to the party?
whose	belonging to whom?	*Whose* socks are on the sofa?
You're/your		
you're	contraction: you are	*You're* in the way.
your	belonging to you	*Your* gift is in the mail.

PRACTICE EXERCISE 1: CONTRACTIONS THAT SOUND LIKE OTHER WORDS

Underline the correct word in the parentheses for the meaning of the sentence.

1. (You're/Your) package was sent yesterday by overnight mail.

2. (It's/Its) in (they're/their/there) best interest to listen to the supervisor.

3. Do you know (whose/who's) socks these are?

4. I forgot where (were/we're) going this afternoon.

5. (Whose/Who's) going to the ice cream shop after dinner?

6. Are you certain that (you're/your) ready to take the driving test?

7. (Their/There/They're) is a trail that (their/there/they're) supposed to walk.

8. Exactly (we're/were/where) did you think the restaurant was located?

9. (It's/Its) engine overheated in the hot, arid Nevada desert.

10. The leaves (we're/were/where) turning colors as autumn approached.

PRACTICE EXERCISE 2: CONTRACTIONS

Underline the correct word in the parentheses.

1. (Your/You're) luck is about to change.

2. He isn't sure (whose/who's) book is under the desk.

3. (Where/Were) did you expect to find happiness?

4. Getting from here to (their/there) is not as easy as it seems.

5. The cat howled for (it's/its) dinner every night at five o'clock.

6. (Were/Where) (your/you're) notes on the computer?

7. (Who's/Whose) leaving early for the concert?

8. (There/They're) are no tickets left!

9. We (were/where) going to camp out over night to get good seats.

10. (It's/Its) not a good idea to wait until the last minute to start an essay.

Words That Sound or Look Almost Alike

The following words may not be spelled exactly alike. However, they sound alike and are often confused.

Words	Definition	Example
Accept/except		
accept (verb)	to acknowledge as true; to receive	She *accepted* his explanation. They *accepted* the wedding gifts.
except	other than	All of the assignments *except* one were easy.
Advice/advise		
advice (noun)	wise suggestions about solutions to a problem	He never listens to *advice*.
advise (verb)	to make suggestions; to give advice	The counselor *advises* the confused freshmen.
Affect/effect		
affect (verb)	to influence	The weather will *affect* your mood.
effect (noun)	end product; result	The *effect* of the accident was obvious for years.
Breath/breathe		
breath (noun)	air inhaled or exhaled by living creatures	The swimmer held his *breath*.
breathe (verb)	to exhale or inhale	The cat *breathes* silently.
Choose/chose		
choose (verb, present tense)	pick/select	They could not *choose* a restaurant.
chose (past tense)	picked/selected	They *chose* to order pizza.
Conscience/conscious		
conscience	thought process acknowledging right and wrong	He has no *conscience*.
conscious	aware of being/ existence; thinking	The students were not *conscious* after lunch.
Council/consul/counsel		
council (noun)	group which meets/ plans/governs	The city *council* meets each month.
consul (noun)	government official in foreign service	The German *consul* met with the President.
counsel (verb)	to advise	The department chair *counseled* the frustrated student.

Words	Definition	Example

Desert/dessert

desert (noun)	dry, barren land	The sunsets on the *desert* are spectacular.
desert (verb)	to leave alone/abandon	His friends *deserted* him.
dessert (noun)	last dish of a meal; often sweet	They decided to avoid sweet, fat *desserts*.

Diner/dinner

diner (noun)	a long narrow type of restaurant with counters and booths; a person who is eating	At the *diner*, they have an old juke box. The *diners* enjoy listening to oldies from the juke box.
dinner	the large, important meal of the day‖ (mid-day or evening)	The fried chicken is for *dinner*.

Emigrate/immigrate

emigrate	to leave a country	They *emigrated* from China.
immigrate	to enter a new country	*Immigration* is very complex.

Farther/further

farther (physically)	greater distance	The sprinter ran *farther* than he had to.
further	to advance an ideal/ goal/cause; greater distance (mentally)	The protesters *further* the cause of equality. Most arguments can be *further* developed.

Loose/lose

loose	not tight	*Loose* fitting clothing has been in style recently.
lose (verb)	to misplace; to be unable to find; to fail to win	I always *lose* my earrings. He *lost* the tennis match.

Personal/personnel

personal	pertaining to the individual; private concerns	*Personal* information should remain confidential.
personnel	employees	*Personnel* should be aware of their benefits.

Quiet/quit/quite

quiet	little noise; peaceful	The class is too *quiet*.
quit	to stop suddenly, to give up	The employee *quit* suddenly.
quite	definitely	You were *quite* right.

Words	Definition	Example
Special/especially		
special (adjective)	unique	Their anniversary was a *special* event.
especially (adverb)	even more; very	Final exams can be *especially* difficult.
Than/then		
than	word to make comparison	Sale prices are better *than* original prices.
then	at that time	First they studied; *then*, they took the exam.
Thorough/though		
thorough	detailed, complete, accurate	Social attitudes changed after several *thorough* studies were made.
though (conjunction)	despite	*Though* the trees are changing colors, the temperature is warm.
through/threw		
through	in one side and out the other	The ball crashed *through* the window.
threw (verb)	to throw/past tense	The president *threw* the first pitch.

PRACTICE EXERCISE: WORDS THAT SOUND OR LOOK ALMOST ALIKE

Underline the correct word in parentheses for the meaning of the sentence.

1. After the race, the swimmer was short of (breathe/breath).

2. The county (council/consul/counsel) met shortly after the disaster occurred.

3. The members of the symphony orchestra ate (diner/dinner) at the (diner/dinner).

4. I need to (loose/lose) weight before my next physical exam.

5. Shanika ran (further/farther) than her brother Latrelle.

6. The Surf Shop clerk didn't (except/accept) the shipment of dogsleds.

7. The library was (quiet/quit/quite) (quiet/quit/quite).

8. The officer's talk about drugs had quite an (affect/effect) on the seventh grade class.

9. The (personal/personnel) office's task was to evaluate all employees.

10. In the (desert/dessert), nuts and dates often are eaten for (desert/dessert).

Confusing Verbs That Sound Alike:
Lie/Lay; Rise/Raise; Sit/Set

These six verbs are often confused. In order to understand how to use them correctly, it is important to understand the difference between *reflexive verbs* which *do not* take an object (the verb needs no noun to complete the meaning of the sentence), and *transitive verbs* which *do* take and object. *Lie, rise,* and *sit* are reflexive; *lay, raise,* and *set* are transitive.

Lie, Rise, Sit

Meaning	Present	Present Participle	Past	Past Participle
lie (to rest or recline)	lie	lying	lay	has/have lain
rise (to move upward)	rise	rising	rose	has/have risen
sit (to move body into sitting position)	sit	sitting	sat	has/have sat

The family dog loves *to lie* by the front door.

The bread dough *rises* well on the warm kitchen counter.

She *sits* in front of a computer for eight hours every day.

Reflexive verbs are often followed by a prepositional phrase, not a stand-alone noun.

Lay, Raise, Set

Meaning	Present	Present Participle	Past	Past Participle
lay(to put an object down)	lay	laying	laid	has/have laid
raise (to lift or move something up)	raise	raising	raised	has/have raised
set (to carefully place something)	set	setting	set	has/have set

She *lay* the flowers carefully on the table.

Please *raise* the window shades.

She *sets* a lovely table.

The object (underlined) is necessary to complete the meaning of these sentences.

PRACTICE EXERCISE 1: USING LIE/LAY, RISE/RAISE, SIT/SET

Fill in the blanks with the correct form of the above verbs.

1. The book has _____ (lie/lay) out in the rain all day.

2. Steam is _____ (raise/rise) from the hot pavement.

3. He _____ (lie/lay) the knife carefully on the counter.

4. _____ (sit/set) the boxes down before you hurt yourself!

5. She is feeling ill suddenly, so she is _____ (lie/lay) down in the guest room.

6. He had to move because the landlord _____ (raise/rise) the rent.

7. Don't _____ (sit/set) on those chairs!

8. His clothes are _____ (lay/lie) all over the room.

9. _____ (Rise/Raise) in unison, the students left the classroom.

10. They are _____ (sit/set) the chairs in the park for the picnic.

PRACTICE EXERCISE 2: USING LIE/LAY, RISE/RAISE, SIT/SET

Write your own sentences, using each verb correctly.

1. Lie/Lay

_____

_____

2. Rise/Raise

_____

_____

3. Sit/Set

_____

_____

Two- and Three-Word Verb Phrases

These phrases are often difficult for non-native speakers. Many of them are idiomatic expressions, and they need to be studied or memorized.

Phrasal Verbs (Two-Word and Three-Word Verbs)

The term *phrasal verb* refers to a verb and preposition which together have a special meaning. For example, ***put + off*** means "postpone." Sometimes a phrasal verb consists of three parts. For example, ***put + up + with*** means "tolerate." Phrasal verbs are also called *two-word verbs* or *three-word verbs*.

Separable Phrasal Verbs	A phrasal verb may be either *separable* or *nonseparable*.
(a) **I *handed*** *my paper* ***in*** *yesterday.*	
(b) **I *handed in*** *my paper yesterday.*	With a separable phrasal verb, a noun may come either between the verb and the preposition or after the preposition, as in (a) and (b).
(c) **I *handed it in*** *yesterday.* *(INCORRECT: I handed it in yesterday.)*	A pronoun comes between the verb and the preposition if the phrasal verb is separable, as in (c).
Nonseparable Phrasal Verbs	With a nonseparable phrasal verb, a noun or pronoun must follow the preposition, as in (d) and (e).
(d) **I *ran into*** *an old friend yesterday.*	
(e) **I *ran into*** *her yesterday.* *(INCORRECT: I ran an old friend into.)* *(INCORRECT: I handed her into yesterday.)*	

Phrasal verbs are especially common in information English. Following on pages 342–344 is a list of common phrasal verbs and their usual meanings. This list contains only those phrasal verbs used in the exercises in the text. The phrasal verbs marked with an asterisk (*) are nonseparable.

A   ask out .... *ask someone to go on a date*

B   bring about, bring on .... *cause*

           bring up .... (1) *rear children;* (2) *mention or in-*
                                          troduce a topic

C   call back .... *return a telephone call*

           call in .... *ask to come to an official place for a*
                                          specific purpose

           call off .... *cancel*

           *call on .... (1) *ask to speak in class;* (2) *visit*

           call up .... *call on the telephone*

           *catch up (with) .... *reach the same position or level*

           *check in, check into ...... *register at a hotel*

           *check into .... *investigate*

           check out .... (1) *take a book from the library;*
                                          (2) *investigate*

           *check out (of) .... *leave a hotel*

           cheer up .... *make (someone) feel happier*

           clean up .... *make clean and orderly*

           *come across.................. *meet by chance*

           cross out .... *draw a line through*

           cut out.......................... *stop an annoying activity*

D   do over .... *do again*

           *drop by, drop in (on) .... *visit informally*

           drop off .... *leave something/someone at a place*

           drop out (of) .... *stop going to school, to a class, to a*
                                          club, etc.

F   figure out .... *find the answer by reasoning*

           fill out .... *write the completions of a question-*
                                          naire or official form

           find out .... *discover information*

G   *get along (with) .... *exist satisfactorily*

           get back (from) .... (1) *return from a place;* (2) *receive*
                                          again

           *get in, get into.............. (1) *enter a car;* (2) *arrive*

           *get off .... *leave an airplane, a bus, a train, a*
                                          subway, a bicycle

           *get on .... *enter an airplane, a bus, a train, a*
                                          subway, a bicycle

           *get out of..................... (1) *leave a car;* (2) *avoid work or*
                                          an unpleasant activity

           *get over .... *recover from an illness*

---

*Indicates a nonseparable phrasal verb.

	*get through	*finish*
	*get up	*arise from bed, a chair*
	give back	*return an item to someone*
	give up	*stop trying*
	*go over	*review or check carefully*
	*grow up (in)	*become an adult*
H	hand in	*submit an assignment*
	hang up........................	*(1) conclude a telephone conversation; (2) put clothes on a hanger or a hook*
	have on	*wear*
K	keep out (of)	*not enter*
	*keep up (with)	*stay at the same position or level*
	kick out (of)	*force (someone) to leave*
L	*look after......................	*take care of*
	*look into	*investigate*
	*look out (for)	*be careful*
	look over......................	*review or check carefully*
	look up	*look for information in a reference book*
M	make up	*(1) invent; (2) do past work*
N	name after, name for	*give a baby the name of someone else*
P	*pass away	*die*
	pass out........................	*(1) distribute; (2) lose consciousness*
	pick out........................	*select*
	pick up	*(1) go to get someone (e.g., in a car); (2) take in one's hand*
	point out	*call attention to*
	put away	*remove to a proper place*
	put back	*return to original place*
	put off	*postpone*
	put on	*put clothes on one's body*
	put out	*extinguish a cigarette or cigar*
	*put up with...................	*tolerate*
R	*run into, *run across......	*meet by chance*
	*run out (of).................	*finish a supply of something*
S	*show up	*appear, come*
	shut off	*stop a machine, light, faucet*
T	*take after......................	*resemble*
	take off	*(1) remove clothing; (2) leave on a trip*

*Indicates a nonseparable phrasal verb.

take out	(1) *take someone on a date;* (2) *remove*
take over	*take control*
take up	*begin a new activity or topic*
tear down	*demolish; reduce to nothing*
tear up	*tear into many little pieces*
think over	*consider carefully*
throw away, throw out	*discard; get rid of*
throw up	*vomit; regurgitate food*
try on	*put on clothing to see if it fits*
turn down	*decrease volume or intensity*
turn in	(1) *submit an assignment;* (2) *go to bed*
turn off	*stop a machine, light, faucet*
turn on	*begin a machine, light, faucet*
turn out	*extinguish a light*
turn up	*increase volume or intensity*

Readings

▼
THE MUTE SENSE

Diane Ackerman

In the following essay, "The Mute Sense," Diane Ackerman creates strong, visual images by using very specific verbs, by modifying nouns with descriptive adjectives, and by making comparisons through the use of metaphor. The author also uses many specific examples to develop the picture being described and supports this development through the particular sensory device of smell.

Pre-reading exercise: Meaning comes primarily from words. Before reading the essay, look up the definitions of the following words that appear in the text. The numbers in parentheses refer to the paragraph number of the essay.

curd (1)	larder (2)
decipher (2)	paraphernalia (2)
detonate (1)	poignant (1)
etymology (3)	succulent (1)
exaltation (3)	vigilant (2)
inarticulate (3)	

1   Nothing is more memorable than a smell. One scent can be unexpected, momentary, and fleeting, yet conjure up a childhood summer beside a lake in the Poconos, when wild blueberry bushes teemed with succulent fruit and the opposite sex was as mysterious as space travel; another, hours of passion on a moonlit beach in Florida, while the night-blooming cereus drenched the air with thick curds of perfume and high sphinx moths visited the cereus in a loud purr of wings; a third, a family dinner of pot roast, noodle pudding, and sweet potatoes, during a myrtle-mad August in a midwestern town, when both of one's parents were alive. Smells detonate softly in our memory like poignant land mines, hidden under the weedy mass of many years and experiences. Hit a tripwire of smell, and memories explode all at once. A complex vision leaps out of the undergrowth.

2   People of all cultures have always been obsessed with smell, sometimes applying perfumes in Niagaras of extravagance. The Silk Road opened up the Orient to the western world, but the scent road opened up the heart of Nature. Our early ancestors strolled among the fruits of the earth with noses vigilant and precise, following the seasons smell by smell, at home in their brimming larder. We can detect over ten thousand different odors, so many, in fact, that our memories would fail us if we tried to jot down everything they represent. In "The Hound of the Baskervilles," Sherlock Holmes identifies a woman by the smell of her notepaper, pointing out that "There are seventy-five perfumes, which it is very necessary that a criminal expert should be able to distinguish from each other." A low number, surely. After all, anyone "with a nose for" crime should be able to sniff out culprits from their tweed, Indian ink, talcum powder, Italian leather shoes, and countless other scented paraphernalia. Not to mention the odors, radiant and nameless, which we decipher without even knowing it. The grain is a good stagehand. It gets on with its work while we're busy acting out our scenes. Though most people will swear they couldn't possibly do such a thing, studies show that both children and adults, just by smelling, are able to determine whether a piece of clothing was worn by a male or a female.

3   Our sense of smell can be extraordinarily precise, yet it's almost impossible to describe how something smells to someone who hasn't smelled it. The smell of the glossy pages of a new book, for example, or the first solvent-damp sheets from a mimeograph machine, or a dead body, or the subtle differences in odors given off by flowers like bee balm, dogwood, or lilac. Smell is the mute sense, the one without words. Lacking a vocabulary, we are left tongue-tied, groping for words in a sea of inarticulate pleasure and exaltation. We see only when there is light enough, taste only when we put things into our mouths, touch only when we make contact with someone or something, hear only sounds that are loud enough. But we smell always and with every breath. Cover your eyes and you will stop seeing, cover your ears and you will stop hearing, but if you cover your nose and try to stop smelling, you will die. Etymologically speaking, a breath is not neutral or bland—it's *cooked air;* we live in a constant simmering. There is a furnace in our cells, and when we breathe we pass the world through our bodies, brew it lightly, and turn it loose again, gently altered for having known us.

Descriptive Technique Questions

1. What is the dominant sensory area that the author uses to develop the essay? Point out some examples.

2. Is the essay more subjective or objective? Point out examples to support your point of view.

3. Ackerman uses many active, vivid verbs to help the descriptive quality of the essay. Point out several, and explain how they help to make the description more effective.

Suggestions for Writing

1. Choose a sensory area (touch, smell, taste, sight, hearing), and write a paragraph describing it. To make the assignment more challenging, do not mention the name of the sense you are describing. See if your reader can guess what it is by the way you describe it.

2. Write a paragraph describing a particular sense area that you associate with a famous person, place, or thing.

▼
THE ROOMMATE'S DEATH

Jan Harold Brunvand

In his essay, "The Roommate's Death," Jan Harold Brunvand relates one of a series of stories he calls "urban legends" because they have found their most popular and long-lived run in America and because, like all legends, they have been passed on from one person to another as having really occurred. The one telling the story usually states that he or she knew the person involved or that it was someone that a close friend or family member had known. As Brunvand unveils the story and makes comments about it, see if you can recognize any larger contemporary fears held by society that might be captured by the specific incidents in the story.

Pre-reading exercise: Meaning comes primarily from words. Before reading the essay, look up the definitions of the following words that appear in the text. The numbers in parentheses refer to the paragraph number of the essay.

adornments (12)	plausible (3)
assailant (1)	refuge (1)
commission (1)	resolve (12)
elicit (7)	variants (10)
generalization (12)	venture (13)
motifs (4)	

1 Another especially popular example of the American adolescent shocker story is the widely-known legend of "The Roommate's Death." It shares several themes with other urban legends. As in "The Killer in the Backseat" and "The Baby-sitter and the Man Upstairs," it is usually a lone woman in the story who is threatened—or thinks she is—by a strange man. As in "The Hook" and "The Boyfriend's Death," the assailant is often said to be an escaped criminal or a maniac. Finally, as in the latter legend, the actual commission of the crime is never described; only the resulting mutilated corpse is. The scratching sounds outside the girl's place of refuge are an additional element of suspense. Here is a version told by a University of Kansas student in 1965 set in Corbin Hall, a freshman women's dormitory there:

2   These two girls in Corbin had stayed late over Christmas vacation. One of them had to wait for a later train, and the other wanted to go to a fraternity party given that night of vacation. The dorm assistant was in her room—sacked out. They waited and waited for the intercom, and then they heard this knocking and knocking outside in front of the dorm. So the girl thought it was her date and she went down. But she didn't come back and she didn't come back. So real late that night this other girl heard a scratching and gasping down the hall. She couldn't lock the door, so she locked herself in the closet. In the morning she let herself out and her roommate had had her throat cut, and if the other girl had opened the door earlier, she [the dead roommate] would have been saved.

3 At all the campuses where the story is told the reasons for the girls' remaining alone in the dorm vary, but they are always realistic and plausible. The girls' homes may be too for away for them to visit during vacation, such as in Hawaii or a foreign country. In some cases they wanted to avoid a campus meeting or other obligation. What separates the two roommates may be either that one goes out for food, or to answer the door, or to use the rest room. The girl who is left behind may hear the scratching noise either at her room door or at the closet door, if she hides there. Sometimes her hair turns white or gray overnight from the shock of the experience (an old folk motif). The implication in the story is that some maniac is after her (as is suspected about the pursuer in "The Killer in the Backseat"); but the truth is that her own roommate needs help, and she might have supplied it had she only acted more decisively when the noises were first heard. Usually some special emphasis is put on the victim's fingernails, scratched to bloody stumps by her desperate efforts to signal for help.

4   A story told by a California teenager, remembered from about 1964, seems to combine motifs of "The Baby-sitter and the Man Upstairs" with "The Roommate's Death." The text is unusually detailed with names and the circumstances of the crime:

5   Linda accepted a baby-sitting job for a wealthy family who lived in a two-story home up in the hills for whom she had never baby-sat before. Linda was rather hesitant as the house was rather isolated and so she asked a girlfriend, Sharon, to go along with her, promising Sharon half of the baby-sitting fee she would earn. Sharon accepted Linda's offer and the two girls went up to the big two-story house.

6   The night was an especially dark and windy one and rain was threatening. All went well for the girls as they read stories aloud to the three little boys they were sitting for and they had no problem putting the boys to bed in the up-stairs part of the house. When this was done, the girls settled down to watching television.

7   It was not long before the telephone rang. Linda answered the telephone, only to hear the heavy breathing of the caller on the other end. She attempted to elicit a response from the caller but he merely hung up. Thinking little of it and not wanting to panic Sharon, Linda went back to watching her television program, remarking that the caller had dialed a wrong number. Upon receiving the second call at which time the caller first engaged in a bit of heavy breathing and then instructed them to check on the children, the two girls became frightened and decided to call the operator for assistance. The operator instructed the girls to keep the caller on the line as long as possible should he call again so that she might be able to trace the call. The operator would check back with them.

8   The two girls then decided between themselves that one should stay down-stairs to answer the phone. It was Sharon who volunteered to go upstairs. Shortly, the telephone rang again and Linda did as the operator had instructed her. Within a few minutes, the operator called back telling Linda to leave the house immediately with her friend because she had traced the calls to the up-stairs phone.

9   Linda immediately hung up the telephone and proceeded to run to the stair-way to call Sharon. She then heard a thumping sound coming from the stair-way and when she approached the stairs she saw her friend dragging herself down the stairs by her chin, all of her limbs severed from her body. The three boys also lay dead upstairs in their beds.

10   Once again, the Indiana University Folklore Archive has provided the best published report on variants of "The Roommate's Death," Linda Dégh's summary of thirty-one texts and several subtypes and related plots collected since 1961. The most significant feature, according to her report, is the frequent appearance of a male rescuer at the end of the story. In one version, for example, two girls are left behind alone in the dorm by their roommate when she goes downstairs for food; they hear noises, and so stay in their room all night without opening the door. Finally the mailman comes around the next morning, and they call him from the window:

11   The mailman came in the front door and went up the stairs, and told the girls to stay in their room, that everything was all right but that they were to stay in their rooms [sic]. But the girls didn't listen to him cause he had said it was all right, so they came out into the hall. When they opened the door, they saw their girlfriend on the floor with a hatchet in her head.

In other Indiana texts the helpful male is a handyman, a milkman, or the brother of one of the roommates.

12   According to folklorist Beverly Crane, the male-female characters are only one pair of a series of significant opposites, which also includes home and away, intellectual versus emotional behavior, life and death, and several others. A male is needed to resolve the female's uncertainty—motivated by her emotional fear—about how to act in a new situation. Another male has mutilated and killed her roommate with a blow to her head, "the one part of the body with which women are not supposed to compete." The girls, Crane suggested, are doubly out of place in the beginning, having left the haven of home to engage in intellectual pursuits, and having remained alone in the campus dormitory instead of rejoining the family on a holiday. Ironically, the injured girl must use her fingernails, intended to be long, lovely, feminine adornments, in order to scratch for help. But because her roommate fails to investigate the sound, the victim dies, her once pretty nails now bloody stumps. Crane concluded this ingenious interpretation with these generalizations:

13   The points of value implicit in this narrative are then twofold. If women wish to depend on traditional attitudes and responses they had best stay in a place where these attitudes and responses are best able to protect them. If, however, women do choose to venture into the realm of equality with men, they must become less dependent, more self-sufficient, more confident in their own abilities, and, above all, more willing to assume responsibility for themselves and others.

14   One might not expect to find women's liberation messages embedded in the spooky stories told by teenagers, but Beverly Crane's case is plausible and well argued. Furthermore, it is not at all unusual to find up-to-date social commentary in other modern folklore—witness the many religious and sexual jokes and legends circulated by people who would not openly criticize a church or the traditional social mores. Folklore does not just purvey the old codes of morality and behavior; it can also absorb newer ideas. What needs to be done to analyze this is to collect what Alan Dundes calls "oral-literary criticism," the informants' own comments about their lore. How clearly would the girls who tell these stories perceive—or even accept—the messages extrapolated by scholars? And a related question: Have any stories with clear liberationist themes replaced older ones cautioning young women to stay home, be good, and—next best—be careful, and call a man if they need help?

Narrative Technique Questions

1. Narrative storytelling is most effective when the tale appears realistic (that it really happened)—not made up or too fantastic to have actually happened. Pick one of the stories that Brunvald relates and point out elements that convinced you that the stories are based on real events.

2. What do you think of Beverly Crane's interpretation of the "Roommate's Death"? Are her ideas about feminist themes convincing?

Suggestions for Writing

1. Think of a horror story that scared you. Write a paragraph explaining what elements of the story had the greatest effect on you.

2. By yourself or in a group, create your own "urban legend." Write a narrative paragraph detailing the action.

THE EYE OF THE BEHOLDER

Grace Suh

> In "The Eye of the Beholder" Grace Suh recounts a visit she made to a cosmetic's counter for a facial makeover guaranteed by the "priestesses of beauty." However, after the process is complete, Suh does not like what she sees. Pay particular attention to the difference between "Estée's" idea of beauty and that eventually expressed by the author.

Pre-reading exercise: Meaning comes primarily from words. Before reading the essay, look up the definitions of the following words that appear in the text. The numbers in parentheses refer to the paragraph number of the essay.

astringent (9)	imperious (6)
bourgeoisie (3)	reclamation (5)
emulsifier (9)	renounce (3)
entropy (5)	reverie (11)
epiphanous (4)	scythe (5)
icons (5)	stark (2)

1   Several summers ago, on one of those endless August evenings when the sun hangs suspended just above the horizon, I made up my mind to become beautiful.

2   It happened as I walked by one of those mirrored glass-clad office towers, and caught a glimpse of my reflection out of the corner of my eye. The glass on this particular building was green, which might have accounted for the sickly tone of my complexion, but there was no explaining away the limp, ragged hair, the dark circles under my eyes, the facial blemishes, the shapeless, wrinkled clothes. The overall effect—the whole being greater than the sum of its parts—was one of stark ugliness.

3   I'd come home from college having renounced bourgeois suburban values, like hygiene and grooming. Now, home for the summer, I washed my hair and changed clothes only when I felt like it, and spent most of my time sitting on the lawn eating mini rice cakes and Snickers and reading dogeared back issues of *National Geographic.*

4   But that painfully epiphanous day, standing there on the hot sidewalk, I suddenly understood what my mother had been gently hinting these past months: I was no longer just plain, no longer merely unattractive. No, I had broken the Unsightliness Barrier. I was now UGLY, and aggressively so.

5   And so, in an unusual exertion of will, I resolved to fight back against the forces of entropy. I envisioned it as reclamation work, like scything down a lawn that has grown into meadow, or restoring a damaged fresco. For the first time in ages, I felt elated and hopeful. I nearly sprinted into the nearby Nieman Marcus. As I entered the cool, hushed, dimly lit first floor and saw the gleaming counters lined with vials of magical balm, the priestesses of beauty in their sacred smocks, and the glossy photographic icons of the goddesses themselves—Paulina, Linda, Cindy, Vendella—in a wild, reckless burst of inspiration I thought to myself, Heck, why just okay? Why not BEAUTIFUL?

6   At the Estée Lauder counter, I spied a polished, middle-aged woman whom I hoped might be less imperious than the aloof amazons at the Chanel counter.

7   "Could I help you?" the woman (I thought of her as "Estée") asked.

8   "Yes," I blurted. "I look terrible. I need a complete makeover—skin, face, everything."

9   After a wordless scrutiny of my face, she motioned me to sit down and began. She cleansed my skin with a bright blue mud masque and clear, tingling astringent and then applied a film of moisturizer, working extra amounts into the rough patches. Under the soft pressure of her fingers, I began to relax. From my perch, I happily took in the dizzying, colorful swirl of beautiful women and products all around me. I breathed in the billows of perfume that wafted through the air. I whispered the names of products under my breath like a healing mantra: cooling eye gel, gentle exfoliant, night time neck area reenergizer, moisture recharging intensifier, ultra-hydrating complex, emulsifying immunage. I felt immersed in femininity, intoxicated by beauty.

10   I was flooded with gratitude at the patience and determination with which Estée toiled away at my face, painting on swaths of lip gloss, blush, and foundation. She was not working in vain, I vowed, as I sucked in my cheeks on her command. I would buy all these products. I would use them every day. I studied her gleaming, polished features—her lacquered nails, the glittering mosaic of her eyeshadow, the complex red shimmer of her mouth, her flawless, dewy skin—and tried to imagine myself as impeccably groomed as she.

11   Estée's voice interrupted my reverie, telling me to blot my lips. I stuck the tissue into my mouth and clamped down, watching myself in the mirror. My skin was a blankly even shade of pale, my cheeks and lips glaringly bright in contrast. My face had a strange plastic sheen, like a mannequin's. I grimaced as Estée applied the second lipstick coat: Was this right? Didn't I look kind of—fake? But she smiled back at me, clearly pleased with her work. I was ashamed of myself: Well, what did I expect? It wasn't like she had anything great to start with.

12   "Now," she announced. "Time for the biggie—Eyes."

13   "Oh. Well, actually, I want to look good and everything, but, I mean, I'm sure you could tell, I'm not really into a complicated beauty routine . . . " My voice faded into a faint giggle.

14   "So?" Estée snapped.

15   "Sooo . . . " I tried again, "I've never really used eye makeup, except, you know, for a little mascara sometimes, and I don't really feel comfortable ———"

16   Estée was firm. "Well, the fact is that the eyes are the windows of the face. They're the focal point. An eye routine doesn't have to be complicated, but it's important to emphasize the eyes with some color, or they'll look washed out."

17   I certainly didn't want that. I leaned back again in my chair and closed my eyes.

18   Estée explained as she went: "I'm covering your lids with this champagne color. It's a real versatile base, 'cause it goes with almost any other color you put on top of it." I felt the velvety pad of the applicator sweep over my lids in a soothing rhythm.

19   "Now, being an Oriental, you don't have a lid fold, so I'm going to draw one with this charcoal shadow. Then, I fill in below the line with a lighter charcoal color with a bit of blue in it—frosted midnight—and then above it, on the outsides of your lids, I'm going to apply this plum color. There. Hold on a minute . . . Okay. Open up."

20   I stared at the face in the mirror, at my eyes. The drawn-on fold and dark, heavy shadows distorted and reproportioned my whole face. Not one of the features in the mirror was recognizable, not the waxy white skin or the redrawn crimson lips or the sharp, deep cheekbones, and especially, not the eyes. I felt negated; I had been blotted out and another face drawn in my place. I looked up at Estée, and in that moment I hated her. "I look terrible," I said.

21   Her back stiffened. "What do you mean?" she demanded.

22   "Hideous. I don't even look human. Look at my eyes. You can't even see me!" My voice was hoarse.

23   She looked. After a moment, she straightened up again, "Well, I'll admit, the eye shadow doesn't look great." She began to put away the pencils and brushes, "But at least now you have an eyelid."

24   I told myself that she was a pathetic, middle-aged woman with a boring job and a meaningless life. I had my whole life ahead of me. All she had was the newest Richard Chamberlain miniseries.

25   But it didn't matter. The fact of the matter was that she was pretty, and I was not. Her blue eyes were recessed in an intricate pattern of folds and hollows. Mine bulged out.

26   I bought the skincare system and the foundation and the blush and the lip liner pencil and the lipstick and the primer and the eyeliner and the eyeshadows—all four colors. The stuff filled a bag the size of a shoebox. It cost a lot. Estée handed me my receipt with a flourish, and I told her, "Thank you."

27   In the mezzanine level washroom, I set my bag down on the counter and scrubbed my face with water and slimy pink soap from the dispenser. I splashed my face with cold water until it felt tight, and dried my raw skin with brown paper towels that scratched.

28   As the sun sank into the Chicago skyline, I boarded the Burlington Northern Commuter for home and found a seat in the corner. I set the shopping bag down beside me, and heaped its gilt boxes and frosted glass bottles into my lap. Looking out the window, I saw that night had fallen. Instead of trees and backyard fences I saw my profile—the same reflection, I realized, that I'd seen hours ago in the side of the green glass office building. I did have eyelids, of course. Just not a fold. I wasn't pretty. But I was familiar and comforting. I was myself.

29   The next stop was mine. I arranged the things carefully back in the rectangular bag, large bottles of toner and moisturizer first, then the short cylinders of masque and scrub and powder, small bottles of foundation and primer, the little logs of pencils and lipstick, then the flat boxed compacts of blush and eyeshadow. The packages fit around each other cleverly, like pieces in a puzzle. The conductor called out, "Fairview Avenue," and I stood up. Hurrying down the aisle, I looked back once at the neatly packed bag on the seat behind me, and jumped out just as the doors were closing shut.

Narrative Technique Questions

1. What are the factors that influence Suh to seek out a facial "makeover"?

2. At what point in the story does Suh realize that what she is doing is not going to solve the problem she thought she was correcting?

3. What does Suh finally realize about herself, and how do her final thoughts relate to the essay's title?

Suggestions for Writing

1. Write a paragraph about some part of your looks that you would like to change, or a change that you had contemplated but decided not to complete.

2. Write a paragraph about how you think the culture influences people to want to change their appearance. Explore how this can be a negative or positive experience.

▼

THE CULTURE OF VIOLENCE

Myriam Miedzian

In "The Culture of Violence," Myriam Miedzian inspects the culture that is influencing our children. The essay creates a fictional situation in which a group of anthropologists from Australia examine contemporary America. Pay particular attention to the variety of examples the author makes available for the visitors to evaluate.

Pre-reading exercise: Meaning comes primarily from words. Before reading the essay, look up the definitions of the following words that appear in the text. The numbers in parentheses refer to the paragraph number of the essay.

acculturate (3)	exacerbated (23)
anthropology (10)	indignation (7)
chaste (3)	intricately (1)
collateral (5)	intuitively (3)
detrimental (4)	laissez-faire (34)

1   Anyone who has ever taken a cultural anthropology course is aware that different societies weave different patterns of culture, and that the different threads—religion, music, sports, children's games, drama, work, relations between the sexes, communal values, and so on—that make up the cultural web of a society are usually intricately related.

2   If a tribe's songs and dramas are centered on violence and warfare, if its young boys play war games and violently competitive sports from the earliest age, if its paintings, sculptures, and potteries depict fights and scenes of battle, it is a pretty sure bet that this is not a peaceful, gentle tribe.

3   Every child in the world is born into a particular culture and "from the moment of his birth the customs into which he is born shape his experience and behaviour," we are told by anthropologist Ruth Benedict.[1] Throughout history people have known this intuitively and so they have been careful to acculturate their children from the youngest age into a pattern of behavior that is acceptable to the group. We have in our own society some very clear and simple examples: Christian groups like the Hutterites and the Amish, or Jewish groups like the Hasidim want their children to grow up to be devoted primarily to religious rather than material values, to be sexually modest and completely chaste before marriage. They share a strong sense of community and commitment to taking responsibility for the well-being of all their members. Among the Hutterites and Amish there is a strong emphasis on non-violence. None of these groups allows their children to participate in the mainstream culture.

4   Sometimes societies develop customs that become highly detrimental to their members. A cultural trait that may be of considerable value in a limited form or that was of value at an earlier point of history is elaborated and continued in a form that is socially deleterious. Ruth Benedict refers to this as the "asocial elaboration of a cultural trait."

5   A prime example is the incest taboos and marital customs of the Kurnai tribe of Australia. Many a student of anthropology has laughed or at least chuckled at Benedict's descriptions. Benedict explains that all human societies have incest taboos, "but the relatives to whom the prohibition refers differ utterly among different peoples."[2] The Kurnai, like many other tribes, do not differentiate "lineal from collateral kin." Fathers and uncles, brothers and

cousins, are not distinguished, so that "all relatives of one's own generation are one's brothers and sisters."[3]

6   The Kurnai also have an extreme horror of "brother-sister" marriage. Add to this their strict rule with respect to locality in the choice of a mate and the right of old men to marry the attractive young girls, and a situation is created in which there are almost no mates for young people, especially young men. This does not lead the Kurnai to change their incest taboos or rules of marriage. Quite to the contrary, "they insist upon them with every show of violence."[4]

7   As a result, the usual way for tribe members to marry is to elope. As soon as the villagers get wind of this crime, they set out in pursuit of the newlyweds with the intent to kill them if they catch them. That probably all the pursuers were married in the same way does not bother anyone. Moral indignation runs high. However, if the couple can reach an island traditionally recognized as a safe haven, the tribe may eventually accept them as husband and wife.

8   Cultural webs and irrationalities are simpler and easier to see in small, isolated tribes or small communities than in large industrial societies, but they exist in both.

9   Industrialized societies are made up of different socioeconomic classes, and often different ethnic groups. In a large country like ours, differences in geography and climate affect people. Nevertheless, there are certain aspects of our culture, besides a common language, that are widely shared. Children and adolescents from coast to coast play with the same toys, see many of the same films and TV shows, listen to the same rock music, play many of the same sports.

10   I suspect that if the Kurnai were to send a few anthropologists over to study contemporary American society, they would be as amused by our irrationalities as we are by theirs.

11   On the one hand, they would find in our Declaration of Independence a deep commitment to life, liberty, and the pursuit of happiness. An examination of the Constitution would reveal that the goals of our government include "justice," "domestic tranquility," and "the general welfare." An examination of contemporary society would reveal that we deplore murder, assault, wife- and child-battering, sexual abuse of children, and rape.

12   On the other hand, our newspaper headlines, our TV news with its daily roundups of murders and rapes, our crime statistics, and the fact that over six hundred thousand of our citizens—mostly male—are in prison would inform them just how deeply these problems afflict us. Having established this strong contradiction between our professed goals and beliefs, and our reality, our Kurnai anthropologists would begin to wonder what we teach our boys that makes them become such violent men. They would ask, "Who are your young boys' heroes, who are their role models?"

13   Rambo, Chuck Norris, Arnold Schwarzenegger, would be high on the list.

14   "Do your boys watch only violent adventure films?"

15   No. They like comedies too, but when they reach adolescence many of them become particularly fond of "slasher" films in which they can watch people being skinned, decapitated, cut up into chunks. Wanting to experience all aspects of our culture, the Kurnai anthropologists would undoubtedly watch a few slasher films. They would find out that the perpetrators are practically all male, and the films frequently center on the victimization of females.

16   "What about the rest of their leisure time, what do your boys do with it?"

17   Our young boys spend about twenty-eight hours a week watching TV. By the time they are eighteen, they have seen an average of twenty-six thousand TV murders, a vast majority of them committed by men.

18   "Do they listen to much music?"

19   They certainly do. They spend billions of dollars a year on records and tapes, not to mention radio and MTV. The Kurnai anthropologists might be advised to turn on MTV to see what the young boys like. They would find that the programming often consists of very angry-looking young men singing lyrics that are hard to make out, but the music sounds as angry as the men look. Women on the shows are often scantily clad, and sometimes it looks as if they are about to be raped.

20   "Can we see the texts of some of these lyrics?"

21   Samples of popular hits might include an album by Poison that reached number three on the Billboard pop charts and has sold over two million copies. Its lyrics include, "I want action tonight . . . I need it hot and I need it fast/*If I can't have her, I'll take her and make her* [my emphasis]."

22   Switching channels from MTV, the Kurnai would find that a considerable amount of American television is devoted to sports. Brawls and fistfights are common at these events, particularly in hockey but also in baseball and basketball. The main tactics in football, tackling and blocking, look exactly like bodily assault.

23   The anthropologists would find out that our high rates of violent crime have been exacerbated by an ever-growing drug problem. In light of this they would note that drug and alcohol abuse are common among athletes and the heavy metal musicians that many young people admire and emulate.

24   "What about your sons' toys?" the Kurnai might ask next.

25   A trip to the playground or a look under Christmas trees—religious symbols used to commemorate the birth of the deified founder of the nation's leading religion who preached a gospel of love and nonviolence—would reveal that while little girls get dolls and carriages and dollhouses; little boys get guns, "action figures" like GI Joe, and violent space-age toys and games.

26   By now the Kurnai would no doubt have discovered that rates of violence in our society are highest among boys and men raised by single mothers. Being anthropologists they would not be surprised since they would be aware of cross-cultural data indicating that the presence of a caring, involved father decreases the chances of a son being violent.

27   Delving deeper, they would find out that many boys who start out with fathers lose them along the way through divorce. They would hear divorced women, [as well as] social workers, psychiatrists, and other professionals complain bitterly that a large percentage of divorced fathers never or rarely see their children, nor do they make child support payments.

28   Increasingly stunned by the irrationalities of our society, they might inquire of these professionals: In light of the lack of interest of so many of your men in nurturing and taking responsibility for their children, and the subsequent increases in rates of violence and other social problems, why don't you encourage your little boys to become good fathers by buying them dolls and baby carriages and dollhouses? Why don't you encourage them to play house instead of training them to become warriors?

29   "Parents would never stand for that," professionals and parents would explain. "They are much too afraid that their sons might grow up to be gay if they played with 'wimpy' girls' toys."

30   At this point the visiting anthropologist might emit a cry of disbelief. Is it not obvious to these strange people who deplore violence, yet do everything possible to encourage it in their sons, that gay men do not have children? They don't push baby carriages, change diapers, or give bottles to their babies. Only heterosexual men become fathers and do these things. What could be more absurd than to think that little boys will become gay by rehearsing the quintessentially heterosexual role of being a father?[5]

31   Having established the deep contradictions and absurdities of our customs, the Kurnai would look for their origins. They would find that like many

warrior societies, we have a long tradition of raising our boys to be tough, emotionally detached, deeply competitive, and concerned with dominance.

32 These traits, they would note, have gotten out of hand. The enormous escalation of violence that Americans are experiencing seems to coincide with the development of a vast system of communications technology that has led to the creation of a culture of violence of unprecedented dimensions, much of it directed toward or available to children. Instead of treasuring their children as a precious national resource to be handled with the utmost care, Americans have allowed them to be exploited as a commercial market.

33 How could they let this happen? the Kurnai would wonder. Surely they must understand that one of society's most important tasks, the socialization of the next generation, should not be left in the hands of people whose main concern is financial gain, people who will not hesitate to exploit the basest human tendencies for profit?

34 In their efforts to understand this puzzle they would be helped by their understanding of their own culture. The Kurnai would see that our "laissez-faire" attitude toward our children can be traced to the asocial elaboration of some of our most beneficial and admirable values, just as their absurd marital rules can be traced to originally useful taboos.

35 A system of largely unfettered free enterprise led to the extraordinary economic development of the nation. The subsequent commitment to free enterprise is so deep that the economic exploitation of children is taken for granted. Companies manufacture toys for six-year-olds that encourage reckless violence, sadism, and torture, and few people question their right to do so.

36 The Kurnai would turn next to the First Amendment, the embodiment of the national commitment to free speech.

37 It would not escape their attention that with respect to pornographic and "indecent" material, it has long been acknowledged that the First Amendment cannot apply equally to children and adults. Long-standing laws protect children from such material. That is why there are no Saturday morning pornographic TV programs.

38 For some strange reason, the Kurnai would conclude, these people have blinded themselves to the fact that what makes sense with respect to sex makes at least as much sense with respect to violence. And so they have allowed their children to be raised on tens of thousands of TV murders, detailed depictions of sadistic mutilations on the screen, and song lyrics that advocate rape.

39 What a perfect example of an asocial elaboration, they might exclaim! Everything is justified in terms of free enterprise and free speech, but this freedom as interpreted in present-day society contributes to the nation's enslavement!

40 Don't these Americans see that boys raised in a culture of violence are not free? Their basest, most destructive tendencies are reinforced from the youngest age to the detriment of their altruistic, pro-social tendencies. Then when they commit serious acts of violence they are sent to prison.

41 Don't they see that millions of Americans, especially women and elderly people, live in great fear of being mugged, raped, or murdered? Many are afraid to leave their homes after dark.

42 A survey of national crime statistics published by U.S. government agencies would inform the Kurnai that about twenty-thousand Americans a year suffer the greatest loss of freedom. They are deprived of their lives through violent deaths. Their families and friends are permanently deprived of someone they love.

43 How long will it take these people, the exasperated anthropologists might wonder, until they realize that an interpretation of freedom that allows for no restraints with respect to the commercial exploitation of children is self-destructive?

44   The Kurnai would note that in other areas Americans acknowledge there is no such thing as absolute freedom. Ordinances prohibit people from playing loud music in the middle of the night if in doing so they deprive others of sleep. Laws restrict the freedom of chemical companies to dump pollutants into streams and rivers. But when it comes to producing a culture of violence that pollutes the minds of their young and encourages violence, these strange people act as if freedom were an absolute!

Notes

1. Ruth Benedict, *Patterns of Culture* [New York: Mentor Books, 1946 (1934)], p. 18.
2. Ibid., p. 42.
3. Ibid., p. 43.
4. Ibid.
5. I owe this point to Letty Cottin Pogrebin in *Growing Up Free: Raising Your Child in the 80's* (New York: Bantam Books, 1981).

Example Technique Questions

1. How does the culture influence young people's behavior? Point out some elements in the first three paragraphs that Miedzian identifies.

2. What is the single, most important source that the author identifies as the cause for most violence (paragraphs 34 and 35). Can you think of other reasons?

3. The essay focuses on male experiences, from boys to men. How do female experiences differ as girls grow into womanhood?

Suggestions for Writing

1. Write a paragraph describing how a group you are associated with influences your behavior. The group can be friends, an athletic team, your family, etc.

2. Write about a movie you have seen or a story you have read that deals with violence and young people. Are the reasons for the young people's behavior similar to or different from what Miedzian describes?

HEROINE WORSHIP: THE AGE OF THE FEMALE ICON

Holly Brubach

In this essay, Brubach inspects women as role models in a culture that increasingly values the rich and famous. She concludes, however, that today's female has many more role models from which to choose. She begins the essay with an extended list of famous role models. As you read the remainder of the essay, pay attention to the number and variety of other famous females she uses as examples.

Pre-reading exercise: Meaning comes primarily from words. Before reading the essay, look up the definitions of the following words that appear in the text. The numbers in parentheses refer to the paragraph number of the essay.

apotheosized (1)	modulate (14)
contemporaneous (1)	oblique (12)
deployed (10)	pantheon (1)
enigma (2)	proliferation (11)
genre (8)	reproach (6)
icon (2)	synonymous (2)
idiosyncrasies (13)	ubiquitous (3)
inculcated (6)	

1   It's the 90's, and the pantheon we've built to house the women in our minds is getting crowded. Elizabeth Taylor, Eleanor Roosevelt, Oprah Winfrey, Alanis Morissette, Indira Gandhi, Claudia Schiffer, Coco Chanel, Doris Day, Aretha Franklin, Jackie Onassis, Rosa Parks—they're all there, the dead and the living side by side, contemporaneous in our imaginations. On television and in the movies, in advertising and magazines, their images are scattered across the landscape of our everyday lives. Their presence is sometimes decorative, sometimes uplifting, occasionally infuriating. The criteria for appointment to this ad hoc hall of fame that takes up so much space in our thoughts and in our culture may at first glance appear to be utterly random. In fact, irrespective of their achievements, most of these women have been apotheosized primarily on the basis of their ability to appeal to our fantasies.

2   An icon is a human sound bite, an individual reduced to a name, a face and an idea: Dale Evans, the compassionate cowgirl. In some cases, just the name and an idea suffice. Few people would recognize Helen Keller in a photograph, but her name has become synonymous with being blind and deaf to such an extent that she has inspired an entire category of jokes. Greta Garbo has gone down in collective memory as an exalted enigma with a slogan about being alone. Asking a man if that's a gun in his pocket is all it takes to invoke Mae West. Catherine Deneuve's face, pictured on a stamp, is the emblem of France. Virginia Woolf has her own T-shirt. Naomi Campbell has her own doll. Celebrity being the engine that drives our culture, these women have been taken up by the media and made famous, packaged as commodities and marketed to a public eager for novelty and easily bored. . . .

3   Our icons are by no means exclusively female, but the male ones are perhaps less ubiquitous and more accessible. The pedestals we put them on are lower; the service they are called on to perform is somewhat different.

4   Like women, men presumably look to icons for tips that they can take away and apply to their lives. The men who are elevated to the status of icons are the ones who are eminently cool, whose moves the average guy can steal. They do not prompt a fit of introspection (much less of self-recrimination), as female icons often do in women. What a male icon inspires in other men is not so much the desire to *be* him as the desire to be accepted by him—to be buddies, to shoot pool together, to go drinking. I have all this on good authority from a man of my acquaintance who insists that, though regular guys may envy, say, Robert Redford for his ability to knock women dead, what they're thinking as they watch him in a movie is not "Hey, I wonder if I have what it takes to do that, too," but "I wonder if Redford would like to hang out with me."

5   Whereas women may look at an icon like Raquel Welch, whose appeal is clearly to the male half of humanity, and ask themselves, "If that's what's required to appeal to a man, have I got it, or can I get it?" (The thought of hang-

ing out with Welch—going shopping together or talking about boyfriends—would, I think it's safe to say, never cross most women's minds.)

6   An entire industry, called fashion, has grown up around the business of convincing women that they need to remake themselves in someone else's image: makeup and clothes and other products are presented not as alterations but as improvements. The notion of appearance and personality as a project to be undertaken is inculcated early on. A man may choose to ignore certain male icons; a woman has no such luxury where the great majority of female icons are concerned. She must come to terms with them, defining herself in relation to them—emulating some, rejecting others. In certain cases, a single icon may exist for her as both an example and a reproach.

7   Our male icons are simply the latest entries in a tradition of long standing, broad enough in any given era to encompass any number of prominent men. But the current array of female icons is a rare phenomenon, the outgrowth of aspirations many of which date back no more than 100 years.

8   What were the images of women that informed the life of a girl growing up 200 years ago? It's hard to for us to imagine the world before it was wall-papered with ads, before it was inundated with all the visual "information" that comes our way in the course of an average day and competes with real people and events for our attention. There were no magazines, no photographs. In church, a girl would have seen renderings of the Virgin Mary and the saints. She may have encountered portraits of royalty, whose station, unless she'd been born an aristocrat, must have seemed even more unattainable than that of the saints. There were picturesque genre paintings depicting peasants and chambermaids, to be seen at the public salons, if anyone thought to bring a girl to them. But the most ambitious artists concentrated on pagan goddesses and mythological women, who, being Olympian, inhabited a plane so lofty that they were presumably immune to quotidian concerns. History and fiction, for the girl who had access to them, contained tales of women whose lives had been somewhat more enterprising and action-packed than those of the women she saw around her, but her knowledge of most women's exploits in her own time would have been limited to hearsay: a woman had written a novel, a woman had played hostess to one of the greatest philosophers of the age and discussed ideas with him, a woman had disguised herself as a man and gone to war. Most likely, a girl would have modeled herself on a female relative, or on a woman in her community. The great beauty who set the standard by which others were measured would have been the one in their midst—the prettiest girl in town, whose fame was local.

9   Nineteenth-century icons like Sarah Bernhardt and George Sand would have imparted no more in the way of inspiration; their careers were predicated on their talents, which had been bestowed by God. It was Florence Nightingale who finally provided an example that was practicable, one to which well-born girls could aspire, and hundreds of women followed her into nursing.

10   Today, the images of women confronting a girl growing up in our culture are far more diverse, though not all of them can be interpreted as signs of progress. A woman who in former times might have served as the model for some painter's rendering of one or another pagan goddess is now deployed to sell us cars and soap. The great beauty has been chosen from an international field of contenders. At the movies, we see the stories of fictional women brought to life by real actresses whose own lives have become the stuff of fiction. In the news, we read about women running countries, directing corporations and venturing into outer space.

11   The conditions that in our century have made possible this proliferation of female icons were of course brought on by the convergence of advances in women's rights and the growth of the media into an industry. As women ac-

complished the unprecedented, the press took them up and made them famous, trafficking in their accomplishments, their opinions, their fates. If, compared with the male icons of our time, our female icons seem to loom larger in our culture and to cast a longer shadow, perhaps it's because in so many cases their stories have had the urgency of history in the making.

12   When it comes to looking at women, we're all voyeurs, men and women alike. Does our urge to study the contours of their flesh and the changes in their faces stem from some primal longing to be reunited with the body that gave us life? Women have been the immemorial repository of male fantasies—a lonesome role that many are nonetheless loath to relinquish, given the power it confers and the oblique satisfaction it brings. The curiosity and desire inherent in the so-called male gaze, deplored for the way it has objectified women in art and in films, are matched on women's part by the need to assess our own potential to be found beautiful and by the pleasure in putting themselves in the position of the woman being admired.

13   Our contemporary images of women are descended from a centuries-old tradition and, inevitably, they are seen in its light. Women have often been universalized, made allegorical. The figure who represents Liberty, or Justice, to say nothing of Lust or Wrath, is a woman, not a man—a tradition that persists: there is no Mr. America. The unidentified woman in innumerable paintings—landscapes, genre scenes, mythological scenes—transcends her circumstances and becomes Woman. It's the particular that is customarily celebrated in men, and the general in woman. Even our collective notions of beauty reflect this: a man's idiosyncracies enhance his looks; a woman's detract from hers.

14   "I'm every woman, it's all in me," Chaka Khan sings, and the chords in the bass modulate optimistically upward, in a surge of possibility. Not all that long ago, the notion that any woman could be every women would have been dismissed as blatantly absurd, but to our minds it makes evident sense, in keeping with the logic that we can be anything we want to be—the cardinal rule of the human-potential movement and an assumption that in America today is so widely accepted and dearly held that it might as well be written into the Constitution. Our icons are at this point sufficiently plentiful that to model ourselves on only one of them would seem arbitrary and limiting, when in fact we can take charge in the manner of Katherine Hepburn, strut in the way we learned by watching Tina Turner, flirt in the tradition of Rita Hayworth, grow old with dignity in the style of Georgia O'Keeffe. In the spirit of post-modernism, we piece our selves together, assembling the examples of several women in a single personality—a process that makes for some unprecedented combinations, like Madonna: the siren who lifts weights and becomes a mother. We contemplate the women who have been singled out in our culture and the permutations of femininity they represent. About to move on to the next century, we call on various aspects of them as we reconfigure our lives, deciding which aspects of our selves we want to take with us and which aspects we want to leave behind.

Example Technique Questions

1. In paragraph 8, the author suggests that a girl several centuries ago would model herself after someone in her community or someone in her immediate family. How is this different than in today's society?

2. In paragraph 14, Brubach gives many examples of famous women. What is the point she is trying to make about how today's modern young woman can use these role models?

Suggestions for Writing

1. Write a paragraph about one of today's female icons. Discuss the qualities that make her famous and/or popular.

2. Write a paragraph about a female you admire. Discuss the qualities that influence her appeal for you.

▼
THE PLOT AGAINST PEOPLE

Russell Baker

> In "The Plot Against People," Russell Baker takes a humorous look at the frustrating relationship that often exists between people and inanimate objects. Pay particular attention to how Baker divides the various objects into distinct categories as he classifies them.

Pre-reading exercise: Meaning comes primarily from words. Before reading the essay, look up the definitions of the following words that appear in the text. The numbers in parentheses refer to the paragraph number of the essay.

conciliatory (12)	invariable (10)
constitutes (11)	locomotion (7)
cunning (3)	plausible (7)
idle (3)	utterly (15)
incapable (6)	virtually (9)
inanimate (1)	

1   Inanimate objects are classified into three major categories—those that don't work, those that break down and those that get lost.

2   The goal of all inanimate objects is to resist man and ultimately to defeat him, and the three major classifications are based on the method each object uses to achieve its purpose. As a general rule, any object capable of breaking down at the moment when it is most needed will do so. The automobile is typical of the category.

3   With the cunning typical of its breed, the automobile never breaks down while entering a filling station with a large staff of idle mechanics. It waits until it reaches a downtown intersection in the middle of the rush hour, or until it is fully loaded with family and luggage on the Ohio Turnpike.

4   Thus it creates maximum misery, inconvenience, frustration and irritability among its human cargo, thereby reducing its owner's life span.

5   Washing machines, garbage disposals, lawn mowers, light bulbs, automatic laundry dryers, water pipes, furnaces, electrical fuses, television tubes, hose nozzles, tape recorders, slide projectors—all are in league with the automobile to take their turn at breaking down whenever life threatens to flow smoothly for their human enemies.

6   Many inanimate objects, of course, find it extremely difficult to break down. Pliers, for example, and gloves and keys are almost totally incapable of breaking down. Therefore, they have had to evolve a different technique for resisting man.

7   They get lost. Science has still not solved the mystery of how they do it, and no man has ever caught one of them in the act of getting lost. The most

plausible theory is that they have developed a secret method of locomotion which they are able to conceal the instant a human eye falls upon them.

8   It is not uncommon for a pair of pliers to climb all the way from the cellar to the attic in its single-minded determination to raise its owner's blood pressure. Keys have been known to burrow three feet under mattresses. Women's purses, despite their great weight, frequently travel through six or seven rooms to find hiding space under a couch.

9   Scientists have been struck by the fact that things that break down virtually never get lost, while things that get lost hardly ever break down.

10   A furnace, for example, will invariably break down at the depth of the first winter cold wave, but it will never get lost. A woman's purse, which after all does have some inherent capacity for breaking down, hardly ever does; it almost invariably chooses to get lost.

11   Some persons believe this constitutes evidence that inanimate objects are not entirely hostile to man, and that a negotiated peace is possible. After all, they point out, a furnace could infuriate a man even more thoroughly by getting lost than by breaking down, just as a glove could upset him far more by breaking down than by getting lost.

12   Not everyone agrees, however, that this indicates a conciliatory attitude among inanimate objects. Many say it merely proves that furnaces, gloves and pliers are incredibly stupid.

13   The third class of object—those that don't work—is the most curious of all. These include such objects as barometers, car clocks, cigarette lighters, flashlights, and toy train locomotives. It is inaccurate, of course, to say that they never work. They work once, usually for the first few hours after being brought home, and then quit. Thereafter, they never work again.

14   In fact, it is widely assumed that they are built for the purpose of not working. Some people have reached advanced ages without ever seeing some of these objects—barometers, for example—in working order.

15   Science is utterly baffled by the entire category. There are many theories about it. The most interesting holds that the things that don't work have attained the highest state possible for an inanimate object, the state to which things that break down and things that get lost can still only aspire.

16   They have truly defeated man by conditioning him never to expect anything of them, and in return they have given man the only peace he receives from inanimate society. He does not expect his barometer to work, his electric locomotive to run, his cigarette lighter to light or his flashlight to illuminate, and when they don't, it does not raise his blood pressure.

17   He cannot attain that peace with furnaces and keys and cars and women's purses as long as he demands that they work for their keep.

Classification Technique Questions

1. According to the author, what is the goal of all inanimate objects?

2. What are Baker's classification categories? You can group them by paragraphs 3–6, 7–12, and 13–16.

3. In the concluding paragraphs, 15–17, Baker suggests that these inanimate objects have defeated both science and humanity. How does this add to the overall tone of the essay?

Suggestions for Writing

1. Write a paragraph about an inanimate object in your life that has caused you problems.

2. Select an inanimate object that "science" has touted as having the ability to save you time and effort in your life. Explain how it had the opposite effect.

▼ RELATIVELY SPEAKING

Jan Borst

> Jan Borst, in her essay "Relatively Speaking," classifies the new relationships created by the phenomenon of blended families caused by remarriages. The problem she confronts is that there are no names or rules for these newly created relationships and responsibilities. Pay attention to the serious issues that Borst raises as she explores these new categories.

Pre-reading exercise: Meaning comes primarily from words. Before reading the essay, look up the definitions of the following words that appear in the text. The numbers in parentheses refer to the paragraph number of the essay.

convoluted (13)	laden (10)
flourish (2)	relinquish (6)
idealism (2)	vernacular (8)
imply (4)	via (9)

1   Our daughter will be getting married soon. My husband and I recently met our future son-in-law, Ed, who seems to be a great guy. He has a good job providing a comfortable income. He's a spiritual man, with many talents, well thought of in the community, and more important, he's head over heels in love with our daughter—as she is with him.

2   We especially pray for their happiness because they're not your average twentysomething couple starting their marital journey with all the idealism of youth. They're in their late 30s, each bringing to this union the baggage of failed prior marriages. They wish to recommit—to try again, in Samuel Johnson's words, "the triumph of hope over experience." As all parents do, we want this marriage not only to succeed but to flourish.

3   Like many other couples starting over, they have children—his daughter, her two girls. Their honeymoon will be brief. Then its instant family. Mothering and fathering children they've known a short time. Two last names on the mailbox. Two girls in the house, a third there every other weekend. Child-support payments going out and coming in. One child's mother across town, a father a state away. Children confused over loyalties to the parents they live with and those they visit. The couple pulled in opposite directions by the wants and needs of their kids and their own need to form a successful, intimate marital relationship.

4   Their situation is pretty complex, but, these days, quite common. Some "step" families are more complicated than the word implies. Ours is one such family. I began by saying that our daughter will be getting married. Techni-

cally this is not true. My husband and I are in a second marriage ourselves, and the bride is my husband's child.

5   He was a widowed father of nine and I the divorced mother of four when we met at Parents Without Partners 16 years ago. Of the 13 children between us, only his four oldest were out of the house and on their own. The other nine children ranged in age from 4 to 19. Even though he and I were crazy about each other, we knew that combining our two households was not a good idea. Too many kids reared with different parenting styles. Two religions. Two income levels. Too much age difference (he is nearly a generation older than I). Yet we loved each other, so we became a weekend family of sorts, courting one another while surrounded by kids. Eventually the kids grew up, and six years ago we married. Our long courtship helped solidify the mutual affection all of us now enjoy. We are a family. But still the bonds are fragile.

6   Questions arise as to who is family. Will our daughter's new family be a family of four, made up of those who live in the house? Or a family of five— the four plus the child who visits on weekends? In their home, who is the real parent? Who sets the rules? When does the mother relinquish some of her parenting role to her husband? When does the stepparent step in; when does he or she back off? How much time should the visiting child spend alone with her father and how much time with her new family?

7   Then there's the question of what they call one another. If a child calls her stepfather "Dad," does this take something away from her real father? When children speak about their parents, whom are they referring to? When parents say "our children," should they explain the relationship?

8   In divorce, some words have taken on new meaning in our vernacular. Most states don't call it "divorce," but rather "dissolution of marriage," as if the process were some chemical reaction. A former spouse is an "ex"—it implies a prior position that no longer exists, but also suggests the unknown in math. Do our former in-laws become "ex-laws"? Or "out-laws"?

9   Whether "joint," "shared," "residential," "sole," or "split," parents either have, lose or give up "custody" of their offspring—custody being a term applied to criminals. "Visitation" used to mean making a call to someone hospitalized or going to a funeral home; now it means seeing your own children via some prearranged schedule, possibly devised with the assistance of a family mediator, perhaps by court order.

10   Our language is even more heavily laden with family terms beginning with "step." Ed will be my stepson-in-law, but there's no simple way to state the relationship between his daughter, Amy, and me. She and I will be related only by the slender threads of two remarriages: her father's to my husband's daughter and mine to my husband. Amy becomes my husband's stepgranddaughter, his daughter's stepdaughter, his granddaughters' stepsister or his son-in-law's daughter. But to me, the linguistic link is truly unwieldy: my husband's stepgranddaughter, my stepdaughter's stepmother, my stepgrandchildren's stepsister!

11   Yet whatever we choose to call this relationship created through two remarriages, Amy will be part of our family. She will likely spend some Christmases at our home. She may join our granddaughters when they come to Kansas for their vacation. We've already begun sending her birthday cards and the same holiday treats and trinkets grandmothers (even stepgrandmothers) send grandchildren throughout the year. We will remember her in our thoughts and prayers as we do the other kids in the family.

12   All this has not escaped Amy, 11 years old going on 35. At our last meeting she asked me, "What shall I call you? You're like a grandmother, but not really my grandmother. I have two grandmothers already, you know." (What she didn't say was that should her mother remarry, she will have one more.)

13 "I know," I said with a sigh, "it is pretty complicated." We talked a bit, trying to make sense of this convoluted, many-branched, pruned and grafted family tree. We discussed some of the choices, tried out some of the step-this, step-that options, even suggested a step/step or double-step something or other. Each sounded more ridiculous than the last. Finally we decided it would be "Amy and Jan, Jan and Amy." That would have to do.

Classification Technique Questions

1. In the opening paragraphs, Borst states that her daughter and her fiancée are very much in love. Why then is she so worried that their marriage might not work?

2. What day-to-day problems will confront the couple after they are married?

3. While the essay has a serious tone, there is some humor interspersed throughout. Pick an example and explain how it adds to the effectiveness of the essay.

Suggestions for Writing

1. Write a paragraph about similar experiences and concerns that have happened to you or someone you know.

2. Write a paragraph suggesting some solutions that might help alleviate some of the difficulties that re-marriages present to couples and their children.

▼

GIVE JUGGLING A HAND!

Joe Buhler and Ron Graham

> In this essay, "Give Juggling a Hand!" Buhler and Graham explain the process of learning how to juggle. The essay is intended to be directional. If you have access to three rubber balls or three pairs of socks rolled into balls, see if you can duplicate the juggling process being explained.

Pre-reading exercise: Meaning comes primarily from words. Before reading the essay, look up the definitions of the following words that appear in the text. The numbers in parentheses refer to the paragraph number of the essay.

apogee (10)	minstrels (3)
asymmetrical (11)	renaissance (2)
entrant (6)	ritual (3)
manipulated (4)	virtuoso (5)
medieval (3)	

1 Nothing could be simpler than a game of catch. But just add another ball or two and the game turns magical—the juggled balls take on a life of their own. Suddenly, simple notions and common objects blur into one stunning display after another.

2   In recent years, juggling has experienced a renaissance. Street performers and skilled amateurs are practicing the ancient art in parks, back yards, and on campuses around the globe. Membership in the largely amateur International Juggler's Association (IJA) has more than doubled since 1979.

3   Juggling is actually 4000 years young. In Egypt, Asia, and the Americas, it was once associated with religious ritual. In medieval Europe, wandering minstrels often juggled; the term derives from these *jongleurs*.

4   Amazing jugglers imported from the Orient—in particular the "East Indian" Ramo Samee, who was said to string beads in his mouth while turning rings with his fingers and toes, and the Japanese artist Takashima, who manipulated a cotton ball with a stick held in his teeth—convinced 19th-century Europeans that juggling could be extraordinary show business.

5   Perhaps the greatest juggler of all time was variety-show virtuoso Enrico Rastelli. By his death in 1931, he had taught himself to juggle eight clubs, eight plates or ten balls; he could even bounce three balls continuously on his head.

6   Most people assume that a skilled juggler can manage up to 20 objects. In fact, even five-ball juggling is very difficult and requires about a year to master. Only a few jugglers worldwide have perfected seven-ball routines. At the 1986 IJA competition, one entrant separately juggled nine rings, eight balls, and seven clubs.

7   Jugglers use a bewildering variety of objects, including bowling balls, whips, plastic swimming pools, cube puzzles, fruit, flaming torches, and playing cards. Performers trying for the largest number of objects usually choose rings, which allow a tighter traffic pattern and are stable when thrown to great heights. Several jugglers can manage 10 or 11 rings, and some are trying for 12 or 13.

8   Clubs are the most visually pleasing objects to juggle. They're especially suited for passing back and forth between performers. Because they take up a lot of space when they rotate and must be caught at one end, juggling even five is tricky. Almost nobody can manage seven, even for a few seconds.

9   Throughout history, all jugglers—from South Sea Islanders to Aztec Indians—have used the same fundamental patterns:

10   *The Cascade.* Here, each ball travels from one hand to the other and back again, following a looping path that looks like a figure eight lying on its side. The juggler starts with two balls in his right hand, using a scooping motion and releasing a ball when his throwing hand is level with his navel. As the first ball reaches its highest point, the other hand scoops and releases a second ball, and as that one reaches *its* apogee, he throws the third. Skilled jugglers can keep three, five, or even seven balls going in a cascade, but never four or six. With an even number, balls collide at the intersection of the figure eight.

11   *The Shower.* In this more difficult pattern, the balls follow a circular path as they are thrown upward by the right hand, caught by the left and quickly passed back to the right. Since the right does all the long-distance throwing, the shower is inherently asymmetrical and, therefore, inefficient; it is difficult with more than three objects.

12   *The Fountain.* This figure allows for a large number of balls. In a four-ball fountain, each hand juggles two balls independently in a circular motion. For symmetry, the number of balls is usually even. If the hands throw alternately and the two patterns interlock, it is surprisingly hard to discern that the fountain is made of two separate components and not one.

13   Because gravity causes objects to accelerate as they fall, a juggler has only a short time to catch and throw one ball before another drops into his hand—even if he throws high. A juggler who throws a ball eight feet in the air, for example, must catch it 1.4 seconds later, but throwing it four times that high only doubles the flight time.

14   The best way to understand juggling is to learn to do it yourself. Some people get the hang of the three-ball cascade in minutes, although most need

at least a few days. Limit your sessions to ten minutes rather than frustrate yourself with a two-hour binge.

15   *Step 1: One Ball.* Practice throwing a ball from your right hand to your left and back, letting the ball rise to just above your head. Make the ball follow the path of a figure eight lying on its side, by "scooping" the ball and releasing it near the navel. Catch the ball at the side of your body, then repeat the sequence.

16   *Step 2: Two Balls.* Put one in each hand. Throw the ball in the left hand as in Step 1, and then, just as the ball passes its high point, throw the right-hand ball. Avoid releasing the second throw too early or tossing the balls to unequal heights.

17   At first it may be difficult to catch the balls. Don't worry. Focus instead on the accuracy and height of the throws. Catching will come naturally as soon as the throws are on target. If things seem hectic, try higher throws.

18   *Step 3: Two Balls Reversed.* Reverse the order of throws so that the sequence is right, then left.

19   *Step 4: Three Balls.* Now put two balls in your right hand and one in your left. Try to complete Step 2 while simply holding the extra ball. Pause, then do Step 3.

20   The third ball can make it difficult to catch the second throw. To solve this, throw the third ball just after the second reaches its high point. The sequence is thus right, left, right. At first it may be tough to persuade your right hand to make its second throw. Remember: catches are irrelevant in the beginning. Throw high, accurately and slowly. Don't rush the tempo, and don't forget the figure-eight pattern.

21   Once you've mastered the three-ball cascade you'll want to try other patterns. A juggler is never finished: there is always one more ball.

Process Technique Questions

1. Juggling appears to be a difficult activity to learn. How do the authors explain the process so that readers will not be intimidated to give it a try?

2. Before moving to a step-by-step explanation of juggling in paragraphs 15–20, the authors define *The Cascade, The Shower,* and *The Fountain.* How do these patterns of juggling help clarify the process in the paragraphs that follow?

Suggestions for Writing

1. Write a paragraph about an activity that most people think is difficult. Explain the process so that your reader will feel less intimidated in trying it.

2. If necessary, do some research at the library, and explain the history of the activity described in question 1.

▼
WE BUILD EXCITEMENT

James B. Twitchell

In this essay, "We Build Excitement," Twitchell explains how the process of advertising influences values and perceptions in our culture. The essay is not meant to be duplicatable, as in directional process, but rather is informational. Notice the many examples the author uses to describe the advertising process.

Pre-reading exercise: Meaning comes primarily from words. Before reading the essay, look up the definitions of the following words that appear in the text. The numbers in parentheses refer to the paragraph number of the essay.

charade (5)	irony (2)
concoct (3)	plummet (5)
conduit (6)	suffused (9)
differentiate (3)	touted (10)
electron (7)	Valhalla (11)

1   *The Hatter in the Strand of London, instead of making better felt-hats than another, mounts a huge lath-and-plaster Hat, seven feet high, upon wheels; sends a man to drive it through the streets; hoping to be saved thereby. He has not attempted to* make *better hats, as he was appointed by the Universe to do, and as with this ingenuity of his he could very probably have done, but his whole industry is turned to* persuade *us that he has made such! He too knows that the Quack has become God.*

THOMAS CARLYLE, *Past and Present, 1843*

2   Thomas Carlyle just didn't get it. The Hatter in the Strand of London was not in the business of making hats to make better hats. He made hats to make money. The Victorians may have commanded the manufacturer to make the best of what he set out to do, but the culture of capitalism does not care so much about what he makes as about what he can sell. Hence the "best" hat becomes the most profitable hat. Ironically, perhaps he cannot make hats profitably unless he can market what he makes efficiently. The selling determines the making. And once he makes those best hats, especially if he has a machine to help him, heaven help him if he makes too many. If he has to spend some of his productive time acting like a nut in order to sell those hats, so be it.

3   The ingredients necessary to concoct an Adcult [culture of advertising, eds.] are not complex. The Hatter in the Strand of London is crucial. Because the Hatter probably has enough hats for his own use, he makes something that has exchange value. Assuming that he can control the retail price, the more he manufacturers, the more he takes advantage of the economies of mass production and the greater the profit. To control that retail price however, he needs some method to differentiate his hat or he will produce more than he can sell. After all, because the product is partially machine made, it is essentially interchangeable with a competitor's product made with the same machinery.

4   The process of differentiation, called branding, is the key ingredient in all advertising. Make all the machine-made felt hats, biscuits, shoes, cigarettes,

automobiles, or computer chips you want, but you cannot sell effectively until you call it a Fedora, a Ritz, a Nike, a Marlboro, a Chevrolet, or an Intel 386. If everybody's biscuits are in the same barrel, and if they look pretty much the same, urging people to buy biscuits probably won't do the trick. Chances are, they won't buy your biscuit. As Thomas J. Barratt said at almost the same time that Carlyle was having at the Hatter, "Any fool can make soap. It takes a clever man to sell it."[1] Barratt was a clever man. He made a fortune by the end of the century by calling his soap Pears' Soap and making sure everyone knew about it by defacing miles of Anglo-American wall and newsprint space with "Have you had your Pears' today?" In many ways, modern culture has been a battle between Carlyle and Barratt. If you aren't sure who won, look around you.

5   Adcult also requires purchasers with sufficient disposable income to buy your product. And it doesn't hurt if your audience members have enough curiosity to listen to you tell them your biscuits are different when they know all biscuits are the same. But watch out: this process is not without risk. When money is tight, brands take flight. For reasons no one can understand, from time to time markets fall apart, advertising loses its grip, and the charade has to be reenacted. Procter & Gamble spent billions building its soap brands, Philip Morris did the same with premium cigarettes, as did IBM with the personal computer, only to have the demand for their brands suddenly plummet. Generics appear to eat up what advertising created. Brands can suddenly become just commodities again. The Hatter in the Strand soon responds by dropping his prices and by making a still larger lath-and-plaster hat.

6   With those ingredients in the pot all an Adcult still needs is a plasma, or conduit, between producer and consumer within which producers can, in the jargon of modern criticism, *inscribe* their message. The ever bigger lath-and-plaster hat is soon subject to diminishing returns. The brand may appear *on* his hat, but its name recognition is created *in* a medium. So along with his sign the Hatter may even decide to hire someone to advertise his product by voice. In the nineteenth century consumers still heard the cries of the costermonger (the coster is a kind of English apple) or other traders announcing their wares:

> *One-a-penny, two-a-penny, hot cross buns!*
> *One-a-penny, two for tup'ence, hot cross buns!*
>
> *Dust, O! Dust O! Bring it out today.*
> *Bring it out today! I shan't be here tomorrow!*
>
> *I sweep your Chimnies clean, O!*
> *I sweep your Chimney clean, O!*
>
> *Buy my Diddle Dumplings, hot! hot!*
> *Diddle, Diddle, Diddle, Dumplings, hot!*
>
> *Maids, I mend old Pans or Kettles,*
> *Mend old Pans or Kettles, O!*
>
> *Muffins, O! Crumpets! Muffins to-day!*
> *Crumpets, O! Muffins, O! Fresh to-day!*

7   Street cries and moving hats "set upon wheels" are no longer major conduits in modern Adcult. True, the urban bus has become a billboard. And the billboard plastered on a truck is making a comeback in clustered cities (the sides of such rolling billboards are lit fluorescently and can change panels every ten minutes), and the human voice can still be heard on street corners.[2] But they are no match for ink and electrons.

8   With the advent of print and paste, signs moved to walls. From the late seventeenth century to the middle of the nineteenth the great cities of west-

ern Europe were nightly plastered over—sometimes twice a night—with what became known as posters. Seventeenth-century London streets were so thick with signs that Charles II proclaimed that "no sign shall be hung across the streets shutting out the air and light of the heavens." Although it was against the law, even Fleet Street Prison was posted. As the "post no bills" regulations took hold, posters became free-standing billboards. The "boards" grew so thick in America that people could barely see Niagara Falls through the forest of Coca-Cola and Mennen's Toilet powder signs. N. W. Ayer Company executives bragged that if all the boards they had erected for Nabisco were painted on a fence, the fence would enclose the Panama Canal on either side, from sea to shining sea.

9   What distinguishes modern advertising is that it has jumped from the human voice and printed posters to anything that can carry it. Almost every physical object now carries advertising, almost every human environment is suffused with advertising, almost every moment of time is calibrated by advertising.

10   *Start the day with breakfast.* What's on the cereal box but the Ninja Turtles, Batman, or the Addams Family? Characters real or imagined once sold cereal; now they *are* the cereal. Once Wild Bill Hickock, Bob Mathias, Huckleberry Hound, and Yogi Bear touted Sugar Pops or Wheaties. Now the sugar gobs reappear every six months, renamed to cross-promote some event. When the most recent Robin Hood movie was released, a Prince of Thieves Cereal appeared on grocery shelves. Alas, the movie did not show Mr. Hood starting the day with his own brand. But Kellogg has tried for this brass ring of promotion anyway. It has marketed cereals with Jerry Seinfeld and Jay Leno on the boxes and then gone on to buy commercial time on their network, NBC. It is of some comfort that while cereals sporting Barbie and Donkey Kong have gone stale on the shelves, the redoubtable Fred Flintstone and his Flintstones cereal survive.

11   *Go to school.* The classroom is the Valhalla of place-based media. Better than the doctor's office, the shopping mall, the health club, the hospital, and the airport, here you have the ideal—a captive audience with more disposable income than discretion. Advertising material is all over the place. For home economics classes Chef Boyardee supplies worksheets on how to use pasta; Prego counters with the Prego Science Challenge complete with an "instructional kit" to test the thickness of various spaghetti sauces. General Mills sends out samples of its candy along with a pamphlet, "Gushers: Wonders of the Earth," which encourages the kids to learn about geysers by biting the "fruit snack." Monsanto donates a video suggesting that the world cannot be fed without using pesticides; Union Carbide does the same, saying chemicals "add comfort to your lives." Exxon has an energy awareness game in which nonrenewable natural resources are not losers. K-Swiss sneakers provides shoes for participants in a video creation of an ad for . . . you guessed it. And Kodak, McDonald's, and Coca-Cola plaster a national essay contest about why kids should stay in school with corporate logos and concern. Clearly, one reason to stay in school is to consume more advertising.

12   *Go shopping.* The war, as they say, is in the store. Food shoppers make almost two-thirds of their buying decisions when they set foot in the aisle. Capitalizing on these last-minute decisions is why grocers don't alphabetize soup sections, why all the raisin bran cereals are not bunched together, and why high-profit toothbrushes are both nestled with toothpastes and stacked almost at random throughout the store. With more than fifteen hundred new items introduced to supermarkets each month, the need to inform and convince the querulous shopper of the new product is intense. The experience of food buying has become an advertising adventure.

13   A company called Ad-Tiles puts its ads on the floors in Pathmark stores, charging what amounts to 50 cents per thousand impressions. Flashing coupon dispensers are omnipresent, except near the upright freezers and open dairy case, because shoppers do not like to open doors to compare prices—too cold. They won't even open the door for coupons. The latest hot places for advertising are the checkout line and the shopping cart. The shopping cart, which revolutionized food shopping as much as self-service, because it determined the amount of food a shopper could buy, has come alive. VideOcart is here, almost. This shopping cart has a six-by-nine-inch screen affixed to what used to be the kiddie rumble seat, and infrared censors on the ceiling cause it to flash ads, messages, and recipes as you pass various products. The same technology that scans the Universal Product Code on your can of beans now scans the shopper. You are the can.

14   *Go to a sporting event.* It's football season. Let's go to a bowl game. Which one? Or which product? The Orange Bowl has become the Federal Express Orange Bowl, the Cotton Bowl has become the Mobil Cotton Bowl, the Sugar Bowl has become the USF&G Sugar Bowl, and the Sun Bowl has become the John Hancock Bowl. Not to mention the Sunkist Fiesta Bowl (now the IBM OS/2 Fiesta Bowl), the Mazda Gator Bowl (now the Outback Steakhouse Gator Bowl), the Sea World Holiday Bowl, the Domino's Pizza Copper Bowl, the California Raisin Bowl, and everyone's favorite, the Poulan/Weed Eater Independence Bowl. For a while even the Heisman Memorial Trophy was up for grabs. Merrill Lynch paid $1.5 million for promotional rights but not for a name change. Not yet. No matter: Merrill Lynch already has a golf tournament.

15   *Take a trip.* Get away from Adcult. Weren't we told in the famous Cunard advertisement that getting there is half the fun? Hop in a taxi. Some urban cabs have alphanumeric signs that scroll ten ads per minute across a panel on the back of the front seat. Gannett, the billboard-and-newspaper conglomerate, has been experimenting with installing these "electronic gutters" in subway cars and has contracted with the Transit Authority of New York to put them in six thousand cars. Nothing revolutionary here, just the electrifying of the advertising card, which has been a staple of public transportation since the first trolley. The company has also introduced what it calls the brand train and the brand bus in which a sponsor can buy all the ad space on a particular vehicle that runs a specific route. So Donna Karan's DKNY line has taken over an entire ten-car train that runs under Lexington Avenue on Manhattan's East Side, endlessly running beneath DKNY's superstore at Bloomingdale's. Gannett also installed radio equipment in bus shelters around midtown Manhattan for a news and business station. The New York City Department of Transportation ordered Gannett to pull the plug—too much noise.

16   No destination is safe. The Russian government has even sold space inside Red Square. For something less than $1 million your message can be part of the May Day celebration. Coca-Cola and Pepsi are already in Pushkin Square. For $100,000 the side of GUM, the largest department store in the world, is yours. Lenin's tomb is off-limits, but above Lenin's tomb is OK. For about $30,000 you can float a blimp. Who's itching to get onto Russian space? The usual suspects: AT&T, Reebok, Sara Lee, and of course the ever-present tobacco companies.[3]

17   Finally, no matter where you go in this world or beyond, when you get home, your credit card bill for the trip will eventually appear. When it does, it may have that tear-off tag on the envelope upon which is printed yet another ad.

18   Almost as interesting as where advertising is, is where it might be. Here are some of the more interesting venues contributed by advertising men and women who make hundreds of thousands of dollars thinking up and trying out some of these locations:

- ▼ Subway tokens.
- ▼ The backs of chairs in commuter trains.
- ▼ The Gateway Arch in St. Louis.
- ▼ Postage stamps and paper currency.
- ▼ In place of the telephone dial tone.
- ▼ Polo ponies.
- ▼ The bottom of golf holes, to be observed while putting and then while removing the ball.
- ▼ Self-serve gasoline pumps. Messages scroll along with the amount of gas pumped.
- ▼ Rural mailboxes. Although the Postal Service prohibits advertising on boxes, John Deere has produced a green and yellow version that retails for about $50.
- ▼ Astronauts' uniforms.
- ▼ Postcards. Laden with advertising, they are given to patrons by restaurants.
- ▼ School buses.
- ▼ Slot machines. Why should they come up cherries and oranges? Why not boxes of Tide?
- ▼ Catalogs. This has been done, most notably by *The Sharper Image*, but the reverse is almost as interesting—a recent *Lands' End* catalog included a story by David Mamet.
- ▼ Video games. "Cool Spot" is a game like "Pac Man," except it stars "Spot," the 7-Up mascot: "Yo! Noid!" is a game centered around the Domino's Pizza character. "Mick and Mack: Global Gladiators" has a black hero who battles pollution. To get from level to level the player has to collect golden arches passed out by a gate-tending Ronald McDonald.

19   It may be of some comfort to critics of this use of the human imagination that a new advertising medium has begun appearing *inside* advertising agencies. Called Media News, it appears on a never ending fifty-four-by-eight-inch alphanumeric display similar to the Dow Jones market ticker. Running across the board is information interspersed with thirty seconds of commercials. Advertisers pay $5,000 for thirteen weeks of ads in a medium described by its creators as "invasive without being aggravating." Poetic justice?

20   The rise of place-based (as it is known in the trade), in your face (as it is experienced), or new media (as it is presented to the public) follows the principle that where blank space exists, there shall advertising be. The triumph of Adcult is attributable not so much to new products as to new media reaching new audiences. Each new invasion by commercialism is greeted with an outcry, followed by tentative acceptance, assumption, and expectation. And, finally, of course, neglect.

Notes

1. E. S. Tuner, *The Shocking History of Advertising* (New York: Dutton, 1953).
2. In a sense, of course, advertising in various media is ancient. Commercial speech starts with the snake's spiel in the Garden of Eden, is heard in the cries of vendors in ancient Persia, is seen on walls of Pompeii as the marks listing prices of various prostitutes, is carried in our surnames (as with Smith, Weaver, Miller, Taylor, Baker . . .), and remains in the coats of arms over European hostelries with names like the Red Crown, the Gold Fox, and the Three Stars as well as in the symbolic images of the barber's pole or the golden balls of a pawn shop.
3. Nor would you be ad free in outer space. For $500,000 NASA agreed that Columbia Pictures could cover a rocket with an ad for Arnold Schwarzenegger's *Last Action Hero* (the movie bombed before the missile flew). And Joel Babbit, an Atlantic ad exec, almost succeeded in launching a billboard high in the heavens. The space billboard was to be an unfolding screen set in geosynchronous orbit 250 miles above the equator; in the evening it would appear to be about the size of the moon—just right for a logo. The usual suspects were interested, but the U.S. Department of Transportation nixed the idea.

Process Technique Questions

1. According to Twitchell, how does the process of modern advertising differ from advertising of bygone years?

2. How does the list of italicized labels that begin paragraphs 10–15 help organize the modern advertising process?

3. What is Adcult, and how does it affect our culture?

Suggestions for Writing

1. Write a paragraph about an advertising campaign or single advertising spot that influenced you to purchase a product or service.

2. Select a product or service, real or one you create, and write a paragraph explaining the advertising you would use to market it.

▼

GRANT AND LEE: A STUDY IN CONTRASTS

Bruce Catton

> In this essay, "Grant and Lee: A Study in Contrasts," Catton contrasts the two great American Civil War military leaders. However, while he recounts the basic differences between the two men, he also is making commentary on the significance the two men had in shaping the two sides embroiled in the conflict. By doing so, Catton makes understandable the reasons why the Union and the Confederacy came to war.

Pre-reading exercise: Meaning comes primarily from words. Before reading the essay, look up the definitions of the following words that appear in the text. The numbers in parentheses refer to the paragraph number of the essay.

aspiration (13)	indomitable (14)
burgeoning (12)	obeisance (7)
diametrically (12)	sinewy (7)
fidelity (14)	tenacity (11)
implicit (8)	

1 When Ulysses S. Grant and Robert E. Lee met in the parlor of a modest house at Appomattox Court House, Virginia, on April 9, 1865, to work out the terms for the surrender of Lee's Army of Northern Virginia, a great chapter in American life came to a close, and a great new chapter began.

2 These men were bringing the Civil War to its virtual finish. To be sure, other armies had yet to surrender, and for a few days the fugitive Confederate government would struggle desperately and vainly, trying to find some way to go on living now that its chief support was gone. But in effect it was all over when Grant and Lee signed the papers. And the little room where they wrote out the terms was the scene of one of the most poignant, dramatic contrasts in American history.

3   They were two strong men these oddly different generals, and they represented the strengths of two conflicting currents that, through them, had come into final collision.

4   Back of Robert E. Lee was the notion that the old aristocratic concept might somehow survive and be dominant in American life.

5   Lee was tidewater Virginia, and in his background were family, culture, and tradition . . . the age of chivalry transplanted to a New World which was making its own legends and its own myths. He embodied a way of life that had come down through the age of knighthood and the English country squire. America was a land that was beginning all over again, dedicated to nothing much more complicated than the rather hazy belief that all men had equal rights and should have an equal chance in the world. In such a land Lee stood for the feeling that it was somehow of advantage to human society to have a pronounced inequality in the social structure. There should be a leisure class, backed by ownership of land; in turn, society itself should be keyed to the land as the chief source of wealth and influence. It would bring forth (according to this ideal) a class of men with a strong sense of obligation to the community; men who lived not to gain advantage for themselves, but to meet the solemn obligations which had been laid on them by the very fact that they were privileged. From them the country would get its leadership; to them it could look for the higher values—of thought, of conduct, or personal deportment—to give it strength and virtue.

6   Lee embodied the noblest element of this aristocratic ideal. Through him, the landed nobility justified itself. For four years, the Southern states had fought a desperate war to uphold the ideals for which Lee stood. In the end, it almost seemed as if the Confederacy fought for Lee; as if he himself was the Confederacy . . . the best thing that the way of life for which the Confederacy stood could ever have to offer. He had passed into legend before Appomattox. Thousands of tired, underfed, poorly clothed Confederate soldiers, long since past the simple enthusiasm of the early days of the struggle, somehow considered Lee the symbol of everything for which they had been willing to die. But they could not quite put this feeling into words. If the Lost Cause, sanctified by so much heroism and so many deaths, had a living justification, its justification was General Lee.

7   Grant, the son of a tanner on the Western frontier, was everything Lee was not. He had come up the hard way and embodied nothing in particular except the eternal toughness and sinewy fiber of the men who grew up beyond the mountains. He was one of a body of men who owned reverence and obeisance to no one, who were self-reliant to a fault, who cared hardly anything for the past but who had a sharp eye for the future.

8   These frontier men were the precise opposites of the tidewater aristocrats. Back of them, in the great surge that had taken people over the Alleghenies and into the opening Western country, there was a deep, implicit dissatisfaction with a past that had settled into grooves. They stood for democracy, not from any reasoned conclusion about the proper ordering of human society, but simply because they had grown up in the middle of democracy and knew how it worked. Their society might have privileges, but they would be privileges each man had won for himself. Forms and patterns meant nothing. No man was born to anything, except perhaps to a chance to show how far he could rise. Life was competition.

9   Yet along with this feeling had come a deep sense of belonging to a national community. The Westerner who developed a farm, opened a shop, or set up in business as a trader could hope to prosper only as his own community prospered—and his community ran from the Atlantic to the Pacific and from Canada down to Mexico. If the land was settled, with towns and highways and accessible markets, he could better himself. He saw his fate in terms

of the nation's own destiny. As its horizons expanded, so did his. He had, in other words, an acute dollars-and-cents stake in the continued growth and development of his country.

10   And that, perhaps, is where the contrast between Grant and Lee becomes most striking. The Virginia aristocrat, inevitably, saw himself in relation to his own region. He lived in a static society which could endure almost anything except change. Instinctively, his first loyalty would go to the locality in which that society existed. He would fight to the limit of endurance to defend it, because in defending it he was defending everything that give his own life its deepest meaning.

11   The Westerner, on the other hand, would fight with an equal tenacity for the broader concept of society. He fought so because everything he lived by was tied to growth, expansion, and a constantly widening horizon. What he lived by would survive or fall with the nation itself. He could not possibly stand by unmoved in the face of an attempt to destroy the Union. He would combat it with everything he had, because he could only see it as an effort to cut the ground out from under his feet.

12   So Grant and Lee were in complete contrast, representing two diametrically opposed elements in American life. Grant was the modern man emerging; beyond him, ready to come on the stage, was the great age of steel and machinery, of crowded cities and a restless burgeoning vitality. Lee might have ridden down from the old age of chivalry, lance in hand, silken banner fluttering over his head. Each man was the perfect champion of his cause, drawing both his strengths and his weaknesses from the people he led.

13   Yet it was not all contrast, after all. Different as they were—in background, in personality, in underlying aspiration—these two great soldiers had much in common. Under everything else, they were marvelous fighters. Furthermore, their fighting qualities were really very much alike.

14   Each man had, to begin with, the great virtue of utter tenacity and fidelity. Grant fought his way down the Mississippi Valley in spite of acute personal discouragement and profound military handicaps. Lee hung on in the trenches at Petersburg after hope itself had died. In each man there was an indomitable quality . . . the born fighter's refusal to give up as long as he can still remain on his feet and lift his two fists.

15   Daring and resourcefulness they had, too: the ability to think faster and move faster than the enemy. These were the qualities which gave Lee the dazzling campaigns of Second Manassas and Chancellorsville and won Vicksburg for Grant.

16   Lastly, and perhaps greatest of all, there was the ability, at the end, to turn quickly from war to peace once the fighting was over. Out of the way these two men behaved at Appomattox came the possibility of a peace of reconciliation. It was a possibility not wholly realized, in the years to come, but which did, in the end, help the two sections to become one nation again . . . after a war whose bitterness might have seemed to make such a reunion wholly impossible. No part of either man's life became him more than the part he played in their brief meeting in the McLean house at Appomattox. Their behavior there put all succeeding generations of Americans in their debt. Two great Americans, Grant and Lee—very different, yet under everything very much alike. Their encounter at Appomattox was one of the great moments of American history.

Comparison and Contrast Technique Questions

1. Catton calls both Grant and Lee symbols of their respective sides. Point out some of the differences between the two men.

2. Beginning with paragraph 13, Catton changes his mode of development of Grant and Lee. Point out the similarities the two leaders share.

3. Catton has two paragraphs (paragraphs 3 and 4) consisting of only one sentence each. Do you find these effective or not? Explain.

Suggestions for Writing

1. Select two of today's world leaders, and write a paragraph either comparing or contrasting them.

2. Using yourself and someone you know or two other people you know, write a paragraph describing how their differences actually make their relationship better, not worse.

HASTA LA VISTA, ARNOLD

Margaret Talbot

> In this essay, "Hasta la Vista, Arnold," Talbot compares familiar male action heroes, like Stallone, Schwarzenegger, and Willis, with the new emerging female action hero. Notice that while her main interest is the difference between male and female movie heroes, she is also comparing whether cultural attitudes are changing or whether old cultural stereotypes are being reinforced.

Pre-reading exercise: Meaning comes primarily from words. Before reading the essay, look up the definitions of the following words that appear in the text. The numbers in parentheses refer to the paragraph number of the essay.

forged (3)	rapacious (6)
mantle (10)	tensile (5)
marauding (13)	uncanny (14)
prowess (2)	

1 When I was eight or nine, I'd sometimes fantasize about single-handedly saving my classmates—all 32 of them—from some impending doom. Say we had a fire drill or a bomb scare at school, but this time the fire or the bomb was real. And only I knew about it.

2 Unlike my other girlhood fantasies of omnicompetence, though, this one was always a little fuzzy at the center, where the various feats of physical prowess should have been. How, exactly, was I to save them? I'd seen a few action-hero movies, but they never had women or girls in the action-hero

roles. Could a woman wield fists of fury if she had to? Or bolt through a wall of flame, grateful classmates in tow? What if she were wearing platform shoes? I wanted to be brave—spiritually, I was pretty sure I could be—but the physicality of bravery eluded me.

3   That was 1970 or so, and not even Charlie's ultra-coiffed Angels had been set in motion yet. Whatever the song said, not everybody was kung-fu fighting. Maybe now it's easier for girls to imagine themselves in postures of defiance. Maybe their fantasies of derring-do aren't quite so likely to sputter out. They've seen movies, like *Terminator 2* and *Speed* and the *Alien* series in which women—tough, buff, inexhaustibly resourceful women—play the central roles. They've seen *Xena: Warrior Princess,* the syndicated TV show that brings the Amazon virtues to *Baywatch* territory. ("In a time of ancient gods, warlords, and kings," the voice-over intones each week, "a land in turmoil cried out for a hero. She was Xena, a mighty princess forged in the heat of battle.") If they're nerdy-cool types, they may have seen some Hong Kong action movies—dizzy, kinetic kick-fests that have long made room for actresses trained in the martial arts to give as good as they get.

4   And as it happens, they are about to see many more female icons like these. For this, you might say, is the year of the action heroine, the year when women steer the blockbusters—the blow-hard, die-hard behemoths, the intergalactic star vehicles, the box-office bonanzas. This summer's *Speed 2: Cruise Control* has Sandra Bullock, as the plucky-by-nature Annie, fending off terrorists who have hijacked a cruise ship. The fourth *Alien* movie, due this fall, has Sigourney Weaver and Winona Ryder in the starring roles. The new *Batman* movie features Alicia Silverstone as (the perhaps inevitable) Batgirl. Actresses who seem to have been genetically engineered to play grimly determined action leads are playing them (Demi Moore as a Navy SEAL), and so are actresses who don't (Mira Sorvino in *Replacement Killers,* Minnie Driver in *The Flood*). There's even a spoofy send-up of the action genre, *Austin Powers: International Man of Mystery,* that costars Elizabeth Hurley as a trained fighter in Emma Peel rig-out.

5   Among other things, the new gender-bent action movie will bring us unprecedented displays of female grit. The wondrous Michelle Yeoh, a veteran of Hong Kong movies who upends her opponents with the tensile grace of the dancer she once was, will be starring as "a good guy" (her words) in the next James Bond movie. And though she's small (five foot four inches and 103 pounds) and beautiful (she's a former Miss Malaysia), Yeoh has a wicked roundhouse kick and a charming "Oh, do I have to save his sorry ass again?" expression. (See the Jackie Chan vehicle *Police Story III: Supercop,* in which she hops around like a Mexican jumping bean, hurling grenades and sucker-punching various mainland Chinese baddies—all the while trussed up in a bulletproof vest strapped with explosives.) Yeoh describes herself, simply, as "an actress who likes to do her own stunts. I like to be challenged. What can I say? I like strong women. I don't like wimps—of either sex."

6   Several of the actresses starring in the upcoming action movies said they relished the chance to show their stamina. "You really have to be in pretty great shape to do this part," says Sigourney Weaver, whose latest incarnation of Ripley has her swimming out of the flooded kitchen of a spaceship while battling ever-rapacious aliens. By all accounts, Weaver, at 47, *is* in great shape and does most of her own stunts.

7   Not so long ago, women hovered at the edges of action movies. They were the sacrificial lambs whose rapes or murders set our hero on his quest. Or they were the decorative gewgaws who offered proof of his heterosexuality. If they had power, it was the nefarious power of the spider woman, the vagina dentata, the comically wicked Bond villainess. (My favorite sub-B-grade version of this is the fifties sci-fi classic *Attack of the 50-Ft. Woman,* in which a neurotic

housewife gets irradiated, grows to colossal proportions, and handily pulver-
izes the puny blond who stole her husband. "No, no, Mrs. Archer!" the sher-
iff keeps shouting into the wind created by her Brobdingnagian crop top.)

8   Good women in action movies were never powerful, and powerful
women were never good enough. Now, though, all that has begun to shift.
Women are occupying the center of the story, almost as likely to play the
avengers as the avenged. If an actress is strong—physically strong, especially—it's likely to be a sign of her character's integrity. Or as Iris Grossman,
senior vice president of talent and casting at Turner Broadcasting, puts it, "The
studios have finally woken up to the fact that women are as capable of running and jumping and slamming cars around as anyone else."

9   Not that this is exactly a feminist awakening. Conscience is nice, but
money comes through a lot clearer on a cell phone. And the fact is that
women have more power to make or break a film than ever before—or at
least that's how the studios see it these days. Like soccer moms in last year's
political campaigns, women moviegoers, especially those over 25, are the new
swing constituency, sought after, fought over, and patronized. Women have
been going to movies somewhat more often recently, according to figures
from the Motion Picture Association of America. Female audiences were crucial to the success of several of this past year's most profitable films—including *The First Wives Club* and *Jerry Maguire.*

10   Besides, in this era of girl power and "work-life issues" and fashionable
breast cancer fund-raisers, there is a kind of ineffable sense that catering to
women, or being seen to do so, will earn you a mantle of virtue. Women are
a "minority," but they are the biggest minority around; speaking feelingly of
their special needs can be an easy way for politicians or companies or
moviemakers to broadcast their compassion and rack up cultural brownie
points for what George Bush memorably called "the vision thing."

11   When it comes to the new crop of action movies, the thinking goes something like this. On the one hand, big loud blockbusters with lots of things ex-
ploding in them are what Hollywood mostly does these days; the studios are
in thrall to their money-making potential. On the other hand, women seem
to like more character-driven movies and have turned some of those into big
hits. So why not glom the two together? Put women in action movies, rejig-
ger the genre slightly to accommodate the tastes of female audiences and
voilà—you've got what you hope is a new sure-fire formula. "The aim is to do
action films that are more women-friendly; that is, having strong women in
top roles and taking out a lot of the violence," William Mechanic, chairman
and CEO of Fox Filmed Entertainment, told *The New York Times* recently.
"Women are not only driving the box office but also video-cassette rentals and
sales and TV watching. Not respecting their taste level is silly." (And probably
a lot harder to do now that so many more women executives are making
green-light decisions at the major studios. At Paramount Pictures for example,
close to half the top creative executives are women; at 20th Century Fox,
about a third are, and many more women are making production deals.)

12   Maybe, too, we're at a cultural moment when we're willing, even eager
to see women in strong roles—but we'd just as soon they be strong in space,
or the future, or at least some pretty outlandish, exceptional circumstances in
the here and now. Let them be queens for a day, just not every day. "I know
that Ripley has become a feminist icon," says Sigourney Weaver when I ask
her if she conceives of her *Alien* character that way. "But I've always thought
that was kind of strange because everywhere I go, I see women doing everything, all kinds of physically demanding jobs. The fact that in general movies
don't reflect that day-to-day reality is a measure of how out of it Hollywood
is."

13   For actresses, the new availability of action roles is a boon, but not an un-mitigated one. Action movies propel a few of them into the salary strato-sphere as nothing else can. They still don't occupy the same gilded bracket as, say, Schwarzenegger, Stallone, or—God help us—Jim Carrey, all of whom make $20 million a film. But Sandra Bullock did take home $12.5 million for *Speed 2: Cruise Control,* and Sigourney Weaver got $11 million for *Alien Resur-rection.* On the other hand, the roles can be, well, a bit robotic. Elizabeth Hur-ley had fun playing a jokey action heroine in silver lamé boots but says she's not especially eager to sign up for a lot of rock-'em-sock-'em blockbusters. "I really prefer to do a scene that you can get your teeth into, rather than just waiting around for things to blow up. Action films can be a little tedious." Minnie Driver agrees. In *The Flood,* she plays, of all things, a church restorer who manages to save her work and her town from rising waters and ma-rauding robbers. She says she liked playing a character who was "definitely not a damsel in distress," and she's encouraged by the prospect of more parts for "women who can be strong across the board without being bitches." Still, Driver says she "wouldn't necessarily do another action thriller," because she's "interested in movies that are more about character. Though I have to say that if it involved somebody more like Sigourney Weaver's character in the *Alien* movies, I'd make an exception. That role, and Sigourney in it, has such grace and passion. It's never cheesy." Weaver herself worries that action movies may not embrace women who, like Ripley, project a sinewy tenacity rather than something more traditionally feminine. "The important thing in intro-ducing new female action heroes," Weaver says, "is that they don't try to make us too glamorous, put us all in see-through uniforms or something."

14   The great strength of the *Alien* movies is their relative psychological com-plexity—above all, their ability to evoke a Freudian sense of the uncanny. All three of the previous *Alien* movies, with their dominant metaphor of violent birth, muck about in that mire. The next one, directed by Jean-Pierre Jeunet (*Delicatessen, City of Lost Children*), takes cloning as its dominant metaphor. The plot has Ripley, who plunged to a self-sacrificing death in the last installment, brought to life by the usual nefarious military-industrial complexers, who aim only to get at the alien inside her and to clone it for their own uses. That no-tion, too, has a primal pull. "I found the idea of being brought back to life against your will quite seductive," Weaver says. (The producers and publicists on *Alien Resurrection* may be among the few people who are positively cheer-ful about the recent cloning of a sheep and its implications for human exper-imentation. Everybody on the set is talking about it. Morally troubling, sure, but good box office.) Still, none of this would move us or scare us if we didn't have a central character—a woman pressing hard against her bodily limitations, not escaping her femaleness but letting her heroism transcend it—whose fate we care about and whose strength we trusted.

15   On a recent visit to the *Alien Resurrection* set, I thumbed through a stack of stills from the movie. There she was again, the nearly six-foot-tall Weaver as the larger-than-life Ripley. In the last movie, *Alien 3,* the bleakest and least successful of the series, poor Ripley was more beaten down than she'd been before. Still, even with her head shaved and her options spooled out, she at least had the charisma of her exhaustion—hollowed-eyed, sallow, a bruise blooming like a rose tattoo at her temple. She won't rest until it is vanquished. This time Ripley has hair, and her costume for most of the movie, a tunic and pants of dark, glistening leather, hugs her like a second skin. (Winona Ryder as a mechanic on a raging spaceship gets the somewhat humbler outfit—a blue-gray jumpsuit.) But even slightly glamorized, Weaver manages to look austere and haunted, her face an irreducible sliver of recognizable emotion in a technoslimed wasteland.

16   How important is it, I asked Bill Badalato, the producer of *Alien Resurrection,* to have a woman in the central role? Does it ensure greater audience appeal, bigger box office? Badalato, who produced *Broken Arrow,* among other noisy action films, steepled his fingers and thought for a bit. "Well, the *right* woman in the role is very appealing to an audience," he said at last. "Sigourney manages to convey this steely persona that is feminine at the same time. It's a delicate balance: If a woman acts too tough and macho, an audience isn't going to buy it. If she acts too girly and gushy, they aren't going to buy it."

17   He's right, too. The best women action heroes aren't doing comic-book turns as girls with brawn *and* breasts. And they aren't doing Steven Seagal in drag, either. What you like about them is the sense that they are playing women, just women who might be a little—OK, a lot—stronger than you and me. Or, as Badalato put it of the ideal women's action role, "If men admire it and don't giggle at it and women admire it and aspire to it, then you've got it right." That's all I wanted when I was eight, after all. Is it too much to ask?

Comparison and Contrast Technique Questions

1. Point out some of the elements of contrast that Talbot makes in her discussion of female and male action heroes.

2. While some of the discussion in paragraph 13 has to do with the characteristics of female versus male action heroes, what other topic is being contrasted?

3. According to Talbot, how do the *Alien* movies, starring Sigourney Weaver, exemplify the best opportunity for women to establish a heroic identity as acceptable to audiences as are the traditional male heroes?

Suggestions for Writing

1. Select a female and a male "action hero" from recent movies and discuss how they compare or contrast to those in the essay.

2. Compare or contrast a female and male action hero of today with ones from 20 or 30 years ago.

▼

DISCRIMINATION IS A VIRTUE

Robert Keith Miller

In this essay, "Discrimination Is a Virtue," Miller defines "discrimination" in a very unconventional manner. Miller states that the term's true meaning is often misused and misunderstood. Pay particular attention to his use of *denotative* meaning (the conventional, literal meaning) and *connotative* meaning (the meanings evoked or suggested beyond a word's essential meaning).

Pre-reading exercise: Meaning comes primarily from words. Before reading the essay, look up the definitions of the following words that appear in the text. The numbers in parentheses refer to the paragraph number of the essay.

arbitrary (14)   notion (7)
euphemistically (12)   obsessed (7)
hypocrites (3)   radically (11)
irony (9)   realm (2)

1   When I was a child, my grandmother used to tell me a story about a king who had three daughters and decided to test their love. He asked each of them "How much do you love me?" The first replied that she loved him as much as all the diamonds and pearls in the world. The second said that she loved him more than life itself. The third replied "I love you as fresh meat loves salt."

2   This answer enraged the king; he was convinced that his youngest daughter was making fun of him. So he banished her from his realm and left all of his property to her elder sisters.

3   As the story unfolded it became clear, even to a 6-year-old, that the king had made a terrible mistake. The two older girls were hypocrites, and as soon as they had profited from their father's generosity, they began to treat him very badly. A wiser man would have realized that the youngest daughter was the truest. Without attempting to flatter, she said, in effect, "We go together naturally; we are a perfect team."

4   Years later, when I came to read Shakespeare, I realized that my grand-mother's story was loosely based upon the story of King Lear, who put his daughters to a similar test and did not know how to judge the results. Attempting to save the king from the consequences of his foolishness, a loyal friend pleads, "Come sir, arise, away! I'll teach you differences." Unfortunately, the lesson comes too late. Because Lear could not tell the difference between true love and false, he loses his kingdom and eventually his life.

5   We have a word in English which means "the ability to tell differences." That word is *discrimination*. But within the last 30 years, this word has been so frequently misused that an entire generation has grown up believing that "discrimination" means "racism." People are always proclaiming that "discrimination" is something that should be done away with. Should that ever happen, it would prove to be our undoing.

6   Discrimination means discernment; it means the ability to perceive the truth, to use good judgment and to profit accordingly. The *Oxford English Dictionary* traces this understanding of the word back to 1648 and demonstrates that for the next 300 years, "discrimination" was a virtue, not a vice. Thus, when a character in a nineteenth-century novel makes a happy marriage, Dickens has another character remark, "It does credit to your discrimination that you should have found such a very excellent young woman."

7   Of course, "the ability to tell differences" assumes that differences exist, and this is unsettling for a culture obsessed with the notion of equality. The contemporary belief that discrimination is a vice stems from the compound *discriminate against*. What we need to remember, however, is that some things deserve to be judged harshly: we should not leave our kingdoms to the selfish and the wicked.

8   Discrimination is wrong only when someone or something is discriminated against because of prejudice. But to use the word in this sense, as so many people do, is to destroy its true meaning. If you discriminate against something because of general preconceptions rather than particular insights, then you are not discriminating—bias has clouded the clarity of vision which discrimination demands.

9   One of the great ironies of American life is that we manage to discriminate in the practical decisions of daily life, but usually fail to discriminate when we make public policies. Most people are very discriminating when it comes to buying a car, for example, because they realize that cars have differences. Similarly, an increasing number of people have learned to discriminate in what they eat. Some foods are better than others—and indiscriminate eating can undermine one's health.

10   Yet in public affairs, good judgment is depressingly rare. In many areas which involve the common good, we see a failure to tell differences.

11   Consider, for example, some of the thinking behind modern education. On the one hand, there is a refreshing realization that there are differences among children, and some children—be they gifted or handicapped—require special education. On the other hand, we are politically unable to accept the consequences of this perception. The trend in recent years has been to group together students of radically different ability. We call this process "mainstreaming," and it strikes me as a characteristically American response to the discovery of differences: we try to pretend that differences do not matter.

12   Similarly, we try to pretend that there is little difference between the sane and the insane. A fashionable line of argument has it that "everybody is a little mad" and that few mental patients deserve long-term hospitalization. As a consequence of such reasoning, thousands of seriously ill men and women have been evicted from their hospital beds and returned to what is euphemistically called "the community"—which often means being left to sleep on city streets, where confused and helpless people now live out of paper bags as the direct result of our refusal to discriminate.

13   Or to choose a final example from a different area: how many recent elections reflect thoughtful consideration of the genuine differences among candidates? Benumbed by television commercials that market aspiring officeholders as if they were a new brand of toothpaste or hair spray, too many Americans vote with only a fuzzy understanding of the issues in question. Like Lear, we seem too eager to leave the responsibility of government to others and too ready to trust those who tell us whatever we want to hear.

14   So as we look around us, we should recognize that "discrimination" is a virtue which we desperately need. We must try to avoid making unfair and arbitrary distinctions, but we must not go to the other extreme and pretend that there are no distinctions to be made. The ability to make intelligent judgments is essential both for the success of one's personal life and for the functioning of society as a whole. Let us be open-minded by all means, but not so open-minded that our brains fall out.

Definition Technique Questions

1. How does Miller define "discrimination"? How does he say most other people define it? What problems does this cause in various areas of society?

2. How does the personal story at the beginning of the essay help you understand what Miller is saying about the problems that misunderstanding terms can cause?

3. What is "one of the great ironies of American life" (paragraphs 9–13)? How does this affect American culture?

Suggestions for Writing

1. Select two words that you commonly confuse, and write a paragraph clarifying their definitions. Has confusing the words ever caused you any problems?

2. Write a paragraph about words you and your friends use that could be misunderstood by adults. Would most of the misunderstandings be innocent, or might some of the misunderstandings cause problems?

▼
STYLE IN REVOLT: REVOLTING STYLE

Dick Hebdige

> In this essay, "Style in Revolt: Revolting Style," Hebdige defines a subculture of young people who act, speak, and dress differently from society's mainstream. Pay attention to how the author broadens the meaning of why punk members dress and act outrageously as not merely surface affectations but a means of revolt and protest against the "normal" society's conventional style.

Pre-reading exercise: Meaning comes primarily from words. Before reading the essay, look up the definitions of the following words that appear in the text. The numbers in parentheses refer to the paragraph number of the essay.

caricature (3)	metaphor (7)
context (1)	province (1)
intrinsic (3)	*reductio ad absurdum* (3)
jettisoned (2)	sordid (2)
juxtaposed (2)	strident (10)
kitsch (2)	succinctly (5)
manifesto (9)	zealous (4)

Nothing was holy to us. Our movement was neither mystical, communistic nor anarchistic. All of these movements had some sort of programme, but ours was completely nihilistic. We spat on everything, including ourselves. Our symbol was nothingness, a vacuum, a void.

—George Grosz *on Dada*

We're so pretty, oh so pretty . . . vac-ant.

—The Sex Pistols

1   Although it was often directly offensive (T-shirts covered in swear words) and threatening (terrorist/guerilla outfits) punk style was defined principally through the violence of its "cut ups." Like Duchamp's "ready mades"—manufactured objects which qualified as art because he chose to call them such, the most unremarkable and inappropriate items—a pin, a plastic clothes

peg, a television component, a razor blade, a tampon—could be brought within the province of punk (un)fashion. Anything within or without reason could be turned into part of what Vivien Westwood called "confrontation dressing" so long as the rupture between "natural" and constructed context was clearly visible (i.e., the rule would seem to be: if the cap doesn't fit, wear it).

2   Objects borrowed from the most sordid of contexts found a place in the punks' ensembles: lavatory chains were draped in graceful arcs across chests encased in plastic bin-liners. Safety pins were taken out of their domestic "utility" context and worn as gruesome ornaments through the cheek, ear or lip. "Cheap" trashy fabrics (PVC, plastic, lurex, etc.) in vulgar designs (e.g., mock leopard skin) and "nasty" colours, long discarded by the quality end of the fashion industry as obsolete kitsch, were salvaged by punks and turned into garments (fly boy drainpipes, "common" mini-skirts) which offered self-conscious commentaries on the notions of modernity and taste. Conventional ideas of prettiness were jettisoned along with the traditional feminine lore of cosmetics. Contrary to the advice of every woman's magazine, make-up for both boys and girls was worn to be seen. Faces became abstract portraits: sharply observed and meticulously executed studies in alienation. Hair was obviously dyed (hay yellow, jet black, or bright orange with tufts of green or bleached in question marks), and T-shirts and trousers told the story of their own construction with multiple zips and outside seams clearly displayed. Similarly, fragments of school uniform (white brinylon shirts, school ties) were symbolically defiled (the shirts covered in grafitti, or fake blood; the ties left undone) and juxtaposed against leather drains or shocking pink mohair tops. The perverse and the abnormal were valued intrinsically. In particular, the illicit iconography of sexual fetishism was used to predictable effect. Rapist masks and rubber wear, leather bodices and fishnet stockings, implausibly pointed stiletto heeled shoes, the whole paraphernalia of bondage—the belts, straps and chains—were exhumed from the boudoir, closet and the pornographic film and placed on the street where they retained their forbidden connotations. Some young punks even donned the dirty raincoat—that most prosaic symbol of sexual "kinkiness"—and hence expressed their deviance in suitably proletarian terms.

3   Of course, punk did more than upset the wardrobe. It undermined every relevant discourse. Thus dancing, usually an involving and expressive medium in British rock and mainstream pop cultures, was turned into a dumbshow of blank robotics. Punk dances bore absolutely no relation to the desultory frugs and clinches which Geoff Mungham describes as intrinsic to the respectable working-class ritual of Saturday night at the Top Rank or Mecca.[1] Indeed, overt displays of heterosexual interest were generally regarded with contempt and suspicion (who let the BOF/wimp[2] in?) and conventional courtship patterns found no place on the floor in dances like the pogo, the pose and the robot. Though the pose did allow for a minimum sociability (i.e., it could involve two people) the "couple" were generally of the same sex and physical contact was ruled out of court as the relationship depicted in the dance was a "professional" one. One participant would strike a suitable cliché fashion pose while the other would fall into a classic "Bailey" crouch to snap an imaginary picture. The pogo forebade even this much interaction, though admittedly there was always a good deal of masculine jostling in front of the stage. In fact the pogo was a caricature—*a reductio ad absurdum* of all the solo dance styles associated with rock music. It resembled the "anti dancing" of the "Leapniks" which Melly describes in connection with the trad boom. The same abbreviated gestures—leaping into the air, hands clenched to the sides, to head an imaginary ball—were repeated without variation in time to the strict mechanical rhythms of the music. In contrast to the hippies' languid, free-form dancing, and the "idiot dancing" of the

heavy metal rockers, the pogo made improvisation redundant: the only variations were imposed by changes in the tempo of the music—fast numbers being "interpreted" with manic abandon in the form of frantic on-the-spots, while the slower ones were pogoed with a detachment bordering on the catatonic.

4   The robot, a refinement witnessed only at the most exclusive punk gatherings, was both more "expressive" and less "spontaneous" within the very narrow range such terms acquired in punk usage. It consisted of barely perceptible twitches of the head and hands or more extravagant lurches (Frankenstein's first steps?) which were abruptly halted at random points. The resulting pose was held for several moments, even minutes, and the whole sequence was as suddenly, as unaccountably, resumed and re-enacted. Some zealous punks carried things one step further and choreographed whole evenings, turning themselves for a matter of hours, like Gilbert and George,[3] into automata, living sculptures.

5   The music was similarly distinguished from mainstream rock and pop. It was uniformly basic and direct in its appeal, whether through intention or lack of expertise. If the latter, then the punks certainly made a virtue of necessity ("We want to be amateurs"—Johnny Rotten). Typically, a barrage of guitars with the volume and treble turned to maximum accompanied by the occasional saxophone would pursue relentless (un)melodic lines against a turbulent background of cacophonous drumming and screamed vocals. Johnny Rotten succinctly defined punk's position on harmonics: "We're into chaos not music."

6   The names of the groups (the Unwanted, the Rejects, the Sex Pistols, the Clash, the Worst, etc.) and the titles of the songs: "Belsen was a Gas," "If You Don't Want to F*** Me, F*** Off," "I Wanna Be Sick on You," reflected the tendency towards willful desecration and the voluntary assumption of outcast status which characterized the whole punk movement. Such tactics were, to adapt Levi-Strauss's famous phrase, "things to whiten mother's hair with." In the early days at least, these "garage bands" could dispense with musical pretensions and substitute, in the traditional romantic terminology, "passion" for "technique," the language of the common man for the arcane posturings of the existing élite, the now familiar armoury of frontal attacks for the bourgeois notion of entertainment or the classical concept of "high art."

7   It was in the performance arena that punk groups posed the clearest threat to law and order. Certainly, they succeeded in subverting the conventions of concert and nightclub entertainment. Most significantly, they attempted both physically and in terms of lyrics and life-style to move closer to their audiences. This in itself is by no means unique: the boundary between artist and audience has often stood as a metaphor in revolutionary aesthetics (Brecht, the surrealists, Dada, Marcuse, etc.) for that larger and more intransigent barrier which separates art and the dream from reality and life under capitalism.[4] The stages of those venues secure enough to host "new wave" acts were regularly invaded by hordes of punks, and if the management refused to tolerate such blatant disregard for ballroom etiquette, then the groups and their followers could be drawn closer together in a communion of spittle and mutual abuse. At the Rainbow Theatre in May 1977 as the Clash played "White Riot," chairs were ripped out and thrown at the stage. Meanwhile, every performance, however apocalyptic, offered palpable evidence that things could change, indeed were changing: that performance itself was a possibility no authentic punk should discount. Examples abounded in the music press of "ordinary fans" (Siouxsie of Siouxsie and the Banshees, Sid Vicious of the Sex Pistols, Mark P of *Sniffin Glue*, Jordan of the Ants) who had made the symbolic crossing from the dance floor to the stage. Even the humbler posi-

tions in the rock hierarchy could provide an attractive alternative to the drudgery of manual labour, office work or a youth on the dole. The Finchley Boys, for instance, were reputedly taken off the football terraces by the Stranglers and employed as roadies.

8   If these "success stories" were, as we have seen, subject to a certain amount of "skewed" interpretation in the press, then there were innovations in other areas which made opposition to dominant definitions possible. Most notably, there was an attempt, the first by a predominantly working-class youth culture, to provide an alternative critical space within the subculture itself to counteract the hostile or at least ideologically inflected coverage which punk was receiving in the media. The existence of an alternative punk press demonstrated that it was not only clothes or music that could be immediately and cheaply produced from the limited resources at hand. The fanzines (*Sniffin Glue, Ripped and Torn,* etc.) were journals edited by an individual or a group, consisting of reviews, editorials and interviews with prominent punks, produced on a small scale as cheaply as possible, stapled together and distributed through a small number of sympathetic retail outlets.

9   The language in which the various manifestoes were framed was determinedly "working class" (i.e., it was liberally peppered with swear words) and typing errors and grammatical mistakes, misspellings and jumbled pagination were left uncorrected in the final proof. Those corrections and crossings out that were made before publication were left to be deciphered by the reader. The overwhelming impression was one of urgency and immediacy, of a paper produced in indecent haste, of memos from the front line.

10   This inevitably made for a strident buttonholing type of prose which, like the music *is* described, was difficult to "take in" in any quantity. Occasionally a written, more abstract item—what Harvey Garfinkel (the American ethnomethodologist) might call an "aid to sluggish imaginations"—might creep in. For instance, *Sniffin Glue,* the first fanzine and the one which achieved the highest circulation, contained perhaps the single most inspired item of propaganda produced by the subculture—the definitive statement of punk's do-it-yourself philosophy—a diagram showing three finger positions on the neck of a guitar over the caption: "Here's one chord, here's two more, now form your own band."

11   Even the graphics and typography used on record covers and fanzines were homologous with the punk's subterranean and anarchic style. The two typographic models were graffiti which was translated into a flowing "spray can" script, and the ransom note in which individual letters cut up from a variety of sources (newspapers, etc.) in different type faces were pasted together to form an anonymous message. The Sex Pistols' "God Save the Queen" sleeve (later turned into T-shirts, posters, etc.) for instance incorporated both styles: the roughly assembled legend was pasted across the Queen's eyes and mouth which were further disfigured by those black bars used in pulp detective magazines to conceal identity (i.e., they connote crime or scandal). Finally, the process of ironic self abasement which characterized the subculture was extended to the name "punk" itself which, with its derisory connotations of "mean and petty villainy," "rotten," "worthless," etc. was generally preferred by hardcore members of the subculture to the more neutral 'new wave'.[5]

Notes

1. In his P.O. account of the Saturday night dance in an industrial town, Mungham (1976) shows how the constricted quality of working-class life is carried over into the ballroom in the form of courtship rituals, masculine paranoia and an atmosphere of sullenly repressed sexuality. He paints a gloomy picture of joyless evenings spent in the desperate pursuit of "booze and birds" (or "blokes and a romantic bus-ride home") in a controlled setting where "spontaneity is regarded by managers and their staff—principally the bouncers—as the potential hand-maiden of rebellion."

2. BOF = Boring old Fart; Wimp = "wet."

3. Gilbert and George mounted their first exhibition in 1970 when, clad in identical conservative suits, with metallized hands and faces, a glove, a stick and a tape recorder, they won critical acclaim by performing a series of carefully controlled and endlessly repeated movements on a dais while miming to Flanagan and Allen's "Underneath the Arches." Other pieces with titles like "Lost Day" and "Normal Boredom" have since been performed at a variety of major art galleries throughout the world.

4. Of course, rock music had always threatened to dissolve these categories, and rock performances were popularly associated with all forms of riot and disorder—from the slashing of cinema seats by teddy boys through Beatlemania to the hippy happenings and festivals where freedom was expressed less aggressively in nudity, drug taking and general "spontaneity." However, punk represented a new departure.

5. The word "punk," like black American "funk" and "superbad" would seem to form part of that "special language of fantasy and alienation" which Charles Winick describes (1959), "in which values are reversed and in which 'terrible' is a description of excellence."

    See also Wolfe (1969) where he describes the "cruising" scene in Los Angeles in the mid-60s—a subculture of custom-built cars, sweatshirts and "high-piled, perfect coiffure" where "rank" was a term of approval:

    > Rank! Rank is just the natural outgrowth of Rotten . . . Roth and Schorsch grew up in the Rotten Era of Los Angeles teenagers. The idea was to have a completely rotten attitude towards the adult world, meaning, in the long run, the whole established status structure, the whole system of people organising their lives around a job, fitting into the social structure embracing the whole community. The idea in Rotten was to drop out of conversational status competition into the smaller netherworld of Rotten Teenagers and start one's own league.

Definition Technique Questions

1. While Hebdige spends a lot of time defining "punk" by the clothes, music, and dancing that are outward manifestations, what more serious social movement underlies these symbolic attributes?

2. Point out some words and phrases that indicated the author's feeling about the punk movement and its followers.

3. How does Hebdige expand his definition of the punk movement by comparing it to certain artistic movements?

Suggestions for Writing

1. Write a paragraph defining a group of young people in your community who use dress, music, and dancing as a way of protesting against the mainstream culture.

2. Write a paragraph defining how a group of mainstream adults use clothing, cars, and employment as a means to express their value system.

THE REVOLT OF THE BLACK BOURGEOISIE

Leonce Gaiter

> In "The Revolt of the Black Bourgeoisie," Gaiter argues that the black middle class has to fight negative stereotyping caused mainly by its being associated with the black underclass. He maintains that the black middle class is professionally competent, educated, and culturally talented. Pay attention to the number and variety of examples that the author uses to convince the reader that his point of view is a valid one.

Pre-reading exercise: Meaning comes primarily from words. Before reading the essay, look up the definitions of the following words that appear in the text. The numbers in parentheses refer to the paragraph number of the essay.

authenticity (3)	misogyny (5)
bourgeoisie (11)	monolith (17)
depicted (3)	psyche (9)
idiosyncrasies (17)	stereotype (4)
intelligentsia (11)	superficial (6)

1   At a television network where I once worked, one of my bosses told me I almost didn't get hired because his superior had "reservations" about me. The job had been offered under the network's Minority Advancement Program. I applied for the position because I knew I was exceptionally qualified. I would have applied for the position regardless of how it was advertised.

2   After my interview, the head of the department told my boss I wasn't really what he had in mind for a Minority Advancement Program job. To the department head, hiring a minority applicant meant hiring someone unqualified. He wanted to hire some semiliterate, hoop-shooting former prison inmate. That, in his view, was a "real" black person. That was someone worthy of the program.

3   I had previously been confronted by questions of black authenticity. At Harvard, where I graduated in 1980, a white classmate once said to me, "Oh, you're not really a black person." I asked her to explain. She could not. She had known few black people before college, but a lifetime of seeing black people depicted in the American media had taught her that real black people talked a certain way and were raised in certain places. In her world, black people did not attend elite colleges. They could not stand as her intellectual equals or superiors. Any African-American who shared her knowledge of Austen and Balzac—while having to explain to her who Douglass and DuBois were—had to be *willed* away for her to salvage her sense of superiority as a white person. Hence the accusation that I was "not really black."

4   But worse than the white majority harboring a one-dimensional vision of blackness are the many blacks who embrace this stereotype as our true nature. At the junior high school I attended in the mostly white Washington suburb of Silver Spring, Md., a black girl once stopped me in the hallway and asked belligerently, "How come you talk so proper?" Astonished, I could only reply, "It's proper*ly*," and walk on. This girl was asking why I spoke without the so-called black accent pervasive in the lower socioeconomic strata of black society, where exposure to mainstream society is limited. This girl was asking, Why wasn't I impoverished and alienated? In her world view, a black male like me couldn't exist.

5   Within the past year, however, there have been signs that blacks are openly beginning to acknowledge the complex nature of our culture. Cornel West, a professor of religion and the director of Afro-American Studies at Harvard University, discusses the growing gulf between the black underclass and the rest of black society in his book "Race Matters"; black voices have finally been raised against the violence, misogyny and vulgarity marketed to black youth in the form of gangsta rap; Ellis Cose's book "The Rage of a Privileged Class," which concentrates on the problems of middle- and upper-income blacks, was excerpted as part of a Newsweek magazine cover story; Bill Cosby has become a vocal crusader against the insulting depiction of African-Americans in "hip-hop generation" TV shows.

6   Yes, there are the beginnings of a new candor about our culture, but the question remains, How did one segment of the African-American community come to represent the whole? First, black society itself placed emphasis on that lower caste. This made sense because historically that's where the vast majority of us were placed; it's where American society and its laws were designed to keep us. Yet although doors have opened to us over the past 20 years, it is still commonplace for black leaders to insist on our community's uniform need for social welfare programs, inner-city services, job skills training, etc. Through such calls, what has passed for a black political agenda has been furthered only superficially; while affirmative action measures have forced an otherwise unwilling majority to open some doors for the black middle class, social welfare and Great Society-style programs aimed at the black lower class have shown few positive results.

7   According to 1990 census figures, between 1970 and 1990 the number of black families with incomes under $15,000 rose from 34.6 percent of the black population to 37 percent, while the number of black families with incomes of $35,000 to $50,000 rose from 13.9 percent to 15 percent of the population, and those with incomes of more than $50,000 rose from 9.9 percent to 14.5 percent of the black population.

8   Another reason the myth of an all-encompassing black underclass survives—despite the higher number of upper-income black families—is that it fits with a prevalent form of white liberalism, which is just as informed by racism as white conservatism. Since the early 70's, good guilt-liberal journalists and others warmed to the picture of black downtrodden masses in need of their help. Through the agency of good white people, blacks would rise. This image of African-Americans maintained the lifeline of white superiority that whites in this culture cling to, and therefore this image of blacks stuck. A strange tango was begun. Blacks seeing advancement opportunities allied themselves with whites eager to "help" them. However, those whites continued to see blacks as inferior, victims, cases, and not as equals, individuals or, heaven forbid, competitors.

9   It was hammered into the African-American psyche by media-appointed black leaders and the white media that it was essential to our political progress to stay economically and socially deprived. To be recognized and recognize oneself as middle or upper class was to threaten the political progress of black people. That girl who asked why I spoke so "proper" was accusing me of political sins—of thwarting the progress of our race.

10   Despite progress toward a more balanced picture of black America, the image of black society as an underclass remains strong. Look at local news coverage of the trial of Damian Williams and Henry Watson, charged with beating the white truck driver Reginald Denny during the 1992 South-Central L.A. riots. The press showed us an African-print-wearing cadre of Williams and Watson supporters trailing Edi M. O. Faal, William's defense attorney, like a Greek chorus. This chorus made a point of standing in the camera's range. They presented themselves as the voice of South-Central L.A., the

voice of the oppressed, the voice of the downtrodden, the voice of the city's black people.

11   To anyone watching TV coverage of the trial, all blacks agreed with Faal's contention that his clients were prosecuted so aggressively because they are black. Period. Reporters made no effort to show opposing black viewpoints. (In fact, the media portrait of the Los Angeles riot as blacks vs. whites and Koreans was a misrepresentation. According to the Rand Corporation, a research institute in Santa Monica, blacks made up 36 percent of those arrested during the riot; Latinos made up 51 percent). The black bourgeoisie and intelligentsia remained largely silent. We had too long believed that to express disagreement with the "official line" was to be a traitor.

12   TV networks and cable companies gain media raves for programs like "Laurel Avenue," an HBO melodrama about a working-class black family lauded for its realism, a real black family complete with drug dealers, drug users, gun toters and basketball players. It is akin to the media presenting "Valley of the Dolls" as a realistic portrayal of the ways of white women.

13   The Fox network offers a differing but equally misleading portrait of black Americans, with "Martin." While blue humor has long been a staple of black audiences, it was relegated to clubs and records for *mature* black audiences. It was not peddled to kids or to the masses.

14   Now the blue humor tradition is piped to principally white audiences. If TV was as black as it is white—if there was a fair share of black love stories, black dramas, black detective heroes—these blue humor images would not be a problem. Right now, however, they stand as images to which whites can condescend.

15   Imagine being told by your peers, the records you hear, the programs you watch, the "leaders" you see on TV, classmates, prospective employers—imagine being told by virtually everyone that in order to be your true self you must be ignorant and poor, or at least seem so.

16   Blacks must now see to it that our children face no such burden. We must see to it that the white majority, along with vocal minorities within the black community (generally those with a self-serving political agenda), do not perpetuate the notion that African-Americans are invariably doomed to the underclass.

17   African-Americans are moving toward seeing themselves—and demanding that others see us—as individuals, not as shards of a degraded monolith. The American ideal places primacy on the rights of the individual, yet historically African-Americans have been denied those rights. We blacks can effectively demand those rights, effectively demand justice only when each of us sees him or herself as an individual with the right to any of the opinions, idiosyncracies and talents accorded any other American.

Persuasion Technique Questions

1. How does Gaiter's personal story in the opening paragraphs support his argument about how the black underclass is holding the black middle class back?

2. Paragraph 7 uses statistics as the method of persuasion. How effective are the statistics in convincing you that the author's point of view is valid?

3. In paragraph 5, the author mentions several well-known black men who have spoken out about how successful blacks are treated unfairly. Is this effective support for his argument? How could quoting such successful blacks actually work against his argument?

Suggestions for Writing

1. Gaiter's essay was written almost a decade ago. Write a paragraph arguing for or against the idea that the black middle class is still being identified as having the same goals, attitudes, and abilities as the members of the black underclass.

2. From your own personal experience or knowledge about how successful blacks are accepted into your community, write a paragraph supporting or rejecting Gaiter's contention that attitudes concerning the black underclass affect white society's treatment of the black middle class.

▼
CYBERSPACE: IF YOU DON'T LOVE IT, LEAVE IT

Esther Dyson

> In "Cyberspace: If You Don't Love It, Leave It," Dyson argues for freedom from regulation of the Internet by the government, even in the face of growing problems, such as child pornography and racial hate group sites. Pay attention to how Dyson uses transitional devices ("The first order of business," "First," "Second," "Third," and so on) to help organize her points and to keep the momentum of her argument going.

Pre-reading exercise: Meaning comes primarily from words. Before reading the essay, look up the definitions of the following words that appear in the text. The numbers in parentheses refer to the paragraph number of the essay.

affluent (13)	provoke (2)
alluring (8)	psyche (1)
consensual (9)	terrestrial (15)
hanker (1)	tyranny (15)
metaphor (3)	unsavory (6)
oriented (19)	

1 Something in the American psyche loves new frontiers. We hanker after wide-open spaces; we like to explore; we like to make rules instead of follow them. But in this age of political correctness and other intrusions on our national cult of independence, it's hard to find a place where you can go and be yourself without worrying about the neighbors.

2 There is such a place: cyberspace. Lost in the furor over porn on the Net is the exhilarating sense of freedom that this new frontier once promised—and still does in some quarters. Formerly a playground for computer nerds and techies, cyberspace now embraces every conceivable constituency: schoolchildren, flirtatious singles, Hungarian-Americans, accountants—along with pederasts and porn fans. Can they all get along? Or will fear of kids surfing for cyberspace behind their bedroom doors provoke a crackdown?

3 The first order of business is to grasp what cyberspace *is*. It might help to leave behind metaphors of highways and frontiers and to think instead of real estate. Real estate, remember, is an intellectual, legal, artificial environment constructed *on top of* land. Real estate recognizes the difference between parkland and shopping mall, between red-light zone and school district, between church, state and drugstore.

4   In the same way, you could think of cyberspace as a giant and unbounded world of virtual real estate. Some property is privately owned and rented out; other property is common land; some places are suitable for children, and others are best avoided by all but the kinkiest citizens. Unfortunately, it's those places that are now capturing the popular imagination: places that offer bomb-making instructions, pornography, advice on how to procure stolen credit cards. They make cyberspace sound like a nasty place. Good citizens jump to a conclusion: better regulate it. . . .

5   Regardless of how many laws or lawsuits are launched, regulation won't work.

6   Aside from being unconstitutional, using censorship to counter indecency and other troubling "speech" fundamentally misinterprets the nature of cyberspace. Cyberspace isn't a frontier where wicked people can grab unsuspecting children, nor is it a giant television system that can beam offensive messages at unwilling viewers. In this kind of real estate, users have to *choose* where they visit, what they see, what they do. It's optional, and it's much easier to bypass a place on the Net than it is to avoid walking past an unsavory block of stores on the way to your local 7-11.

7   Put plainly, cyberspace is a voluntary destination—in reality, many destinations. You don't just get "onto the Net"; you have to go someplace in particular. That means that people can choose where to go and what to see. Yes, community standards should be enforced, but those standards should be set by cyberspace communities themselves, not by the courts or by politicians in Washington. What we need isn't Government control over all these electronic communities: We need self-rule.

8   What makes cyberspace so alluring is precisely the way in which it's *different* from shopping malls, television, highways and other terrestrial jurisdictions. But let's define the territory:

9   First, there are private e-mail conversations, akin to the conversations you have over the telephone or voice mail. These are private and consensual and require no regulation at all.

10   Second, there are information and entertainment services, where people can download anything from legal texts and lists of "great new restaurants" to game software or dirty pictures. These places are like bookstores, malls and movie houses—places where you go to buy something. The customer needs to request an item or sign up for a subscription; stuff (especially pornography) is not sent out to people who don't ask for it. Some of these services are free or included as part of a broad service like Compuserve or America Online; others charge and may bill their customers directly.

11   Third, there are "real" communities—groups of people who communicate among themselves. In real-estate terms, they're like bars or restaurants or bathhouses. Each active participant contributes to a general conversation, generally through posted messages. Other participants may simply listen or watch. Some are supervised by a moderator; others are more like bulletin boards—anyone is free to post anything. Many of these services started out unmoderated but are now imposing rules to keep out unwanted advertising, extraneous discussions or increasingly rude participants. Without a moderator, the decibel level often gets too high.

12   Ultimately, it's the rules that determine the success of such places. Some of the rules are determined by the supplier of content; some of the rules concern prices and membership fees. The rules may be simple: "Only high-quality content about oil-industry liability and pollution legislation: $120 an hour." Or: "This forum is unmoderated, and restricted to information about copyright issues. People who insist on posting advertising or unrelated material will be asked to desist (and may eventually be barred)." Or: "Only children 8 to 12, on school-related topics and only clean words. The moderator will decide what's acceptable."

13   Cyberspace communities evolve just the way terrestrial communities do: People with like-minded interests band together. Every cyberspace community has its own character. Overall, the communities on Compuserve tend to be more techy or professional; those on America Online, affluent young singles; Prodigy, family oriented. Then there are independents like Echo, a hip, downtown New York service, or Women's Wire, targeted to women who want to avoid the male culture prevalent elsewhere on the Net. There's SurfWatch, a new program allowing access only to locations deemed suitable for children. On the Internet itself, there are lots of passionate noncommercial discussion groups on topics ranging from Hungarian politics (Hungary-Online) to copyright law.

14   And yes, there are also porn-oriented services, where people share dirty pictures and communicate with one another about all kinds of practices, often anonymously. Whether these services encourage the fantasies they depict is subject to debate—the same debate that has raged about pornography in other media. But the point is that no one is forcing this stuff on anybody.

15   What's unique about cyberspace is that it liberates us from the tyranny of government, where everyone lives by the rule of the majority. In a democracy, minority groups and minority preferences tend to get squeezed out, whether they are minorities of race and culture or minorities of individual taste. Cyberspace allows communities of any size and kind to flourish; in cyberspace, communities are chosen by the users, not forced on them by accidents of geography. This freedom gives the rules that preside in cyberspace a moral authority that rules in terrestrial environments don't have. Most people are stuck in the country of their birth, but if you don't like the rules of a cyberspace community, you can just sign off. Love it or leave it. Likewise, if parents don't like the rules of a given cyberspace community, they can restrict their children's access to it.

16   What's likely to happen in cyberspace is the formation of new communities, free of the constraints that cause conflict on earth. Instead of a global village, which is a nice dream but impossible to manage, we'll have invented another world of self-contained communities that cater to their own members' inclinations without interfering with anyone else's. The possibility of a real market-style evolution of governance is at hand. In cyberspace, we'll be able to test and evolve rules governing what needs to be governed—intellectual property, content and access control, rules about privacy and free speech. Some communities will allow anyone in; others will restrict access to members who qualify on one basis or another. Those communities that prove self-sustaining will prosper (and perhaps grow and split into subsets with ever-more-particular interests and identities). Those that can't survive—either because people lose interest or get scared off—will simply wither away.

17   In the near future, explorers in cyberspace will need to get better at defining and identifying their communities. They will need to put in place—and accept—their own local governments, just as the owners of expensive real estate often prefer to have their own security guards rather than call in the police. But they will rarely need help from any terrestrial government.

18   Of course, terrestrial governments may not agree. What to do, for instance, about pornography? The answer is labeling—not banning—questionable material. In order to avoid censorship and lower the political temperature, it makes sense for cyberspace participants themselves to agree on a scheme for questionable items, so that people or automatic filters can avoid them. In other words, posting pornography in "alt.sex.bestiality" would be O.K.; it's easy enough for software manufacturers to build an automatic filter that would prevent you—or your child—from ever seeing that item on a menu. (It's as if all the items were wrapped, with labels on the

wrapper.) Someone who posted the same material under the title "Kid-Fun" could be sued for mislabeling.

19   Without a lot of fanfare, private enterprises and local groups are already producing a variety of labeling and ranking services, along with kid-oriented sites like Kidlink, EdWeb and Kids' Space. People differ in their tastes and values and can find services or reviewers on the Net that suit them in the same way they select books and magazines. Or they can wander freely if they prefer, making up their own itinerary.

20   In the end, our society needs to grow up. Growing up means understanding that there are no perfect answers, no all-purpose solutions, no government-sanctioned safe havens. We haven't created a perfect society on earth and we won't have one in cyberspace either. But at least we can have individual choice—and individual responsibility.

Persuasion Technique Questions

1. Government regulation of the Internet is an important issue. Does Dyson's argument support or reject this idea.

2. Dyson compares the Internet to real estate, even though it is not a tangible piece of property. Does this comparison help support her point of view?

3. How does Dyson's argument in paragraph 18 support or reject her stated opinion about freedom of speech and freedom of choice? Does this help or hurt her overall argument?

Suggestions for Writing

1. Write a paragraph agreeing or disagreeing with Dyson's contention that parents should be responsible for what their children access on the Internet.

2. Write a paragraph agreeing with Dyson's point of view about whether or not the government should regulate the Internet. Then, write a paragraph that takes the opposite point of view.

HALLOWEEN HAVOC

Erin Nelson

In the following descriptive essay, student writer Erin Nelson creates a spooky night of Halloween fun, filled with all the traditional images of ghosts and goblins that have scared and excited children down through the ages. Pay particular attention to the author's use of figurative language devices (e.g., personification and simile) to create vivid images and sensory emotion.

Pre-reading exercise: Meaning comes primarily from words. Before reading the essay, look up the definitions of the following words that appear in the text. The numbers in parentheses refer to the paragraph number of the essay.

briskly (1)   musty (4)

curdle (5)   prey (2)

grotesque (2)   vicious (3)

gruesome (2)

1 When the wind begins to howl like the wolves and the leaves begin to fall, the time is coming nearer to the creepiest night of the year. The silvery moon is full; the clouds briskly roll across the black sky. A chill is sent down spines, and the neck hairs stand on end. What could it be? Halloween? All Hallows Eve can be the spookiest night of the year because of the creepy decorations, the chilling weather, and the scary goblins.

2 The spooky old houses come to life at night with gruesome decorations. With grotesque carved faces, the Jack-O-Lanterns give off an eerie glow. The tombstones line the sidewalk; beware of the bloody hands, for they may grab intruders. Bats as black as the night sky fly around in the air, and a black cat with razor sharp fangs crosses the path of terrified prey. The ghosts and the goblins sneak around the monster-like trees, ready to grab the next victim with ease.

3 The wind begins to whip, and the branches of the trees begin to sway like the bones of a forgotten skeleton. The fallen dead leaves whirl around like a vicious tornado. When the fog rolls in, the eyes begin to play tricks. A monster! With the fog comes the mist that makes you chilled down to the bone.

4 Screams echo from all directions. A witch, a vampire, and a ghost fly by; consequently, they disappear down the dark, damp street. The hairy werewolf howls, and the musty old mummy moans. Look out! Here comes Freddy—with blood dripping from his razorblade fingers. He's going to get you!

5 One night of the year is all it takes to get the heart pounding and the blood flowing. To be out on this night is quite a fright, so beware of the boogie man. With all the scary sights and the blood curdling sounds on Halloween, a flashlight will come in handy. Happy Halloween!

Description Technique Questions

1. Alliteration is the repetition of the same sounds (e.g., consonants: the willowy, whipping wind; or vowels: as loose as a goose or a moose) usually done to support or help create a particular mood. Point out examples of alliteration in the essay using both consonants and vowels and explain how they help support or create a mood.

2. Brief writing doesn't have to mean underdeveloped writing. All of the paragraphs in this essay are short. However, the author packs each paragraph with vivid descriptions. Point out single words, phrases, similes, metaphors, and sensory images that help create distinct moods quickly and fully.

3. The author refers to "Freddy" in paragraph 4 but does not explain who he is. Is an explanation necessary? Did you know to whom the author is referring? Explain how making such a reference might hurt an essay.

▼ SHATTERED SANCTUARY

Stephanie K. Higgs

> In the following narrative essay, student writer Stephanie Higgs recounts the frightening personal experience of being robbed at knifepoint in her own home. Pay particular attention to how the author builds drama and intensity by moving from internal thoughts and emotions to the external sounds, sights, and events taking place around her.

Pre-reading exercise: Meaning comes primarily from words. Before reading the essay, look up the definitions of the following words that appear in the text. The numbers in parentheses refer to the paragraph number of the essay.

bile (2)	predictable (2)
crescendo (2)	staccato (3)
incapacitated (2)	traumatic (1)
intimidate (1)	vacillate (9)
nook (1)	wielding (2)

1   Time stood still as I tried to reconcile in my mind what was happening in my cheery breakfast nook on that dreary Tuesday morning in September of 1998; a traumatic event happened there; consequently, my life has been changed forever. Before this event, I felt snug and secure in my roomy, comfortable two story- home, peacefully nestled on three gently rolling acres where my loyal and intimidating German shepherds were on patrol, in a private neighborhood near suburban St. Louis. Two young men and their decision to invade my home took all of that away from me.

2   Thunderstorms the previous night had settled into a steady, rhythmic rainshower by daylight. After finally getting the last child out the door and onto the school bus around 7:00 A.M., I was alone in the house following my predictable routine. I had put the dogs in the garage by 7:45 A.M. because I was leaving the house for a college art history class. I heard the scraping of the vinyl floor trim on the French door against the ceramic floor tiles. Now, much like the sound of nails on a chalkboard, it is forever recorded in my memory to come back during waking and sleeping hours alike, to torture me. It makes no difference whether the door is actually opening or not because my mind will always believe that it is. Next, I remember calling out down the hallway to the kitchen, "What did you forget?" I guessed my husband had forgotten some important papers he needed for a meeting he had scheduled in Hazelwood that morning. As I rounded the corner, what I saw made fear rise in my throat like green bile forced up from the pit of my stomach. As soon as I saw them, panic increased my heart rate, bringing it to ear-shattering crescendos until I thought I would go deaf or explode. Incapacitating shock and disbelief bordering on denial paralyzed my entire body as I stared at two masked black men wielding knives standing in my kitchen breakfast room and heading straight toward me.

3   Walking past the wallphone, in one deft move they dropped the receiver to the floor and were right in front of me with a cold steel blade to my throat before I could comprehend what was happening. While looking into the cold dark, eyes of the one who seemed to be in charge, I heard someone who strangely sounded like me, but miles away asking "What are you here for?" I remember thinking he must be a rap singer because of the staccato style in which he answered, "We be axing the questions muthuh fuckin bitch! Don

you scream bitch or we kill you!" He would kill me, I knew with a dull certainty, if I did not obey him. Gripped by the icy fingers of insanity, I heard myself laughing as I was pushed down onto my bedroom floor. I felt like a character in a Dean Koontz thriller. How did I get from the kitchen to here? Surely I made the movements to get there, but I could not recall them from the strange mind that didn't seem like mine anymore. Events were viewed, but from another place before this day unknown to me.

4   They grabbed my hands to tie them behind my back along with my feet. I realized, even though my mind was a tilt-a-whirl seriously out of control, this would more than likely be my last day to live on this earth; my thoughts began to organize as I focused on survival.

5   The men went through my bedroom like a tornado in a springtime storm, tossing my chest of drawers and all its contents, my private possessions, on the floor, crashing the crystal lamps off of night stands, also upending my four poster bed. All the while my shepherds were howling and throwing themselves against the door to the mudroom located off the kitchen in a valiant, yet futile attempt to try and help me.

6   I was told to keep my face down and not to look at them. Even though they were both masked and wore latex gloves, there must have been some fear of discovery; this led me to believe they planned to leave me alive if things went well. At that point, I decided I would do everything in my power to make sure things went well, or I would quite literally die trying.

7   They discovered the gun shells in the nightstand and asked where the guns were. I told them, somewhat reluctantly, while wondering if I was crazy for giving them an even deadlier weapon. I asked what they were looking for. "We looking for money bitch! Where's the gold bitch?" What gold? I thought. Jewelry. A picture began to form in my mind from the things they were taking and asking about, things they could fence to get quick money. For what? Drugs?

8   Surely they were on drugs. How else would they ever work up the nerve to enter another person's house without invitation for the purpose they were carrying out? My mind began to dwell on what brought these young men to this end. I hated them for being the first vile, black people I had ever encountered, yet I pitied them as a mother of young men myself.

9   Suddenly, my mind was rudely snapped back to the present as they left the bedroom to go upstairs and ransack. Even though I couldn't see, I could hear the crashing and tearing; my rage swelled again. How dare they! This was my home, my property. What right did they have? I began to hope the loaded shotgun taken from under my bed would go off as they tried to leave, thereby blowing some part of their anatomy into the next county. I vacillated between hatred and gratitude within mere seconds of each other.

10   Lifting my face, I looked into the kitchen where they were stacking their bounty for a hasty exit. Taking in as many details as I could while I was free to look about, I started to allow myself the luxury of thinking about what I would do after they left. Also, what I could do to help catch them. Details, memorize details. I started to mentally catalog everything about their appearance and what they were taking.

11   Hitching the shotgun up over his shoulder, the leader said, "Let's get outta here." They loaded up and were gone. I lay where I was for what seemed an eternity, too scared to move, yet thrilled to be alive. Working frantically at freeing my hands and feet, I decided to run to the neighbor's house for help. I jumped up and ran like the devil himself was chasing me. What if they were waiting outside to see what I would do? I couldn't let myself think about that, or I would lose my nerve. Safely on my neighbor's porch, I began to heave; I didn't stop until well after the authorities showed up.

12   After taking my statement, it took only two hours for the detectives to take these criminals into custody. They were apprehended within one mile of

my home along with all of the stolen property. Even though they are still in the St. Charles County jail, facing four first degree felony indictments, I have not forgotten their words of warning: "If you call the police bitch, we be back to kill you!"

13   My home is for sale; we are relocating for reasons of personal safety. The peace and comfort known before that day is gone—never to return. My sanctuary has been shattered, and I must try to find a new one.

Narrative Technique Questions

1. The author begins the narrative with a brief description of her home, the rain, and getting her children off to school. Why does the author open the story this way?

2. The author identifies her two assailants as young black men. Would it have made any difference if she had not mentioned their race? Discuss how cultural bias can influence people's perceptions of events.

3. At the end of the story, the author relates that she and her husband have put their house up for sale because they want to find a new sanctuary somewhere else. Point out some examples from the story to support the idea that simply moving will not create peace and serenity for the author.

▼ MICHELANGELO MADNESS

Martin Brink

In the following essay by student writer Martin Brink, tools that are supposed to help humans are classified by their design and by how they actually frustrate us. Pay attention to the examples the author uses; for the most part, they are activities that most people have, unfortunately, experienced.

Pre-reading exercise: Meaning comes primarily from words. Before reading the essay, look up the definitions of the following words that appear in the text. The numbers in parentheses refer to the paragraph number of the essay.

averted (1)	evoke (1)
cloaks (4)	gizmo (1)
contraption (1)	indispensable (5)
cunning (4)	primal (5)
ensue (1)	tedious (3)

1   Since the dawn of man, humanity has striven to enhance the quality of life by inventing and employing gadgets and gizmos to reduce time and labor in everyday chores. Man, consequently, also created maintenance mayhem because of a dependency on machines, not only in the work place, but also at home. The contraptions are truly wonderful when fully functional, but when failing as a result of Murphy's law, frustration and anger ensue. Stress can be averted by avoiding the use of three types of home maintenance tools that are unreliable, counterproductive, and evoke health hazards to the operator.

2   A good rule of thumb (red and swollen by now) to follow is that any tools powered by fossil fuels—weed whackers, lawn mowers, edgers, and snow blowers—are temperamental by design. These helpful devices (a.k.a. "accidents waiting to happen") have starter cords to assist in starting the engine. According to the manual, the happy homeowner should pull the starter cord three or four times to prime the engine with gas. The manufacturer calls this activity "pre-ignition" because on the fifth pull, the engine is supposed to hum into full force. This activity should really be called "aerobic exercise" because the only thing demonstrating full force is the red-faced homeowner who is approaching unconsciousness after pulling on the starter cord fifty-seven times without so much as a puff of exhaust.

3   Believe it or not, science has created tools that are actually counterproductive. One such tool comes to mind: "The Wagner Power Roller Machine." This machine is supposed to save time when applying paint to walls; consequently, anything within ten feet of the operator is painted, too. Apart from dripping paint on everything, cleaning the machine is a tedious and time-consuming task, greater than the job of painting itself.

4   Basic instinct is all that is needed to realize the danger involved with chain saws and 35 foot extension ladders especially when used together. But none are more cunning and unsuspected as a hammer, the most widely used tool. Its simplistic design cloaks its true destructive force; anyone who is experienced in the application of this hand tool knows of the potential hazards or pain of a smashed thumb.

5   Over the years, man's tireless refinement of machines has only made life more complicated. Despite the frustration of mechanical failures and injuries caused by these devices, mankind still finds them indispensable. Humans are enslaved by the notion that bigger is better, faster is fabulous; therefore, the smell of two-cycle exhaust in the morning is addicting. Satisfying primal instincts to mulch, cut, and conquer, machines are embedded in our minds.

Classification Technique Questions

1. The author does not define "Murphy's law." Why not? If you don't know what Murphy's law is, can you figure out what it might mean from the essay? Point out some examples that support your definition of Murphy's law.

2. What is the essay's tone: serious, humorous, sarcastic, or angry? Point out some examples to support your answer.

3. Personification is giving human qualities to inanimate objects. Can you find some examples in the essay? How do they support the tone of the essay you identified in question 2?

4. How many categories does the author use to classify tools? Can you think of some other tools that would fit into the categories in the essay?

Chapter 3

PRACTICE 1

1. airliner
3. lights
5. air traffic controller
7. Passengers
9. Signs

PRACTICE 2

2. It
4. Adler and Sullivan Company
6. philosophy
8. carport
10. Frank Lloyd Wright

PRACTICE 3

1. Yukon Territory
3. mineral wealth and scenic vistas
5. High plateaus
7. Forests
9. climate

PRACTICE 4

Answers will vary

PRACTICE 5

Answers will vary

PRACTICE 6

2. The carton ~~of oranges~~ floated ~~in the water.~~
4. ~~Between the two hills,~~ the houses are made ~~from cedar logs.~~
6. ~~During the week~~ and ~~on the weekend,~~ homework is a constant activity.
8. ~~Over the river~~ and ~~through the woods,~~ the wolf raced ~~to Grandmother's house.~~
10. Three ~~of the guitarists~~ are alternative musicians.

PRACTICE 7

1. ~~In a presidential election,~~ the incumbent has to choose a running mate.

3. ~~At the beginning of the process,~~ many candidates are considered.
5. ~~After the elimination of some candidates,~~ a short list is assembled.
7. ~~Without the interview process,~~ the final choice cannot be made.
9. ~~By the end of the process,~~ the incumbent can make a clear choice ~~for the party.~~

PRACTICE 8

2. The rocking motion ~~of the plane~~ was very relaxing.
4. ~~Outside the cabin,~~ the stars shone like small fireflies ~~in the dark.~~
6. ~~In most cases,~~ smaller children slept ~~on their parents' laps.~~
8. ~~After the flight landed,~~ the passengers walked ~~to the baggage carousel.~~
10. ~~During the trip to the hotel,~~ their bags were carried ~~on the top of the bus.~~

PRACTICE 9

1. ~~As a young child,~~ (he) learned the proper mechanics ~~of the swing.~~
3. The (youngster) progressed rapidly ~~as a golfer.~~
5. ~~Without hesitation,~~ (Woods) won three straight Amateur championships.
7. (He) regularly launched 300 yard drives ~~on the longer holes.~~
9. (Tiger) stunned the golfing world ~~with his outstanding and exciting play.~~

PRACTICE 10

2. (She) opened the letter ~~on the kitchen table.~~
4. (She) unfolded the piece ~~of paper.~~
6. (Tears) ~~of happiness~~ flowed ~~from her eyes.~~
8. ~~After calming down,~~ (Marjorie) called her mother and father ~~on the phone.~~
10. (She) won round trip tickets ~~for four to London.~~

PRACTICE 11

1. Most (people) participate ~~in outdoor activities.~~
3. (Another) skis ~~in the mountains of Colorado.~~

5. A (group) from Vermont searches for rare birds in the deep forests.
7. (Missourians) ride bikes on the scenic Katy Trail.
9. (Others) leap from bridges with bungee cords attached to their ankles.

PRACTICE 12

Answers will vary.

PRACTICE 13

2. The (foyer) (looked) (buffed and polished) from floor to ceiling.
4. (People) in the audience (seemed) (nervous)
6. The symphony (orchestra) (sounded) (confident and well-rehearsed)
8. The (music) (remained) (controlled) throughout the evening.
10. At the concert's end, the (applause) (became) (louder) with each bow.

PRACTICE 14

1. My (life) (was not) (wonderful)
3. My family said (I) (looked) (depressed)
5. Even (food) (smelled) (dull and tasteless.)
7. (I) (felt) (disassociated) with my true self.
9. (I) (turned) to a counselor (for help)

PRACTICE 15

Answers will vary.

PRACTICE 16

2. However, (exercising) must be done on a regular basis.
4. On the other hand, (exercising) too much may be detrimental to your health.
6. (Lifting weights) should be accompanied by an aerobic exercise.
8. (Mental health) also will be stimulated by physical exercise.
10. Regular (exercising) would lower health-related costs nationally.

PRACTICE 17

1. How do (you) start a hobby?
3. Then, (you) should ask your friends and neighbors what hobbies they have.
5. Knowing this may help (you) narrow your choices.
7. (This) could put you in touch with other enthusiasts interested in the same hobby as you.
9. (Being a member) of a club also might get you discounts on materials and publications.

PRACTICE 18

Answers will vary.

PRACTICE 19

2. danced
   dances
   will dance
4. played
   plays
   will play

PRACTICE 20

1. cornered
   corners
   will corner
3. consumed
   consumes
   will consume
5. camped
   camps
   will camp

PRACTICE 21

2. coordinated
   coordinates
   will coordinate
4. juggled
   juggles
   will juggle

PRACTICE 22

Answers will vary.

PRACTICE 23

Answers will vary.

PRACTICE 24

1. The child's ears and nose (looked) just like its mother's.
3. Jupiter, Mars, and Venus (are) planets in our solar system.
5. The antique sofa, the art deco clock, and the abstract painting (were sold) at auction.
7. The slithery snake, the prickly hedgehog, and the colorful parrot (are) the most popular animals at the children's zoo.
9. *Hamlet and Macbeth* (are) two of Shakespeare's most famous plays.

PRACTICE 25

2. Brad Pitt, Harrison Ford, and Tom Cruise (are) popular movie stars.
4. The lawn mower, the edger, and the cultivator (sat) unused in the garage.
6. Either you or I (will have to make) dinner for the cub scouts.
8. In the middle of the night, snoring, cat calls, and crying infants (can reduce) sleep.
10. Nike, Adidas, and Reebok (are) best-selling athletic shoes.

PRACTICE 26

1. The horse trotted and galloped around the track.
3. The audience laughed and cried at the actor's performance.
5. The motel room was clean and smelled of lilacs and roses.
7. Skateboarding is annoying to merchants and fun for skateboarders.
9. The legislature argued and voted on fifty-three bills this current session.

PRACTICE 27

2. In the auditorium, students <u>clapped their hands and stomped their feet.</u>
4. The old fire engine <u>jiggled and rattled</u> down the cobblestone street.
6. After the huge meal, the diners <u>moaned and groaned.</u>
8. Sea birds <u>fly, dive, swim, and float</u> while searching for food.
10. The dancers <u>twirled and leaped</u> in unison with the music.

PRACTICE 28

Answers will vary.

PRACTICE 29

Answers will vary.

PRACTICE 30

Answers will vary.

Chapter 4

PRACTICE 1

1. Jawan hit the ball, but Christie caught the ball.
3. Pang ran quickly to third base, yet Chinua tagged him out.
5. Tom singled four times, and Angie hit two home runs.
7. Joe caused three errors, so the other team scored five runs.

PRACTICE 2

2. , so
4. , for
6. , yet

PRACTICE 3

Answers will vary.

PRACTICE 4

Answers will vary.

PRACTICE 5

Answers will vary.

PRACTICE 6

Sentence corrections will vary.
1. CS
3. C
5. RO
7. C
9. CS

PRACTICE 7

Sentence corrections will vary.
2. RO
4. C
6. CS
8. CS
10. RO

Chapter 5

PRACTICE 1

The surgical team prepared the operating room for the procedure. The surgeon dressed in a green surgical gown; she wore a protective cap covering her hair. Bach's *Toccata and Fugue* was piped into the operating room during the operation; it helped to maintain a relaxed atmosphere during the delicate procedure. The operation was a success. The patient experienced a quick recovery; he was back at work in less than two weeks. His insurance paid for the operation. His family was happy to have him healthy again.

PRACTICE 2

Answers will vary.

PRACTICE 3

Answers will vary.

Chapter 6

PRACTICE 1

Answers will vary.

PRACTICE 2

Answers will vary.

PRACTICE 3

Answers will vary.

PRACTICE 4

Answers will vary.

PRACTICE 5

Answers will vary.

Chapter 7

PRACTICE 1

1. They ordered <u>steak, potatoes, and asparagus</u> at dinner.
3. C
5. The garden consisted of <u>tulips, crocuses, and jonquils</u> during the three months of spring.
7. The fog blanketed the fields <u>in the morning, during the afternoon, and after evening.</u>
9. The orchestra's <u>violins, cellos, and violas</u> answered the woodwinds during the second movement.

PRACTICE 2

Answers will vary.

PRACTICE 3

Answers will vary.

PRACTICE 4

Answers will vary.

PRACTICE 5

Answers will vary.

Chapter 8

PRACTICE 1

2. Jerry enjoyed many activities while vacationing: boating, fishing, and hiking.
4. The librarian reshelved the book left on her desk: *Retire Early: How to Make Money in Real Estate Foreclosures.*
6. The office workers ate lunch in a variety of places: in the employee lounge, on the roof, and out by the lake.
8. Joaquin used three types of peppers to add color to his special salsa: red, yellow, and green.
10. The children enjoyed the party because of the food: hot dogs, hamburgers, and chips.

PRACTICE 2

Answers will vary.

PRACTICE 3

Answers will vary.

Chapter 9

PRACTICE 1

1. Gas prices increase during the summer because many people drive on their vacations.
3. Golfers can play all day and night in Finland since the sun never sets.
5. Before an earthquake sends tremors through the ground, some scientists believe animals can somehow sense it is going to happen.
7. Until their economy failed, the Russians were considered a world power.
9. The students had a study session every Sunday evening unless there was a good concert at the student center.

PRACTICE 2

Answers will vary.

PRACTICE 3

Answers will vary.

PRACTICE 4

Answers will vary.

PRACTICE 5

Answers will vary.

Chapter 10

PRACTICE 1

2. At first, I did not see the need to know CPR for my job as a lifeguard.
4. More often, the traffic is heavier in the evening than in the morning.
6. All in all, it was a very profitable day selling pennants outside the stadium.

8. Being thin and tall, the model easily fit into all the designer's latest gowns.
10. Whether guilty or not, the defendant seemed believable when testifying.

PRACTICE 2

1. After the matinee showing, the tour bus left Las Vegas and headed for Reno.
3. On most sunny days, the students gathered in the quadrangle to read and visit.
5. Over the mountains, the highway trailed away like a giant black snake.
7. Under the viaduct, a homeless person had established living quarters.
9. As lava eventually cools, more living space is realized.

PRACTICE 3

Answers will vary.

PRACTICE 4

2. description
4. comparison
6. definition

PRACTICE 5

Answers will vary.

Chapter 11

PRACTICE 1

1. No, taking the driver's exam is not possible until Monday morning.
3. Nevertheless, we are spending a full week in Toronto.
5. Yes, the mechanic says he can fix the radiator.
7. Hmmm, I can't decide on sausage or pepperoni on my pizza.
9. Well, I might go hang gliding if the weather conditions are good.

PRACTICE 2

2. Nevertheless, (To express a contrast)
4. Ah, (To express surprise or wonderment)
6. However, (To express a contrast)
8. Well, (To express a contemplative pause)
10. Leonardo, (To address someone by name)

PRACTICE 3

Answers will vary.

PRACTICE 4

Answers will vary.

Chapter 12

PRACTICE 1

1. Today, the United States and Japan, however, are considered allies.
3. The United States and Japan, unfortunately, both were after dominance in the Far East.
5. The two nations, subsequently, could not come to common agreement.

7. Although isolationist, the Congress, nevertheless, voted for a Declaration of War.
9. The war, however, had begun in Europe in September of 1939.
11. After six years, the Allies, finally, defeated the Axis powers.

PRACTICE 2

2. Frost, in fact, was from the New England region of the country.
4. His poetry, on the other hand, often dealt with death and alienation.
6. Frost, as a matter of fact, achieved his first success while living in England.
8. Robert Frost, at last, had attained the status of a major poet worldwide.

PRACTICE 3

Answers will vary.

PRACTICE 4

Answers will vary.

PRACTICE 5

Answers will vary.

PRACTICE 6

Answers will vary.

Chapter 13

PRACTICE 1

1. Mud-slinging and personal attacks turn off some people when it comes to politics.
3. Families can help children by being a support system for all their activities.
5. The movie was a success because of the script, the acting, and the special effects.
7. The depletion of the ozone layer might cause global warming and an increase in skin cancers.
9. Helping others can make almost any profession a rewarding experience.

PRACTICE 2

2. The fence was built to keep the coyotes away from the livestock.
4. Great teamwork has made the United States' women's soccer team an international success.
6. Versatility and size make the laptop computer a good business tool for travelers.
8. The Spanish Inquisition impaired scientific thought for decades.
10. A quiet place with good lighting can help students study more effectively.

PRACTICE 3

Answers will vary.

PRACTICE 4

Answers will vary.

PRACTICE 5

Answers will vary.

PRACTICE 6

Answers will vary.

PRACTICE 7

Answers will vary.

PRACTICE 8

Answers will vary.

PRACTICE 9

Answers will vary.

PRACTICE 10

Answers will vary.

PRACTICE 11

Answers will vary.

PRACTICE 12

Answers will vary.

PRACTICE 13

Answers will vary.

PRACTICE 14

Answers will vary.

PRACTICE 15

Answers will vary.

PRACTICE 16

Answers will vary.

PRACTICE 17

Answers will vary.

Chapter 14

PRACTICE 1

Answers will vary.

PRACTICE 2

Answers will vary.

PRACTICE 3

Answers will vary.

PRACTICE 4

1. Halloween—stated in the title, not in the paragraph.
3. Similes add descriptive images that support the "scary" dominant impression. The trees are also personified as they can "snatch their next victim."

PRACTICE 5

2. Excitement

PRACTICE 6

1. Smells
3. "The opposite sex was as mysterious as space travel," and "smells detonate softly in our memory like poignant land mines."

5. These verbs are very dramatic, and they combine to stimulate visual memory because of their ability to elicit memories from sensory stimulation.

PRACTICE 7
Answers will vary.

Chapter 15

PRACTICE 1
Answers will vary.

PRACTICE 2
Answers will vary.

PRACTICE 3
Answers will vary.

PRACTICE 4
Answers will vary.

PRACTICE 5
Answers will vary.

PRACTICE 6
Answers will vary.

PRACTICE 7
1. The writer uses telephone calls to order the events. There are two phone calls and a third is inferred. The first call is introduced in the first sentence: "It was not long before the telephone rang." The second call is introduced in sentence five: "Upon receiving the second call...." And the third call is inferred by the operator in the last sentence: "The operator would check back with them."

PRACTICE 8
1. The writer orders the events chronologically as they occur: first, the writer resolves to do something about her looks; second, how she feels about the project; third, she sprints to the department store; fourth, she goes to the cosmetics counter; and lastly, her decision to broaden her original desire to go for BEAUTIFUL, rather than just attractive.

Chapter 16

PRACTICE 1
Answers will vary.

PRACTICE 2
Answers will vary.

PRACTICE 3
Answers will vary.

PRACTICE 4
Answers will vary.

PRACTICE 5
Answers will vary.

PRACTICE 6
2. The desire is to acculturate children with the values of their own group.

PRACTICE 7
1. Dale Evans (the wife of cowboy star Roy Rogers), Helen Keller (the famous teacher of the blind and deaf), Greta Garbo (a famous movie star who shunned the limelight), Mae West (one of the first movie "sex goddesses"), Catherine Deneuve (the famous French actress), and Naomi Campbell (the famous super model).
3. Only a few: "In some cases," in the second sentence, is used to introduce the listing of famous female examples; and, also in the second sentence, the coordinating conjunction "but" to combine ideas. The writer probably could have used more. Other answers will vary.

Chapter 17

PRACTICE 1
2. b
4. b
6. b

PRACTICE 2
1. d
3. b
5. b

PRACTICE 3
2. "The second category" (sentence 4)

PRACTICE 4
Answers will vary.

PRACTICE 5
Answers will vary.

PRACTICE 6
Answers will vary.

PRACTICE 7
1. They all have "starter cords."
3. Weed whackers, lawn mowers, edgers, and snow-blowers. Yes, because most people probably own at least one of the machines, so they have personal knowledge and experience with them.
5. No, the writer does not use transitional expressions. Other answers will vary.

PRACTICE 8
2. Pile drivers, carpenters, and millwrights. All their jobs are dangerous.
4. "The first type" (sentence 2); "The second kind" (sentence 4); "The last category" (sentence 7). They organize the three types of workers chronologically. This organization helps the reader remain focused on the categories.

PRACTICE 9

1. "Pliers...climbing" with "single-minded determination"; "Keys...burrow"; "Women's purses...travel...to find hiding space." The tone is humorous. It's as if the objects are planning to these things to annoy us.
3. Answers will vary.
5. To entertain by giving us humorous situations that we can identify with because we have all most likely experienced such exasperating activities.

PRACTICE 10

2. Disciplining, rule setting, and visitation.
4. Many readers will come from split families, and they will have their own experiences in similar situations.

Chapter 18

PRACTICE 1

1. D
3. D
5. I
7. D
9. I

PRACTICE 2

2. I
4. D
6. D
8. I
10. I

PRACTICE 3

1. 3, 4, 2, cross out, 1

PRACTICE 4

2. cross out, 5, 2, 4, 1, 7, 6, 3

PRACTICE 5

1. Planning a vacation.
3. Three steps: making a budget, looking for discount packages, and calling hotels for advanced reservations.

PRACTICE 6

2. Informational
4. "first...step" (sentence 2); "while" (sentence 6); "now" (sentence 7)

PRACTICE 7

1. Producing a photograph from a negative.
3. Three: setting the scene, developing the negative, and enlarging the print.
5. Answers will vary.

PRACTICE 8

2. Directional
4. "following" (sentence 1); "starts" (sentence 2); "when his" (sentence 2); "As...first ball" (sentence 3); "as that..." (sentence 3)

PRACTICE 9

1. How advertising has become part of our culture.
3. Two: product ads then (in the past) and now (the present.)
5. Answers will vary.

Chapter 19

PRACTICE 1

Answers may vary, but the following are generally the most popular approaches.
2. Contrast
4. Contrast
6. Compare
8. Contrast
10. Contrast

PRACTICE 2

1. Compare
3. Compare
5. Contrast
7. Contrast
9. Compare

PRACTICE 3

Answers will vary.

PRACTICE 4

Answers will vary.

PRACTICE 5

Answers will vary.

PRACTICE 6

Answers will vary.

PRACTICE 7

2. Point-by-point
4. While the author talks about "character," in general terms, no specific characters are offered as examples.

PRACTICE 8

1. Who pays for the commercial and residential real estate marketing costs—the company or the agent. Yes, the first sentence.
3. By using transitional expressions: "similarly (sentence 1); "like" (sentence 2).

PRACTICE 9

2. Point-by-point
4. Only in general terms—that both men put peace uppermost on the agenda. The writer does not give an specifics.

PRACTICE 10

1. Yes, new (stated) versus traditional (inferred) action roles for women.
3. Yes. "On the other hand" (sentence 4); "like" (sentence 15).

Chapter 20

PRACTICE 1

2. To blunder is to error.
4. Rustic means relating to the rural or country life or people.

PRACTICE 2

1. A robin is a bird having a red breast and gray and black upper plummage.
3. A shark is a marine carnivorous fish having a cartilage skeleton and scratchy skin.
5. A prude is a person who is excessively concerned with appearing proper, modest, or righteous.

PRACTICE 3

Answers will vary.

PRACTICE 4

Answers will vary.

PRACTICE 5

2. Informational process: World War II soldiers returning home. Description: The engine was cheap, plentiful, a popular choice, easy to customize, and a winning combination when coupled to a light-bodied chassis.
4. It was cheap, plentiful, easy to customize, and powerful.

PRACTICE 6

1. Yes, the perfect store. Process—how the customer is sold merchandise and how the customer can evaluate merchandise by price.
3. Sentence 5. It not only honors its own coupons and advertised prices, but it does so for its competitors' coupons and advertised prices as well.

PRACTICE 7

2. Answers will vary.

PRACTICE 8

1. His attitude is negative: "sordid" (sentence 1); "gruesome ornaments" (sentence 2); " 'cheap', trashy fabrics" (sentence 3); "vulgar design" (sentence 3).
3. Objects borrowed out of context; lavatory chains as jewelry; safety pins pierced through cheeks, ear, and lip; obsolete materials worn as clothing; males wore cosmetics intended for females; hair dyed outrageous colors.

Chapter 21

PRACTICE 1

Answers will vary.

PRACTICE 2

2. The writer uses the first sentences to state the opposition's point of view. Then, he uses the next two sentences to refute the opposition's position by introducing the negative aspects of nuclear waste material.

PRACTICE 3

1. An idea many have about a thing, another person, or a group that is often untrue or partially untrue.
3. Black political leaders, whose agenda seems to be limited to Great Society-style programs aimed at the lower class.

PRACTICE 4

Answers will vary.

PRACTICE 5

2. F
4. O
6. O
8. O
10. F

PRACTICE 6

1. Answers will vary.

PRACTICE 7

1. Answers will vary.
2. Answers will vary depending upon the student's answer to #1.

PRACTICE 8

Answers will vary.

PRACTICE 9

Answers will vary.

PRACTICE 10

Answers will vary.

PRACTICE 11

Answers will vary.

Chapter 22

PRACTICE 1

1. Salt and water retention may be related as unhealthy aspects of eating meat versus vegetables, but temperature in not a viable reason supporting a vegetarian diet.
3. These three essay map items do not support why household chores help children in any way.
5. Correct.

PRACTICE 2

2. Playmaking, speed, and bench-clearing brawls make ice hockey an exciting sport.

4. College students go to class, study, and write papers. No attitude.

6. Solar power should be a governmental priority because of diminishing fossil fuels, environmental pollution, and skyrocketing costs.

8. The St. Louis Rams, Green Bay Packers, and Pittsburgh Steelers are football teams. No attitude.

10. <u>Humor, social satire, and musicality</u> have made the <u>Beatles</u> popular long after their breakup as a rock group.

PRACTICE 3

Answers will vary.

PRACTICE 4

Answers will vary.

PRACTICE 5

Answers will vary.

PRACTICE 6

1. A shocking statistic: over six-million people were exterminated.
3. The Holocaust.
5. Horrendous policies; numbers of victims; terrible effects it continues to have on the survivors.
7. Body Paragraph #1: what the horrendous policies led to.

Body Paragraph #2: who was affected by the Holocaust.
Body Paragraph #3: how the liberators and survivors were affected.

PRACTICE 7

2. Exercising the upper body, abdominal muscles, and leg muscles correctly is important for proper functioning.
4. Is important
6. The most important <u>muscles</u> to exercise in the upper body are the triceps, biceps, and pectorals. The <u>abdominal muscles</u> are significant because they support the entire body. The <u>three major muscles</u> in the legs give you the ability to stand, walk, run and jump.
8. Call to action: it is important to exercise. Prediction: If you exercise properly, you will lose weight, have more energy, and feel younger.

GLOSSARY

Absolute phrase: A group of words consisting of a noun or pronoun and a **participle,** (not the regular verb form) plus any other completing words. Absolute phrases modify the entire sentence and cannot be punctuated as a complete sentence.

Active verb: A verb that states what a subject does (in the past, present, or future tense).

Active voice: A verb form in which the subject of the sentence does the acting (using action verb/transitive verb).

Adjective: A word that modifies (or describes) a noun or pronoun. Adjectives come before the nouns they describe; they can also follow the noun. Adjectives can be objective (describing nouns with sensory details) or subjective (describing concepts, feelings, or ideas in more general terms). Both are useful in good writing and enhance meaning, especially in combination.

Adverb: A word that modifies (describes) a verb, or an adjective. Often adverbs end in –ly. Another test to identify adverbs is to ask if it answers one of the questions *where, how,* or *when.* Adverbs describe the action of a passage; in some cases they refer to other adverbs to intensify meaning.

Adverbial conjunction: A word that often follows a semicolon to explain how or in what way the two clauses joined by the semicolon are logically related; often called a *transitional word.*

Antecedent: The noun (or words) to which a pronoun refers in a sentence. (See *Pronoun.*)

Apostrophe: The apostrophe is used to indicate contractions or possession/ownership.

Appositive: A word or phrase which renames the word or phrase preceding it. Appositive words or phrases are often called noun phrases.

Article: A type of word, that introduces a noun and indicates whether the noun is specific or countable. Frequently used articles are *a, an, the.*

Body: The central section of a paragraph or essay that explains the topic sentence of the paragraph or the thesis statement of the essay.

Brackets: Punctuation marks [ ] used in quoted material to set apart editorial explanations.

Brainstorming: A form of freewriting in which the writer lists thoughts freely, at random.

Chronological order: An organization system for events according to how they occur in order of time. This order is used most often in narratives, process analysis, and cause-effect essays.

Classification: An organization system that divides the subject matter into categories determined by one criterion or basis for grouping.

Clause: A group of related words containing both a subject and a verb. There are two types of clauses: *independent clauses* and *dependent clauses.* **Independent clauses** can stand alone as a complete sentence. A **dependent clause** (or subordinate clause) begins with subordinating words/conjunctions and cannot stand alone as a sentence (see Chapter 9 for more information on dependent clauses).

Clustering: A type of pre-writing in which the writer explores and organizes thoughts in a chart that begins with putting the main topic in a circle in the center of the page, then connecting related ideas (in smaller circles) with lines (branches).

Coherence: A quality in which the relationship between ideas is clear throughout a paragraph or essay.

Colon: A punctuation mark [:] that is most often used to show that a list is following a complete introductory sentence.

Comma: A punctuation mark [,] used for separating ideas, independent clauses, items in a list, and enclosing descriptive phrases.

Comma splice: A sentence containing two independent clauses incorrectly joined by a comma.

Comparison-contrast: An organization system showing similarities and differences between two or more subjects/topics. The organization can be blocked by topic, or point by point by criteria.

Complex sentence: A sentence that contains an independent clause and a dependent clause.

Compound verb (predicate): A predicate (the part of the sentence containing the verb) containing two or more verbs.

Compound sentence: A sentence consisting of two or more independent clauses.

Compound subject: A subject consisting of two or more nouns and/or pronouns joined by a coordinating conjunction.

Conclusion: The last sentence of a paragraph or the last paragraph of an essay, which ties together the preceding ideas and smoothly ends the work.

Conjunction: A joining word or phrase. (See *Coordinating conjunction, Adverbial conjunction* and *Subordinating conjunction.*)

Coordinating conjunction: A word that joins grammatically equal structures. There are seven of these conjunctions: *but, or, yet, for, and, nor, so (BOYFANS).*

Coordination: Joining of two or more grammatically equal structures, most often with a coordinating conjunction or a semicolon.

Countable nouns: Nouns that can be either singular or plural.

Criterion: The method used to classify things (basis for grouping, evaluating, comparing, and contrasting).

Dangling modifier: A descriptive phrase or clause that does not modify (describe) any word or phrase in a sentence.

Dash: Punctuation mark [—] used to set apart parenthetical information that needs more emphasis than would be indicated by parentheses.

Definition: An organization system that explains the meaning of a term or concept using a variety of strategies (examples, contrast, description, etc.).

Demonstrative pronouns: The demonstrative pronouns (*this, that, these,* and *those*) are used to point out or specify certain people, places, or things.

Dependent clause: A group of words with a subject and verb but which cannot stand alone and must be joined to an independent clause to complete its meaning. Most dependent clauses begin with subordinating conjunctions or relative pronouns.

Direct object: The word or words (usually nouns or pronouns) following and receiving the action of an action verb, or following a preposition.

Editing: One of the final steps in the writing process during which the writer checks over the draft of the essay for misspelled words, grammatical errors, missing words, and other errors.

Essay: An organized written work on a topic in a series of paragraphs, including an *introduction*, which attracts the readers attention and states the *thesis* of the essay; *body* paragraphs, which present the supporting points of the thesis and develop them with facts, details, and examples; and a *conclusion*, which summarizes the ideas and coherently ends the work.

Exemplification: The use of examples to clarify or illustrate a topic.

Expository writing (exposition): Informative writing, the primary purpose of which is to explain a concept.

Fact: A statement that can be proven to be true.

Fragment: An incomplete sentence because it (1) is missing a subject, a verb, or both; (2) the verb is incomplete; or (3) it is a dependent clause that is not attached to an independent clause.

Freewriting: Writing that is used to explore the author's ideas without concern for grammar, spelling, or organization.

Gerund: The *–ing* form of a verb that functions as a noun in the sentence.

Gerund phrase: A gerund phrase includes a gerund and its completing words.

Helping verb: The part of the verb before the main verb, conveying the most important information about tense or mood of the verb (examples are forms of *have, be, do, will,* etc.).

Hyphen: A punctuation mark [-] used to join descriptive adjectives before a noun, to join compound words and prefixes, or to separate syllables at the end of a line.

Indefinite pronouns: These pronouns do not refer to a specific person; they refer to general or indeterminate people, places, or things. Examples are *everyone, everybody, someone, somebody, everything, something, nothing, anyone,* etc.

Independent clause: A clause that can stand alone as a sentence, containing a complete subject and verb.

Indirect object: A noun or pronoun following a verb that receives a direct object.

Infinitive phrase: A group of words consisting of *to* plus a verb and its completing words. An infinitive phrase can function as a noun, adjective, or adverb.

Interrupters: Sentences may be interrupted by clauses or phrases that clarify or provide additional meaning. These clauses usually begin with the relative pronouns *who, whom, which,* or *that.* See also *Restrictive clauses and Nonrestrictive clauses.*

Irregular verbs: Many irregular verbs (more than 100 in English) do not form the past tense by adding *–ed,* or *–d.* Some verbs do not change form at all, or they form the past tense by changing the spelling of the entire word ("stem-changing verbs").

Linking verb: A verb that does not express action, but links the subject to the word or words that describe the subject. The most common linking verbs are forms of the verb *to be.*

Main verb: The last word in a verb phrase, usually conveying the action of the sentence.

Metaphor: A way to describe a topic in terms of another concept (e.g., love is *a rose*).

Modifier: A word or group of words that functions as an adjective or adverb (providing description).

Narration: A story, usually told in chronological order, that usually builds to a climax and then resolves.

Nonrestrictive clause: A clause that is not essential to complete the meaning of the sentence. If a nonrestrictive clause is removed from the sentence, the basic meaning of the sentence will remain clear. Because it is nonessential, commas always set off this type of clause.

Noun clause: A clause functioning as a noun, usually beginning with *a, the, what, where why,* or *when.*

Nouns: Words that stand for people, places, or things. They can be singular or plural.

Object: A word or words (usually nouns or pronouns) following action verbs, or following words formed from verbs (*-ing* words, past participles, and infinitives); prepositions; or direct objects/indirect objects.

Paragraph: A group of sentences that discuss/develop a topic.

Parallel construction (parallelism): The repetition of the same grammatical structure for coherence or emphasis.

Paraphrase: The writer restating ideas in his or her own words and sentence structure (not directly quoting another author's words).

Parentheses: A mark of punctuation [( )] used to set off specific details giving additional information, explanations, or qualifications of the main idea in a sentence. This would include words, dates, or statements.

Participle: A verb form ending in *–ed* or *–ing,* used as an adjective or used with helping verbs to form present perfect or past perfect forms.

Participial phrase: A group of words (verb phrase) consisting of a participle and its completing words which can function as an adjective or adjective phrase. Participles also are used with helping verbs to clarify tense or voice. All verbs have present participle and past participle forms.

Passive voice: A verb form chosen when the actor of the sentence is not important or when the writer wishes to avoid naming the subject. In the passive voice, the object of an active verb becomes the subject of the passive verb. The form of the verb becomes *be* + past participle.

Past continuous (progressive) tense: A verb tense showing an action in progress in the past, formed from helping verbs *was/were* and adding *-ing* to the verb form.

Past perfect tense: A verb tense used to describe a past action or event occurring prior to a later time in the past. The past perfect is formed from *had* + the verb's past participle form.

Past tense: A verb tense used to discuss completed past actions. All *regular* past tense verbs end in *–ed.* However, there are more than 100 *irregular* verbs (see The Writer's Resources).

Period: A punctuation mark [.] that is used to end a complete statement or is included in an abbreviation.

Personal pronouns: Those pronouns which refer to a person (*I/me, you, he/him, she/her, it, we/us,* and *they/them*). They are divided into three forms, depending on how they are used in a sentence. These forms are *subjective* (pronoun used as a subject), *objective* (pronoun used as an object), or *possessive* (pronoun indicates possession/ownership).

Phrasal verb: A two-word or three-word expression that combines a verb with another word, changing the meaning (e.g., *pick it up*).

Phrase: A group of related words missing a subject, verb, or both subject and verb. Phrases are used in sentences to complete thoughts or add descriptive detail; they may be restrictive or nonrestrictive (see Additional Punctuation Rules, Interrupters in The Writer's Resources). There are several types of phrases used as modifiers in sentences: *prepositional phrases, participial phrases, gerund phrases, infinitive phrases,* and *absolute phrases.*

Predicate: The part of the sentence containing the verb, making a statement or asking a question about the subject.

Prepositional phrase: A **preposition** connects a noun or pronoun to the rest of the sentence, often showing location or time. A **prepositional phrase** contains a preposition (e.g., *in, on, over, before, after,* etc.) and its object.

Present continuous (progressive) tense: A verb tense that discusses actions that are happening now or are planned for the future. This tense is formed by adding a form of the verb to be (*is, am, are*) with the verb + *ing*.

Present perfect tense: A verb tense used to describe an action or condition in the past that continues up to the present. The tense is formed by combining *has/have* + the past participle.

Present tense: A verb tense used to discuss habitual actions, facts, or conditions that are true of the present.

Pre-writing: The step in the writing process in which the writer thinks about the topic, purpose, and audience, and explores ideas for development through **brainstorming, clustering,** or **freewriting.**

Process analysis: An organizational structure that explains how to do something or how something works.

Pronoun: A word that takes the place of, or refers to, nouns. The word or words that the pronoun refers to are known as the **antecedent(s)** of the pronoun. Pronouns can be divided into several categories. The most common categories are *personal pronouns, relative pronouns, demonstrative pronouns, indefinite pronouns,* and *reflexive pronouns.*

Question mark: A punctuation mark [?] that ends direct questions.

Reflexive pronouns: The reflexive form adds *–self* or *–selves* to the pronoun and is used to indicate action performed to or on the antecedent.

Regular verb: A verb ending in *–ed* in the past tense or past participle, or forming its third person singular form by adding *–s* or *–es*.

Relative clause: A clause that functions like an adjective, beginning with a **relative pronoun** (*who, whom, which, that*).

Relative pronouns: Those pronouns used to introduce a qualifying or explanatory clause (*who, whom, which, that, whoever, whichever*).

Restrictive clause: Clause that is essential to identify a noun or to complete the meaning. This type of clause simply follows the noun or idea it is modifying. No commas are used to set off restrictive clauses.

Run-on sentence: A sentence containing two independent clauses with nothing that joins them together (a serious grammatical error).

Semicolon: A mark of punctuation [;] that usually joins two independent clauses, or occasionally separates items in a series containing internal commas.

Sentence: A complete statement or question containing a subject, a verb, and expressing a complete thought.

Simile: A comparison using *like* or *as* (e.g., my love is *like a rose*).

Subject: The topic (who or what) about which a clause makes a statement or asks a question. Usually the subject is a noun or pronoun, and usually the subject precedes the verb.

Subject-verb agreement: Subjects and verbs in the present tense (as well as in the past and future tenses), should agree in number. Thus, singular subjects require verbs with singular endings, and plural subjects require verbs with plural endings.

Subordinating conjunction: A word that joins two clauses by making one clause less in importance and dependent on the second (independent) clause. (Examples: *although, after, because, while,* etc.) See The Writer's Resources for more information.

Subordination: Joining a dependent clause to an independent clause.

Synonym: A word with the same, or close to the same, meaning as another word.

Tense: The form of the verb that shows when in time an action occurred (present, past, future). See The Writer's Resources for more information.

Thesis statement: The sentence, usually included in the introduction, which states the main idea of the essay, and often outlines the subtopics of the essay **(essay map).**

Topic sentence: A sentence stating the main idea of a paragraph.

Transitional word: A word explaining how or in what way two ideas are related. These are often *adverbial conjunctions* (see *Adverbial conjunctions*).

Uncountable nouns: Nouns that represent an idea or concept that cannot be counted (e.g., water, air, fruit), and cannot be made plural.

Verb: A word indicating action, feeling, or being; verbs can be divided into three classes: *action verbs, linking verbs,* and *helping verbs* (see Chapter 3). Additionally the form of the verb can indicate the time of the action: **present, past,** or **future** (also known as **tense**).

CREDITS

Text Credits

"The Hook and Other Horrors," from *The Vanishing Hitchhiker: American Urban Legends and Their Meaning* by Jan Harold Brunvand. Copyright © 1981 by Jan Harold Brunvand. Reprinted by permission of W.W. Norton & Company, Inc.

Grace Suh, "The Eye of the Beholder," Copyright © 1992. Reprinted by permission of the author. First appeared in *A Magazine*, 1992.

Stephanie Higgs, "Shattered Sanctuary," is reprinted by permission of the author.

Matt Grant, "Small Town Views," is reprinted by permission of the author.

"The Mute Sense", from *A Natural History of the Senses* by Diane Ackerman. Copyright © 1990 by Diane Ackerman. Reprinted by permission of Random House, Inc.

Ellery Akers, "Left Sink," *Sierra*, November/December, 1990.

Erin Nelson, "Halloween Havoc," is reprinted by permission of the author.

Amber Barton, "New York-The Big Apple," is reprinted by permission of the author.

"The Culture of Violence," from *Boys Will Be Boys* by Myriam Miedzian. Copyright © 1991 by Myriam Miedzian. Used by permission of Doubleday, a division of Random House, Inc.

"Heroine Worship: The Age of the Female Icon," Copyright © 1996 by The New York Times Co. Reprinted by permission.

Lora Smith, "Seafood Sensation," is reprinted by permission of the author.

Margaret Ewert, "A Stroke of Bad Luck," is reprinted by permission of the author.

"The Revolt of the Black Bourgeoisie," Copyright © 1994 by The New York Times Co. Reprinted by permission.

Paragraph from "The Internet: If You Don't Love It Leave It," Copyright © 1995 by The New York Times Co. Reprinted by permission.

Tim Schuette, "Don't Give Up The Right to Carry," is reprinted by permission of the author.

Danny Butler, "Nuke Nuclear Energy," is reprinted by permission of the author.

Tim Schuette, "The Importance of Exercising Properly," is reprinted by permission of the author.

Nancy Smith, "Childhood Cancer," is reprinted by permission of the author.

Rebecca Eisenbath, "The Holocaust," is reprinted by permission of the author.

"Mute in an English-Only World," Copyright © 1996 by The New York Times Co. Reprinted by permission.

Ynestra King, "The Other Body: Reflections on Difference, Disability, and Identity Politics." First appeared in *Ms.* magazine, 1990.

Photo Credits

page 3, SuperStock, Inc.

page 4, John Coletti/Index Stock Imagery, Inc.; Spencer Grant/Index Stock Imagery, Inc.; Spencer Grant/Index Stock Imagery, Inc.; Paula Lerner/Index Stock Imagery, Inc.; Romily Lockyer/The Image Bank

page 23, (c)AFP/CORBIS

page 44, Reuters/Mike Blake/Archive Photos

page 70, William H. Mullins/Photo Researchers, Inc.

page 99, Archive Photos

page 129, Jeff Greenberg/Photo Researchers, Inc.

page 145, (c)Jeff Vanuga/CORBIS

page 159, Sandy King/The Image Bank

page 172, Bob Kramer/Index Stock Imagery, Inc.

page 186, Superstock, Inc.; Tom Prettyman/PhotoEdit

page 199, A. Ramey/PhotoEdit

page 215, Superstock, Inc.

page 227, Giraudon/Art Resource, N.Y.

page 250, Index Stock Imagery, Inc.

page 273, AFP/Vince Bucci/Corbis

INDEX

Note: Word usage is indicated with lower case italics, e.g. *and, but, for,* etc.

Copyright © 2001 by Addison Wesley Longman, Inc.